A Practical Guide to Private Equity Transactions

This overview of a complex and often misunderstood subject takes the reader through the issues that are faced throughout the life cycle of a private equity investment, from the identification of an opportunity, through the various stages of the transaction and the lifetime of the investment, to the eventual exit by the investor. The analysis of key documentation and legal issues covers company law, employment law, pensions, taxation, debt funding and competition law, taking into account recent legal developments such as the Companies Act 2006, the recent emergence of private equity in the UK and the challenges faced by the industry as a result of the financial crisis.

GEOFF YATES is a corporate partner with Addleshaw Goddard LLP, where he specialises in private equity. He has acted for many years for both private equity houses and management teams on a range of transactions including MBOs, MBIs and 'take private' transactions. A member of the CBI Companies Committee, he is a regular public speaker on private equity and company law matters.

MIKE HINCHLIFFE is a partner at Addleshaw Goddard LLP, with over ten years' experience advising private equity firms, banks and investee companies in the UK on MBOs, MBIs, development capital and venture capital transactions. He also advises a number of private equity investors in relation to the ongoing management of their portfolio companies and exits.

Law Practitioner Series

The *Law Practitioner Series* offers practical guidance in corporate and commercial law for the practitioner. It offers high-quality comment and analysis rather than simply restating the legislation, providing a critical framework as well as exploring the fundamental concepts which shape the law. Books in the series cover carefully chosen subjects of direct relevance and use to the practitioner.

The series will appeal to experienced specialists in each field, but is also accessible to more junior practitioners looking to develop their understanding of particular fields of practice.

The Consultant Editors and Editorial Board have outstanding expertise in the UK corporate and commercial arena, ensuring academic rigour with a practical approach.

Books in the series

A Practical Guide to Private Equity Transactions
Geoff Yates and Mike Hinchliffe

Stamp Duty Land Tax
Michael Thomas; Consultant Editor David Goy QC

Accounting Principles for Lawyers
Peter Holgate

The European Company: Volume 1
General Editors: Dirk van Gerven and Paul Storm

The European Company: Volume 2
General Editors: Dirk van Gerven and Paul Storm

Capital Markets Law and Compliance: The Implications of MiFID
Paul Nelson

Reward Governance for Senior Executives
Edited by Carol Arrowsmith and Rupert McNeil

Prospectus for the Public Offering of Securities in Europe: Volume 1: European and National Legislation in the Member States of the European Economic Area
General Editor: Dirk van Gerven

Prospectus for the Public Offering of Securities in Europe: Volume 2: European and National Legislation in the Member States of the European Economic Area
General Editor: Dirk van Gerven

Common Legal Framework for Takeover Bids in Europe: Volume 1
General Editor: Dirk van Gerven

Accounting Principles for Non-Executive Directors
Peter A. Holgate and Elizabeth Buckley

The Law of Charitable Status
Robert Meakin

The Business Case for Corporate Governance
Ken Rushton

Cross-Border Mergers in Europe: Volume 1
Edited by Dirk Van Gerven

A Practical Guide to Private Equity Transactions

GEOFF YATES

and

MIKE HINCHLIFFE

CAMBRIDGE
UNIVERSITY PRESS

CAMBRIDGE
UNIVERSITY PRESS

University Printing House, Cambridge CB2 8BS, United Kingdom

Published in the United States of America by Cambridge University Press, New York

Cambridge University Press is part of the University of Cambridge.

It furthers the University's mission by disseminating knowledge in the pursuit of education, learning and research at the highest international levels of excellence.

www.cambridge.org
Information on this title: www.cambridge.org/9780521193115

First published 2010
Reprinted 2012

A catalogue record for this publication is available from the British Library

Library of Congress Cataloguing in Publication data
Yates, Geoff.
A practical guide to private equity transactions /
Geoff Yates, Mike Hinchliffe.
p. cm. – (Law practitioner series) ISBN 978-0-521-19311-5 (hardback)
1. Venture capital–Law and legislation–Great Britain. 2. Private equity–Great Britain.
3. Private companies–Great Britain–Finance. I. Hinchliffe, Mike. II. Title. III. Series.
KD2115.Y38 2010
346.410922–dc22
2009053420

ISBN 978-0-521-19311-5 Hardback

Contents

Figures

Foreword

This book runs to some 400 pages and delves into the very heart of how private equity deals work, yet the concepts that it describes and the methods that it unpicks are simple ones. Private equity is not reliant on complex algorithms or other financial wizardry for its successes, but on the expertise of its managers, who know their business sectors intimately and understand what decisions to take and when to take them.

The operating model of private equity is very straightforward and this model can be applied to businesses which possess wildly differing characteristics. This is one of the fascinating aspects of the private equity industry; from a high street clothes shop to a waste treatment plant, a cereal maker to an aerospace parts manufacturer, the fundamentals which govern everything that a private equity firm does remains more or less the same regardless of the industry in which the target company operates. Private equity invests in businesses which have reached a plateau and need private equity expertise and resources to grow, or those which have suffered from underperformance or stagnation due to imperfect management and need to undergo significant change in order to be revived.

In all of these cases, the model works because it aligns the interests of the people running the business with the private equity investor, providing those people with the monetary and operational support they need. The overriding goal is for the private equity firm and the management team it supports to sell the business for a greater sum than that for which it was bought, and the only way to do that is to ensure that what you are trying to sell is an improvement on the entity you originally acquired (a strikingly simple philosophy which debunks the notion that private equity success is down to 'asset stripping'). Management of the company and the private equity firm are both working towards this same goal, and the structure of the fund is such that rewards are always tied to long-term success. This model does not eradicate failure but does focus minds by ensuring that, in the event of failure, no one is rewarded.

Many private equity funds are organised as a fund which has a life of a minimum of ten years, during which the limited partners are locked in. The virtue of this is that it affords a private equity firm the time to take a long-term investment approach. Jittery investors cannot redeem their money and the fund is under no pressure to sell assets for a knockdown price. As tough as this recession has been for some portfolio companies, private equity firms are putting this long-term view into practice by supporting viable companies with injections of new money and hands-on help. For many, this support will ensure they are as prepared as they can be to survive the downturn by saving jobs, preserving value and putting the company in the best position possible to thrive once the upturn begins.

The bottom line, ultimately, is that, for private equity to be able to raise the funds from institutions such as pension funds to buy companies and to improve and sell them, they need to demonstrate that investing in a private equity fund for ten years or more will be more profitable than other routes. This is what private equity has been able to do and, even during this downturn, continues to do.

According to research undertaken by Capital Dynamics and PricewaterhouseCoopers for the BVCA's annual Performance Measurement Survey, private equity funds recorded an IRR of 15.4 per cent over the ten years up to 2008, compared to 3.7 per cent for total pension funds assets and 1.2 per cent for the FTSE All-Share. This level of performance is one that private equity has delivered consistently, according to the same data. From December 2000 to December 2008, IRRs have ranged from a low of 13 per cent to a high of 17.3 per cent, a period which has encompassed the dot com crash and the current recession. This stability is made possible because of private equity's long-term outlook and ability to adapt to changing market conditions.

The adaptability of private equity will ensure continued returns at these levels. The industry is playing a role in helping the economy through the recession by rescuing companies from administration and, as any experienced practitioner will tell you, previous funds raised during downturns have gone on to record outstanding returns to investors. So, those of you reading this book considering a career in private equity, or who have recently begun work in the industry, take heart: this industry is a resilient one, predicated on a simple, yet flexible, model and a downturn is an opportune moment to demonstrate the strengths of this model.

Simon Walker
Chief Executive, British Private Equity and
Venture Capital Association

Preface and acknowledgments

In recent years, the private equity market has experienced dynamic growth in the UK. However, the credit crunch that began in the summer of 2007, and the resulting recession being experienced at the time of writing this book, have created far more challenging market conditions for the industry. The purpose of this book, therefore, is to capture the practice prevailing in the market not only before the market turned, but also in the more challenging environment that has emerged since. To a degree, that latter practice is still developing of course – but, as this book highlights throughout, an understanding of how private equity deals were structured and transacted during the recent boom period will help the reader appreciate how such market practice is adapting, and will continue to adapt, to the more uncertain conditions currently being experienced. It is also our view that private equity will continue to make a significant contribution to UK industry notwithstanding these uncertain market conditions; in all uncertainty lies opportunity.

We have designed this book to guide the reader through the principal issues likely to be faced in transactions in the UK private equity market – from the initial business planning, due diligence and negotiation of the investment, through the life of that investment for the management team and the investors, concluding with a successful (or perhaps less successful) exit. The book also considers in some detail the practical issues that can arise in specialist areas – particularly banking, tax, pensions, competition law and employment law – all of which combine to define the structuring and terms of any transaction. This approach is intended to help the practitioner understand how the pieces of the private equity jigsaw fit together – for example, how decisions made at the time of the original deal can impact on the ability of the private equity investors and the managers to operate the business during the life of the investment, and how the need for a successful exit drives the original deal and informs the attitude of private equity owners when making investment decisions.

This book is not intended to inform the reader of everything that he or she needs to know about buying or selling businesses in the UK, nor does it provide any detailed analysis on the structuring of private equity funds. There are other titles specialising in those fields. Its aim is to give the reader an understanding of how private equity works in practice in the UK, and the practical differences that the nature, structure, motivation and objectives of private equity investors bring to UK deals.

We should like to take this opportunity to thank Michael Carter (share schemes), Matthew Doughty ('take privates' and IPOs), Ed Jenkins (tax), Catherine McAllister (pensions), Phil McDonnell (competition), Phil Slater (banking) and Richard Yeomans (employment) for their invaluable contributions to the relevant sections in this book. We should also like to thank David Ascott, Chris Leonard and Mo Merali of Grant Thornton for their contributions to the sections dealing with the Business Plan and financial due diligence. Last, but by no means least, our sincerest thanks to Carmel Craddock who was not only responsible for typing the vast majority of this book, but has also provided invaluable word processing support on many of the transactions that have contributed towards its content.

Much of this book is informed by market practice in the UK as experienced by the authors. It is hoped that future editions can benefit from the experiences of readers of the book as market practice continues to develop, and therefore any comments, queries or suggestions on the text are both encouraged and welcome.

We have, where relevant, used the section numbers from the Companies Act 2006 which will be fully in force by 1 October 2009. Save for that fact, and unless otherwise stated, this book reflects the law and practice as at 1 July 2009.

Table of cases

1

An introduction to private equity

1 Introduction

In this chapter we aim to provide a general introduction to private equity as it has been practised in the United Kingdom in the period up to January 2009. We will introduce some of the key players that shape the market and the types of deals that they do. This chapter will help to explain how private equity evolved into what it is today and will look at some of the factors that may influence its future. It is designed to set the scene for much of the rest of this book, and to give to the reader who is less familiar with the sector a welcome overview of a typical deal and some of the bigger issues in the private equity marketplace generally, but with a particular focus on the UK mid-market.

Industry terminology exists in all markets and has its place as shorthand for those familiar with the territory. Ever more colourful and elaborate phrases and acronyms are coined. In the private equity market they have (or once had) distinct and separate meanings and nuances. Many are now merging and being used inconsistently, creating an aura of spin and shimmer around the sector, and meaning different things to different people. We will seek to demystify some of the features of the market and the jargon used by practitioners and commentators alike.

This chapter will set out some of the history of the industry and explain the key building blocks with which it has been built. One of these, as we will see, is the focus on the Business Plan. We will go on to consider the significance of the Business Plan in a private-equity-backed transaction, and the ways in which such Business Plan will be assessed by investors to underpin their desired financial returns. In particular, we will look at how management and their advisers put together the Plan, and what factors are of particular interest to private equity funders in the evaluation of the opportunity, including the types of businesses most likely to attract support. We will also explain the importance of the financial return to private equity and some of the ways in which this can be measured.

Much of this may sometimes seem very technical, especially for a reader who does not deal every day in the world of net present values, discount rates and internal rate of return (IRR). However, it matters – knowing what good and bad looks like in the eyes of many private equity investors can be key to understanding how they value potential investments, how they behave on acquisitions and on exits, and how they react to underperformance. It can help you work with them, knowing what buttons to press (and what buttons to leave untouched), and predicting how they may react in any likely scenario. It can also help in negotiations against them where this is in your own, or your client's, commercial interests.

2 Background to private equity in the UK

2.1 What is private equity?

The term 'private equity' is a generic expression for investments in equity securities in companies which are not listed on any public stock exchange. Generally in the UK this means shares in limited companies, although there are exceptions (such as so-called 'vanity plcs', being public limited companies which are not listed on any investment exchange, but maintain plc status in order that the term 'plc' may be used in the corporate name).[1]

There is a wide range of types and styles of private equity, and the term therefore has different connotations depending on the circumstances (and possibly jurisdiction) in which it is used. In the UK, as for most other developed economies, the expression is generally used to describe any type of transaction whereby a fund or group of funds invests monies either directly into an operating company, or for the purposes of acquiring a company or group of companies (for ease of reference, referred to throughout this book as the 'Target'). Funds may be provided from a wide range of sources including pension funds, financial institutions and other institutional investors, companies, public bodies and high net worth individuals (for more on the different types of private equity funders in the UK market see section 2.3 below).

There are many different types of private equity transaction in the UK. Unfortunately, different expressions are sometimes used interchangeably and inconsistently, which can cause confusion. The following labels are most regularly encountered:

(a) Management buyouts (MBOs, or buyouts)

This phrase is generally used to describe the acquisition of a company (Target) by its incumbent senior management team, who up until the time of the buyout may have held either a limited equity stake, or no shareholding at all. MBOs may arise for a variety of reasons, the most usual being a corporate holding

1 There are implications to being a vanity plc rather than a private company. For example, a public limited company must satisfy particular minimum share capital and other requirements set out in sections 4(2) and 761–767 of the Companies Act 2006, and a vanity plc will be subject to the requirements of the City Code on Takeovers and Mergers notwithstanding that it is not listed.

company disposing of a non-core subsidiary, or one or more private sellers looking to unlock the value in their company (e.g. where there is no obvious successor to inherit a family business). Traditionally, such transactions were often sourced by the management teams themselves, who then took the Target business to the market for funding through retained advisers; however, as the private equity industry developed, it became more common for private equity firms to approach the Target, or for the seller(s) concerned to instigate the transaction, with management involvement being minimised until later in the process (see section 2.4 below).

(b) Management buyins (MBIs)

An MBI is identical to an MBO save that the management team that will invest alongside the private equity funds, and run the Target business, has not previously been involved in the management of the Target. The lucrative profits earned by management teams from successful MBOs led to many individual managers researching their own industry sectors, with a view to identifying potential acquisition targets which they could then run with a deal funded by private equity. Individuals who have previously been successful in an MBO often then move on to look for MBI opportunities.

A 'pure' MBI (i.e. where there is no involvement of any member of the management team within the existing business) is now rare in the UK. The lack of any inside knowledge of the Target business means that there is an increased risk to the funders of the transaction; even where a comprehensive due diligence exercise is carried out by external accounting, legal and other advisers, there is no substitute for experience from within the business. As a result, many private equity funders refuse to contemplate MBIs at all.

That said, on a buyout, the existing management team is often complemented by one or more managers from outside the business. In many modern deals in the UK, the team will include a combination of the existing management team and managers from outside the company; such transactions are sometimes referred to as 'buyin management buyouts' (or, affectionately, BIMBOs) – although such deals are often still simply referred to as MBOs or buyouts.

(c) Leveraged buyouts and institutional buyouts (LBOs/IBOs)

The expression 'leveraged buyout', or LBO, is used to describe a buyout where significant debt is utilised by the private equity firm in order to fund the acquisition of Target. The expression originates in America, although it has been used more extensively in the UK market in recent times (particularly as a consequence of the buyout boom between 2005 and 2007 – see section 2.2).

In reality, leverage is used to some degree by private equity firms in all buyouts to deliver the returns that their ultimate funders expect. In chapter 3, a typical deal structure is outlined demonstrating how bank debt (and, indeed, debt investment by the private equity investor) is combined with a relatively small (often, therefore, described as 'pinhead') equity investment. In the UK, therefore, whilst the expression LBO may generally be applied to any buyout, its use tends to be limited to those buyouts with particularly high levels of leverage – often involving several layers of debt funding, as is described in more detail later in this book.[2]

Another expression often used is 'institutional buyout', or IBO. This expression simply describes a transaction where the private equity investors are leading the acquisition process and will hold a substantial majority interest in the buyer vehicle (with the management team holding a relatively small, minority interest). In these cases, the relevant private equity firm or firms are often referred to as 'sponsors'. The terms LBO and IBO often go hand in hand because, as a general rule, as the deal size increases, it is far more likely that significant leverage will be required and that the transaction will be structured as an IBO with majority control in the hands of the private equity investors.

(d) Venture capital

In the UK, the terms 'venture capital' and 'private equity' have often been used interchangeably, causing some confusion. Indeed, the principal trade body for private equity in the UK, the British Venture Capital and Private Equity Association, was simply the British Venture Capital Association until as recently as December 2008, and is still known in its abbreviated form as the BVCA.

However, the term 'venture capital' is now generally used to describe those transactions where private equity firms invest in less mature companies to assist with the development, expansion or start-up of a business. By its nature, venture capital is often found in the technology, biotechnology, healthcare and pharmaceuticals sectors, although its application is not exclusively limited to those areas. Venture capital funding provides much-needed capital to entrepreneurs who would not otherwise have the funding to invest in the development of important products or exciting new business ideas. For this reason, it is often presented as a 'friendlier face' of private equity.

The legal documentation in a venture capital transaction is similar to that required for a buyout, but there are some differences both in form and in structure. Investment agreements typically provide for phased investments once certain milestones are achieved, for example, whilst a buyout typically requires the investors to commit all of their funds to pay the purchase price to the seller(s) on completion of the relevant acquisition. The forms of investment may also vary, with complex provisions to deal with the possibility of dilution on future funding rounds and to provide investors with a priority return on their investment (usually expressed as a multiple of the amount initially invested) before any proceeds are shared with management. This reflects the riskier nature of venture capital – it is far more likely that a venture will fail

2 See chapter 3, section 2.4, and chapter 6, section 6.

and all, or substantially all, of the initial investment will be lost. Equally, however, when a venture capital investment is successful, the returns can be spectacular, and as such it remains an attractive asset class to investors.

(e) Growth capital and development capital

The expression 'growth capital' is generally used to describe investments in relatively mature companies which require funds for future growth and expansion. The expression 'development capital' is also widely used, and can sometimes describe the same situation, although the latter expression is perhaps associated with businesses that have gone past an initial venture or start-up capital phase, but which are still relatively small, whilst the former can be used to describe deals involving extremely mature businesses. Growth capital funds may also finance a restructuring, for example to reduce high leverage that may be a relic of an earlier buyout, or to give an individual shareholder the ability to extract some cash value from his business, as well as for the purpose of funding significant expansion. Other houses specialise in so-called 'buy-and-build' investments; here, markets ripe for consolidation are targeted, with the investors backing a management team to acquire multiple Targets over time to produce a leading market player as that consolidation takes place.

By their nature, growth and development capital deals often result in the investors holding minority stakes, which can have particular implications when drafting the equity documentation. The deal may be structured by way of a direct investment into the company itself, or by the setting up of a new company which then acquires the existing Target in exchange for cash and shares (which is usually necessary for tax reasons where any or all of the existing shareholders are extracting value as part of the transaction).

(f) Secondary buyouts

A 'secondary buyout' describes a transaction where an existing company created as a consequence of a buyout backed by original private equity investors is sold to a new buyer vehicle backed by new private equity investors. The management team may remain the same across the two transactions, or there may be individual changes.

Secondary buyouts were particularly common in the UK during the period from 2003 to 2007. They may arise in a range of circumstances, and give rise to particular issues for the legal adviser – chapter 12 explores these issues in more detail.

2.2 The emergence of private equity

Private equity as it is currently known can be traced back to the end of the Second World War in both the UK and the US, by the establishment of venture capital firms on both sides of the Atlantic (notably the American Research and Development Company and J. H. Whitney and Company in America, and the

Industrial and Commercial Finance Corporation (now 3i) in the UK). Prior to that time, such investment was primarily sourced from wealthy individuals. The success of such institutions was supported by the respective governments at that time to encourage enterprise to help with the post-war rebuilding effort.

Until the 1980s, most investments by these firms, and other investors established in their wake, would largely fall under the modern categories of venture or development capital. Whilst more modern, and leveraged, buyouts did occur between the 1950s and the 1970s, the asset class really came to prominence during the boom years of the 1980s, particularly in America where a number of significant deals were completed. One of the last major buyouts of that decade was also, and probably remains, the most celebrated or controversial (depending on your point of view), being the US$25 billion takeover of RJR Nabisco by KKR. It was at the time the largest buyout in history, and retained that title for nearly twenty years, the events surrounding the buyout being famously documented in the book *Barbarians at the Gate*.[3]

Whilst the recession experienced at the start of the 1990s had the effect of derailing for a time the growing trend towards bigger and bigger buyouts, a number of key private equity players nevertheless emerged or were created during that decade as the market recovered from around 1992. Many still referred to themselves as venture capitalists, and deals in the UK often did have a venture, development or growth element in this period. Many players had a strong focus on venture and start-up capital, with a particular emphasis on technology and dot com businesses towards the end of the twentieth century (with the result that many suffered significant losses with the burst of the dot com bubble in 2000).

The three-to-four-year period leading up to the summer of 2007 saw an unprecedented boom in buyout activity in many developed economies, including the UK. A number of new players continued to emerge – at the time of writing, the latest edition of the BVCA handbook lists over 200 investors in the UK market – but, most notably, the size and scale of leveraged buyouts increased to unprecedented levels. Whilst in America the RJR Nabisco record was finally toppled, in the UK deals, or attempted takeovers, emerged with similar ambition and involving household names such as Alliance Boots, EMI and (unsuccessfully) Sainsbury's. This brought private equity very much into the public eye; the relatively light-touch disclosure requirements of a private-equity-owned business when compared with a listed company, the attractive tax treatment attached to the returns achieved by individuals working in the industry,[4] and inevitable questions around the short-term motives of investors led to considerable political pressure, culminating in a high-profile review by a Treasury Select Committee in June 2007.

3 Bryan Burrough and John Helyar, *Barbarians at the Gate – The Fall of RJR Nabisco* (1990).

4 See also chapter 9, section 2.5.

Since these buoyant times, the fallout from the credit crunch which began in Autumn 2007 has been well documented in the business press and the wider media. The structuring of LBOs has left private equity investors exposed to a significant, or possibly full, write-off of their investments in the event of business failure, whilst the increased leverage of existing businesses to facilitate deals made such failure more likely. At the time of writing it is unlikely that debt funding is going to be readily available to facilitate higher value LBOs in the foreseeable future,[5] and the political pressures on both sides of the Atlantic and in particular at EU level for increased regulation of alternative assets, and the wider financial services industry, is likely to have a significant impact on the private equity landscape.

The Walker Report[6] is a case in point. Commissioned during the boom period in February 2007, and published in November that year, Sir David Walker's guidelines for disclosure and transparency in private equity require additional disclosure and communication by private equity firms and their portfolio companies where particular thresholds apply, namely, where such portfolio companies:

(a) have more than 1,000 UK employees; and
(b) generate more than 50 per cent of their revenues in the UK; and
(c) either had an enterprise value of more than £500 million when acquired by one or more private equity firms or, in the case of a public-to-private transaction, had a market capitalisation together with a premium for acquisition of control of more than £300 million.

Given the substantial nature of these thresholds, the application of these guidelines is limited to a relatively small number of investments held by the larger players. However, private equity firms whose investments fall below the radar may do well to become familiar with the requirements; given the continued political scrutiny (particularly in the European Parliament), and public and media interest, it seems inevitable that similar transparency requirements will emerge in a form that will have implications for a larger proportion of private-equity-backed companies.[7]

That said, there is also little doubt that private equity will continue to play an important role in the UK economy. Whilst critics may highlight excessive leverage, cost-cutting measures or so-called asset-stripping, supporters of the industry will point out that an effective incentive for management to grow,

5 For more detail concerning the impact of the credit crunch on the availability of debt for leveraged deals, see chapter 6, section 2.

6 Sir David Walker, *Guidelines for Disclosure and Transparency in Private Equity* (20 November 2007). The independent review was carried out at the request of the BVCA and a group of private equity firms.

7 A practical checklist of the requirements for a company's accounts incorporating the Walker Guidelines can be found on the BVCA website.

or otherwise improve the performance or competitiveness of, the underlying business is inherent in the buyout model. This in turn can lead to increased employment, and the distribution of a substantial part of the profits to wider society as a result of the considerable participation in private equity funds by many pension schemes.

2.3 Types of private equity investor

In the UK, private equity firms come in a variety of shapes and sizes. It is important at the outset to distinguish between a private equity firm and a private equity fund. A private equity firm is an investment manager which raises pools of capital, typically in the form of private equity funds, to invest. These firms receive a periodic management fee for doing so, as well as a share in the profits known as a 'carried interest' from each of the private equity funds that it manages. As is outlined in chapter 3,[8] the typical arrangement in the UK is for the private equity funds to take the form of limited partnerships, with the private equity firm being the general partner of such limited partnership. A transaction usually involves the private equity firm arranging an investment by two or more limited partnership funds under its management in parallel. As a result of this structure, the investors in private equity funds are often referred to as 'LPs', and the private equity firms themselves as 'GPs', in the business and financial press.

Private equity firms are often ranked based on the value of the funds under management, or typical deal sizes for that investor. Common terminology is to divide the UK buyout market into upper-market, mid-market and lower-market – although the deal sizes falling within each category are not always consistent, and the mid-market is itself sometimes then divided into lower and higher sub-divisions. As a general rule of thumb, as at January 2009 most would describe deals with a transaction size of less than £50 million as lower-market, those with a size of £50 million to £500 million as mid-market, and those exceeding £500 million as upper-market.

The upper-market is dominated by the larger American and UK firms. Firms operating in the UK in the mid-market are often distinguished based on whether they are 'captive', 'semi-captive' or 'independent'. A captive investor obtains their funds exclusively from a parent company – usually a financial institution. These include those firms investing on behalf of the well-known UK banks. An independent firm will source all of its capital from external investors. A semi-captive combines the two approaches – investing the parent company's money alongside externally raised funds. Many of the independent firms operating in the mid-market in the UK were established by individuals who had previously worked in the larger buyout houses or within a captive or semi-captive environment, and similarly a number of such independents

8 See chapter 3, section 3.3.

were created as a result of the buyout of a captive or semi-captive firm by its managers.

Another way to categorise the UK market is by the sectors in which the various firms invest. Some firms will state that they do not focus on specific sectors, preferring a general approach, whilst others limit their investments to a particular sector or small number of sectors. In reality, the generalists will still have certain sectors in which they prefer to invest, or would like to invest, influenced by their existing funds, the sector experience of their key managers, and their view of where the best returns may be made.

Venture capital investment is typically the focus of distinct venture capital houses. Some investors in the upper-market and mid-market buyouts sector will also provide a separate venture capital offering too (especially where the firm is captive or semi-captive), although this may be presented using a similarly named but separate venture capital brand. Many venture capital investments are made by venture capital trusts (VCTs), a quoted entity which offers individuals the opportunity to participate in venture capital with particular tax advantages. The requirements for such investors are not detailed in this book, which focuses on the buyout market rather than the venture capital market, but it should be noted that there are strict requirements for the structuring of VCT investments which must be adhered to if the favourable tax treatment is to be obtained. These requirements can result in a VCT being less flexible than an LP structure.

Unsurprisingly in the economic climate subsisting at the time of writing, an increasing number of distressed and special situation funds have emerged, although this is by no means a new concept; successful specialist investors have existed for many years. In a private equity context, the expression is generally used to describe those investors who look to acquire distressed businesses (often at a significantly discounted, or even negligible, price arising from an insolvency process), and then implement strategic and operational improvements with a view to a successful *turnaround* of the fortunes of the business. Whilst many investors may claim interest in this particular area, quite different skills and expertise are required when compared with more conventional buyouts. It should also be noted that a range of alternative asset classes exist in the distressed and special situation arena outside these types of transaction – for example, hedge funds and other investors often employ strategies for dealings in debt in distressed companies.

Other sources of funding are also available to businesses which, in the broader sense, constitute private equity. For example, 'business angels' (high net worth individuals, often investing via an informal syndicate led by a recognised intermediary) often fund investments in the so-called 'equity gap' – a phrase typically used to describe transactions requiring equity investment of less than £1 million which most mainstream private equity investors have moved away from. At the other end of the scale, 'sovereign wealth funds' have emerged as key players in the upper market, often competing with the more traditional large private equity firms in the higher profile deals during the 2003–7 buyout boom. This book focuses on the typical requirements, and issues faced, in a more traditional buyout – although a number of these points will still be relevant to these alternative investors. The legal practitioner should, however, always be mindful of the need to fit the legal documentation to the deal, rather than the other way around; the principals will become frustrated if excessive cost is incurred negotiating comprehensive content on a smaller deal, particularly if the issues are not of concern to the investor, or worse still simply not relevant.

2.4 Sourcing the deal

One of the most important aspects of any management buyout process from the private equity funder's perspective is the identification of a suitable opportunity. This will vary according to the circumstances in which each particular deal arises – although general trends also emerge based on the prevailing market conditions.

For example, in the bullish market in the UK leading up to the summer of 2007, the opportunities often presented themselves – that is to say, the sellers (whether corporate or private individuals) instructed corporate finance advisers to undertake a formal marketing process, typically involving an extensive auction. An information memorandum relating to the Target, its business affairs and prospects would be prepared by the sellers' corporate finance advisers and made available to potential bidders. The bidders approached would often include both trade buyers and private equity or other financial buyers (in the latter case, these would usually be selected having regard to their interest and credentials in relation to that particular sector, and at the relevant deal size). Assuming there was significant interest, an aggressive deal process ensued, with tight timescales for completion of the transaction.

Although this formal marketing process, and resulting wider auction, has its attractions to any seller seeking to maximise value from disposal, it can be unattractive to private equity buyers and trade buyers alike (with the result that, during that bullish market, many credible buyers were reluctant to participate in such auctions). Some private equity funds have been set up, formally or informally, on the basis that they will not take part in auction processes. The strength of bargaining power of the seller demonstrated by a strict process, designed both to maximise value and to achieve a high level of execution certainty before agreeing to proceed exclusively with a particular bidder (or even without granting such exclusivity at all) meant that each potential bidder had to undertake ever increasing amounts of preparatory work including, in many cases, the incurring of legal, accounting and other professional costs. The fact that each potential bidder was exposed to these considerable costs and expenses, and also seeking to maximise its offer in such a way as to exclude other bidders, meant that many interested parties decided simply not to embark on the process at all. Bidders who did pursue the process diligently could still find themselves frustrated if a particular bidder was able to come in with a credible 'knockout' bid (with a unique ability to see value in the business, or a reckless misreading of that value, depending on your point of view).

Contrast this with the changing mood to reflect the more challenging market conditions experienced since summer 2007, and it is clear that the balance of negotiating power has swung back in favour of the buyer. On the one hand, this assists those buyers who were reluctant to participate in auctions for the reasons outlined above, by ensuring that exposure to costs and expenses before exclusivity can be minimised, and allowing sufficient periods of exclusivity to ensure a transaction can be fully assessed. However, the absence of formal auction processes and a shortage of willing sellers (understandably reluctant to sell their businesses for a significant discount on their perceived value at the height of the market) makes the identification of potential transactions more challenging. A distressed seller may have no choice but to accept the best price he can in a difficult market; however, not all buyers are interested in distressed assets (which, as mentioned above, requires a particular approach and skill set). In any event, the structuring of any buyout relies on debt funding, and the difficulties in raising debt (or relatively unattractive terms on which debt is offered) makes the execution of deals, or matching of private equity offers with sellers' aspirations, increasingly difficult.[9]

In these challenging situations, however, the door is left open to possibilities for those private equity firms with the skills to source or develop what might be considered the Holy Grail for a private equity buyer – an exclusive (or near exclusive) introduction to an attractive business. Private equity firms will use their own internal research capabilities, and their network of contacts (including accounting and legal advisers, as well as those in industry) to source opportunities for direct discussions with sellers and/or the incumbent management teams. In the ideal scenario, a deal might be concluded without the competitive tension of other bidders in a formal process. More realistically, not least to ensure that sellers can feel comfortable that the correct deal has been struck, a formal sale process may follow such approaches – although quite possibly to a more limited audience. In any event, the earlier introductions may well put the private equity house in a strong position to win the race, especially if a rapport has been achieved with the sellers or the managers whose ability to influence the deliverability of any offer should not be underestimated.

A comparison of the deal processes involved in an originated transaction versus an auction is set out in chapter 2.[10]

9 See chapter 6, section 2, for more background on the impact of the credit crunch on debt financing in the UK.

10 See chapter 2, section 2.

3 The Business Plan and financial returns

3.1 General

The Business Plan is a cornerstone requirement for any private equity proposition. It is a critical document outlining management's strategy for the business, key milestones (and how these will be achieved), and an assessment of the outlook for the business within its market.

In very general terms, the private equity investors are typically searching for a business which satisfies the following criteria, all of which should be addressed by the management team within a robust and well-structured Plan:

(a) experienced and committed management;
(b) good product/service;
(c) strong market position;
(d) high/predictable margins;
(e) the potential to double the money within three years (generating an IRR of 25–35 per cent);[11]
(f) running yield and the capacity for the payment of arrangement and monitoring fees; and
(g) foreseeable exit opportunities.

Typically, the management team will appoint corporate finance advisers to help compile the Business Plan. The corporate finance advisers bring a robust discipline to this process – acting as devil's advocate, challenging management's assumptions and preparing professional documents (including the critical selling points) to help attract interest and support from private equity firms. The preparation of the Business Plan is in many ways a balancing act. On the one hand, it must describe the Target's business and opportunity accurately and with appropriate prudence; however, it must also help sell the opportunity to potential funders. Members of the management team may have strength in either of these areas, but only very talented or experienced managers (or well-balanced teams) combine the two effectively. Corporate finance advisers are there to help management achieve this balance, as well as to provide ongoing guidance throughout what is invariably a challenging transaction process.

The facts and opinions expressed in the Business Plan will, by necessity, remain those of management. Given the fundamental importance of the Business Plan to the decision of the investors to invest, the management team will be required to warrant the content of the Business Plan to the investors in the legal documentation.[12] Typically, the managers must confirm that the factual information in the Business Plan concerning the Target is correct, and that the opinions and assumptions expressed in the document are reasonable

11 For an outline of the meaning of IRR, see section 3.4 below.
12 See further chapter 5, section 3.4.

1. Executive summary
2. Background
3. Products and production
4. Operations
5. Market analysis
6. The management team and organisation
7. The strategy
8. Financial summary
9. Funding requirements
10. Milestones
11. Risk assessment and sensitivity analysis
12. Exit review
13. Appendices

Figure 1.1 Typical contents of a Business Plan

(having made suitable enquiries, and otherwise having given such opinions and assumptions appropriate consideration).

3.2 Business Plan contents

Although the Business Plan is a bespoke document addressing specific areas relating to the business and its markets, there are a number of general areas that are invariably covered. Figure 1.1 shows the typical contents that private equity firms would expect to see – interested private equity investors will review each section with a particular focus.

Executive summary. The executive summary provides a brief, but comprehensive, overview of the key points in the Business Plan. This is a critical section of the document – as it is the first section that is read by recipients, and is likely to determine whether private equity investors are sufficiently interested to consider the remainder of the document in any detail. The executive summary will usually consider each of the following: the nature of Target's business; the ultimate goal(s) of the management team with Target, and strategy underpinning such goal(s); a summary of the market and Target's position in it; significant features relating to the existing, or planned, products or services of Target; the management team; financial highlights (both in relation to historic results and future projections); and the funding requirements including projected returns. It is worth noting that private equity firms typically receive hundreds of Business Plans every year; a strong executive summary is therefore critical to grab the attention of the investors, particularly at a senior (usually decision-making) level.

Background. This section will include a brief history of the creation, development and growth of the business, including reasons for its inception, and the current (and perhaps historic) group structure and ownership details. The track record of Target in its market will be of vital importance to the private equity house in assessing the risks of the potential investment opportunity.

Products and production. An explanation of the products and/or services should be included, with details of applications, principal features and any unique selling points. Any technology, intellectual property and research and development activities would also be covered in this section. As noted in section 2.3 above, many private equity houses will be interested in businesses in specific sectors, either to build on their positive experiences and expertise as a result of historic and existing investments in the same sector, or to expand their portfolio into a new sector which it has identified as particularly attractive.

Operations. This section will include details of all premises, facilities and plant and machinery (including capacity), supplier relationships, quality control, and IT and management information systems. Private equity investors will consider whether the company can demonstrate adequate capabilities and capacity for Target to be able to deliver its outlined strategy, and the extent of any capital expenditure requirement, which in a growing business will underpin the valuation of Target to the investors. Investors are also interested in the strength of the balance sheet – in particular whether Target owns the premises, plant and machinery and other significant fixed assets. This will be a significant factor in determining the extent to which secured borrowings can be raised to fund the transaction, and might also provide a means for generating cash to reduce borrowings post-acquisition (for example, by way of a transaction to sell and lease back any substantial property).

Market analysis. Areas covered in this section include: identification and characteristics of the market and Target's position in it; the size of the specific market segment and forecast market growth; current and forecast market share, with details of how increases in market share will be achieved; research on customers and potential customers, explaining their needs and decision-making factors; a marketing and selling strategy, including pricing policy; and an assessment of competitors in the market.

This section is of vital importance to any private equity investor. An attractive growth market, and a strong defensive position within that market, will help to build the investment case for the investor. The anticipated growth in a market, and the correlation to the forecast sales, will have a direct impact on the investment return and will therefore be subject to considerable scrutiny, including commercial due diligence.[13] For example, businesses with a particular niche in the market are often of great interest to investors, but the robustness of management's strategy will be challenged. Frequent issues raised are whether the Target truly has a unique offering and position in its market, and whether there are sufficient barriers to prevent new entrants coming into that market.

The potential investor will want to know any information about the customers and competitors that could prevent Target from delivering on its strategy. For example, is there over-reliance on any one particular customer, which

13 See further chapter 2, section 4.5.

would increase the risk profile of Target? What factors and influences exist in the market which are beyond Target's control? Will Target compete effectively with its competitors, and what is the likely response of competitors to Target's strategy? Pricing policy, and anticipated pricing movements in the future, will be equally important; not only to assess the prospects for the market as a whole, but also to assess the likely impact of such trends on Target's own market share (and the resulting impact on margin, profitability and ultimately the anticipated investment return).

Management. An equally critical section of the Business Plan to a private equity house is the 'Management' section. The achievement of the objectives and strategy within the Business Plan depends upon the capabilities of management to execute that strategy. This section should include the key members of the management team, their specific skills, sector credentials, achievements and experience. Brief details of the other staff should also be included along with an organisational chart showing responsibility and reporting lines. A private equity house is likely to be particularly interested in the quality and strength of the managing director and the finance director.

Private equity houses may, however, put in place their own management team as part of the transaction, or will add to the existing team if they do not believe the existing management team can deliver the Plan themselves. This is particularly the case if the private equity firm already has an investment, and therefore a management team, in the same business sector, and has adopted a 'buy-and-build'[14] strategy.

Strategy. The Plan will include an overview of the team's strategy for Target including objectives, implementation, ultimate exit routes and a timetable. The timing and manner of exit is of particular importance to private equity investors, as they rely on those exits to generate their expected return (see further section 3.4 below).

Financial. The Plan will include both historical financial analysis and financial projections, along with the key assumptions, and justification of those assumptions, underpinning the projections. The data will encompass profit and loss statements, balance sheets and cash flows for, typically, a three-year period on a historic basis, and up to five years on a forecast basis. The main body of the Plan usually includes a summary of key data, with the full financial model being supplied as an appendix (see further section 3.3 below).

The financial data underpins the determination of the funding requirement, and the calculations of the projected investment return. The financials need to reflect management's strategy and objectives, and so must be consistent with the rest of the content of the Business Plan. This financial data will be subject to stringent due diligence, and ultimately the performance of the management team will be measured against these projections.

14 See section 2.1 above.

Investors are understandably attracted to projections which forecast a trend of increased profitability, with such increases being achieved as soon as possible. Investors also speak of their attraction to a *high visibility* of earnings, meaning future turnover of sufficient certainty to enable the investors to feel comfortable that the financial projections will be delivered; as a result, businesses with significant long-term contractual commitments are often well received. Strong operational cash flows are essential, particularly in a more challenging economic climate, to ensure that Target can satisfy debt interest and capital repayments as they fall due without this resulting in a breach of banking covenants (which breach might, in turn, necessitate further equity investment or cause the investment to fail).[15]

Funding requirements. The Plan will outline the current financial structure, and the immediate and future funding requirements (and their intended uses), along with anticipated sources of funding. The returns which investors look to achieve are explained in more detail in section 3.4 below, whilst the way in which such investments are typically structured to generate those required returns is explained in chapter 3.

Milestones. The key stages necessary to achieve the Plan, and how they should be attained, will be detailed in the Plan. Private equity houses will need to understand the key milestones envisaged as part of their ultimate exit route, to assess whether the strategy is achievable, and be in a position to monitor progress against those objectives post-investment. It is now customary for investors to require the production of a 90 or 100 Day Plan setting out the activities which must be undertaken in that period immediately after the investment is made, to ensure a seamless transfer of ownership so that Target can 'hit the ground running'. This is often prepared also to address any urgent or important issues that are highlighted by due diligence.

Risk assessment and sensitivity analysis. The Plan should include details of the critical success factors for the achievement of financial projections, including a SWOT analysis (assessing the strengths, weaknesses, opportunities and threats applicable to Target). It should explain in some detail how the risk, and impact on financial projections, of weaknesses and threats can be minimised. Investors will want the management team to demonstrate that they have been thorough in their analysis and are well prepared.

A Business Plan is normally accompanied by a number of appendices, the nature of which will vary depending on the investment opportunity, and the nature of Target. Typically, they will include the more substantial detail and analytical data required to support the information in the body of the document, particularly the historic financial information, financial projections and assumptions underlying those projections, all of which will also be encapsulated in the financial model.

15 On banking covenants, see also chapter 6, section 4.1(g).

3.3 The financial model

The financial model is at the core of the Business Plan. The model incorporates all of the financial information that underpins the Plan in an integrated, electronic form, using spreadsheet and accounting software. The model will include historical financial analysis and financial projections along with the key assumptions made. The projected figures usually encompass historic monthly profit and loss statements, balance sheets and cash flows for three years and, at the very least, quarterly projections for at least a further two years. Once the operating model incorporating all of this historical data and current management forecasts is complete, the deal structure agreed to fund the transaction can be superimposed on the model, enabling private equity and debt funders to analyse the envisaged returns. Inputs to the model can then be altered to reflect changing views on projections as the financial due diligence exercise is undertaken.

The financial model will generally include a comprehensive sensitivity analysis. The projections will be shown both as a 'base case' (which is based on a conservative estimate of anticipated future sales and profits), and an 'upside' scenario (based on sales and profit forecasts reliant on more optimistic assumptions). From there, different *sensitivities* (in simple terms, 'what if?' scenarios) can then be inputted into the model, showing the financial impact of each material risk associated with Target both in general terms, or specific to the strategy itself. The number of scenarios presented can be tailored to suit the particular situation; for example, where there is more than one approach under consideration by the management team, the alternatives can be included as different scenarios within the model, sensitivities can be run against each scenario to demonstrate the implications for each, and then a final strategy chosen.

Responsibility for the production of the model usually falls to the finance director in the management team. However, the corporate finance advisers will again assist in its construction and presentation. This can be particularly important in the later stages of a transaction, when the scope and extent of the due diligence exercise, combined with the other demands on the finance director's time to facilitate the transaction (not to mention continuing to run Target's business), will see the finance director put under considerable strain.

Prior to the execution of the transaction, but most likely after exclusivity has been granted, the private equity house will undertake extensive due diligence to validate the content of the Business Plan and the financial model. Due diligence is considered in chapter 2.

3.4 Investor returns

The Business Plan will need to demonstrate that the private equity funders can expect to achieve a return on their investment which is attractive when compared to other opportunities in the market, and which will satisfy the requirements of their own investors. The measure generally used to assess the return achieved is the internal rate of return (IRR). When fundraising, independent and semi-captive private equity firms tend to market themselves to their own investors based on the IRRs which they have delivered on their previous investments.

Understanding the detailed calculations involved in determining the IRR can be complicated. However, the basic principles applied are relatively straightforward. In its simplest form, the IRR takes into account all of the cash flows which the investor receives in connection with its investment, and the timescale in which such cash flows will be received, and expresses those returns as an average annual percentage return based on the amount of the original investment.

A more technical definition usually states that an IRR is the discount rate applied in order to ensure that the net present value of the relevant cash flows is zero. This can be confusing to non-accountants – perhaps because they do not understand the concepts of a discount rate or net present value, or why the cash flows should ultimately amount to zero when it is applied. A discount rate is an annual percentage rate which is applied to a cash flow which occurs in the future in order to ascertain the value of that future cash flow today (such discounted value being described as that cash flow's net present value). For the purposes of an IRR calculation, amounts invested are treated as a negative cash flow, and cash receipts as a positive cash flow. Accordingly, an IRR calculation requires the calculation of the rate at which any cash invested is discounted to produce a (negative) net present value for such investment which is equal to the (positive) net present value of any cash returns to the investor when discounted at the same rate – the aggregate sum of the positive and negative net present values will be zero when the correct IRR rate has been applied. If it is assumed that the only negative cash flow (i.e. amount invested) is that amount which is invested at the outset of a transaction, then the net present value of that amount, as at the date of the original investment, is simply the amount of that investment – meaning that the IRR is effectively an average annual percentage return achieved on that initial investment when all the cash returns the investor receives in the future, and the date upon which each is received, have been taken into account.

Various cash flows may be received by investors during the life of the investment. As is explained in more detail in chapter 3, the investors typically invest by way of a mixture of equity and debt, and may therefore be entitled to receive interest on their loans, and possibly (although it is more unusual in modern buyouts than was historically the case) dividends on their shareholdings. Cash flows are also received by the investors in the form of arrangement and monitoring fees, although this is often ignored by investors when calculating the IRR achieved. However, it should be borne in mind that interest and dividend payments are often effectively deferred due to the restrictions imposed on the investee company by its bank funders; by delaying the payment in cash terms, the IRR achieved by the investors is effectively reduced, notwithstanding that the interest paid is ultimately the same. The IRR is a measure which reflects the time value of money, as well as the money actually received.

The majority of the investors' return, therefore, will generally take the form of proceeds from the ultimate exit – whether by way of an IPO (or flotation), trade sale, a secondary buyout or some other route. The main exit transactions are considered in more detail later in this book.[16] During times when bank debt is readily available, it may also be possible for investors to achieve a partial exit through a refinancing – for example, by paying down existing debt from profits earned during the initial life of the investment, and then refinancing the remaining debt later (with the investors, and possibly management, extracting the additional cash raised). However an exit may be anticipated to arise, the valuation of that exit and its timing will be critical for the investors to understand the IRR they are likely to achieve.

Two different approaches to achieving an attractive exit (and therefore IRR) might be considered:

(a) *Growing profits*, and therefore the enterprise value of the business on exit. It would be unusual for any Business Plan to be prepared which does not envisage some growth in profits over the lifetime of the investors' holding. Assuming that the strategy set out in the Business Plan will be successful in achieving such growth, the investors would expect to sell (or otherwise exit) Target at a more attractive valuation than that at which it was acquired. That profit growth might be organic, or by way of acquisitions in a 'buy-and-build' strategy.

(b) *Multiple arbitrage*. Profitable businesses are typically valued by reference to a multiple of profits; the precise accounting measure used varies, but is most usually earnings before interest, taxation, depreciation and amortisation of goodwill. The multiple of profit paid will depend on current market sentiment; generally speaking, far lower multiples will be paid for businesses in an economic downturn when confidence is low, whilst higher multiples will be paid in better times. Multiples may also reflect a shifting perspective on the future prospects of a particular sector – witness the high valuations attributed to internet-based companies at the end of the twentieth century, followed by the bursting of the dot com bubble in 2000. Therefore, investors may achieve an attractive exit simply by virtue of exiting at a higher multiple than that used to determine the value of Target on the original investment, even if the actual earnings remain the same.

The reality is that, whilst investors hope to achieve an element of both, multiple arbitrage is a factor outside their control. Most investors will want to ensure they are paying a sensible valuation for an attractive asset – and the impact of multiple arbitrage will often therefore be discounted by investors in

16 See chapters 12 and 13.

Cash multiple	Year 1	2	3	4	5	6	7	8	9	10
2	100%	41%	26%	19%	15%	12%	10%	9%	8%	7%
3	200%	73%	44%	32%	25%	20%	17%	15%	13%	12%
4	300%	100%	59%	41%	32%	26%	22%	19%	17%	15%
5	400%	124%	71%	50%	38%	31%	26%	22%	20%	17%
6	500%	145%	82%	57%	43%	35%	29%	25%	22%	20%
7	600%	165%	91%	63%	48%	38%	32%	28%	24%	21%
8	700%	183%	100%	68%	52%	41%	35%	30%	26%	23%
9	800%	200%	108%	73%	55%	44%	37%	32%	28%	25%
10	900%	216%	115%	78%	58%	47%	39%	33%	29%	26%

Figure 1.2 IRR based on date on which exit is achieved

assessing any Business Plan. Whilst many private equity firms have undoubtedly made spectacular returns as a result of arbitrage, it is not the case that private equity deals grind to a halt in buoyant markets as investors recognise that arbitrage may not be achievable; quite the opposite was true in the UK in the boom period to 2007, when the availability of cheap debt fuelled higher and higher multiples by private equity bidders, with trade buyers often being priced out of the market as a result.

The IRR targeted by private equity investors is typically between 25 per cent and 40 per cent per annum. Exactly what percentage is required by investors within this range will depend on the associated risk of the project, the then prevailing market conditions, and the relative bargaining position of the various funders and management.

To give a simple illustration of what the IRR means in practice, suppose that a private equity investor requires a return of 25 per cent over a five-year period. This might be simplified to a statement that such investors need to realise three times their original investment at the end of that period. Based on this simple example, Figure 1.2 shows the cash multiple required on exit, depending on when that exit is actually achieved.

A typical period for exit on a UK buyout is between three and five years, although, dependent on market conditions, an exit may well take longer in practice. Certainly, most Business Plans will envisage an exit within that period, and investors will be anxious to challenge the assumptions on timing and deliverability of exit given the significant impact this has on the IRR.

The example given above for determining an investor's IRR is, of course, oversimplified. There will be numerous cash flows involved, and the precise timing of each cash flow must be taken into account to provide an accurate measure. Future cash investments may also be necessary to finance future growth and expansion in a positive scenario, or to enable continued trade without a breach of the banking documentation in more difficult times – all such negative cash flows must be taken into account in determining the IRR. Unfortunately, this is not a detail which the legal practitioner can ignore, as the IRR is a common measure used in structuring a ratchet arrangement (which will have to be documented in the articles of association of the Newco[17] bidder).[18] However, whilst this can lead to rather complex drafting, modern accounting software has made the calculation of the IRR ultimately achieved more straightforward – provided that actual cash flows paid are accurately captured in the accounting model during the lifetime of the investment.

4 Conclusion

As we have seen from this brief introduction to the industry, private equity has matured in the UK over the last sixty years, whilst still adapting to a complex and ever-changing business and regulatory environment. It has its supporters and its critics, its champions and its detractors. Its successes at times have led to an image problem in the minds of many, and it has not always seen the need to explain its actions to the wider business community or to the public, or the need to be that concerned with what others think about it. However, that it has played a very major part in the recent business history of the UK and many other developed markets, and that it is playing an increasing role in many emerging economies, is indisputable.

The future is always uncertain. The industry has changed over the years, and the combined effects of the credit crunch and the increased spotlight in which private equity must operate will change it further. As long as good business opportunities can be put forward that need more money than the owners (or would-be owners) and debt lenders can provide, and all that they can realistically offer to attract that extra money is a share in the future with great upside potential but little downside protection, there will be private equity investors trying to make a turn by bridging that gap. It seems highly likely that private equity will always have a role to play in any capitalist system where the capital of some players can combine with the ambitions, potential, ideas and skills of others to share the resultant success.

We will now begin to examine in more detail how that combination has been realised in the recent market in the UK. Practice in the future will change – but the factors that have created the current market will continue to underpin how practice will develop going forward.

17 The creation of one or more new companies (Newcos) to facilitate buyouts is explained in chapter 3.

18 See further chapter 3 section 3.2, and chapter 5 section 4.6.

2

The deal process and preliminary matters

1 Introduction

In this chapter, we will look in more detail at the deal process and certain preliminary matters encountered in a typical private equity deal. This will set the scene for the more detailed analysis of deal structures in chapter 3, and the discussion of the key transaction areas and documentation that follow in the later chapters of this book. We also look at the advisers retained by the parties in a deal, and some of the commercial issues and tensions that can arise in respect of their terms of engagement. Market practice has developed over time in this area, and professional and trade bodies have played a role in resolving some of these aspects – enabling the parties and their advisers to align themselves with less friction and delay to the process.

This chapter also considers the early stages in the relationship between the potential sellers and the potential buyers – what risks each faces as a result of the deal process, and the protections they may seek to mitigate these risks. Heads of agreement are used to structure the deal itself (to some extent) and also to set the expectations of the parties in relation to the deal process, giving the parties the confidence to commit the time and expense needed to reach a final, binding contract. In the period leading to the summer of 2007, auction processes became ever more favourable to sellers, having a significant impact on deal processes as sellers looked to exploit the competitive tension that could be created between competing bidders. Changes in the market since then will undoubtedly lead to a significant swinging back of bargaining power towards buyers.

Finally in this chapter, we begin to consider the risks that a private equity investor may face in acquiring a business, and look at the importance of due diligence in identifying and addressing these concerns.

2 The deal process: an overview

The deal process for any given buyout will vary according to the circumstances in which the transaction opportunity has arisen, and the market conditions prevailing at the time. However, the general nature of the required steps is relatively consistent and it is only the order in which those steps are taken, and the detail behind those general steps, that will vary. Corporate finance advisers on the transaction will include such steps in a detailed timetable which is circulated to all of the relevant advisers; in the case of a seller-led auction this may well be prepared by the seller's advisers (who will also strictly control adherence to such timetables by competing bidders by way of comprehensive process letters). In other cases, the advisers to the private equity house will take the lead. The steps will include:

- preparation/completion of an information memorandum concerning Target's business by the seller's advisers (save, perhaps, where a deal is originated by the private equity bidder and progresses on an exclusive basis[1] with no need for marketing);
- preparation/completion of the Business Plan;
- management presentations to interested investors and banks (where there is a competitive process);
- appointment of advisers;
- selection of a preferred bidder (where relevant) and agreement of heads of terms/granting of exclusivity (discussed later in this chapter);
- due diligence, which will invariably include financial, legal, taxation and commercial due diligence, and (depending on the house style of the relevant investors, and the particular requirements of the deal and sector) may also include insurance, property, environmental, pensions, operational, IT and, increasingly, management due diligence;
- approaches to, and selection of, bank funders, and necessary work for the setting of appropriate bank covenants;
- legal documentation, including acquisition, equity and debt documents;[2] and
- legal completion (the completion meeting).

The way in which these consistent steps can be incorporated within very different processes is best illustrated by contrasting a deal originated by a private equity funder 'off-market' with a seller-led auction. Figure 2.1 compares possible outline timetables for the two processes.

This comparison of admittedly simplistic timetables – the comprehensive timetable issued by the relevant corporate finance adviser will include detailed steps in relation to each stage of the process – demonstrates a number of reasons why auctions are generally so unattractive to private equity buyers (as mentioned in chapter 1). In an auction, a seller usually controls the information that will be made available to bidders, and the timing of the release of that information, including the use of vendor due diligence and a controlled data room.[3] The seller(s) will approach possible bank funders to

1 See further chapter 1, section 2.4.
2 For an overview, see chapter 3, section 4.
3 See further section 4.2 below.

Week	Originated Deal (Buyer-led)	Auction (Seller-led)
1	Initial offer or letter of intent submitted [Note: Such offer is often facilitated by a 'headline' financial due diligence exercise]	Information Memorandum (IM) issued
2 3	Advisers appointed **Heads of terms agreed and exclusivity granted**	Advisers appointed Banks approached/selected by seller(s) Bidders submit initial offers
4 5 6 7	Financial, legal and other due diligence Banks approached/selected by buyer Investors may issue equity termsheet and first draft legal documents	Vendor due diligence released and data room made available to 'second round' bidders with management presentation Draft SPA and management termsheet 'Stapled' bank offers communicated to bidders Bidders submit proposed management terms, and mark up of SPA
8 9 10 11	Legal documentation negotiated and agreed Final (confirmatory) due diligence work Business Plan finalised	**Heads of terms agreed, and exclusivity granted, to preferred bidder** Finalisation of SPA Equity/bank funding documented Final (confirmatory) due diligence work Business Plan finalised
12	Completion	Completion

Figure 2.1 Auctions versus originated deals: a comparison

secure banking offers, and provide details of those offers to private equity bidders (a so-called 'stapled' debt package), on an understanding that bidders will be strongly favoured if they can demonstrate deliverability of their final offers by agreeing to fund the transaction with one of these preferred lenders. Draft legal documentation and detailed termsheets setting out the proposed terms for management's equity package will also be issued by the seller before a single preferred bidder is selected, encouraging buyers to put their best foot forward in submitting their final offers. Critically, as highlighted by the bold text in Figure 2.1, the private equity firm is selected and granted exclusivity far later in the transaction process (resulting in an increased costs exposure for bidders), with the seller encouraging the buyer to complete the transaction in a short timescale once that exclusivity has been granted based on the significant work and negotiations that have already taken place – whilst the example above suggests a three-week timetable to completion, in the bullish buyout market experienced up to the summer of 2007 the periods were often far shorter. The timing of the granting of exclusivity is key; in many ways, at that point, the balance of negotiating power switches from the seller(s) to the buyer (although, as is discussed in section 3.3 below, the granting of exclusivity does not amount to a legal agreement on the part of the seller(s) to negotiate should they subsequently become dissatisfied).

Originally, exclusivity was designed to protect the buyer, who is likely to invest considerable time and expense (including professional fees) in negotiating the legal documentation and undertaking substantial due diligence. Private equity investors are also very keen to ensure that there is an obligation to talk only to them as early in the process as possible in order to ensure that they are not being used as a stalking horse, and to minimise their exposure to a situation where multiple potential bidders are being played off against each other. The advantages of an originated deal, rather than an auction, in terms of process should be obvious in both respects.

Whilst auctions were particularly prominent until the credit crunch had such a significant impact on UK transactions, it will be informative to see the deal process that emerges once transaction activity increases again. Clearly, the market has become more favourable to buyers, and it is likely that the desire of bidders for exclusivity at an early stage will become ever more compelling. Private equity firms will place an increased emphasis on origination (when they are not preoccupied dealing with difficulties in their existing portfolio of investments); however, sellers will still expect a fair price for valuable businesses, and there is a high level of awareness of how a good corporate finance adviser and a well-run deal process can be instrumental in securing this. Low market confidence causes an increased risk of buyers walking away, which a well-run sale process can also help to manage. Therefore, a transaction process which contains elements of both extremes should be expected in many cases; sellers may well prepare an information memorandum, and approach a selection of possible bidders from both private equity and trade, but the target audience will most likely be selected after considerable thought, and be smaller in number. Similarly, banks may well still be approached by the sellers, but this may be to ensure that a business is actually 'bankable' in a difficult climate (to ensure an approach to private equity bidders is credible), rather than an attempt to present a specific debt package as 'stapled' to the sale process in itself. Most importantly, sellers are more likely to be sympathetic to arguments that exclusivity should be granted before any detailed legal or other advisory work is undertaken.

It should also be clear that a buyout is a significant project. Lawyers and other advisers must manage complex issues relating not only to the Target business and acquisition terms, but also to securing the necessary debt and equity funding. Project management is key and, provided it is structured sensibly, a comprehensive timetable should assist with this. Completion meetings are often particularly fraught, in many cases simply because the parties and their lawyers have convened the meeting prematurely. The legal adviser must work closely with the corporate finance adviser throughout the process both to keep the project on track and to manage their mutual client's expectations. It is often worthwhile scheduling a 'dummy run', lawyers-only, completion meeting a day or so ahead of the suggested completion date, which will help identify and iron out the issues or identify and allocate tasks which otherwise might arise at the last moment, to everybody's frustration.

Much of the legal adviser's time will be spent drafting and negotiating the key legal documentation towards the end of the transaction process. However, there are various preliminary matters where a legal adviser will often be asked to provide input by a client (whether a seller, private equity firm or management team), or by a client's corporate finance adviser. Indeed, such preliminary input can be particularly helpful in ensuring that the more substantial legal process that follows later runs more smoothly.

3 Preliminary matters

3.1 Engaging advisers

At an early stage in the process, the private equity investor will usually engage a number of key advisers. Not all advisers will be engaged at the same time, and not all advice is needed in the early stages – generally, as the negotiation advances and the transaction becomes more certain, the private equity investor will look to appoint additional advisers and to extend the role of those already appointed. The range of advisers needed for a transaction will vary depending upon the nature and extent of the business, the jurisdictions in which it operates and, later in the process, on the particular issues or concerns that are identified by due diligence.

The two key advisers will, generally speaking, be the accounting advisers (who may undertake accounting due diligence, corporate finance advisory work and tax due diligence), and the legal advisers who will undertake the legal due diligence and negotiate the acquisition, equity and banking documents as part of the overall client team. Sometimes, either or both of these firms will have been instrumental in originating the deal, and accordingly may already have secured a role in the transaction.

An important consideration for private equity investors when engaging advisers is the question of costs. In completed deals, adviser costs are generally met by the buyer (or possibly another company in the buyer group, where there is a more complex group structure[4]), and accordingly the amount of such aggregated costs are taken into account in determining the funding required for the deal and a suitable provision will be included in the relevant section of the financial model. As we have seen, many potential private equity opportunities that are investigated do not lead to a concluded transaction for the party investigating, however. Accordingly, there is an increased risk for private equity investors that they will have a liability for the costs of any advisers retained personally if a transaction ultimately aborts or is closed by another bidder.

In the competitive auction processes seen in the period up to summer 2007, this became an increasing concern for private equity investors – as highlighted in section 2, the methods in which these auctions were run required potential bidders to do an ever increasing amount of work before exclusivity. Every transaction has some abort risk, although if exclusivity is obtained there is usually a fair chance that the transaction will proceed. However, the auction processes had effectively increased the costs exposure, in many cases to significant levels, even before exclusivity.

In the UK, as a result of this exposure, an emerging dynamic in the relationship between private equity investors and their retained advisers has been the sharing of this transaction risk between them. For example, certain advisers may agree to carry out work for a limited fee (or even at no cost) up to the stage of exclusivity. In the more orthodox market operating before the height of auction processes, this may well have been a reasonable exposure for the advisers to accept (as highlighted in section 2, the work required before exclusivity may have been limited to a very preliminary review of data, a very limited amount of due diligence, and negotiation of the heads of agreement or perhaps only an indicative offer letter). As the auction processes became more prominent, however, the amount of work the potential bidder had to do before getting exclusivity (and the risk of not getting exclusivity) significantly increased; as a result, the costs exposure before exclusivity tended to escalate, and therefore other arrangements were sometimes agreed. Those firms with strong links with trusted advisers might negotiate a contingent arrangement, on an understanding that any fees accrued from an aborted deal would be carried forward to the next engagement until a deal was ultimately concluded. Others would be left incurring far more significant costs on aborted transactions.

It is important to note in this context that the professional rules applicable to certain advisers limit or preclude the undertaking of certain work on a contingent basis, particularly in the area of financial due diligence. Practice in this respect also differs in certain jurisdictions and, accordingly, where advisers

4 See further chapter 3, and in particular section 3.4 concerning transaction costs.

are retained overseas for a cross-border transaction, the local rules in relation both to market practice and to professional conduct should also be checked.

It remains to be seen whether the abortive costs risks associated with carrying out significant work before exclusivity is granted will be reduced in the more buyer-friendly market conditions prevailing since summer 2007. Rather than the competitiveness of auctions leading to a number of disappointed buyers on the chase for exclusivity, it is likely that other factors will cause potential transactions not to proceed (for example, scarcity of debt funding, or an inability to meet or modify the seller's price expectation).

3.2 Engagement letters

A lawyer appointed by investors will clearly need to agree the terms of that firm's engagement by way of an engagement letter with the relevant private equity firm. However, in addition to this, it is usual for any engagement letters proposed by other advisers or due diligence providers to be passed on to the law firm for review on the investors' behalf. This review exercise can be substantial, particularly in the case of accountancy firms or investment banks where a detailed engagement letter is often accompanied with 'small print' standard terms and conditions. In addition to general advice concerning the scope of work, fees payable and other key contractual terms, there are certain areas of negotiation where some background information and context is helpful to the lawyer.

(a) Limitations on liability

The Big Four[5] (or, as they were previously, the Big Six) accountancy firms have, like many other advisers, sought over the years to limit their professional liability where possible. This became an increasingly contentious matter in the mid-1990s in the UK, and led to delays on transactions (or at least on agreeing engagement letters) until this issue was addressed. Partly to reduce the time spent on these matters, a Memorandum of Understanding was agreed between the Big Six (as they then were) and the BVCA in February 1998.[6] Whilst this is not a legally binding document, in practice it has gained acceptance throughout the private equity and banking industries and beyond, and throughout accountancy practices both within and, in some cases, outside the current Big Four.

The most notable content of the Memorandum of Understanding is the prescribed amounts given for the cap on the accountancy firms' overall liability from an engagement based on the transaction value. The liability caps prescribed by the Memorandum of Understanding are as follows:

- if the transaction value is less than £10 million, the transaction value;

5 Deloitte, Ernst & Young, KPMG and PricewaterhouseCoopers.

6 Memorandum of Understanding, 18 February 1998.

- if the transaction value is greater than £10 million, but less than £55 million, an amount equal to £10 million plus one-third of the amount by which the transaction value exceeds £10 million; and
- for transactions with a value of more than £55 million, £25 million.

For these purposes, the 'transaction value' is defined as the aggregate of the new equity and debt being invested relating to the transaction. Some commentators have suggested (in response to the larger deals transacted in the period since the Memorandum of Understanding) that these limits, and especially the overall cap at £25 million, should be revised to reflect the increasing size and complexity of many of the more recent deals. However, advisers have generally been able to hold the line on this (in the mid-market at least). In the more buyer-friendly markets prevailing into 2009, with fewer deals and a greater keenness on the part of advisers to win advisory work, it will be interesting to see if attempts to reopen these thresholds meet with any more success.

(b) Proportionality

The Memorandum of Understanding also includes provisions relating to proportionality wording in accountants' engagement letters. Many advisers have historically tried to include a proportionate liability clause that seeks to mitigate the adviser's liability to the extent that the courts might consider it just and equitable to view some other person as principally responsible for the losses in question. Such clauses are an attempt to extend further the general defences that are available to adviser firms in respect of such matters, such as causation principles, contributory negligence, the ability to join in or seek contributions from third parties and common law duties to mitigate loss. Such clauses have therefore proved to be contentious, with many investors (or their legal advisers) arguing that such general principles should be relied on, without the need for an additional contractual defence.

Proportionality matters to advisers, however, because, without it, all advisers who contributed to a loss are generally jointly and severally liable to the claimant for the full amount of that loss (with a right on the part of the advisers to pursue each other adviser for a contribution). Accordingly, one adviser who might be considered to be, say, 20 per cent at fault may nevertheless face 100 per cent of the claim – and any right of contribution in favour of that adviser from other advisers might be worthless (for example, if the other responsible parties, or their insurers, are no longer trading or otherwise not good for their share).

In the Memorandum of Understanding it was agreed that no specific proportionality provisions would be included in smaller or mid-market transactions (at that time defined as transactions with a value of up to £55 million). Beyond this amount, however, it is stated that proportionality wording may be included, given the larger exposure on such transactions. In any such case, it may be necessary to consider and negotiate such wording (which can vary from accountancy firm to accountancy firm) having due regard to the nature of the transaction and the bargaining position of the relevant parties.

(c) 'Hold harmless' provisions

One final clause which is often found in an adviser's engagement letter is an indemnity or 'hold harmless' provision. This should be distinguished from the hold harmless or indemnity provisions often included in a separate letter for the release of audit papers for due diligence purposes, which is referred to in section 4 below. This provision in the engagement letter is intended to ensure that the relevant client will indemnify the adviser firm for any losses it suffers as a result of a claim by a third party against it relating to the transaction. Some of these provisions are drafted very widely, so care is needed in their negotiation, although most firms will be sensible in limiting the recovery to those situations which they are really trying to cover.

Private equity investors and banks may well be subject to their own internal rules and policies as to whether they are able to provide any such hold harmless provision at all, or whether they are able to give such an undertaking on an indemnity basis, in which case it may be necessary for such qualification only to be given by the management team personally and/or by the buyer Newco (which is of limited value unless and until the transaction actually completes, and even then Newco may offer little comfort if the dispute which has arisen is significant and reduces the value of that company).

3.3 Heads of agreement and exclusivity

In order to give some structure to the transaction, and to satisfy both the seller(s) and the buyer that the time and professional costs to be incurred (in negotiating an acquisition agreement, carrying out due diligence, securing funding and negotiating funding documents) are likely to be justified, it is usually the case that the parties will seek to agree heads of agreement (often referred to simply as 'heads') at an early stage in the acquisition process. With certain important exceptions, the provisions in these heads are usually expressly stated to be non-binding, and accordingly do not amount to a contractual commitment. However, they are important in satisfying each party that the key commercial terms are being addressed and that there is, in principle, a transaction in reach.

The heads will set out the nature of the transaction (for example, whether it is to proceed by way of a share sale or an asset sale), the consideration payable, and any conditions attached to that consideration (for example, any net asset or working capital test, or earn out arrangements[7]). It may also contain outline details in relation to the warranties and limitations, the restrictive covenants to be provided by the seller(s) and any other important commercial arrangements to be entered into between the seller(s) and the buyer.[8]

There has been a tendency for heads to become ever more complicated and protracted. Clearly, there is a balance to be struck between ensuring that

7 See chapter 4, section 2.2.

8 These matters are considered in more detail in chapter 4.

there is agreement in principle on the key points (thereby reducing the risk that the transaction may fall over during due diligence and negotiation of the detailed legal documentation), and making the heads such an exhaustive document that it starts to resemble the acquisition agreement itself. In particular, in the absence of substantial vendor due diligence,[9] the buyer is unlikely to be in a situation where it has all the material facts necessary to agree all of the key terms. Accordingly, heads are inevitably expressed to be conditional upon the outcome of due diligence. For this reason, there is usually a desire (on the buyer's part in particular) to move on from discussing the heads so that this due diligence process may be undertaken once the key commercial terms (and particularly the price) have been agreed, rather than seeking to agree absolutely everything upfront. The buyer is particularly driven to secure exclusivity, which is usually dealt with in the heads.

Although the heads are generally non-binding for this reason, there are certain key clauses which the parties (or at least one of them) will insist should be legally binding.

(a) Confidentiality

The seller(s) and the Target have a keen interest in protecting the confidential information of the business. Although this is perhaps a more obvious issue when dealing with a trade buyer, a similarly cautious approach is nevertheless usually adopted when the buyer is a private-equity-backed company. Accordingly, it will be usual for the seller(s) to require any interested buyer to enter into a formal confidentiality letter at an early stage, sometimes as a prerequisite for access to the information memorandum or other details of the sale process. In the case of a private equity bidder, this may be signed not only by the private equity investors themselves, but also by the buyer Newco (if that company is already established, which is not always the case at this preliminary stage). Assuming such a confidentiality letter or agreement (also referred to as a 'non-disclosure agreement', or NDA) was in place prior to the heads being entered into, it is customary for the parties to confirm that such arrangements continue to bind them in respect of their ongoing negotiations.

Prior to 1999, the form of confidentiality agreement was often an area of detailed and time-consuming negotiation between the parties. Whilst the core principles of the agreement seem simple enough, the legal detail can become demanding where provisions are proposed and negotiated to deal with every possible exposure. For example, the inclusion of clauses designed to make the private equity investor responsible for any breach of confidentiality by its advisers or other agents, or requiring it to indemnify the seller(s) in the event of any breach, often led to protracted legal debate – it could sometimes take a week or even a fortnight simply to agree the confidentiality terms to allow commercial discussions and information sharing to begin.

9 See section 4.2 below.

Confidentiality is clearly important – but it should not be allowed to introduce any unnecessary delay into a transaction which the parties otherwise wish to explore, or to create unwanted early friction between the parties. For this reason, in 1999, the BVCA produced a standard form confidentiality agreement, which it has since revised and amended in minor ways. Although this is not binding on parties wishing to participate in buyouts in any legal or regulatory sense, it has achieved a high level of acceptance, and now is often the basis used for confidentiality terms (even in deals with no private equity involvement). Indeed, many private equity investors are willing to sign a confidentiality agreement in this standard form for the purpose of initial exploratory talks before involving their own legal advisers. Accordingly, if the sellers are willing to accept this form of agreement, it can accelerate the process and enable the parties to focus on what are usually more important matters.

Irrespective of whether confidentiality arrangements are stated in full in the heads, or the heads simply make reference to an existing document, the parties will wish to ensure that such provisions are legally binding. A buyer may also wish to include an obligation on the part of the seller(s), and *vice versa*, that the fact that negotiations are taking place is treated in confidence.

(b) Exclusivity

The principle of exclusivity has already been referred to, namely, an arrangement between the parties that negotiations will take place only between the seller(s) and that particular party to have been granted exclusivity. Under these provisions, the seller(s) are obliged not to negotiate with any other party or provide information to them, and to break off any such discussions that are already taking place. English law draws a distinction between an obligation actively to negotiate with the particular preferred bidder (which is generally too vague to be enforceable as a matter of law) and a negative obligation not to speak to or have any dealings with any other bidder. This latter obligation will generally be enforceable under English law – see the House of Lords decision in *Walford* v. *Miles*.[10]

In considering the detailed terms of any exclusivity arrangement, the seller(s) must have regard not only to whether the price and other terms set out in the heads are acceptable, but also to related factors concerning deliverability. As well as the obvious question of for how long exclusivity will be granted, sellers may also require certain milestones to be achieved at particular stages in the transaction for exclusivity to remain in place, or particular evidence of the availability of appropriate funding (including debt finance) to fund the acquisition to be provided or confirmed at such stages. Exclusivity may then be revoked before the agreed end date if certain milestones are not achieved, or if the buyer seeks to renegotiate key commercial terms. This is particularly important to sellers who feel that the buyer may look to reduce the

10 [1992] AC 128.

price; sellers are often of the view that private equity buyers have a habit of 'chipping' the headline price during (and often late on in) the acquisition process. Whether this is entirely a fair reputation (and whether they are any more 'chippy' than trade buyers) are moot points – it is perhaps fairer to say that the negotiating styles of different buyers will vary, whether they are private equity firms or not. Tying exclusivity to milestones and continued deliverability in this way at least gives the sellers the opportunity to consider other approaches if the favoured bidder does start to chip.

(c) Costs underwrites and indemnities

The heads may include some form of costs underwrite or indemnity, usually in favour of the buyer, which is often linked with the exclusivity terms. Under these provisions, the buyer's costs (or costs up to a capped amount) are underwritten by the seller(s) if the transaction does not proceed because of a breach of exclusivity.

In a public-to-private transaction (where the Target is a public limited company) special rules apply, as discussed in chapter 10.[11] In other circumstances, a costs underwrite is usually only available in the context of exclusivity, such that a contribution to the buyer's costs (often a fixed amount, or limited by way of a cap) is payable in the event that the seller(s) breach the terms of the exclusivity clause. In a seller-friendly market, costs underwrites are of course less common, or may be capped at relatively low amounts in the context of the potential abortive costs of the buyer. As the market becomes more buyer-friendly, there is likely to be an increasing emphasis on these costs underwrites, especially if more time and attention will be needed (and accordingly more fees and costs potentially incurred) to get the banking in place and the deal over the line.

It is possible that costs underwrites may be triggered in other circumstances. A common proposition is that either party should be protected where the other seeks materially to change the terms set out in the heads. This is most obviously introduced by sellers to mitigate the risk of 'chipping', although it can work both ways; however, private equity buyers are often unwilling to provide such underwrites, and in any event the fact that an offer is usually subject to broad conditions such as satisfactory due diligence means that the effectiveness of such protection is limited anyway.

In negotiating a costs underwrite, it is important to bear in mind that there are many reasons why a transaction may not proceed other than because the sellers seek to back out or breach exclusivity. These could include any of the following:

- problems identified in due diligence which cannot be addressed in negotiation or in the legal agreements;
- competition or other regulatory consents or approvals not being received;

11 See chapter 10, section 3.1.

- shareholder approval (for example, where the seller is a listed company[12]) not being obtained;
- debt or other funding not being available on suitable terms or being withdrawn; and
- failure to agree the key equity terms or ancillary documentation.

All of these factors should be taken into account when advising clients on the effectiveness of a costs underwrite. Generally speaking, clients should understand that a costs underwrite will only protect them if a deal does not proceed for the specific reasons covered. The other party will be extremely diligent in trying to ensure that they do not breach the relevant obligations, and in any event it can be very difficult to prove that a breach actually occurred. For this reason, recovery under a costs underwrite is extremely rare; however, the focus that it imposes on the parties to ensure strict compliance with the relevant terms means that they are nevertheless of some value.

4 Due diligence

4.1 Overview of due diligence

The buyer of a business will rely on his legal advisers to ensure (insofar as possible) that he is afforded sufficient protection in the acquisition agreement or other legal documents in the event that the Target acquired does not perform as was envisaged in the Business Plan, or if a material issue arises within the business post-acquisition which, had he been aware of such risk before completion, may have affected his decision to proceed at the originally offered price, or possibly at all. However, the limitations of a buyer relying on such legal protection alone should be obvious. For example:

- A buyer would prefer to know about any such issues before transacting, and to negotiate with the seller to reflect the implications of those issues, rather than chasing the seller for financial compensation by way of an action for damages after the deal.
- The ability of the buyer to pursue such an action under general law is limited. In theory, an action may be possible based on deceit, misrepresentation or possibly a breach of statutory duty,[13] but this will generally be limited to more extreme cases of dishonesty, so in most circumstances the principle of *caveat emptor* prevails.
- The prospect of a successful contractual action against either the seller(s) or the management team for a breach of the warranties set out in the relevant transaction documents may also be severely limited. As is outlined later in

12 See further chapter 4, section 2.5(b).

13 For example, section 397 of the Financial Services and Markets Act 2000 provides that persons making misleading, false or dishonest statements may in certain circumstances be guilty of a criminal offence.

this book, such warranties will be subject to comprehensive limitations of liability on the part of the relevant warrantors, and proving that an actual breach has occurred and the damages that have arisen as a consequence is a significant hurdle (not to mention the fact that an investor would prefer not to sue the management team, and a seller may no longer be 'good for the money' even if a claim were to be successful).[14]

A private equity firm (like most other buyers) will therefore insist on a thorough process of due diligence before completing any proposed acquisition or investment. For the lawyer, the most relevant process is that of legal due diligence. However, a lawyer advising on private equity transactions must understand the nature and function of all types of due diligence carried out by the investors and their advisers.

4.2 Vendor due diligence and data rooms

As was highlighted earlier in this chapter, the auction processes which became so prominent during the boom period up to the summer of 2007 invariably included an increased level of control by sellers on the scope and extent of due diligence.

Wherever there is an auction process, or the sellers are otherwise sufficiently sophisticated to undertake a measured and controlled process for the release of due diligence information, it would be usual to find that the sellers and their advisers have established a data room as part of the transaction process. The traditional data room takes the form of a secure and continually monitored room, normally in the offices of the sellers' lawyers, which the bidders and their advisers will visit in order to inspect and report on the various documents included in the room.

The traditional hard copy data room has now largely been replaced by virtual data rooms – essentially an internet site with secure, controlled access being made available to possible bidders. Although some sellers may be nervous as to the security of such sites, the industry is now well developed and the protection afforded to sellers is probably more substantial than in a traditional data room. For example, the ability of persons accessing the site to forward, copy or print any of the materials supplied can be restricted. There are also commercial advantages – the amount of time that each bidder team is spending in the site can be monitored, and multiple bidders can have access to the site at the same time without knowing the identities of each other.

By preparing a data room, sellers can ensure that all bidders receive consistent information. They can also control the addition of new data to the data room in stages, as the more credible bidders emerge – this is particularly important where bidders include trade competitors, to whom the sellers may

14 For more on warranties and limitations, including the practical considerations before pursuing a claim against management, see chapter 4, section 2.7, and chapter 5, section 3.4.

well be reluctant to provide sensitive or confidential financial information until a very late stage. The corporate finance adviser for the sellers will often begin the process of compiling the data room, setting out the scope of information to be included which the sellers then provide in relation to Target. However, if possible, it is preferable for the sellers' lawyers to supplement this list of required information with comprehensive enquiries from their own standard information request. This reduces the possibility of the data room being criticised for being inadequate or incomplete by the lawyers acting for the buyer (who may, in turn, advise their client significantly to renegotiate terms later in the deal process when these issues emerge, reducing the competitive advantage which the data room process can otherwise provide to the sellers). Vendor due diligence also allows problematic issues to be identified before detailed discussions begin, enabling sellers to be better prepared in negotiating those aspects or, better still, to take action to resolve them.

The sellers may go further than this and ask its accounting, and possibly legal, advisers to prepare a vendor due diligence report. A due diligence report is prepared by those advisers, based on the information provided in the data room, as if they were acting for the buyer, and such draft reports are made available to bidders as part of the data room content. Bidders are asked to put forward final offers based on the content of those reports, and, once a preferred bidder is selected, an already prepared form of engagement letter is signed which allows that bidder to rely on the report as that adviser's own client; in essence, the adviser switches sides at that point for the purpose of its due diligence work.

Whilst a vendor due diligence exercise allows sellers to exercise a further level of control over the deal process, there are disadvantages. In a less competitive market, buyers may be more bullish about wanting their own advisers to conduct the due diligence, which can make vendor due diligence wasteful in terms of cost and time. Even if a bidder is prepared to accept vendor due diligence, the question of how the costs of preparing that report will be met must still be addressed. Whilst sellers may argue that a bidder would have to cover the cost of a due diligence exercise in any event, buyers may be reluctant to pay all or any of the cost involved when they have not been involved in choosing the adviser or scoping their review, particularly where they feel that some 'top up' work is needed once they are selected as preferred bidder to address any gaps or specific areas of concern (as is usually the case). Accordingly, the additional control provided to sellers may well come at a price.

4.3 Legal due diligence

The key objective of legal due diligence is to enable the private equity investors (and the bank funders, who are usually also an addressee of the report) to understand and, where possible, quantify any legal risks associated with completing the transaction or within Target itself. It is essentially a legal audit; each key area of Target's business is investigated, and a report is produced highlighting any issues or areas of risk, typically arising as a result of disputes or non-compliance with laws, the nature of which may be relatively insignificant or substantial.

For the practitioner, undertaking a controlled yet comprehensive review of this nature can be challenging. By its nature, the exercise requires the involvement and co-ordination of numerous specialist colleagues, and as a consequence the process can have a tendency to run away with itself. However, a carefully managed and timely legal due diligence exercise can not only facilitate the transaction, but also add value to private equity clients and their investments.

Sometimes, the process of legal due diligence can become confused with the process of disclosure.[15] There is similarity in subject matter, in that both result in a fairly detailed document being prepared highlighting various legal issues that may be of concern to the buyer. However, the distinction between the two processes must be carefully maintained. The process of legal due diligence is generally buyer-led, with the buyer's advisers usually providing a questionnaire with comprehensive enquiries the responses to which form the basis of the report. Even where a vendor legal due diligence exercise is undertaken (which is, in itself, more rare than vendor accounting due diligence), the buyer will usually reserve the right to ask more detailed or probing questions to supplement that exercise. As a result, the adequacy of legal due diligence is entirely dependent on the accuracy and comprehensiveness of the responses provided – if any such responses are inadequate or misleading (whether through deliberate withholding, recklessness or otherwise), this will be reflected in the quality of the due diligence. In contrast, the disclosure exercise is seller-led, requiring the relevant seller(s) to provide details of any material facts which give rise to a breach, or potential breach, of the warranties. Therefore, whilst the exercises are distinct, there is a continuing interaction between the two. The findings of due diligence will inform the warranties that should be sought in the sale agreement; equally, the fact that formal disclosure is necessary to qualify those warranties means that information either validating or supplementing the responses to the legal due diligence enquiries is flushed out by that process.

Understanding the scope of the legal due diligence exercise is very important; such scope should be agreed with the client in some detail. Certain issues which are material for a retail business will not be at all relevant for an engineering business, and *vice versa*. As well as giving careful thought to the areas which are of most importance to the business, it is usual to agree a concept of materiality (typically, a financial limit fixed as a sensible proportion of the deal size) below which issues need not be raised in the report. This limitation, and any other limitations proposed by the lawyer in allowing addressees to rely on the report, should ideally be approved by the bank funders as well as the equity funders wherever that is possible.

By way of overview, the areas covered by legal due diligence include the following matters.

15 For disclosure generally, see chapter 4, section 3.

(a) Constitutional matters and accounts

Copies of the memorandum and articles of association will be reviewed for each group company, and cross-checked against those filed at Companies House or any relevant overseas registries. Details of all existing shareholders, option holders and directors and officers will also be checked by reference to such public records, and Target's statutory books. Particular interest will be taken in Target's existing funding arrangements, and the documentation for any previous acquisitions and disposals, joint ventures or similar transactions.

(b) Contracts and trading

Legal due diligence should identify the basis on which Target carries on its business in the ordinary course. Any material customer and supplier contracts will be reviewed, together with standard terms of sale and supply. Any contracts or arrangements which are outside the ordinary course will also be carefully scrutinised, especially where they involve dealings with other group companies or family members of the shareholders where relevant, to ensure that the terms are at arm's length and assess whether such arrangements should continue or be altered.

(c) Licences and consents

It is important that due diligence identifies any licences or consents that are necessary for Target to continue to trade. Even assuming that the Target company is to be acquired rather than its business and assets (such that those arrangements will be in the name of the correct legal entity that continues to trade post-completion), there may be notification or renewal processes triggered by virtue of the change of control, or any changes to Target's board. Any correspondence relating to the establishment or maintenance of any licences or consents must also be reviewed.

(d) Assets

Target's title to all material assets will be clarified. This will include inspection of the fixed asset register, and a review of any relevant hire purchase, factoring, invoice discounting or leasing contracts.

(e) Employees and pensions

The current terms of key employees will need to be reviewed. Usually, senior staff will be party to stand-alone service agreements, which in the case of the managers will be replaced with new contracts in a form acceptable to the private equity investors on completion,[16] but the employment terms for all employees should in any event be checked to ensure compliance with laws. Supporting documentation such as staff handbooks, details of bonus or

16 See chapter 7, section 2, for more on the content of such service agreements.

profit-sharing schemes or other benefits, and health and safety policies should also be checked. The presence of trade unions adds a further complexity, where there may be binding collective agreements to review and other customs and practices to consider.

As mentioned above, legal due diligence will also identify the nature of Target's pension scheme(s), and will include a review of all relevant documentation including, where appropriate, the trust deed and rules, latest actuarial valuations and details of scheme members. The complexities of a transaction with a final salary pension scheme are considered in detail in chapter 8.

(f) Investigations, disputes and litigation

Details will be requested of any current, or pending or threatened, litigation or disputes. Due diligence should distinguish between disputes that might be considered ordinary course (for example, minor employee disputes will be viewed as inevitable in a business with a large workforce; likewise some degree of customer complaint in a retail business) and those which are material either because of the amount in dispute in itself, or the knock-on implications that dispute may have for Target if it suggests an underlying flaw in Target's business. This area overlaps with insurance due diligence (as the availability of insurance to cover any such claims will be assessed), and also financial due diligence (as adequate provision for such liabilities will need to be included within Target's financial records, and the Business Plan).

(g) Intellectual property

Details of both registered and unregistered intellectual property will be investigated. The former is relatively straightforward, as the responses to the preliminary enquiries can be verified by searches the relevant public registries, but understanding the ownership of unregistered intellectual property (particularly copyright) can be more difficult, particularly where external consultants have been involved in the design of key brochures or literature, or bespoke IT systems. Relevant intellectual property licences granted by the Target group and those granted to it will also be reviewed.

(h) Property and environmental

Target's title to any freehold or leasehold properties will be investigated. There are two possibilities here: the buyer's solicitors may investigate title themselves and provide a report on such title to their clients; or, alternatively, the sellers' solicitors might be willing to provide a certificate of title to the buyer and its funders. Whilst a buyer generally resists accepting due diligence from the sellers' advisers, there can be particular advantages to this approach in relation to property, as the solicitors in question may be very familiar with the title from previous dealings (and this advantage is magnified if the Target has a large number of separate properties, for example if it is a retail chain). In any event, time is of the essence, as the investigation of title necessitates various searches and enquiries with the Land Registry, local authorities and so on. It should also be borne in mind that bank funders will be concerned to ensure that any investigation of title to properties forming a substantial part of its security is sufficiently thorough.

Irrespective of whether the buyer undertakes specialist environmental due diligence, the buyer's solicitors' questionnaire will ask for copies of any relevant licences, consents and permissions, and seek confirmation that Target is trading in a manner which is compliant with those documents, and otherwise with current environmental legislation.

A criticism often raised by private equity and bank funders (and, regrettably, often with some validity) concerning legal due diligence is that it can be difficult to identify the actual advice that emerges from the exercise. Due diligence reports are often lengthy, and a good executive summary highlighting the key issues and concerns is essential. Even then, legal due diligence all too often reports on the factual content of the documents or responses so as to highlight the possible issue, but does not then go on to sensitise such issue or to recommend the action necessary to deal with it. If an issue is so significant as to be a deal-breaker, or to require a fundamental change to the deal terms, then it should be raised with the client without delay, rather than awaiting the conclusion of the full, final report. Where an issue is not so significant, the legal due diligence report should still distinguish those matters which must be addressed before completion (for example, by seeking a suitable confirmatory warranty in the sale and purchase agreement) from those which can be addressed after completion (such as suggested improvements to Target's standard terms and conditions, which might be incorporated within the 100 Day Plan).

The overlap that exists between legal due diligence and other parts of the buyer's due diligence process has already been highlighted. One final area which needs particular care in its scoping is the subject of tax due diligence. It is usual for the legal due diligence questionnaire to request some fundamental tax information such as copies of tax returns, details of any audits, investigations, discussions or disputes with tax authorities, a history of reliefs and exemptions claimed and so on. However, it is nevertheless more usual for a detailed assessment of the tax position of Target to form part of the financial due diligence exercise rather than legal due diligence. That said, the relevant members of the legal and accounting teams should ensure they are in direct contact as soon as possible in the transaction process, to ensure that the information they are receiving is consistent, and the scope of their respective roles is understood (to avoid unnecessary duplication or, worse still, areas of investigation being missed altogether).

4.4 Financial due diligence

The key aim of financial due diligence is to support, validate, challenge or modify the financial data, assumptions and assertions made in respect of

Target and its business in the Business Plan. As for legal due diligence, a comprehensive scope is prepared by the relevant accountancy firm and agreed with the investors prior to the commencement of the due diligence exercise. The relevant information is then compiled by Target's directors or employees and reviewed by the accountancy firm, with the findings ultimately being communicated in a report format, with a draft report usually being issued towards the end of the initial due diligence stage of the process, and a final report being issued prior to completion (or, if a vendor due diligence exercise is undertaken, the first draft report is made available in the data room, with a final 'top up' report being provided at completion).

The key elements of the financial due diligence exercise include the following matters.

(a) Historic trading and net assets

Historic trading and net assets are typically reviewed over a three-year period. The key areas of review include the sustainability of revenues and profits, drivers of growth, product or customer reliance, profit margins, working capital and cash flows. Work in this area forms a key input into the evaluation of forecast trading and cash flow assumptions (see below).

(b) Business operations

A review is undertaken to understand the nature of Target's customer base (and associated contracts), key sales and production processes, products, suppliers and marketing methods. Again, such diligence will inform the evaluation of trading and cash flow forecasts.

(c) Accounting procedures

The procedures for financial reporting, and accounting policies, will be reviewed to assess whether the financial information is reliable or sufficient to allow an accurate understanding of the performance of the business. The consistency with which accounting policies have been applied will be a key area, as well as compliance with generally accepted accounting practice – inconsistent application or changes in policies can have a significant impact on trading results and future reported performance. As with legal due diligence, adverse findings might impact on the deal structure, including price, or highlight areas requiring attention post-completion. The latter is particularly relevant if a Business Plan envisages expansion, which may put strain on the continued adequacy of the systems in place.

(d) Management/staff review

Financial due diligence will look to identify those employees who are key to the business – whether due to technical knowledge, marketing expertise or significant customer or supplier relationships. Consideration will be given to whether such individuals will be adequately motivated to remain in the business and support its growth post-acquisition which, in turn, will have a bearing on the allocation of equity amongst members of the management team, and possibly within a tier beneath that team.[17]

(e) Tax due diligence

As mentioned above, the financial due diligence exercise will usually include a detailed review of the tax history of Target, and an analysis of the implications for the buyer of acquiring Target from a tax perspective.

As we saw in chapter 1, the financial model forms an integral part of the Business Plan. Financial due diligence looks to understand the key risks in the future trading of the business, both by challenging the forecasts themselves (and the assumptions behind them), and by establishing the appropriate sensitivity tests that should be applied to the model in order to understand the impact of particular circumstances on trading performance and cash flows. Those sensitivities should then inform the setting of appropriate financial covenants with the debt funders to the transaction.

As well as understanding the ways in which the findings from financial due diligence may impact on the content of the legal documentation, lawyers may become involved in debates concerning the possible exposure of the accountancy firms involved to legal claims. In the leading case of *Caparo Industries plc* v. *Dickman*,[18] it was established that auditors owe a duty of care to the company itself, and not to its present or future shareholders, unless particular circumstances exist such that the auditors are aware or intend that another party will rely on the report. This decision led to an increasing anxiety on the part of accountants to limit their exposure (as we have seen in relation to the negotiation of accountancy firms' engagement letters generally).[19]

A particular area in which a lawyer may become involved in a financial due diligence context is the agreement of a hold harmless letter with Target's existing auditors. It is common for the investigating accountants appointed to conduct financial due diligence to request access to those working papers which were prepared by the existing auditors of Target for the purpose of preparing the most recent audited accounts. Access to such papers will make the process far more efficient and cost-effective. However, auditors are generally concerned that providing third parties with access to such papers may expose them to an additional litigation risk. As a consequence, the auditors will therefore request a hold harmless letter from both the proposed buyer (often the private equity firm itself, as a Newco may not have been created or will only be a shell company), and the financial due diligence provider, to ensure that the basis on which such papers have been provided is clear.

17 See also chapter 7, section 5.

18 [1990] 2 AC 605.

19 See section 3.2 above.

Historically, the Institute of Chartered Accountants in England and Wales (ICAEW) had drawn up a standard letter for accountants to use for this purpose. The original example dates back to 1995, and was drafted in a manner which many private equity firms felt placed unreasonable and onerous obligations on the buyer. As a consequence, this standard hold harmless letter inevitably became a very contentious issue, with significant delays being caused to the transaction process as such terms were negotiated. As the precedent was effectively ICAEW approved, many firms were extremely reluctant to accept any amendments to its terms – with the effect that on many transactions private equity bidders were left with the choice of either accepting what they considered to be an unreasonable level of risk in order to have access to the working papers, or alternatively conducting the due diligence exercise without such access (making such due diligence less reliable, and causing additional delay and expense).

After further consultation between the ICAEW and the BVCA, and other related parties, an updated standard hold harmless letter was released in 2003[20] which supersedes the previous version. The provisions in this letter are generally viewed in the industry as more reasonable (in fact, the standard reflects the final position which was often negotiated between private equity firms and the accountants from the starting-point of the previous version), and therefore will usually be acceptable to bidders. The letter provides many detailed provisions seeking to limit the auditors' liability, but the key provisions are as follows:

(a) an acknowledgment by the buyer and the investigating accountants that they are not owed any duty of care by the auditors as a consequence of the working papers being released to them;
(b) a requirement that the buyer and investigating accountants keep the contents of such working papers, and information derived from them, confidential, save that the investigating accountants and buyer may disclose and discuss the same with the Target company to obtain further information or verification in relation to the proposed due diligence report, the buyer's legal advisers, or otherwise as required by a court or by statute;
(c) an undertaking on the part of the buyer and the investigating accountants that they will not bring any action, proceedings or claims against the auditors arising from their use of, or reliance on, the information provided or the audit reports contained in Target's financial statements;
(d) finally, and crucially, the buyer will agree to indemnify and hold harmless the auditors against any claims which may be brought as a consequence of the failure of the buyer or any of its advisers (including the investigating accountants) to comply with the terms of the letter.

Later in the financial due diligence process, the issue of the accountant advisers' liability may again arise in the delivery of the final report. It is usual

20 See ICAEW Release Audit 04/03.

for management to be asked to review the report, and, as we will see, the investors will also ask the managers to warrant the content of that report in the investment agreement.[21] What is also becoming increasingly common, however, is for the accountants undertaking the financial due diligence exercise to require the managers to sign a side letter which effectively warrants the content and truth of the due diligence report directly to those accountants. Managers and investors should both be wary about the signing of such letters. Ultimately, if there is an error in the financial due diligence, investors may be prevented from making a claim against the accounting advisers if, in making such a claim, there is a real prospect of the managers being joined into any action. Where a letter is necessary to procure the release of the report, it should be reviewed by the lawyers acting for management and for the investors, so that the implications of the confirmations requested in that letter can be understood.

4.5 Other due diligence

In addition to the financial and legal due diligence carried out by the accountants and lawyers respectively, the following types of due diligence may also be conducted:

(a) *Commercial due diligence.* A firm of consultants are instructed to assess and validate the market analysis and strategies set out in the Business Plan.

(b) *Operational and IT/systems due diligence.* This involves a review of the operational aspects of Target to confirm whether the Business Plan is achievable with the existing operational facilities when combined with the capital expenditure identified in the Plan. Good operational due diligence will also consider whether there is the potential for additional value within Target by improving its operations. Operational due diligence may be carried out by a firm of accountants (possibly the same firm offering financial due diligence), or by a consulting firm. A detailed review of Target's IT capabilities and infrastructure may be included within operational due diligence, or may be carried out separately by a specialist consultant.

(c) *Insurance due diligence.* This involves a firm of insurance brokers assessing the adequacy of the current insurance arrangements of Target, and making recommendations as to the policies which should be in place for Target post-deal. Such policies are usually then arranged by those brokers carrying out the review. There is an important overlap with legal due diligence here, as the adequacy of insurance cover for any historic liabilities identified will be of relevance to both parties in assessing who should be 'at risk' for those liabilities in negotiations. It is also of particular significance in those buyouts involving the purchase of a subsidiary business from a

21 See further chapter 5, section 3.4.

larger group – such businesses will usually benefit from wider group insurance policies, and that cover will most likely not be available when the business leaves the group, necessitating the arrangement of stand-alone cover in anticipation of completion.

(d) *Pensions due diligence.* Where a defined benefits pension scheme is in place, a firm of actuaries will be instructed to assess the funding of the scheme, and to advise on recommendations for dealing with that scheme both before and after completion alongside the legal advisers. The specific issues that arise on the acquisition of a business with such a scheme are considered in detail in chapter 8. Where a defined contribution scheme exists, then such specialist advice may not be necessary, although legal and financial due diligence will investigate matters relevant to such schemes.

(e) *Environmental due diligence.* Again, there is significant overlap with legal due diligence here. Whilst the legal process will usually begin the assessment of any specific environmental issues, environmental consultants will often be brought in to at least carry out a desktop assessment of the risks associated with the properties occupied by the business (where those premises are limited to offices or similar commercial properties) or, where properties of a more industrial nature are involved, this may be extended to a more detailed investigation including a site visit and even the taking of ground samples.

(f) *Management due diligence.* It is now common for private equity firms to require the individuals proposed for the management team to be subject to a due diligence exercise themselves. This typically involves the completion of psychometric and similar written tests, followed by a comprehensive interview and discussion, carried out by specialist HR consultancies. The reviewer will produce a report highlighting the strengths and weaknesses of each individual in the team, and setting out recommendations for their development during the life of the investment. Unsurprisingly, the intrusive nature of this investigation often makes it controversial with some individual managers.

On a successful transaction the individual due diligence processes form part of an integrated exercise, and the outputs from all due diligence exercises will inform the legal protections that the investors require in the key transaction documents. The legal due diligence will usually contain the most immediately relevant issues to be addressed, but there may be key recommendations in the other reports which are equally, or possibly more, significant.

5 Conclusion

In outlining the initial stages of a transaction process, and setting out an overview of the process as a whole, the importance of the relationships between the parties and their respective advisers should already be apparent. Some issues arise again and again on each transaction, whilst others vary according to the particular deal. The recurring issues often relate more to process, rather than the commercial terms or desired outcome from the transaction, and we have noted the role played by the BVCA and relevant professional bodies in an attempt to standardise an acceptable practice relating to the liability of advisers and their engagement terms, and access to the audit papers of the Target. This reflects a consistent desire to remove the repetitive and avoidable process issues common to many deals which are sometimes seen as of interest only to lawyers or to insurers, and which have tended to delay deals and distract parties from the buyout process itself. Industry norms cannot answer all the questions, but they can help the parties focus on the matters of relevance to them and their deal. This initiative has been welcomed in the industry.

Due diligence plays a critical role in underwriting the Business Plan, and flushes out those issues which the buyer and its advisers must consider. It is rare for due diligence to have no effect on a deal – it may well lead to some price or structuring change, or at the very least to the negotiation of bespoke warranties, indemnities or other contractual remedies to address any concerns raised but not resolved during the deal process. Sellers may attempt to limit this erosion of the headline deal terms by the use of structured data rooms, vendor due diligence and tight auction timetables. Whilst this has been effective during stronger market conditions, at the time of writing the balance has undoubtedly swung back towards more formal and comprehensive buyer-led due diligence, in order to give the private equity investors and the banks more confidence to do the deal. It will be interesting to see if this process now favours trade buyers, especially those who do not need new debt funds to close the deal. In some cases, the sector knowledge of those buyers may enable them more easily to take a view on a matter raised in due diligence, or to cut due diligence corners in a manner that a financial investor or a bank would not be prepared to accept in the present climate.

3

Transaction structures and deal documents

1 Introduction

In this chapter, we will look at some typical structures for transactions featuring private equity funding in the UK. This has become an increasingly complex area in recent years for a number of reasons. As private equity investors have looked to acquire larger target companies, and utilised leverage as much as possible in doing so (as we saw in chapter 1), so structures have become more complex to accommodate that debt. A growing number of transactions involve the acquisition of a target with substantial operations outside the UK, which may necessitate a more complicated deal structure. Tax matters dominate, however, as rules governing the taxation of returns payable to both managers and investors must be borne in mind, in addition to any specific tax issues in respect of the target group.

These issues now have such a far-reaching impact that even a relatively low-value and simple private equity deal may nevertheless involve a complex structure. As a result, it can be difficult for anyone embarking on a private equity transaction for the first time to appreciate the fundamental commercial dynamics of a deal, and how a particular deal structure accommodates them. For that reason, this chapter will begin by examining the key players in a simple transaction, and the most straightforward deal structure that might emerge in that situation, which helps to demonstrate how private equity investors look to achieve the returns referred to in chapter 1.[1] From this starting-point, it is then easier to explore the additional factors that may influence the structure, and the consequences that result. This, in turn, helps the lawyer to appreciate the key requirements for the structuring of any particular transaction (and, indeed, to advise on whether all appropriate considerations have been borne in mind).

The chapter considers, in the first instance, a typical MBO or MBI transaction. However, many of the principles apply equally to venture capital and development/growth capital transactions, and certain specific implications applying to secondary buyouts are also touched upon later in the chapter.

1 See chapter 1, section 3.4.

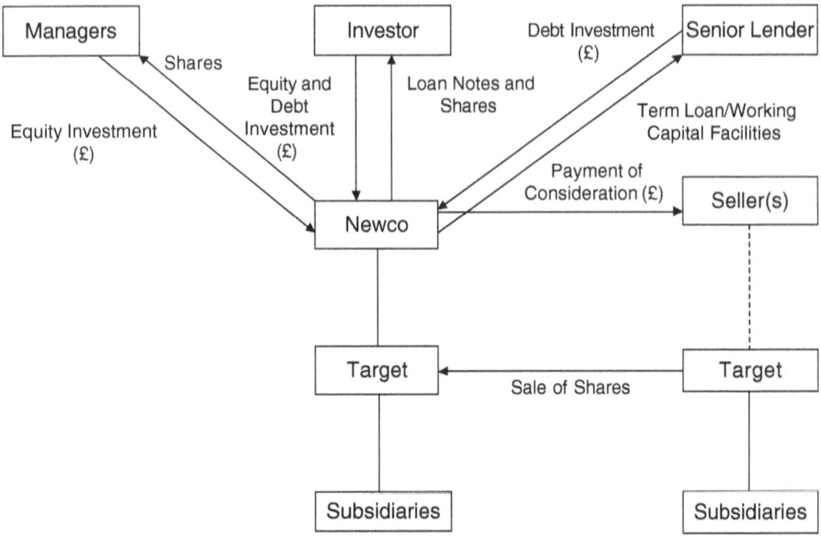

Figure 3.1 Typical single Newco structure

Similarly, this chapter principally looks at the downstream activity of private equity funders investing, rather than the numerous structures involved in the establishment of private equity funds themselves (which is outside the scope of this book), although certain features of the most common form of private equity investor in the UK (being a limited partnership model) are highlighted where this assists the understanding of the structuring of the investment deal. The chapter concludes by providing an overview of the main transaction documents, which are then considered in more detail in the chapters that follow.

2 A typical MBO/MBI deal structure

2.1 A simple structure

A simple starting-point is to consider a transaction whereby a management team wishes to acquire Target utilising funding from a single senior bank funder (which we will refer to in this chapter as the 'senior lender') and a single private equity investor.

In order to achieve this, each of the providers of funding (being the managers, the investor and the senior lender) will provide the funding required for the acquisition of Target, together with such further funding as may be necessary for the ongoing working capital requirements of Target, to a newly incorporated company (Newco) which can then acquire the shares or assets of Target (as the case may be).

Assuming that Newco acquires the entire issued share capital of Target (which, in turn, will therefore result in any subsidiaries of Target being incorporated within the newly formed group of companies), Figure 3.1 shows the typical instruments used (together with a flow of funds) for such a deal.

2.2 The players and their instruments (risk and return)

In this straightforward deal structure there are three parties providing funding for the transaction, and each investment takes a different form. Those investments can be distinguished by reference to the risk (per pound) in making the investment, and the return (per pound) that the party expects for taking such risk with the parties taking the most risk expecting the higher return.

(a) The senior lender

A more simple transaction will involve Newco taking debt facilities from a single bank, often sourced via the acquisition finance team of one of the main clearing banks. Where the debt is limited to a single layer of debt, from a single bank, then this usually comes in the form of a first-ranking secured term loan, together with ongoing working capital facilities.

The term loan is the acquisition finance, that is, the finance required to purchase Target, and is often split into a range of alphabetically identified tranches (i.e. Tranche A, Tranche B, etc.), each with its own repayment and/or interest profiles. Repayment may be by a single 'bullet' repayment at the end of the term, by instalment repayments on scheduled dates over time, or a combination of the two. Interest tends to be charged at a fixed number of percentage points above LIBOR.[2]

The working capital facilities are those facilities required to fund the day-to-day requirements of Target, and so will vary according to the underlying business, but often include an overdraft facility, letters of credit, bank guarantees or revolving credit facilities. Note that the first secured position of the bank would typically extend to all monies owed under all facilities, unless there are unusual commercial reasons for certain parts of the overall package to be carved out of the first-ranking security.

The risk and return profile of the senior lender's investment is therefore relatively straightforward. The relevant bank will expect first-ranking security for the amount loaned, and will apply their then current lending criteria to determine the extent of the facilities it is prepared to offer, and the interest margin it requires in offering such facilities, based on forecasted profits and cash flows as set out in the Business Plan and as tested by financial due diligence.

(b) The investor

A private equity investor will usually invest by way of two different instruments. A loan investment will be made (or, possibly, a preference share investment with economic features similar to a loan investment) alongside a subscription for equity shares.

2 For more on senior banking terms, see chapter 6, section 2.

In most modern UK transactions the loan investment typically takes the form of loan notes. A loan note is simply a loan security (in effect, a sophisticated IOU) issued by Newco entitling the registered holder to receive interest, capital repayments and any other payments as they fall due. The loan note may well be unsecured, or alternatively any security granted will be subject to an intercreditor agreement or deed of priority which effectively subordinates such security behind the senior lender.[3] Payments of interest or repayment of capital on the loan notes will be restricted pursuant to the relevant intercreditor agreement. In any event, repayment of capital on the loan notes would not usually be scheduled until a time when all loans advanced by the senior lender have been repaid in full (typically, twelve months after the due date of the last repayment to the senior lender).

It is also common for the interest accruing on the loan notes to remain outstanding either throughout the life of the loan notes, or at the very least for an initial period. The interest which would usually have been paid on a particular interest payment date (usually a quarter date) is instead added to the capital sum outstanding on the loan notes (or 'rolled up'). Interest then continues to accrue, at the agreed interest rate, on the increased rolled-up amount. The extent to which any interest may be payable to the investor, or should be rolled up, will be a matter for discussion and negotiation between the senior lender and the investor, and their respective advisers, by reference to what seems feasible based on the Business Plan prepared by the managers (and supporting financial due diligence exercise). As larger private equity transactions may utilise a significant amount of leverage from one or more senior lenders, or other priority debt funders (see further below), it is not unusual for interest to continue to roll up until the date of redemption of the loan notes. In any event, even where loan note interest may be payable, the intercreditor documentation will invariably allow the interest payment only if Newco is up to date with all amounts payable to the senior lender (whether capital or interest), and where the payment will not result in a breach of the banking covenants set out in the bank facilities.

The rolling up of interest on investor loan notes in this way has significant tax implications for both the Newco group and the investor. For that reason, other more complex forms of loan note are often utilised such as PIK notes, deep discounted bonds and Eurobonds.[4]

Prior to 1997, it was quite common for the 'debt' element of the investor's investment to be made by way of subscription for redeemable preference shares in the share capital of Newco. The preference shares would be redeemable by Newco on certain agreed dates set out in Newco's articles of association, which would match the dates on which capital repayments would be repayable under a more modern loan note structure. Similarly, the holder of the

3 For more detail concerning intercreditor arrangements, see chapter 6, section 4.3.

4 For more on the tax implications, including these forms of loan note, see chapter 9, section 2.

preference shares would be entitled to a fixed priority dividend on a quarterly or half yearly basis (analogous to the interest payments under loan notes). The intercreditor agreement would then set out restrictions prohibiting the payment of any such dividends, or redemption of the preference shares, other than in agreed circumstances, to afford the senior lender the same protection as is achieved in the loan note scenario described above. With careful drafting in the articles of association of Newco, it is also possible for preference share dividends to be 'rolled up' in the same way as interest on loan notes.

In addition to the restrictions set out in any intercreditor agreement, the ability of Newco to pay any dividends or to redeem any preference shares is limited by the Companies Act. In general terms, a company may only lawfully pay dividends[5] or redeem any redeemable shares[6] where there are distributable reserves enabling it to do so. As a consequence, even where there is no senior lender for whatever reason (perhaps because the senior facilities have been repaid), or a senior lender is willing to permit a payment to the investor, it may not be possible for Newco lawfully to make the payment. Where an investment is to be refinanced or restructured in a situation where preference share dividends or redemptions are in arrears, this can be a hindrance to a refinancing or restructuring proposal that would otherwise be commercially acceptable to the parties.

Another advantage of a loan note investment rather than a preference share investment is that, if structured in the correct way, it may be possible for Newco to claim tax deductibility on the interest payments due under the loan notes, whereas preference share dividends will be paid after tax from Newco's distributable reserves. The rules governing the deductibility of interest are complex, and have been subject to recent change, and so must be considered with great care (and are a dominant factor in determining the type of loan note instrument, and final transaction structure).[7]

As a consequence of these factors, a loan note structure is almost invariably preferred to a preference share structure on modern UK transactions. However, preference share subscriptions do still occur, as the tax and accounting considerations in each particular transaction will differ. They have the advantage of presenting Newco with a stronger balance sheet, and therefore may often be created as part of an agreed restructuring or refinancing. A legal practitioner may also come across companies which secured private equity investment prior to 1997 (the date of abolition of advanced corporation tax), when preference share subscriptions were far more common.

5 Section 830(1) of the Companies Act 2006.

6 Companies Act 1985, section 160, to be superseded by Companies Act 2006, section 687, on 1 October 2009. Note that a redemption is possible without reserves from the proceeds of a fresh issue of shares to facilitate the redemption, or from capital where a strict statutory procedure is followed.

7 See chapter 9, section 2.2.

In terms of risk and return, the investor will expose itself to a higher risk than the senior lender as its investment ranks entirely behind the senior lender on any insolvency event. As a consequence, the investor requires a greater reward on its investment. In part, this is often achieved by charging a higher rate of interest than the senior lender. More significantly, though, the investor expects to make a significant return on exit, so for that reason its loan investment is accompanied by a subscription for equity shares in Newco. Whilst the proportion of the total amount invested by the investor which is used to subscribe for equity is low, the investor will expect a significant percentage equity stake in Newco.[8] If the transaction takes the form of an institution-led buyout, rather than a more traditional management-led buyout, the investor will determine what proportion of the equity must be offered to management to ensure they are sufficiently motivated, but will usually retain a significant majority stake.

Whilst the investor equity may entitle the investor to receive dividends from any profits earned by Newco,[9] it is common for the investor and other shareholders not to receive any dividends, as the key return the investor is looking to obtain from its equity investment is the proceeds from exit whether by way of the sale of Newco, its flotation, or a disposal by Newco of its assets followed by a winding up (although the latter situation is uncommon save for an insolvency situation, where the likelihood is that there would be no proceeds for distribution to shareholders in any event). The proportion of the equity which the investor holds in Newco will, accordingly, be directly derived from the return which the investor expects on exit, determined by reference to the Business Plan. As explained in chapter 1, investors measure the return achieved by reference to the internal rate of return (IRR).[10] Financial advisers to the investor and the managers will negotiate the appropriate split of the equity share capital between their respective clients as the Business Plan and due diligence is finalised, and terms of the bank funding are understood and worked through the financial model.

(c) The managers

The managers in a private equity transaction will typically invest only a small proportion of the total funding required to finance the acquisition of Target. That is not to say that it is necessarily a small investment in the eyes of the managers – on a mid-market private equity deal[11] each of the main managers would usually be expected to contribute sums to the order of tens of thousands of pounds. The investor will be concerned to see that the managers are financially committed to the success of Target post-acquisition, and that their faith in the underlying Business Plan is given a meaningful context.

8 See also section 3.1 below.
9 See further chapter 5, section 4.4.
10 See chapter 1, section 3.4.
11 See chapter 1, section 2.3, for definitions of market sizes.

This investment by the managers normally takes the form of a subscription for ordinary shares in the issued share capital of Newco.[12] As such, the entirety of their investment is subordinated behind all creditors of Newco, including the senior lender and the debt instruments held by the investor and general trade or other creditors. In addition, the articles of association of Newco may also state that on any winding up or other return of capital all amounts subscribed by the investor for its equity shares in Newco must be repaid before any monies are distributed to the managers as shareholders (often referred to as the investor's 'liquidation preference', although *pari passu* ranking on such a return of capital is also seen). In that sense, the managers take the most significant risk, as all of their investment will rank behind the senior lender and investor in the event of a business failure.

However, the managers stand to make the highest return per pound invested on any successful exit. After repayment of the debt obligations, all proceeds from exit will usually (subject to any ratchet arrangement – see further section 3.2 below) be shared between the investor and the managers on a *pro rata* basis. As the managers have not usually subscribed for loan notes, preference shares or similar instruments alongside their equity (unlike the investor), the return received by the managers on a successful exit, per pound invested, is significantly greater. For this reason, the equity issued to managers is often described as 'sweet equity', whilst the combined debt and equity funding provided by the investor is sometimes described as the 'institutional strip'.

Figure 3.2 provides a simple illustration of the risk and return profile for each type of investor on a successful, or unsuccessful, transaction. This highlights the very different perspectives each party has when investing.

2.3 Multiple Newcos

For the purposes of most private equity transactions in the UK, the transaction structure set out above is too simplistic. In many cases, there will be more than one bank funder and/or more than one private equity funder (see section 3.3 below). Similarly, there may be additional leverage in the form of junior debt (see section 2.4). Finally, most transactions will require the incorporation of more than one new company in a structure (although it is often only one of those Newcos, sometimes referred to as 'Bidco', that acquires Target). Multiple Newcos may be required in a transaction structure to facilitate the acquisition of multiple Targets (especially where overseas Targets are involved), as a consequence of tax planning, or to achieve structural subordination of the various debt instruments. Some examples of circumstances in which multiple Newcos arise are set out below.

12 As discussed later in this chapter, in some circumstances (particularly secondary buyouts), the managers may hold debt investments in addition to ordinary shares.

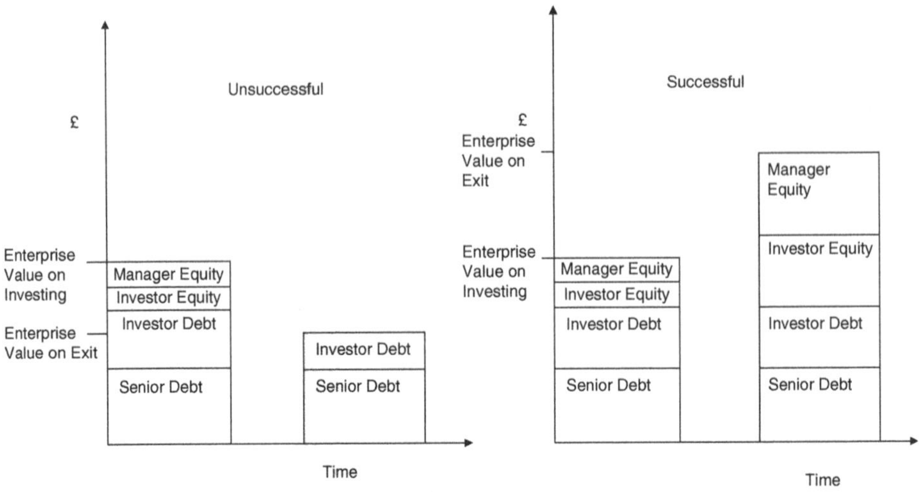

Figure 3.2 Risk and return

(a) Multiple Targets

A transaction may involve the acquisition of more than one Target, for example combining two separate businesses with particular synergies, or the consolidation of one or more businesses in a fragmented market sector. Larger deals may involve the acquisition of separate parent companies in two different jurisdictions, for example a UK and Dutch parent company with trading groups underneath each.

In many such deals, the different Targets may all be acquired by a single Bidco. However, there may be tax or accounting reasons which require one or more additional Newcos to be incorporated to acquire the different Targets. For example, where the Targets are incorporated in different jurisdictions, there may be reasons for the senior debt funders to provide part of its loan to an overseas Newco directly in a local currency. In those transactions, a separate Bidco might be incorporated in each of the two jurisdictions, with a common parent Newco in which the investor and managers will subscribe for shares.

(b) Structural subordination

As noted above, the senior lender and the investor will enter into a deed of priority or intercreditor agreement which ensures that the investor loan notes are effectively subordinated behind the bank debt. However, the senior lender may also want the comfort of achieving such subordination structurally. This involves a separate Newco being incorporated to receive the senior lender debt funding, which sits beneath the Newco in which the investor loan note funding is provided.

Subordination is effectively achieved on a contractual basis by way of the intercreditor agreement. The senior lender also has prior-ranking security to

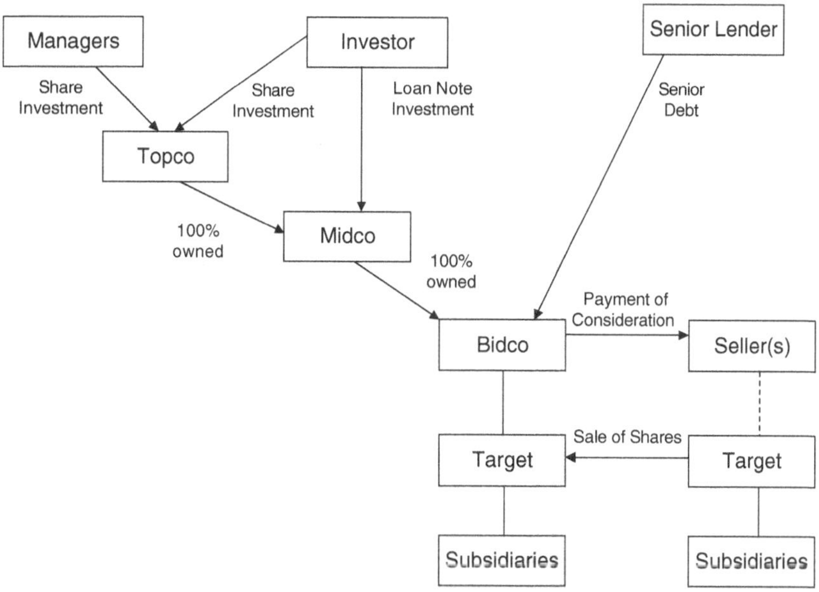

Figure 3.3 Structural subordination (single lender, with subordination of investor debt)

protect it on any business failure. However, a legal or accounting adviser to the senior lender may insist that subordination is achieved structurally, in case the validity of the security may be challenged. This is particularly likely in transactions of a more significant value (i.e. in upper-market and larger mid-market transactions), although it has become such a common practice that it might also be encountered on smaller deals.

Figure 3.3 shows a deal structure incorporating structural subordination between a senior lender and investor, as well as separation of the investor's debt and equity investments for the reasons described in section (c) below.

Where structural subordination is required, intercompany loan arrangements are utilised to ensure that the relevant funds are passed down to the ultimate Bidco to acquire Target. Such loan accounts may then be capitalised, whereby each parent company subscribes in cash for shares in its subsidiary, with such cash subscriptions immediately being satisfied by settling the sum payable against the intercompany loan which is owed. By structuring the transaction in this way, the senior lender would rank ahead of the investor upon any winding up or other distribution of assets by the Newco to which the senior lender has advanced its facilities (Bidco in this example), even if the security of the senior lender is unenforceable. The investor will only be able to participate in such assets after all creditors of Bidco (or other companies below Bidco in the group, depending on how assets are realised on the insolvency) have been paid, as its loan is entirely to Midco. If Midco gets nothing as a shareholder in

Bidco as a result of the insolvency of the companies below it, the loan that the private equity investors have in Midco is worthless.

(c) Tax: loan note interest

Another reason for the creation of additional new companies within the buyer group is to try to ensure that the relevant Newco will obtain a tax deduction for interest payable on the investor's loan notes. As is explained in more detail in chapter 9,[13] where there is a connection between the shares held by the investor and the investor's debt instrument, then HM Revenue & Customs (HMRC) may treat the whole of the interest upon the debt as a distribution. This conclusion is commonly considered to be avoided if the investor's debt investment is in a separate company to its shareholder investment, which can be achieved by introducing another company into the group, as shown in Figure 3.3. However, it should be noted that such measure will not mitigate an attack under the UK transfer pricing and other rules, which are also discussed in chapter 9.[14]

2.4 Higher leverage: junior debt

As has already been mentioned, private equity funders have used increasing levels of debt funding to facilitate acquisitions which would otherwise be out of reach due to the significant enterprise values involved. This necessitates debt being introduced to the transaction ranking behind the senior lender, but ahead of the investor loan notes, which is often described as 'junior debt'. Whilst the turbulent credit markets encountered in recent times generally mean that debt is less readily available for transactions, it does not necessarily follow that all junior debt will cease to feature in deals. Indeed, the reduced availability of senior debt might result in the more established (and often perceived to be less risky) form of junior debt, being 'mezzanine debt', featuring with increased prominence.

As the name implies, mezzanine debt sits between the investments by the senior lender and those of the investor in terms of both risk and return. Accordingly, the investment typically takes the form of a secured loan, which is subordinated fully behind the senior debt pursuant to the relevant inter-creditor agreement, and will usually be repayable in one bullet instalment a short period (six to twelve months) after the senior lender's term debt has been repaid in full but ahead of the investors' loan notes.

Given the additional risk attached to its loan investment, the mezzanine lender seeks a higher reward than the senior lender (typically, mezzanine lenders target a return on an IRR basis of between 20 per cent and 25 per cent per annum). It achieves this by way of a combination of arrangement fees and a higher margin on its loan (typically, around 7–10 per cent greater than the senior lender), together (in most cases) with an equity interest by way of warrants to acquire shares in Newco.

13 See chapter 9, section 3.2.
14 See chapter 9, section 3.3.

A warrant is a security issued by a company which entitles the bearer to subscribe for shares in that company at a pre-determined price. A warrant instrument is entered into by Newco at completion of the transaction entitling Newco to issue warrants, and then warrants are issued to the mezzanine funder over an agreed number of shares at the then prevailing issue price (that is, the price at which the managers subscribe for their sweet equity, or lower if possible). Accordingly, on exit, the mezzanine lender is able to exercise its warrants and participate in a proportion of the equity returns (typically, between 2 per cent and 5 per cent of the full equity value on exit). It is important to note that the warrant is not a security or protection to the mezzanine funder – if the company in question becomes insolvent, the right to own shares in it becomes worthless. The warrant is only of value if there is a successful exit with value for the equity. A warrant enables the mezzanine lender to balance risk over its portfolio. The valuable shares it receives for the warrants on a successful exit help to improve its overall return. It should also be noted that the warrant is normally a permanent feature – it does not cease to exist if the mezzanine debt is fully repaid.

The issues arising in the negotiation of mezzanine facilities and warrant instruments are set out in more detail in chapter 6.[15] For the purposes of structuring, however, it should be noted that, whilst the warrant will entitle the mezzanine lender to subscribe for shares in the ultimate parent company alongside the managers and the investor, for the reasons set out in section (b) above a further Newco may sometimes be introduced into the transaction structure which receives the debt funding, in order to achieve the appropriate structural subordination. This is illustrated in Figure 3.4.

Chapter 6 also explains how other forms of junior debt came to prominence in larger UK buyouts. In the economic and political climate existing at the time of writing, such instruments are far less likely to be encountered. Nevertheless, for the purposes of understanding any proposed deal structure, the lawyer should identify each different layer of debt funding at the outset, and clarify with any appropriate advisers (whether accounting, taxation or legal) how many different new companies may need to be incorporated within the structure to deal with those layers of debt.

3 Some common issues on deal structuring

3.1 Pricing the equity: the safe harbour

One overriding consideration in the structuring of the transaction will be a desire on the part of the managers to ensure that any gains on their equity investment fall within the capital gains tax, rather than income tax, regime. It should also be borne in mind that a manager may be subject to an income tax

15 See chapter 6, section 4.2.

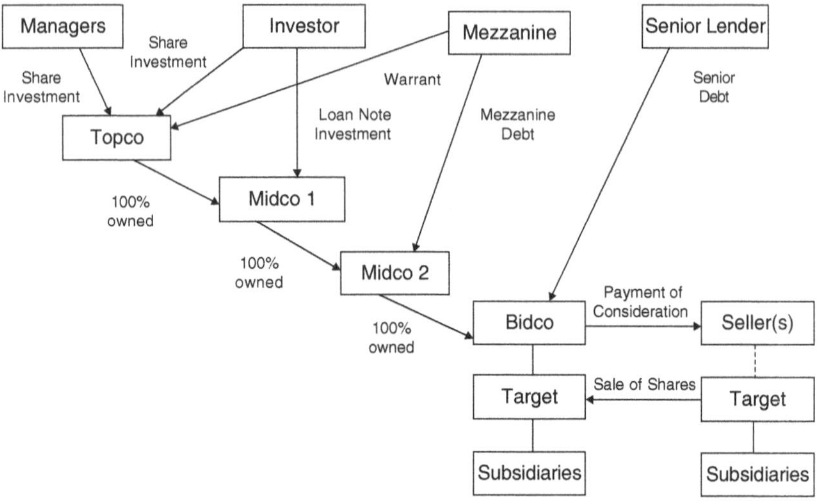

Figure 3.4 Structural subordination (with mezzanine)

charge in the event that the manager acquires shares at a price which is less than the market value of those shares on the date on which he acquires them. These issues are considered in more detail in chapter 9, including the further complexity arising as a result of the new rules concerning 'restricted securities' in the Income Tax (Earnings and Pensions) Act 2003,[16] and the requirements of the 'safe harbour' agreed between the BVCA and HMRC.

The safe harbour generally requires the managers and the investor to invest at the same time, with the price paid by the investors for their equity shares being no greater than the price paid by the managers for their equity shares (in practice, the price paid for the equity is usually the same share for share). Accordingly, the pricing of the equity on any transaction is usually a relatively simple calculation once the commitment that the investor wishes to see invested by the managers has been ascertained. The investor and managers will simply pay the same price per percentage stake in the overall equity, and the balance needed from the investor will be invested by way of loan notes. The managers and the investor will therefore negotiate what is the appropriate split of the equity based on the returns which the investor is expecting to obtain by reference to the Business Plan.[17]

There may, however, be commercial reasons for the various managers to pay a different price for their percentage stake. For example, the investors may wish to see wealthier or key managers committing substantial capital sums, but be more sympathetic to those managers with limited financial resources,

16 See chapter 9, sections 4.2 and 4.3.

17 In certain cases where there is a ratchet, the amount payable per share by a manager may be greater than that payable by an investor: see chapter 9, section 4.4(c).

or who will play a less critical role in delivering the Business Plan. In those situations, it is possible that loan notes or redeemable preference shares will be introduced, to be subscribed for by those manager(s) required to pay a higher price to reflect the premium required over the cost per share paid by the investor. Such instruments may rank either alongside or behind the investor loan notes or preference shares. To satisfy the safe harbour requirements, however, any such instruments must carry a coupon which is no lower than any other debt provider (including any bank).[18] This can prove particularly problematic on any transaction involving mezzanine debt, given the higher margin charged by providers of such debt.

Issues around the safe harbour are not only of concern to the managers and their advisers. The investor will usually be concerned to ensure that the managers have the maximum likelihood of being subject to tax under the more favourable capital gains tax regime, provided there is no material cost or inconvenience to the investor, in order to ensure that managers are most effectively motivated to achieve a favourable exit. Further, if income tax is payable, it may well be Newco's obligation to account for the same through PAYE, in which case employees' and employers' NIC will also be payable – which is potentially disadvantageous for the investor as a shareholder in Newco as the cost will normally reduce the value of Target on the exit. Finally, many investors look to motivate their own employees via a co-investment scheme or similar arrangement, whereby the employees of the investor may have a direct financial interest in the equity of Newco via such scheme. Accordingly, depending on exactly how such a scheme is structured, the individual employees at the private equity firm may need to ensure that the relevant safe harbour requirements have been satisfied, and that appropriate joint elections[19] are entered into, in respect of those investments. For all of these reasons, therefore, the investor will typically ensure that appropriate advice is sought to confirm that the proposed transaction structure does satisfy the safe harbour requirements.

3.2 Ratchets

In structuring any transaction, the parties will consider whether a ratchet mechanism is appropriate. A ratchet is a mechanism which enables the managers to participate in an increased share of the exit proceeds in the event that an exit is ultimately achieved on more favourable terms.[20] Usually, the trigger point at which the managers become entitled to a greater share of the exit proceeds is the target IRR which the investor is looking to achieve from its investment (so that, by way of example, an investor may say that the managers are entitled to x per cent of the exit proceeds up to the point where those proceeds

18 This is another safe harbour requirement: see chapter 9, section 4.4.

19 Section 431 elections: see further chapter 9, section 4.3.

20 For details of how a ratchet is provided for in the relevant investment documentation, see chapter 5, section 4.6.

give the investor an IRR of 35 per cent, but then the share will increase to *y* per cent on any exit proceeds achieved beyond that point). A 'dual test' is often incorporated, whereby the investor expects to achieve a minimum return as a multiple of the initial investment (say twice money invested), as well as hitting the target IRR, with the tipping-point being that exit value at which both of these tests are first satisfied.

Managers may find the IRR concept difficult to understand,[21] and in those circumstances the parties may feel that the ratchet will not have the desired effect of motivating managers towards achieving a higher return for the investor. Therefore, it is sometimes possible for a ratchet (particularly on a smaller deal) to be structured on a more straightforward time and/or valuation basis (for example, a ratchet will be triggered if an exit is achieved for a value of greater than £*x* million within the next *y* years). However, it is more common to see ratchets structured by reference to an IRR trigger, perhaps combined with a separate money multiple threshold. Ultimately, these are the performance measures by which the investor will be judged and rewarded, and an IRR mechanism has the added advantage of taking into account all cash flows to or from the investor during the life of the investment, thus avoiding the need to revisit the relevant threshold in the event of follow-on investment.

Whilst a ratchet is often negotiated in terms of giving the managers more if the relevant exit threshold is exceeded, the Memorandum of Understanding between the BVCA and HMRC[22] originally stated that to fall within the safe harbour the amount subscribed by the managers must reflect the maximum possible entitlement of the managers in respect of their equity shares. This means that it has become more common to see ratchets which are dilutive or negative in their effect (so, using the IRR example above, the managers may begin with an equity share of *y* per cent, but this will then reduce *pro rata* to *x* per cent in the event that the relevant threshold is not exceeded, rather than the other way around). Where a ratchet is stated to operate in the more traditional 'positive effect' terms, then in order to ensure compliance with the safe harbour the managers may have to pay a premium on their equity when compared with the investor, to reflect the fully enhanced value, although there has been more recent guidance on this point, as is explained in chapter 9.

As a result of these complexities, ratchets have been less common in transactions since 2003. Many financial advisers have concluded that it is better to negotiate the overall split of the equity between the managers and the investor to a firm number, than to have the uncertainty for all parties that the ratchet may result in an unfortunate tax treatment. Further, even with an IRR ratchet with carefully thought through multiple thresholds, the financial performance of the business may be such as to produce a distorted result for the managers

21 See chapter 1, section 3.4, for details of how an IRR is determined.

22 Section 6 of the MOU referred to in section 3.1 above. For more detail on the MOU, see chapter 9, section 4.4.

(in situations of positive performance), or may soon become redundant as a motivational tool (in cases of negative performance). However, ratchets are still encountered, as they are often a helpful compromise where the investor and the managers have differing views as to the likely future performance of the business.

3.3 Multiple investors: understanding the parties

For simplicity, throughout this chapter we have made reference to a single investor. However, in the vast majority of cases, there will be more than one investor entity.

In smaller transactions, private equity funding may be provided by one single private equity institution. However, the investments will almost invariably come from a small number of investment funds managed by the private equity house concerned. The main exception to this is those private equity houses which are captives and invest from the parent entity's own balance sheet.[23]

Therefore, in the investment documentation it is usual to see a number of different investing funds providing the appropriate equity and loan note investments on a *pro rata* basis. Often, these funds are structured as limited partnerships, registered under the Limited Partnership Act 1907. A limited partnership will include one general partner (although there can be more than one, this is rare in a private equity context), which is liable for all the debts and obligations of the partnership.[24] The general partner will usually take the form of a limited company or, increasingly frequently, a limited liability partnership (LLP). There will then be various limited partners who contribute capital as and when required for investment, which might include pension funds, insurance companies, local authorities and other national and international corporates. The liability of these entities is limited to the amount contributed, provided they do not participate in the management of the business of the fund.[25]

Each private equity house will regularly undertake fundraising, to raise monies for each new vintage of fund. Funds typically have an expected life of around ten years, meaning that a successful UK private equity firm will usually undertake a new fundraising exercise every three or four years. Each vintage of fundraising may well include more than one limited partnership, investing alongside each other. Often, this is in order that different limited partnerships can be established by those partners sharing particular characteristics – for example, it is common for American investors that are subject to the requirements of ERISA to form a separate limited partnership vehicle so that particular rights can be vested in that fund to qualify for ERISA.[26]

23 See further chapter 1, section 2.3.

24 Section 4(2) of the Limited Partnership Act 1907.

25 Sections 4(2) and 6(1) of the Limited Partnership Act 1907.

26 Employee Retirement Income Security Act 1974, US legislation which imposes particular requirements on certain types of US investor.

As noted in section 3.1 above, this investment by the various limited partnerships may also be accompanied by an investment by a co-investment scheme which invests on behalf of the individuals employed by that private equity firm, and which will often invest only for a proportion of the equity shares without the accompanying subscription for loan notes. Effectively, the members of the investment team are subscribing for a proportion of 'sweet equity' alongside the managers, in a proportion which the limited partners have agreed is appropriate to ensure that they are sufficiently motivated to find successful investment opportunities. The relevant individuals will benefit from the capital gains achieved on such shares, in addition to such individuals benefiting (to the extent they are stakeholders in the general partner) from the management fees and carried interest payable to the general partner under the limited partnership agreement.

It should be noted that not all private equity investors in the UK are structured as limited partnerships under the 1907 Act. Investors may be structured as foreign partnerships, UK companies, venture capital trusts, investment trusts or in a range of other forms based on the investor's origins, and the tax residence and status of the private equity firm and its underlying investors.

The investment documents will normally define a 'Lead Investor'; in a limited partnership structure, this is more often than not the general partner entity. That is the legal entity which will deal with day-to-day management of the investment, including the giving or withholding of investor consents, receipt of relevant information, appointment of investor directors, and so on. It should also be noted that a limited partnership is not in itself a recognised legal entity under English law, and as a result it is usual for a nominee company to be established to hold the relevant shares and loan notes on behalf of the relevant funds.

In many transactions, private equity investors may well combine to form a syndicate. Syndication is not exclusive to larger deals; a syndicate of investors is sometimes found in venture capital transactions, where investors look to spread the higher risk associated with those types of investment. In those cases, the structure may become more complicated to accommodate the specific requirements of each individual funder. At the very least, one would expect to see far more detailed terms regarding the extent to which each member of the syndicate has a right to consent to and/or veto any particular investor consent. As an alternative, an initial investor may wish to reserve a right to syndicate some or all of its investment post-completion, which would need to be accommodated within the initial transaction documents.

Similarly, in larger transactions, one will often be confronted with a syndicate of senior lenders, or an initial senior lender may look to syndicate its debt investment following completion of the transaction.[27]

27 See further chapter 6, section 3.4.

3.4 Investor/management fees

Any private equity investor will look to charge the relevant investee company a fee for arranging its investment. This is in addition to any ongoing monitoring fee, or other fee payable for the ongoing services of any appointed investor director(s). The private equity investor will also expect the investee company to pay any professional fees incurred by the private equity house in relation to the transaction, including accountancy and legal fees, and other due diligence costs.

Prior to October 2008, the payment of such fees attracted a great deal of attention amongst lawyers on the question of whether the same might constitute unlawful financial assistance for the purposes of the Companies Act 1985.[28] In principle, it was possible that the payment by a company of fees incurred by a party for the purpose of subscribing for shares in a company might constitute financial assistance – whilst it is more common to consider the question of financial assistance in the context of the acquisition by a party of shares from another, it might have been argued that a subscription for new shares can constitute an acquisition of shares for the purposes of section 151 of the 1985 Act.

As a result of these concerns, the BVCA has on separate occasions taken advice from counsel as to whether any arrangement to pay such fees is unlawful. These concerns increased as a consequence of the Court of Appeal decision in *Chaston* v. *SWP Group plc*,[29] in which Arden LJ suggested a relatively strict 'but for' approach for determining whether financial assistance has occurred. Since the abolition of financial assistance for private companies with effect from 1 October 2008, however, most of such analysis is now redundant (although still available on the BVCA's website for subscribing members). Such issues may still be of relevance in the event that any transactions entered into prior to that date are challenged in the future. It is also relevant if for some other reason a public limited company is used as the Newco; this is very rare.

A related point, however, which remains of concern is whether any of such fee arrangements might constitute a breach of section 580 of the Companies Act 2006, which prohibits the issue of any company's shares at a discount to their nominal value. In advising the BVCA on the financial assistance issues, counsel also highlighted that, where an investor subscribes for shares at par value, and the investee company then pays fees connected to such subscription, it might be argued that such shares have been issued at a discount in contravention of that section.

There are two steps which might be taken by the diligent legal adviser to a private equity investor to deal with this issue. First, the relevant fees may be invoiced to a company below the ultimate holding company in the relevant structure. Whilst such an approach would not have addressed the financial assistance issues (as financial assistance by a subsidiary for its ultimate

28 Companies Act 1985, sections 151 *et seq.*

29 [2002] EWCA Civ 1999.

holding company was also prohibited),[30] it should be sufficient to demonstrate that such payment cannot be treated as a discount for the share subscription if payment comes from a separate legal entity within the group. Alternatively, where the ultimate parent company must pay the fees for whatever reason, then those fees payable in connection with the equity investment may be identified separately from those fees invoiced in connection with any loan investments, or due diligence or other acquisition advice. The share capital in that parent company is then issued incorporating a share premium which is sufficient to satisfy the full amount of such fees (i.e. so that such deduction cannot in any event be of such an amount which results in the shares being offered at a discount). To be successful in this approach, it follows that the share premium created must exceed the aggregate amount of fees payable to or on behalf of a particular shareholder, which can be difficult when deals are structured with a relatively low equity subscription amount.

3.5 Secondary buyouts and other 'rollover' sellers

There are often circumstances where an existing shareholder in Target will become an investor in the acquiring Newco (or, in a multiple group structure, the ultimate holding company). Common examples include a secondary buyout (discussed in more detail in chapter 12), and development capital transactions where a founder may remain alongside the private equity investor (either with or without extracting some value in cash as part of the transaction).

In these cases, the structure will need to accommodate the relevant seller taking the relevant loan and equity stake in Newco. The simplest way to achieve this is by the buyer simply issuing consideration loan notes or consideration shares. However, this will not work where the funding structure involves multiple Newcos, as the buyer company will not be the company where that seller will be expected to hold his equity interests, and possibly his loan note interests, going forward.

In those cases, the solution is usually for the buyer Newco (i.e. Bidco) to issue loan notes to the relevant seller(s) as part of their consideration for the sale of shares. A series of documents are then entered into by which the relevant seller agrees to exchange his loan notes in Bidco for loan notes in that Bidco's holding company. If required, subsequent exchanges of loan notes may then continue up the chain of companies (often referred to as a 'flip up') until such point as the investment is in the correct entity. As a final step, the relevant proportion of loan notes will then be exchanged for shares in Topco, leaving the seller with equity shares in the correct entity. This is illustrated in Figure 3.5.

Whilst it is possible for Topco to issue shares in consideration for the sale of the shares to Bidco (and for Bidco to agree to procure such share issue within the sale documentation, or even for Topco to be a party to the relevant sale

30 Section 151(1) stated that it was not lawful for a company or any of its subsidiaries to give financial assistance directly or indirectly for the purpose of that acquisition.

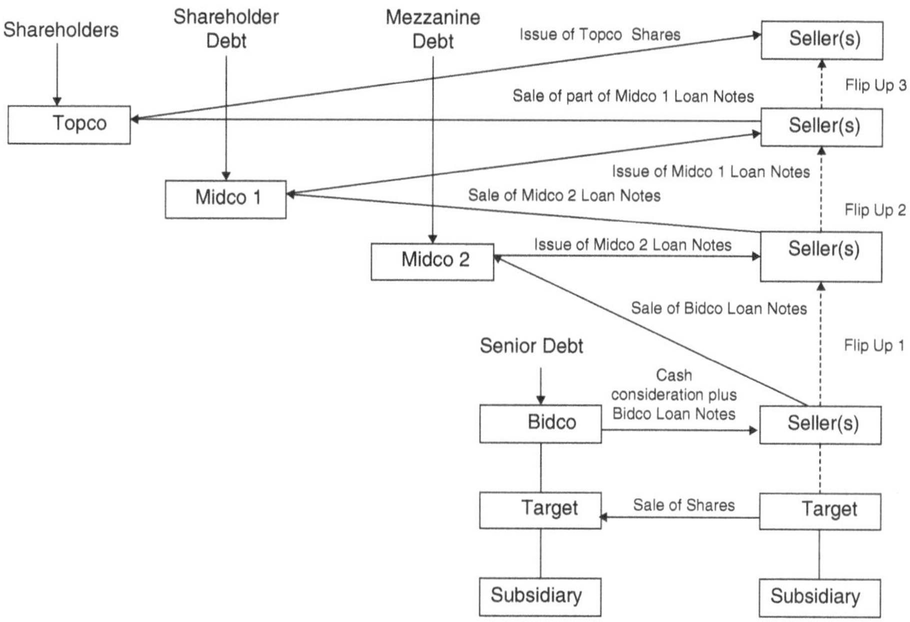

Figure 3.5 'Flip up'

agreement for that purpose) to avoid the need for numerous 'flip up' documents, this approach is not usually followed. One key reason for this is that the relevant seller will usually want to roll over any capital gains in the existing shares into the new investment, which requires the 'flip up' approach to be taken, and with particular care to ensure that the relevant legislative requirements are satisfied.

In any transaction where one or more sellers are rolling part of their consideration into the new investment vehicle, such a seller may try to negotiate that such investment should be on like terms to the investor. That seller might argue that the proportion of the total amount which is invested in the form of equity rather than loan notes should be in the same proportion as is the case for the institutional strip. Taking these arguments further, it might be possible for such rollover shares to be free from some of the punitive restrictions (such as leaver provisions) which attach to the sweet equity. Such participation in the institutional strip might also stand alongside a separate subscription for sweet equity, subject to the same terms and restrictions as the other managers, where the relevant seller is also a key member of the management team going forward (as in a secondary buyout). These issues are discussed in more detail in chapter 12.

4 The deal documents

The chapters that follow discuss the key points to be negotiated on the principal legal documentation on a UK private equity transaction. Whilst the precise

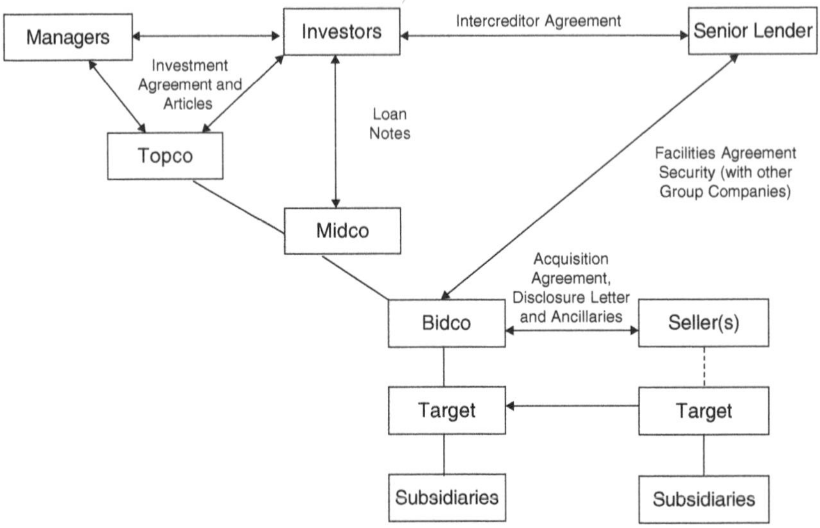

Figure 3.6 Key transaction documents

documentation required will vary depending on the nature and structure of the particular transaction, Figure 3.6 is included here as it shows (by reference to a simple deal structure diagram) the relationships that are governed by those principal documents. A brief overview of the documents in each category is provided below.

4.1 The acquisition documents

The documents governing the acquisition by Bidco of the Target, include:

- the acquisition agreement, entered into by the seller(s) of the Target and Bidco, and possibly other parties (for example, in the case of a disposal by a corporate group of a subsidiary, a guarantee may be required by Bidco from the parent company);
- a separate tax deed (although the tax provisions may alternatively be included within a tax schedule in the acquisition agreement);
- the disclosure letter from the seller(s) of Target to Bidco, qualifying the warranties set out in the acquisition agreement;
- stock transfer forms in favour of Bidco for the shares in Target, together with any ancillary transfer documents or agreements required for the transfer of any assets not covered by the acquisition agreement (for example, to assign assets held by an individual seller personally but used in the business);
- any commercial agreements required to be entered into by such parties to facilitate the continued running of the business (for example, concerning interim accounting, IT or other services to be provided for an initial period from completion);

- any leases, licences or similar documentation that may be required concerning any properties;
- any relevant consents, authorisations, powers of attorney or similar documents; and
- all appropriate board minutes, resolutions of shareholders, and letters of appointment or resignation from office as director, secretary or auditors, together with relevant Companies House forms.

4.2 The equity documents

The documents which are entered into between the investors, the managers and the relevant Newcos are usually referred to as the equity documents. These will include:

- the investment agreement setting out the terms on which the investors agree to invest, and various obligations on the Newco companies and the managers;
- the articles of association of Topco, which set out the different rights attached to the shares held by the managers and the investors;
- a disclosure letter from the managers (and often Topco) to the investors, setting out matters qualifying the separate warranties given to the investors by those parties in the investment agreement;
- the loan note instrument(s) to be entered into constituting the loan notes to be issued to the investor(s), and any relevant managers or sellers as may be applicable;
- the service agreements to be entered into by each of the managers and Topco (or the relevant company in the group employing such managers);
- declarations given by the managers to the investors as to their personal circumstances, employment history and similar matters;
- resolutions, board minutes and Companies House forms dealing with the incorporation of each relevant Newco, including the appropriate structuring of the share capital of Topco and adoption by Topco of the relevant articles of association; and
- any 'flip up' documentation that may be necessary, as referred to in section 3.5 above.

4.3 The debt documents

The debt documents (also often referred to as the banking documents) set out the terms on which any debt funding is to be provided to the acquiring Newco group, for example:

- the facilities agreement(s) with the relevant bank funder(s) setting out the terms of any term loan, working capital and other facilities;
- where applicable, a mezzanine facilities agreement together with any accompanying share warrant instrument and certificate(s);

- the intercreditor agreement and/or deed(s) of priority, setting out the appropriate subordination of the various debt instruments;
- debentures and related cross-guarantees giving all secured lenders the relevant security;
- such documentation as may be necessary for the capitalisation of any intra-group debt, together with an appropriate intra-group loan agreement to govern the ongoing loan accounts between members of the Newco group;
- fees letters setting out the various fees payable to the bank lenders;
- any accession documents or side letters as may be necessary to deal with any syndication of debt; and
- board minutes and shareholder resolutions of each member of the Newco group approving the entering into of the various banking documents.

Chapters 4, 5 and 6 outline the nature and content, and key points for negotiation, on each category of documents in turn.

5 Conclusion

Whilst there may be particular issues on any transaction necessitating a specific structuring requirement, there are equally some common considerations which are relatively simple for a legal practitioner to follow once the basic principles and objectives of the parties are understood. As we have seen, the instruments held by each party are derived from a particular perspective on risk and return.

More complex structures involving the incorporation of a number of new companies are also fairly commonplace. Ideally, the exercise of finalising the deal structure should be undertaken, comprehensively, at the outset of a transaction. It can be particularly frustrating, in the pressured environment leading to a legal completion, to find that the full suite of deal documentation requires amendment to accommodate one or more additional companies within a structure, especially where this is to address a requirement that could have been identified at an early stage. Significantly, this will also often need to be settled as quickly as possible in order to ensure that any relevant tax clearance applications are sufficiently accurate to be reliable.

4

Acquisition issues

1 Introduction

In this chapter, we will examine the issues that typically arise in relation to the acquisition documentation on a UK management buyout. As has already been explained, there is more to a management buyout than simply the acquisition. The whole exercise requires considerable project management, combining the acquisition process with the funding elements of the transaction, both equity and banking, which are explored in the chapters that follow. The issue is further complicated in a secondary transaction (see chapter 12), where some of the sellers are also part of the buyer team.

We will concentrate on the issues that arise on the acquisition of a private limited company in the UK. Whilst buyouts may be structured such that the assets of Target are acquired rather than the share capital, such instances are relatively rare (other than in distressed or insolvency situations, which are outside the scope of this book), so a share acquisition is assumed. The key contractual document that regulates the terms for the sale and purchase of Target is the acquisition agreement, and much of this chapter highlights the issues arising in the drafting and negotiation of that document which are different as a result of the transaction being a buyout rather than a sale from one trading company to another. This chapter is not intended to be a complete or exhaustive manual on the issues that arise on the acquisition of a private company; whilst it does set out some of the features of a typical deal, the focus is very much on those specific considerations which arise in a private-equity-backed transaction.

In addition to the acquisition agreement, this chapter will examine the important role of the tax covenant in share purchase transactions, and the competition law issues that can arise with a private-equity-backed buyer. The particular issues that arise on the acquisition of a publicly traded company via a public-to-private transaction are considered separately in chapter 10.

2 The acquisition agreement

2.1 Parties

The parties to the acquisition agreement will usually be limited to the seller(s) and the buyer. In the context of a private-equity-backed transaction, the buyer will invariably be a new company incorporated specifically for the purpose, and, where a group of new companies is established for structural reasons, the buyer will typically be the lowest in the hierarchy in that structure.[1]

In certain situations, other parties may also join in to the acquisition agreement. These situations may include:

(a) *Guarantors*. If the seller is, for example, an intermediate holding company in a group of companies, it is likely that the ultimate parent company may also be asked to enter into the acquisition agreement as a guarantor of the seller's obligations (or, at least, of certain key obligations) in the document. Similarly, the beneficiaries of any trust selling shares may be required to act as guarantors. It is possible that a guarantor may also be required to enter into other contractual provisions directly in addition to guaranteeing the obligations of the relevant seller (for example, a parent company in relation to restrictive covenants[2]).

(b) *Target itself*. Although rare, there are sometimes situations in which it is appropriate for the Target to join into the transaction. This is often suggested so that Target may be contractually obliged to satisfy particular obligations. Examples include the discharge by Target of existing debt on completion, whether to the seller or to external funders.

Traditionally, Target, being a party to the agreement, or otherwise entering into contractual obligations on its own behalf at the time of the acquisition of its shares, tended to raise alarm bells (at least for lawyers) due to the prohibition on Target giving financial assistance in respect of the acquisition of its own shares under what was then the regime set out in sections 151–158 of the Companies Act 1985. Since 1 October 2008, the prohibitions on financial assistance (now found in section 678 of the Companies Act 2006) relate only to public limited companies. Accordingly, in many transactions, the risks of financial assistance no longer arise. It is important, however, to bear in mind that there can be other legal issues arising as a result of Target being a party to the acquisition agreement or otherwise undertaking certain actions at the time of the sale. For example, it is important to consider whether there is a corporate benefit to Target itself of entering into the arrangements, or whether the discharge of any such obligation or the making of payments for the benefit of its shareholders might be interpreted as a distribution that may be unlawful. As a result, most practitioners still avoid Target being a party to such obligations

1 For further details on the structuring of transactions, see chapter 3.

2 For restrictive covenants, see section 2.10 below.

where possible, instead relying on the respective obligations of the buyer and the seller(s) to procure that Target will perform the relevant action.

It should also be noted that every public limited company is subject to the continuing financial assistance regime – not just a public company which is the ultimate parent company in a particular group, or whose shares are traded in the public markets. Where the Target is such a 'vanity' public company (i.e. a public company whose shares are not publicly traded, and which does not have any other legal justification for being a plc), the Takeover Code will nevertheless still apply on the acquisition of its shares. Accordingly, there may well be situations in which there is a desire to re-register such a public company Target as a private company as part of the transaction, with the resultant need (after discussion with the Takeover Panel) to obtain a waiver from the relevant shareholders to recognise that the provisions of the Takeover Code will not apply once it is no longer a plc.

2.2 Price and price adjustment

The price payable will be debated in some detail during the initial negotiation of any offer letter or heads of terms. This debate not only concerns the amount of the consideration, but also will usually extend to the form of the consideration (i.e. whether the price is to be satisfied entirely in cash, or whether all or part of the consideration will be in non-cash form), and any mechanism for adjusting the price. Part of the price may be satisfied by the issuing of loan notes in the buyer (usually bank guaranteed) or, in some cases, shares in the buyer, for example.[3]

In this section, we will consider some of the pricing issues that are regularly encountered on private equity deals.

(a) Completion accounts

Buyers will regularly state that any offer made is on an assumption that Target is cash and debt free, and has a normalised level of working capital. Completion accounts are often used to test the level of cash and debt, working capital or net assets (or such other key balance sheet measure as may be relevant for the business concerned) as at completion of the transaction. This is a mechanism which allows buyers to check the actual state of the business at the time of purchase by carrying out an accounting exercise in a brief period of time following completion, and to adjust the price (usually on a pound-for-pound basis) if the level of net assets (or such other measure as is relevant) delivered at completion is found to be below the specified target level, or to be more than an agreed tolerance below that level. Sometimes, the mechanism will be an either-way mechanism, with the price also increasing if the net assets (or other relevant measure) transpires to be higher than expected.

3 In these cases, certain of the issues outlined in chapter 12 for a secondary buyout may be equally relevant to a non-manager seller taking an ongoing stake in the buyer.

Completion accounts mechanisms can be complex in their drafting – particularly where the mechanism seeks to spell out in detail the precise practices, policies and principles to be used, and the procedure to be followed in the event of any dispute. The starting-point is usually the practices, policies and principles adopted by the Target in its last statutory accounts, but this may be challenged by the buyer, for example if there has been a change in law or accounting practice since then, or if the buyer has identified an issue from due diligence which suggests another treatment is appropriate. A common compromise is to include the detail of the policies in a schedule (in so far as they can be agreed and documented), and then provide that last accounting policies may be followed (where no express provision is stated) so long as these are compliant with generally accepted accounting practice. This can remove the scope for doubt or disagreement after the event, although it requires a comprehensive and co-ordinated approach by the legal and accounting advisers on both sides, to ensure that the mechanism does not produce an outcome adverse to their respective client's expectations.

In the event that there is more than one seller, the question of how any reduction to the price arising from the completion accounts mechanism should be apportioned between them may arise. In many cases, this will simply be a reduction in proportion to their entitlement to receive the headline consideration – which is usually the more equitable approach. However, there may be sensitivities for some sellers – as noted in chapter 13, this is particularly the case where one or more of the sellers are private equity investors without a detailed knowledge of the business and its affairs on a day-to-day basis.[4] Similarly, it is worth noting that some sellers can be particularly sensitive to agreeing to a completion accounts mechanism in a management buyout, on the basis that the managers may well be better placed to know that there are issues which may ultimately favour the buyer by leading to a reduction in the headline price agreed. As the management team for the seller(s) before completion will become the management team for the buyer after completion, the seller(s) may be less able actively to participate in and oversee the exercise of preparing the completion accounts (although a completion accounts mechanism will invariably give the seller(s) an opportunity to review and object to the buyer's draft accounts, with any issues that cannot be resolved directly between them being referred to an independent accountant).

The questions of whether there should be any cap on the potential price adjustment pursuant to the completion accounts exercise, whether the adjustment should operate on an either-way basis or a downwards-only basis, and whether there should be any tolerance (in the form of an agreed *de minimis*) around the relevant accounting target before any price adjustment is triggered will all be subject to negotiation on a deal-by-deal basis. Generally, this will depend on the relevant bargaining strengths of the parties in negotiation,

4 See chapter 13, section 3.4.

although the underlying business and commercial drivers for the exercise will also be relevant. For example, where a completion accounts mechanism is suggested because the seller(s) have expressed extreme confidence in delivering the proposed balance sheet target, and the buyer is only prepared to pay an agreed price on that basis, this is far more likely to lead to a downward-only adjustment; in contrast, where both parties are of the view that the fluctuations in working capital are such that they are difficult to measure on a day-to-day basis, so that an adjustment mechanism is needed to protect both parties, then an either-way mechanism is more reasonable.

As the completion accounts mechanism is expected to lead to an adjustment to the price in a reasonably short timescale (usually between one and three months), this is often supported by a retention from the purchase price (see further section 2.4 below).

(b) Locked box mechanism

A locked box mechanism is sometimes used as an alternative to completion accounts. Here, the buyer investigates the financial affairs of Target and is persuaded to be comfortable on the net asset position (or other financial yardstick) as at a date before completion of the acquisition, and the sellers effectively promise that they have not received any payment or otherwise extracted value from Target since that date except for permitted payments (such as salary in the case of managers, or interest on loan notes in the case of investors). This exposes the buyer to the general risks of trading since the agreed earlier date (as no completion accounts are prepared), but protects it against value extraction by the sellers. Sellers normally give a several commitment, so that each is only liable for the value which that particular seller has received that was not a permitted payment.

A locked box mechanism is, generally speaking, more attractive than completion accounts to the sellers because each seller knows that, provided it has not had any payment except for a permitted payment (as defined in the agreement), there will be no adjustment to the price. This gives certainty, saves cost and delay, and maximises the ability of any investor seller(s) to return proceeds promptly and fully to clients. As noted above, however, a completion accounts process may still be preferred by the sellers if the net asset or working capital fluctuations are such that there may be additional value generated for which the sellers would not be compensated under a locked box arrangement.

Locked box mechanisms were particularly common in the auction and other seller-led processes which typified the seller-friendly markets of 2006 and 2007 in the UK. The shift in bargaining power towards buyers since then, and a greater caution on the part of buyers as a result of general market uncertainty, may well lead to a return to more traditional completion accounts.

(c) Earnouts and similar arrangements

Deals sometimes include an earnout mechanism, where part of the price is to be determined by a future event (for example, the profits achieved by Target in a future period, or the gain on the disposal of some asset within Target). Earnouts can be complex, especially in a sale to a private-equity-backed business given the different roles of the management team in the deal. If the transaction is a secondary buyout for example, management have an interest in the outcome of the earnout as sellers, as officers of Target going forward, and potentially as shareholders in the buyer.

Where a seller agrees to an earnout, such seller will usually want some contractual protection in relation to how Target is to be run, and how the outcome of the earnout is to be measured and paid. This often extends to a detailed schedule of matters that cannot be implemented by the Target group without the consent of the seller(s) for fear that this might distort the amount of the earnout payment, for example by entering into contracts or incurring significant expenditure outside the ordinary course of business. The extensive controls which the funders of a buyout will require under the equity and senior debt documents, as outlined in chapters 5 and 6 respectively, can conflict with the earnout protections that a seller requires. The gearing and other costs resulting from the buyout itself can also complicate the measuring of the earnout payment, necessitating detailed accounting advice in order to agree the relevant earnout formula.

The additional amount payable under an earnout mechanism will generally be capped on a private equity transaction, as the buyer's funders will want to know that the funding they are arranging for the buyer will be sufficient to discharge that liability if it matures. Also, the time period for the earnout would normally be no longer than, say, two or three years. This is because the ultimate exit of the investment will be easier if the earnout is resolved before that exit. A seller should also consider how best to protect itself if the exit happens sooner, and what effect (if any) this should have on the earnout itself.

One key issue for a seller would be security for the payment of any earnout consideration, especially if the buyer will be highly geared. The protections typically sought by a buyer in order to address security for any unexpected liabilities in the other direction (such as a retention: see section 2.4 below) would be rare here – the funders to the buyer would not normally be able to tie up their cash resources by funding such retention. However, guarantees from a bank or even security over Target (or the shares in Target) ranking behind that of the secured bank funder(s) could be considered. Practice varies, however, and in many situations the earnout consideration is simply left as an unsecured liability payable by Newco. Similar situations can sometimes arise when a price adjustment is 'unwound' – for example, if the seller has agreed a price adjustment because of a particular issue (for example, a suspected tax liability in the Target not provided for), and subsequent events show that the issue did not materialise or resulted in a lower cost to Target than that which was expected. Often, a seller will have negotiated to recover part of the adjustment in these circumstances. Security is less of an issue here, however, as it is more likely that a retention will be used to secure the monies funded by the price adjustment.

2.3 Other risk allocation during negotiation

As was highlighted in chapter 2, the price set out in the original heads of agreement or offer letter is often revisited during the transaction process, most usually as a result of adverse findings from the extensive due diligence processes.[5] It is not uncommon for due diligence to identify areas of difficulty or concern in the Target or its business (for example, potential litigation, pensions or tax issues, or material capital or other expenditure required to satisfy particular regulatory requirements). Generally, when these matters can be clearly quantified, they will lead to a price negotiation.

The extent to which the parties will agree a price reduction depends, among other factors, on their relative bargaining power. In a more buyer-friendly market (such as has prevailed in the UK as a consequence of the credit crunch and the resulting difficult economic climate), a buyer is likely to be in a stronger position to agree a price reduction in its favour to reflect any issues identified during due diligence. In contrast, in a seller-friendly market with significant competitive tension for an asset (as was typical in the two years leading up to the credit crunch), a seller might be in a position to resist any reduction to the initial headline offer. Some sellers can become emotionally attached to the headline price stated in the heads of terms or offer letter, and in their own minds may feel that they are already entitled to it. Where there are potentially many competing buyers, this emotion can sometimes be justified. However, in a market where buyers are few and funding is tight, too much addiction to the headline price can prove to be counter-productive. This is particularly the case where the problem identified is something real and material of which the seller was not already aware. If the reality of the situation is that the seller must either agree a price reduction or walk away from the sale, the seller should remember that a decision not to sell does not solve the problem. If there is a genuine issue in Target, then the seller will face the issue of addressing that problem in any event, even if the particular sale does not proceed at that time. Accordingly, in some situations, a seller can often be persuaded to accept a price reduction for an identified and quantifiable problem.

Sometimes, the issue cannot be quantified in a way which allows the implications to be fully or accurately reflected in the price. For example, in the event that Target is subject to actual or threatened litigation, there will be a risk that a particular claim will succeed, but it is often not practicable to measure the extent of that risk, or to identify the monetary amount involved. In other situations (for example, the risk of a pension shortfall), the matter may well be ascertainable and quantifiable in theory, but the timescale for calculation of the relevant monetary amounts before signature would protract the sale negotiation for many months (and cause the figure to be out of date even when it has been determined). In these situations, the parties may agree a compromise

5 See further chapter 2, section 4.

price adjustment such that there is a one-off reduction in the price to reflect any agreed quantification of the risk. If such an agreement can be reached, then the simplicity is attractive, although it is important that the seller(s) review the acquisition agreement carefully to ensure that such adjustment is not 'double counted' as a result of any warranties, indemnities or price-adjustment mechanism. In many situations, such an agreement cannot be reached due to the uncertainty of the particular situation, and in that case some form of wait-and-see approach, or risk allocation, will be agreed. For example, the seller(s) may agree to indemnify the buyer for any liabilities arising as a result of the issue, but only once the liabilities have been incurred and are quantified. Alternatively, the parties may agree each to make a contribution towards such liabilities, or to pay only within certain cost bands, such that the seller underwrites only part of the exposure.

The precise solution will depend on the nature of the issue concerned. The question of how any relevant litigation or disputes will be conducted also arises; as a party agreeing to indemnify the other for losses suffered will wish to ensure that appropriate steps are taken to mitigate such losses.[6]

2.4 Retention accounts

Where any of these price adjustment mechanisms require a party to make a payment to the other after completion, there is credit and security risk for the recipient party. The same point arises for claims under the warranties and tax covenant, or claims under any indemnity or other specific risk-allocation mechanism. The fact that there may well be a valid contractual claim against a seller some months (or possibly years) later is of little comfort if by then such seller cannot be found, or the consideration received has been spent. Accordingly, where there is a significant likelihood that the sellers could be required to make a monetary payment at a later date, the buyer will usually require some form of security.

One possible solution would be for the buyer to defer part of the price, such that it becomes payable only on the occurrence of a specified later event (or the date when it is clear that the liability concerned will have passed), and subject to an adjustment to take into account any liability suffered as a result of the matter concerned. However, this, in turn, exposes the seller(s) to the risk that the buyer may not be good for the balance once it is finally due and payable. A typical compromise, therefore, is that some of the purchase price is placed into a blocked retention or escrow account held between the respective lawyers to the parties, or by an independent escrow agent service. This is designed to protect either party against any insolvency or similar risk on the part of the other once the mechanism unwinds and the monies become payable.

6 For limitations generally, see section 2.9 below.

The basic structure of a retention account is that a sum of money is placed (usually by the buyer) into the blocked account held by the solicitors or escrow agent as the case may be. The terms of appointment of the solicitors or escrow agent in respect of such sum are then designed to ensure that the relevant sum (and any interest earned on it, less charges) are paid over to the entitled party or parties as appropriate. The terms of the agreement, and of the appointment of the solicitors or escrow agent, are drafted in a way that ensures that the monies must be released on the happening of the relevant events on the basis that has been agreed, and cannot be released in any other circumstances without the consent of both parties.

A retention account is often used to secure liability under the warranties or tax covenant given on the acquisition for a period, or at least certain obligations under them. There can sometimes be more than one retention in a deal; for example one for a price adjustment mechanism such as completion accounts, one for a specific liability such as a pension shortfall that the seller is covering against the price, one for general warranty claims, and so on. The issue can then arise of whether monies not used to meet one type of claim can be used to meet another. For example, if there is a retention for the completion accounts that is not actually needed (or not fully needed) to satisfy a shortfall in the tested figures, what should happen if, by the time the completion accounts are agreed, a claim is made under the general warranties? These areas can lead to tricky negotiations, or can become complicated if multiple seller(s) are only subject to some, but not all, of the relevant liabilities.[7]

2.5 Conditionality

The acquisition agreement will specify any pre-conditions applicable to the purchase of Target. Inclusion of such a condition will usually result in a delay between exchange of the acquisition agreement and its completion. Typical conditions encountered in practice include:

(a) competition clearances;
(b) shareholder approval;
(c) tax clearances; and
(d) other regulatory consents.

(a) Competition clearances

Generally speaking, the granting of approval from a competition authority allowing a transaction to proceed is less likely to be a condition in private-equity-backed acquisitions than in an acquisition by a trade buyer. A trade buyer is more likely than a private-equity-backed buyer to be increasing its

7 For example, a private equity investor as seller may agree to contribute to a completion accounts price adjustment mechanism, but would not expect to have any liabilities under the general warranties; see further chapter 13.

market presence, reducing customer choice, or otherwise having an adverse impact on the competitiveness of a market by virtue of the merger of two competing businesses.

Special issues can, however, arise in certain overseas jurisdictions depending upon the nature and extent of the trade and market presence of Target. A more detailed review of the competition issues that can arise on an acquisition by a private-equity-backed buyer is set out in section 4 of this chapter.

A competition review must be conducted at an early stage; not least as, in some jurisdictions, approval may need to be obtained before a contract is even exchanged. In cases where a contract may be exchanged conditionally on clearance being granted, the delays and complexities caused will still be of significant concern to both parties, and for that reason seller(s) will often require competing buyers to confirm the likelihood of such a clearance application being necessary at an early stage in the process.

The outcome of that review may well lead to the need for one or more competition conditions in the agreement. There is often a commercial sensitivity which prevents a clearance application being made before agreement has been reached in writing between the parties that the acquisition should proceed, and sellers in particular are usually keen to see as much commitment as possible from the buyer(s) by way of a conditional agreement as quickly as possible, whilst the clearance application may take weeks or even months before it is concluded.[8]

(b) Shareholder approval

In certain transactions, it will be necessary for the shareholders of the seller, or a parent company of the seller, to approve the sale.

This typically arises where the sale is of a subsidiary company or business in a group where the ultimate parent company is traded on a stock exchange. Where the seller is listed on the Official List, the following provisions of the Listing Rules of the Financial Services Authority may be relevant.

(a) *Related party transactions.* Chapter 11 of the Listing Rules requires that any related party transaction (disregarding a very small *de minimis*) be subject to shareholder approval. This would require the relevant listed company to issue a circular to shareholders, and to convene a general meeting at which the necessary ordinary resolution will be proposed to approve the transaction. Under the relevant rules, the related party and its associates are not allowed to vote on the resolution. On the acquisition by a private-equity-backed Newco, the related party transaction requirements will be triggered if Newco is an associate of a director of the seller (or of any of its subsidiaries), or of any person who holds at least a 10 per cent equity stake in the seller (or of any person who satisfied any of

8 For more details, see section 4 below.

those conditions at any time in the preceding twelve months). In order for Newco to be such an associate, it is necessary that the directors and their associates together have at least 30 per cent of the voting rights in Newco. In a larger buyout, this would be unusual, but it is not impossible in a smaller transaction and, accordingly, whenever the seller group is listed, this must be considered.

(b) *Class 1 transactions.* Even if there is no related party in the transaction or if the stake of the related parties in Newco is not sufficient to make it an associate, it is possible that a shareholder vote may be required if the transaction is sufficiently large to satisfy the criteria for a Class 1 transaction.[9] If the deal does constitute a Class 1 transaction, then the relevant public limited company is required to issue a circular to its shareholders and to convene a general meeting at which the necessary ordinary resolution will be proposed to approve the transaction. Assuming that it is not also a related party transaction, there is no reason why any existing interested related parties and their associates cannot vote on the Class 1 resolution.

If the seller is listed on AIM, the similar related party rule only requires notification and not shareholder approval. However, if the Target constitutes more than 75 per cent of the listed company (applying the various class tests specified for AIM), this constitutes a fundamental change of business and the same requirement for a shareholder approval arises. In that event, the related parties and their associates are not prohibited from voting.[10]

Even if the seller (or ultimate parent company) is not listed on the Official List or traded on AIM, or if it is only a private company, the fact that the managers will be shareholders in the buyer can, in certain cases, trigger the requirement for shareholder approval of the transaction under section 190 of the Companies Act 2006. For this section to be relevant, it is necessary that the buyer is a connected person of a director of the seller (or of a director of the seller's holding company). Under section 252 of the Companies Act 2006, this will arise where the director (and certain related parties) has a stake of at least 20 per cent of the voting equity in the buyer. In larger transactions where the private equity investors have a majority equity stake in the buyer, it is less likely that any one director will have such a significant minority stake, but this point should be checked. If section 190 does apply, the transaction must be approved by an ordinary resolution of the members of the seller (or, as the context may require, of its ultimate holding company). There is no prohibition under the Companies Act 2006 on the director or other related party voting on the resolution.

9 For more details of these tests, see chapter 10 of the Listing Rules and the Annex to that chapter.

10 See Rule 15 of, and Schedule Three to, the AIM Rules.

It is possible in this context to make the transaction conditional upon such approvals being obtained (so that the sale agreement can at least be signed); however, the necessary shareholder consent must be obtained before completion occurs. The risk that completion may not occur due to approval not being granted can be mitigated to some degree before signing by seeking irrevocable commitments from significant shareholders of the seller (or the seller's holding company, as applicable) to vote in favour of the proposal. Where the shares are publicly traded, there can be issues of confidentiality in seeking such irrevocables, and the specific market conduct rules which regulate this practice will need to be complied with.

(c) Tax clearances

In certain transactions, one or more sellers may seek a tax clearance from HMRC to ensure that the desired tax treatment will arise on disposal. Usually, these clearances will be sought in good time to ensure they are in place before the contract is signed; however, where that is not possible, the sellers may seek to make the disposal conditional upon the clearances being granted.

Generally, HMRC will be able to provide tax clearances in a relatively short period; however, they do have up to thirty days to provide necessary clearances, and the timescale to secure a clearance may be longer if further queries are raised in response to the application. In some circumstances, therefore, the sellers may be left without formal clearance at a time when signing could otherwise occur. In that situation the question of whether a deal should proceed on a conditional basis, be delayed until clearance has been obtained, or be completed immediately (leaving the seller(s) exposed to a risk that the relevant tax treatment will not be obtained) will be determined on a case-by-case basis, depending on the extent of the risk, bargaining power of the parties and overall deal momentum.

(d) Other regulatory approvals

There may be sector-specific regulatory approvals required for the transaction to proceed. In certain situations, the buyer or its directors require regulatory approvals to own the Target or to carry on the business, or the change of control arising from completion of the transaction means that existing approvals held by Target are revoked or at risk of review. In many cases, the continuity of management that flows from a management buyout may well mean that these regulatory consents are already in place, or that the regulator will be more readily persuaded to re-grant them. A legal adviser should ensure that the extent of any regulatory approvals are verified as part of legal due diligence, and identify any approvals which require either the consent of a regulator, or notification of the transaction, as the case may be. A typical example would be a change of controller for the purposes of the Financial Services and Markets Act 2000 (and related rules) if the business being acquired is, for example, an insurance company.

Ideally, the parties will seek to resolve all such regulatory matters before signature, so that there does not need to be a condition in this respect, even where consent and not merely notification is required. However, whether this is practicable will depend on the regulatory body concerned; in many cases, the authority may not be familiar with the nuances of corporate transactions, which can lead to a delay in approval being given, and the parties may be nervous about disclosing any details concerning the proposed transaction before signing to maintain confidentiality.

2.6 Consequences of conditionality

Whenever there is a condition precedent to completion of the transaction, the following points (of general application) must be borne in mind when drafting the relevant provisions.

- What are the precise terms of the condition? It is important that the condition is drafted so as to be sufficiently clear and certain as to whether, and when, it is met.
- Whether any party is under any obligation to procure or assist in satisfying the condition. Often, there is a requirement on both parties to use their respective reasonable endeavours to ensure its satisfaction, although the onus may be placed on one of the parties more extensively, depending on the nature of the condition and the party likely to be most instrumental in ensuring its satisfaction.
- Whether either party is entitled to waive the condition, although, by definition, the implications are usually sufficiently serious for neither party to be able to do so unilaterally.
- A longstop date for satisfaction of the condition, which may be driven by the timescale prescribed for the relevant external approval process (where applicable), and the length of time for which the buyer's funding remains available.
- Consequences if the condition is not met (for example, does either party have any form of cost exposure to the other). This will very much depend on the bargaining power of the parties, and the circumstances in which the need for a conditional contract has arisen. A condition which is inserted for the benefit of the seller or required by the seller (for example, shareholder approval) may well lead to a cost underwrite in favour of the buyer, or at least a partial abortive payment if the transaction does not proceed due to lack of shareholder approval. If the approval is related more to factors associated with the buyer, there may be a suggestion that the buyer should pay abortive costs, although, in general, a private-equity-backed buyer will be reluctant to do this, not least because the transactional funding to meet such a cost underwrite will not be available if the transaction has not proceeded.

The fact that the deal is conditional, and that there may well be a delay before the conditions are satisfied, also results in other practical issues for the process.

(a) Conduct of Target during the delay

The Target remains in the ownership of the seller(s) following exchange of the acquisition agreement. If the condition is never actually met or waived, it will remain with the seller(s), whereas the buyer will take over the Target if the conditions are met or waived. Both parties therefore have a legitimate interest in how Target is run and in maintaining it as a going concern. This issue is even more acute if the circumstances of the delay also makes the transaction public (for example, the need for a circular and shareholder approval). This aspect is normally regulated by agreeing a set of rules for the conduct of the business, including certain matters requiring the consent of the buyer during this interim period. Where the management team is in day-to-day operational control of the Target (as is often the case in a buyout), this also gives some practical comfort to the buyer and its funders, although the specific rules would still be prescribed in any event. The scope of such rules is a matter for detailed negotiation, but in general terms they will seek to ensure that the business is carried on in the ordinary course following exchange, and that no significant actions are taken that could have an adverse impact on the value of Target's business or the sale shares without the consent of the buyer. The restrictions will include both constitutional matters, such as making alterations to the share capital, and operational issues, such as entering into material contracts or significant capital expenditure commitments.

(b) Risk in the business during the delay

Even if the sellers comply with the rules for the running of the business, there is a risk that something may change adversely in the business or the wider sector. It may be that there is an adverse reaction from key customers, suppliers or employees to the news of the imminent sale. A major issue from the past may come to light or material litigation may be threatened. Something may occur or become known which suggests the possibility of a claim under the warranties given on exchange. A key employee may leave the business, or become ill in a way that prevents him from carrying on working. There may well be some incident that causes major disruption to the business of the Target, or to that of a key customer or supplier. All these matters may well have resulted in a material change in the terms of the deal if they had become known before exchange, or may even have resulted in the sale not being exchanged at all.

A seller would normally wish to hold the buyer to the terms already agreed, and to put the parties into the same position as if the deal had actually completed when signed. For example, a seller might argue that any such events should be at the buyer's risk assuming the agreed conditions, and those conditions only, are satisfied. If such an event is so serious as to give rise to a claim under the warranties or other price adjustment mechanism in the agreement, then the buyer should still be expected to complete the transaction, and then to pursue any warranty claim or price reduction afterwards.

A buyer (and, most significantly in a private equity deal, its funders) may well take a different view, especially in a market that favours a buyer. Such funders will usually insist that:

(a) the seller(s) should repeat the warranties set out in the acquisition agreement as at completion; such repetition of warranties may result in the seller(s) being required to prepare and deliver a supplemental disclosure letter on completion, setting out details of any matters that have arisen between exchange and completion which have resulted in a breach of warranty;[11]
(b) a contractual right for the buyer to rescind the acquisition agreement if any breach of warranty arises during the period between exchange and completion (perhaps with a materiality threshold);
(c) similarly, a right to rescind in the event that there is any other material breach of the acquisition agreement by the seller(s), for example as a result of a breach by the seller(s) of the obligations for the conduct of the business between exchange and completion as referred to in (a) above; and/or
(d) possibly, a right to rescind in the event that there is any other material adverse change (often abbreviated to MAC) which has an adverse impact on Target and its business between exchange and completion.

This debate can result in real tension between the parties. Where there is insufficient protection for the buyer in the event of an adverse change in the business, this will cause particular concern to the funders of the buyer, particularly the senior lender(s). Whilst in a seller-friendly market there may be sufficient bargaining power to resist any right to walk away from the transaction, there will generally be strong pressure from the bank funders in particular, who would often seek indirectly to enforce any agreed MAC provisions by having a right to withdraw its debt commitment in those circumstances. Accordingly, the precise negotiation of any right to rescind or walk away, the circumstances in which that right can be exercised, and the contractual consequences if it is exercised or not exercised, can be the most difficult aspects of a conditional private equity deal.[12]

11 On warranties in the acquisition agreement, see further sections 2.7 to 2.9 below. On disclosure, see section 3 below.

12 The interaction of the banking documents, equity documents and acquisition agreement when including any MAC clause or other walk away rights must also be considered carefully: see further chapter 5, section 3.2.

2.7 Warranties, indemnities and risk allocation

As highlighted in sections 2.2 and 2.3 above, where a specific and quantifiable risk is identified as part of the acquisition process (typically, as part of due diligence), it is likely to lead to an adjustment to the price, or some form of mechanism to determine which party will bear the risk or the basis upon which the risk is to be shared. It is a known problem; the only question is whether and how it affects the deal (or whether the deal can be agreed at all, if the issue is sufficiently serious).

However, it is inherent in many businesses that problems caused in the past will only become known or relevant in the future. Often, issues cannot be identified fully (or even at all) during due diligence. For example, there may well be claims not yet notified to or anticipated by the seller(s) as a result of contracts already entered into by Target, or liabilities to employees for occupational illnesses of which people are not yet aware.

The allocation of the risk arising as a result of these unknowns (and, indirectly therefore, the means for adjusting the price after the event to reflect the effect of such unknowns on the value of the sale shares) is effected by the warranties set out in the acquisition agreement. It is important to bear in mind that, in the absence of formal contractual warranties, there are no implied terms to protect a buyer of shares. In particular, in the absence of fraud or negligent misstatement, the buyer will have no claim against the sellers if the business is not as the buyer expected and there is no appropriate warranty or other protection in the acquisition agreement. An acquisition agreement will almost invariably include an express provision that no warranty is given save as is set out in the agreement.

For this reason, the buyer of a private company will seek to negotiate extensive warranties from the sellers. The warranties in the acquisitions agreement are commonly referred to as fulfilling two functions:

(a) to allocate risk; and
(b) to elicit disclosure.

The warranties are given subject to matters disclosed to the buyer pursuant to a disclosure letter provided by the seller(s). The process of disclosure is considered further in section 3 of this chapter, and requires the warranting seller(s) to disclose details of any matter of which they are aware which would breach the warranties given. For a seller to give a warranty which he knows to be breached at the time the warranty is given may constitute a criminal offence. Further, the acquisition agreement will provide that no seller will be liable under the warranties to the extent a matter is disclosed, motivating any seller to enter into a comprehensive disclosure exercise. To this extent, therefore, the warranty schedule will elicit information about the Target and identify potential difficulties and actual problems. This will support the buyer's own due diligence in identifying any areas which require the acquisition price to be revisited, or which may need a specific indemnity or some other contractual risk-allocation mechanism to be agreed.

Accordingly, the warranties are not the principal mechanism for allocating the known risks. They are, however, very important in allocating the unknown risks – or at least the risks which have not been disclosed. The warranties serve a useful function to enable a buyer to bring a claim against the seller(s) for any matters to which the warranties relate, if such warranties subsequently prove to have been inaccurate and diminish the value of the acquired shares. This risk allocation function is the principal purpose of the warranties once the agreement has actually been signed. For this reason, the precise form of the warranties and, in particular, whether they are given in absolute form or to the knowledge of the seller (or subject to some other qualification) forms a key part of the negotiation of the acquisition agreement, as does the extent of any limitations on the buyer's ability to claim under those warranties.

The precise areas covered by warranties will vary deal by deal, but they typically include (in the buyer's first draft at least):

- the title of the seller(s) to the sale shares and capacity to contract;
- the legal status of the company;
- the proper preparation of accounting records and the statutory accounts of the Target;
- Target's title to its assets (including property) and their state and condition;
- Target's contracts, including both material and long-term arrangements, and standard terms of trading;
- Target's employees;
- Target's tax affairs;
- Target's compliance with laws, and any relevant regulatory requirements, whether of general application to all businesses (e.g. environmental, health and safety) or sector specific (e.g. requirements of industry regulators such as the Financial Services Authority);
- Target's pension schemes and any related exposures;
- Target's litigation and litigation risk;
- Target's intellectual property rights and IT systems;
- Target's solvency; and
- interests of the seller(s) in Target and its affairs, any dealings between them and any ongoing reliance by Target on any seller, or *vice versa*.

2.8 Warranties and knowledge/awareness

One very significant area of negotiation in relation to warranties (and the limitations which apply to any warranty claims) is that of the knowledge or awareness of the parties. This will be the case on any arm's length UK off-market transaction, but there is a particular focus on these aspects in a management buyout.

(a) Awareness of the seller

Many sellers will seek to limit the warranties (or at least certain of them) so that they are only given 'so far as the seller is aware', or are otherwise qualified by reference to the knowledge, awareness or belief of the seller. Particular warranties are often referred to in negotiations as being acceptable if given 'to knowledge', or using similar shorthand. Clearly, this can be an important protection for a seller, particularly in respect of matters outside the knowledge of the day-to-day internal management of the company. For example, a seller may be unaware that a regulatory body is considering an investigation into the affairs of Target, or that a customer or supplier is contemplating a claim against it.

Where the warranties are qualified by reference to seller awareness, this creates an additional hurdle for the buyer in bringing a successful claim. The buyer must first prove that the substantive issue has arisen resulting in a loss (for example, that there is a potential investigation into the affairs of the Target, which has diminished the value of the sale shares), and must then prove that the seller was aware of this at the relevant time. In the absence of a clear 'smoking gun', it can be difficult, therefore, for the buyer to show that the seller had actual knowledge of circumstances giving rise to the breach of the awareness-based warranty.

Where the seller is a company or other body corporate, it is usual to specify that the knowledge of the seller for this purpose means the knowledge of certain named individuals (and it follows that, in a buyout context, this may include any or all of the managers: see further below). Buyers may seek to extend seller awareness to include matters of which any employee is aware, or other agents of Target (particularly advisers) are aware, or even of which such persons ought to have been aware. Clearly, a seller is likely to try to limit this list such that it is as short as possible, and to resist any language which implies knowledge on the part of any such person in any event.

It is also important, in this context, to differentiate between imputing to the seller the knowledge of any such party, and requiring the seller to make enquiry of the third party. For example, if the knowledge of particular employees is imputed to the seller, then it is sufficient to prove that one of the employees knew of the matter, even if the seller did not know (or cannot be proved to have known). In contrast, if warranties are stated to be given by a seller based on that seller's knowledge 'after making due and careful enquiry of the employees' or similar, then the risk that an employee did not mention something (perhaps because he forgot the matter, did not realise its relevance, or had his own reasons for not mentioning it) is effectively borne by the buyer and not by the seller. Sellers are inevitably reluctant to see knowledge extended beyond the actual knowledge of the sellers themselves (or, in the case of a corporate seller, of designated individuals), and will certainly seek to resist imputed knowledge, whereas buyers will normally seek to extend the concept as widely as possible. The wider the scope of knowledge, the more the seller must do to rely on it and, conversely, the less the buyer needs to do to overcome the hurdle.

(b) Awareness of the buyer

The seller can also seek refuge against possible warranty claims by limiting the ability of the buyer to make a claim based on matters of which the buyer is aware at the time of contract. To an extent, this is already implicit in the structure, in the sense that matters disclosed (or, at least, fairly disclosed) in the disclosure letter cannot give rise to a warranty claim.[13] However, sellers will often seek to extend this to other matters of which the buyer is aware, whether disclosed by the sellers or otherwise.

As the buyer is a body corporate (i.e. Newco), awareness here is usually again defined by reference to the actual awareness of named individuals, with sellers typically seeking comfort that specific individuals at the relevant private equity house (and, they may also argue, the managers: again, see below) are not aware of any matters giving rise to a claim. A number of the arguments referred to above in the context of the awareness of a seller can be reversed in this area to try to extend the knowledge of the buyer, by suggesting that a buyer should be unable to claim in respect of matters in the knowledge of their advisers (for example, from their due diligence, even if not arising as a result of information supplied by, or known to, the sellers), or that a buyer should be imputed with the knowledge of such persons. In the same way that the buyer seeks to extend seller awareness (if accepted as a defence) beyond actual knowledge, so the sellers will seek to extend the buyer's knowledge beyond actual awareness to seek to have a broader warranty defence.

A related variant of the 'buyer's knowledge as a defence' argument concerns the buyer's commissioned due diligence.[14] Rather than debate what the buyer knows or could have known, and whose actual knowledge constitutes the buyer's knowledge for this purpose, the seller may argue that there can be no claim for what is mentioned in the buyer's due diligence reports. Some buyers (and especially private-equity-backed buyers) can become concerned where this argument is advanced by the seller(s), particularly if the due diligence reports contain information that the buyer may not wish the seller(s) to see (for example, details of an undervaluation of Target's assets or an overprovision in Target's accounts, or details of savings and benefits that the buyer may in future gain from Target which the seller(s) had failed to identify). This debate is sometimes revisited as part of the disclosure process, if the seller(s) seek to incorporate the content of any due diligence reports as a deemed general disclosure in the acquisition disclosure letter. The buyer should be vigilant against both of these arguments, and many private equity firms will simply not accept

13 For disclosure, including fair disclosure, see section 3 below.

14 On due diligence generally, see chapter 2, section 4.

such a position as a matter of policy. If the concept is accepted, it would almost certainly only be agreed on the basis that the buyer will not actually show the reports to the seller(s) pre-contract, such that disclosure only becomes relevant in the event that there is a claim.

Whilst these arguments concerning awareness qualifications are encountered in most share sale agreements, the issue is particularly acute in a management buyout, given that some or all of the senior management of the seller or the Target are to become officers or shareholders in the private-equity-backed buyer. There are two aspects which complicate the typical negotiations.

In relation to seller awareness, many sellers try to argue that all warranties (or a substantial part of them relating to the trading activities of Target) should be given on an awareness basis. In most deals, a buyer will limit awareness qualifications to those warranties which are outside the knowledge of anybody in the Target company (for example, that no third party is intending to cease trading with Target, to commence litigation and so on). However, in a buyout, a parent company or private seller may suggest that the onus should be on the managers to provide comfort to the investors on day-to-day trading matters by way of the warranties in the investment agreement. This is particularly the case where the day-to-day running of the business is in fact carried on by the managers, and the seller is a 'hands off' holding company or otherwise a distant, less involved shareholder. An investor would not normally accept this proposition. For obvious reasons, an ability to sue the incumbent management team which that investor is now backing is not an attractive remedy; if a substantial loss is suffered within Target, then the preferred remedy will be against the seller who extracted value from the transaction, and with whom the investors may no longer have an ongoing relationship. These issues are considered in more detail in the context of the investment agreement warranties in chapter 5.[15] However, if a seller has significant bargaining power, it is possible that a private equity buyer will take a slightly more pragmatic view on knowledge qualification in some areas, particularly if it can take comfort from a diligent and trusted management team that there are unlikely to be any skeletons in the closet. For the particular conflict of interest that can arise in the context of a secondary buyout here, see further chapter 12.

Similarly, the issue of the awareness of the managers can arise in the context of buyer knowledge, where the seller seeks to impute knowledge of the management team on the buyer so as to prevent a claim. Most private equity buyers will strongly resist this argument too, for the reasons referred to above and in chapter 5. Warranties in the investment agreement will provide no comfort at all to the banks or other debt funders – they will not have access to the managers as a means of recourse in any event – so the investors will often use this understandable position from their lenders to justify a firm position. Where the private-equity-backed investor is paying a more attractive price than

15 See chapter 5, sections 3.4 and 3.5.

any other interested party (perhaps as a result of an auction in a more seller-friendly market, or by virtue of being the only runner in the race in a more buyer-friendly market), it may well query why it should receive less protection than the outbid, or absent, trade buyer. For these reasons, if any qualification based on buyer awareness is accepted, such awareness is typically limited to the actual knowledge of specific individuals at the private equity house; this gives a seller comfort that the buyer does not have a warranty claim 'waiting in the wings', without imputing the knowledge of the management team or any advisers or other third parties to the buyer.

A similar protection often seen (commonly referred to as a 'reverse warranty') is a statement from the buyer that it does not know of any claim under the warranties. This is potentially a dangerous confirmation for the buyer to give, for the same reasons that a limitation to prevent or restrict warranty claims based on the buyer's knowledge is undesirable. The buyer may not always fully appreciate the implications of matters of which it is aware, and the question of which individuals' knowledge (whether investors, management team members, their advisers and so on) should be classified as buyer knowledge once again becomes a point for debate. In the context of a management buyout, where the seller(s) will often be nervous of selling Target to a management team who know the business better than they do, some form of protection for the seller(s) based on the buyer's knowledge is usually agreed, although the definition of what is meant by the buyer's knowledge will be precise and limited. In any event, however, the buyer should look to include such knowledge qualification in the agreement as a limitation preventing a claim (usually in the limitation schedule referred to in section 2.9 below) rather than a warranty. The buyer should certainly not leave itself exposed to a warranty claim from the seller(s) in circumstances where it is not pursuing a claim itself – the 'buyer awareness' defence should operate only as a shield for the seller(s), and not as a sword.

Irrespective of whether a defence based on buyer knowledge is accepted, how far a buyer can contract out of its actual knowledge and bring a claim for something of which it was aware at the time of contract from a source other than the disclosure letter is a moot point, and is explored further in section 3 below in the context of the disclosure letter. Certainly, where a buyer has actual knowledge of a problem (whether from the disclosure letter or otherwise), it is normally best advised to address the concern through a price adjustment, specific indemnity or other risk-allocation mechanism, so that the sellers bear, or at least share, the risk rather than relying solely on the warranties to provide a remedy.

2.9 Limitations

It is customary for the acquisition agreement to include a schedule of limitations that apply to any claim for a breach of the warranties (and, in the case of certain specific limitations, to other claims against the sellers under the acquisition documentation). These limitations provide a second line of defence for the sellers – or, to put it another way, a more sophisticated refinement of the allocation of the risk of the unknown. Rather than negotiate into each warranty certain parameters (e.g. the size of claim that is relevant or the ability, if any, of the seller to cause the Target to dispute some third party claim), the sellers rely on a schedule of limitations to act as an overarching layer of protection, setting out the caveats and exclusions which will apply to whichever warranty proves ultimately to have been breached.

Lawyers should ensure that it is clear whether all the limitations, or only some specific limitations, should apply to each particular type of claim (whether pursuant to warranties, specific indemnities, the taxation provisions,[16] or otherwise under the agreement). Generally, the application of the full schedule of limitations is reserved for warranty claims, with time limits and (possibly) some financial limitations being extended to other parts of the agreement, but this will vary according to the nature of the liabilities concerned and the bargaining power of the parties. Certain limitations will not be relevant for any claim other than a warranty claim; there is no point in qualifying a particular indemnity by reference to the content of the disclosure letter if the purpose of the indemnity is to allocate the liability between the parties for the very matter that is disclosed, for example. It is important to note that these monetary and other limitations in the agreement would generally not apply in the case of fraud or wilful non-disclosure.

Whilst the precise content of the limitations will vary from deal to deal, the areas covered by warranty limitations is relatively settled in UK practice. Typically, these include the following matters.

(a) Monetary limits

There will usually be three monetary limits relevant to the warranties:

(a) *Small claims limit.* This *de minimis* provision is designed to ensure that individual small issues arising in connection with the Target cannot form the basis of a warranty claim, however many of such claims or issues may arise. In the UK, as a very general rule of thumb, the small claims limit is typically around 0.1 per cent of the overall consideration, although this will vary from deal to deal. Often, wording will be included to ensure that similar claims (that is, claims arising from the same facts, matters or circumstances) are aggregated for this purpose. For example, if the small claims figure is £5,000, and there are twenty employees who have not received their annual bonus of £3,000 each, then the issue would be treated as one claim of £60,000 (which would exceed the limit) rather than twenty claims each of £3,000 (each of which separately would not exceed the limit).

16 See also section 5 below.

(b) *A claims threshold, also referred to as the 'basket' threshold.* This provides the seller(s) with a second layer of protection. Here, the value of the qualifying claims (i.e. claims exceeding the small claims limit) must still exceed a particular aggregate threshold before a warranty claim can be brought. From the seller's perspective, this ensures that the buyer accepts a level of risk before pursuing a protracted claim, introducing a further principle of materiality. A typical limit would be 1 per cent of the consideration, but practice does vary. One point which is sometimes negotiated here is what should happen once the threshold is exceeded? Is the seller only liable for the excess over the threshold, or do all claims count once the threshold has been exceeded (other than small claims, which do not count towards the basket in any event)? Generally speaking, in most acquisition agreements in the UK, the threshold might be described as a 'tipping basket'; that is to say that, once the relevant threshold has been exceeded, all claims (other than those below the small claims limit) can proceed – although a strong seller may insist that claims are limited to the excess of claims beyond the threshold.

(c) *Maximum liability cap.* Typically, there will be a maximum liability stated, which is at the very least equal to the consideration received by the seller(s). In a seller-friendly market, it may be possible for the sellers(s) to reduce this exposure to a proportion of their consideration received. Some sellers may have no liability under the commercial warranties at all (see in particular chapter 13 in respect of the attitude taken by private equity investors when selling).

(d) *Joint and several liability.* Where there are multiple sellers, a more protracted negotiation will usually take place to determine how warranty risk is to be allocated as between them, and who accepts the risk that one of the sellers becomes insolvent before a claim is made, or is otherwise unwilling or unable to satisfy a claim. A buyer will prefer the discretion to pursue any seller for the full amount of any claim (leaving that seller in a position where he must try to claim a contribution from the others), whereas sellers prefer their liability to the buyer to be apportioned between them on an agreed basis (usually *pro rata* to the consideration received). It follows that a seller will prefer his liability to be capped at the consideration received by that seller, and not the consideration received by all sellers. A typical compromise is that the sellers would be jointly and severally liable (meaning that the buyer can proceed against any one or more of the sellers for the loss without the need to split up individual claims as between the sellers), but that the maximum amount recoverable from any one seller would be the consideration received by that particular seller. However, it is not unheard of for buyers to accept that sellers will be severally liable for their proportion of a warranty claim, particularly in a seller-friendly market.

(b) Time limits

It would be unusual for the agreement not to include appropriate time limits for the bringing of any warranty claims. Without such a limit, the normal period would be six years under most agreements, or twelve years if the agreement is entered into as a deed. As a general rule, claims under the tax covenant or under warranties relating to the tax matters of the Target may be brought within a period of seven years after the date of the acquisition. The other commercial warranties usually have a shorter limitation period, typically between eighteen months and three years, although the time period can be shorter than this if the seller has the bargaining power to limit the timescales further. The time period for claims under the general warranties is often linked to a particular financial year end, allowing the buyer to carry out two audits (or sometimes audits for two complete financial years since acquisition), together with a brief period following that second audit to review the results and identify any areas of concern.

There may also be a provision designed to ensure that the buyer brings a claim as soon as he is aware of it (or at least gives notice of the potential claim to the seller(s)). This is designed, in part, to allow the seller(s) to have a chance to influence the conduct of the claim by the Target if that might help mitigate the loss. A strong buyer will usually resist an obligation to notify immediately, especially if any delay in doing so could cause the warranty claim to fail even though the loss from the warranty breach was real, and the seller(s) suffered no prejudice by the delay. A typical compromise would be that the longstop date agreed for notifying a claim would be rigid, but that the buyer accepts a duty to notify the seller(s) of the claim as soon as it is reasonably practicable upon the buyer becoming aware of the claim, with express wording providing that any delay in doing so does not prejudice the claim and is only relevant to the question of mitigation of the buyer's loss.

A further debate normally arises as to whether the claim (even if notified within the relevant period) should still lapse if legal proceedings are not commenced within a given period following the notification (or, in some cases, following the longstop date). A buyer will resist this, but the seller is normally able to prevail on the point, with a typical period being between six and twelve months after notification of the claim.

(c) Conduct and the right to fight

A major area for disagreement can arise over conduct and the right to fight, i.e. how the parties and Target should act if the circumstances of the claim are connected to a claim against the Target by a third party (for example, a customer claim, a claim by an ex-employee or a demand by a taxation authority), or where the circumstances of the claim would entitle Target itself to pursue a third party (for example, a supplier or adviser to Target). This issue is not limited to warranty claims (where the buyer in any event has a general duty to mitigate its loss), but arises also in the tax covenant or any specific indemnities agreed for a particular matter in the agreement (where there is no duty to mitigate). Whatever the circumstances, the common issue for the seller(s) is a fear that the buyer would rather bring a claim against the seller(s) (especially if the liability is backed up by a retention, or by a right of set-off against any earnout consideration for example), rather than resist a claim from a key customer or pursue a supplier or other third party and prejudice relations with that party. The buyer, in return, is concerned that the seller(s) could pursue all manner of defences or claims in Target's name either to delay its own payment, or because it has no ongoing reason to be concerned about the goodwill of Target.

A typical compromise in respect of general warranty claims would be that the seller(s) have the right to make requests to the buyer as to how it believes the claim should be handled, but the buyer has the ultimate say on how to handle it. Where the buyer chooses not to follow the recommendations of the seller(s), the question then becomes one of mitigation.

Where the claim in question relates to a claim pursuant to the tax covenant, or a specific indemnity, there may be more willingness for the seller(s) to have conduct of the matter (provided it is acting reasonably) on a basis that the seller(s) will bear all of the losses suffered fully, or it may be even more appropriate for the buyer to have exclusive conduct without any regard for the seller(s) (where the protection is for a specific issue that concerns the buyer, but on which the seller(s) have assured the buyer that there is no need for concern, for example). The conduct provisions for indemnities and similar protections will therefore be a matter for bespoke negotiation, depending on the precise subject matter.

(d) Other typical limitations

Other limitations typically seen include:

- no claim for matters in the last statutory accounts or the completion accounts;
- no claim to the extent that any monies are actually recovered under any insurance policies in place;
- no claim for matters resulting from the buyer's or Target's own actions following completion outside the ordinary course;
- no claim for matters arising as a result of the parties carrying out their obligations under the terms of the agreement;
- no claims for any change in law or regulatory practice.

Whilst customary limitations have emerged in the UK market, it is important to remember that the parties to any transaction will often have particular 'must haves', or 'cannot gives', based on their own experience and general approach to risk on transactions. This is particularly the case in the private equity arena, where firms often have established policies based on the requirements of their ultimate investors, or perhaps as a result of a painful experience on a previous transaction.

2.10 Restrictive covenants and confidentiality

Most acquisition agreements will contain restrictive covenants from some or all of the sellers that seek to prevent those sellers competing with the Target for a limited period in any relevant territories, and also to prevent the sellers from soliciting the customers, suppliers or employees of the Target.

The nature and extent of these covenants are matters for negotiation, and will vary according to the particular circumstances of the deal. It is important that the buyer bears in mind that any such restriction operating in restraint of trade is *prima facie* void under English law, unless the buyer can prove that it is designed to protect a legitimate interest (in this context, the goodwill acquired in the business), and is no more onerous than is reasonably necessary in the interests both of the parties and of the public to protect that interest. Accordingly, it is not generally possible for the buyer to seek restrictions intended to restrict the sellers from competing beyond the extent of Target's activities at the time of acquisition (for example, to cover future expansion plans into new territories or product markets, or to indirectly protect other businesses that may exist in similar markets in the investors' portfolio). Typically, restrictive covenants in a UK share sale would subsist for a period of between two and four years.

Certain sellers will generally resist giving restrictive covenants – this will typically include institutional sellers (such as private equity houses: for details on the institutional stance on a sale see chapter 13). Other individual sellers may seek to argue that restrictive covenants would not be reasonable in their situation, on the basis that they have had no real involvement in the business, or have no information which could harm it, for example shares which are held by passive family investors, or the trustees of family trusts or an employee benefit trust. It is important that the restrictive covenants and their reasonableness are tested in the context of each seller. A covenant which may be reasonable against a full-time managing director and controlling shareholder may not be as reasonable in the context of a 2 per cent stakeholder who has never been personally involved in the business or the sector, and whose only reason for holding the shares is that he or she is a relative of the original founder.

Most sellers (including, in some cases, private equity sellers) will accept obligations of confidentiality – to keep confidential the information of the Target group of which they have become aware during their share ownership – and will also accept restrictions not to use trading names or brands used in the Target company or its business. These would usually be perpetual, with (in the case of confidential information) customary carve-outs enabling disclosure where the information has entered the public domain (other than by virtue of disclosure by the seller), or is required to comply with law or the requirements of any regulatory body.

Where one or more of the managers are existing shareholders in Target, and therefore selling shares as well as becoming shareholders in the Newco buyer (in a secondary, for example), they may give restrictive covenants in the investment agreement and their service agreements, as well as in the sale agreement. The scope and extent of the covenants will not be consistent across the three documents, as each is usually tailored to suit the particular context in which the restrictions are given. For further discussion of the interaction of these different restrictive covenants and the particular factors relevant to each of them, see section 3.7 of chapter 5.

2.11 Assignment

Acquisition agreements have increased in their complexity and volume in recent years. It is beyond the scope of this book to review all of the content of such agreements in detail; however, one of the typical 'boilerplate' provisions does have particular relevance in a buyout.

The banks providing senior debt will normally expect to have a charge over all the assets of the buyer, and one of such assets is the benefit of the acquisition agreement itself and related documents, and the right to pursue claims under the various warranties and other protections set out in those documents. In many share sales, the seller will seek to argue that the benefit of the warranties and similar protections should not be assigned, as the seller should not have to face the possibility of a claim from any party other than the buyer, with whom a relationship will have been developed in the course of the transaction.

However, senior debt providers in private equity buyout transactions will normally insist that the benefit of the acquisition agreement (including any rights to claim for any breach of the warranties) may be assigned by way of security, and then dealt with by an administrator or other office holder as part of the realisation and enforcement of any such security if necessary. Sellers will usually accept this as a necessary concession in order for the buyer to secure the funding needed for the transaction to take place. Typically, however, they will seek to include clauses designed to ensure that an assignee can have no greater claim than the buyer itself would have had, and that the seller(s) may take advantage of any defences or protections against such assignee in exactly the same way as would have been the case had the claim been brought by the original buyer.

3 Disclosure and the disclosure letter

3.1 Disclosure: principles

One of the most important protections for the seller(s) arises from the disclosure process. As highlighted in section 2.7 above, the general principle is that the buyer cannot bring a claim under the warranties in the acquisition agreement to the extent that any matters are disclosed in the disclosure letter. Rather than negotiate each individual warranty by reference to the particular circumstances – say, for example, 'except for matter X and matter Y the Target is not engaged in litigation' – the individual warranties are not amended, and the content of the disclosure letter will qualify the warranties instead. As well as easing the drafting of the warranties, placing all the significant or material disclosures in one letter makes it easier for the buyer to consider whether any issues are sufficiently serious to justify a price negotiation or other measure – and, as a result, the disclosure letter is invariably a document in which the private equity and bank funders take great interest.

It follows that the negotiation of the disclosure letter itself (which is considered below), and the provisions in the acquisition agreement setting out the hurdle which has to be met in the preparation of the disclosure letter for it to be effective, are two of the most important aspects of the acquisition process. These aspects are also very closely linked to the issue of awareness qualifications on warranties discussed in section 2.8 of this chapter.

In the earlier part of this decade, there was an opinion that, as a rule of law, for disclosure to be effective it needed to be fair – that is to say, it needed to set out in reasonable detail and clarity what the seller knew on the matter which was being referred to and, probably, the context and relevance of it to the overall affairs of the Target. However, the decision in *Infiniteland Ltd* v. *Artisan Contracting Ltd*[17] has confirmed that there is no principle of law that a disclosure has to be fair, and it is entirely a matter of contract between the parties. Accordingly, if the parties provide that it is enough that something is simply 'disclosed', then providing that the relevant information is 'disclosed' it will operate as a disclosure in the context of the warranties, and limit or prevent a warranty claim by the buyer for the matter that has been disclosed. For this reason, buyers invariably set a standard for what constitutes a valid disclosure. Typically, this is achieved by incorporating an 'adverbial hurdle' in the clause or definition dealing with disclosure in the acquisition agreement – for example, 'save as fairly disclosed', 'save as fully and fairly disclosed', 'save as accurately disclosed', or similar wording. The precise wording will be a matter of negotiation, with the most common outcome being a provision requiring that, for a matter to qualify the warranties, it must be 'fairly disclosed'.

In many cases, a buyer will go on to seek to define what constitutes fair disclosure (or whatever other adjective or adverb is included to set the hurdle). This has the advantage to the buyer (and, it might be argued, also to the sellers) of clarifying precisely how extensive a disclosure must be to qualify the warranties. When advising sellers, it is important to check that an expansive definition does not push the boundaries of what might be considered 'fair disclosure' towards a more stringent 'full disclosure' concept. A favoured (and balanced) definition typically refers to disclosure being sufficient to enable the buyer to make a reasonably informed assessment of the matter concerned, and its likely impact on Target and its business.

17 [2005] EWCA Civ 758.

3.2 The acquisition disclosure letter

Generally, disclosure letters come in three parts. The first section sets out some general principles, recitals and interpretation provisions concerning the disclosure letter; the second sets out general disclosures intended to qualify all of the warranties; and the third sets out disclosures of specific issues, cross-referencing the specific disclosure against the particular warranty to which it is relevant.

(a) General principles/interpretation

The introductory part of the letter will identify the document and its attachments as the disclosure letter, and may set out some context as to how it should be construed (for example, by borrowing defined terms from the acquisition agreement). There is a tendency for advisers to the seller(s) to seek to explain its purpose in some detail: for example, to include wording such as: 'This letter sets out the disclosures for the purposes of the acquisition agreement and no claim may be made against the seller(s) for any matter disclosed in it.' Such expansive attempts to define the legal effect of the disclosure letter should generally be resisted – its purpose should be set out in the agreement not in the letter, and such additional wording can undermine the carefully considered definition of the adverbial hurdle, such as fair disclosure, in the agreement itself. Less objectionable to the buyer are provisions such as 'Nothing in this letter shall be taken as extending the meaning of any warranty or as an acknowledgment that the disclosure needs to be made to qualify the warranty', which simply clarifies that the disclosure letter should not, in itself, increase the liability of the seller(s).

(b) General disclosures

General disclosures represent an attempt by the seller(s) to disclose to the buyer information which is available outside the text of the specific disclosures in the disclosure letter itself. Typical examples include:

- the contents of the statutory books of Target;
- information appearing in respect of Target at Companies House;
- contents of an agreed bundle of documents, documents from any data room, or any other written diligence information handed over (for example, any information memorandum or other 'selling' document produced by the seller(s) as part of the sale process);
- the contents of Target's accounts;
- matters that could be obtained from any public search or registry in respect of Target, its properties or intellectual property;
- anything set out in the buyer's due diligence reports;
- anything said or communicated between the parties' advisers in respect of the transaction; and
- anything in the public domain.

As a general guide, the above list sets out an order of likely palatability – that is to say that the lower a matter is in the list, the less likely it is that the buyer will accept the general disclosure. However, there are some exceptions to this. For example, some buyers take a particularly robust stance in resisting the disclosure of any data room contents or a large bundle of disclosed documents, irrespective of how tightly the concept of 'fair disclosure' (or similar wording) has been defined.

There is some area of overlap between certain limitations and certain general disclosures – for example, should the buyer be precluded by a limitation from claiming to the extent that any matter is set out in Target's accounts, or should the contents of Target's accounts be generally disclosed. It is in part a matter of taste, but, generally speaking, the seller(s) should usually prefer a limitation to a general disclosure, as in the former case it is possible that the adverbial hurdle set for a disclosure to qualify the warranties can be avoided or mitigated. In any event, it is important to ensure consistency – for example, a buyer who insists that a limitation which seeks to prevent claims in respect of any matters revealed by the buyer's due diligence investigations cannot be accepted should not then allow the content of any due diligence reports to reappear as a general disclosure.

The essence of a general disclosure is that it does not in particular seek to pull out from that information source exactly what is relevant to the Target, or explain how the disclosure is relevant in the context of any particular warranty. The effect of a general disclosure is that a claim cannot be brought for a matter which is within that particular source of information. As a general disclosure can have the effect of limiting warranty claims without necessarily identifying any particular problem (which the buyer can then take into account in price negotiation or other contractual protections), buyers will often resist extensive general disclosures. However, custom and practice has allowed certain general disclosures to be made in UK deals at least. Some general disclosures are generally accepted to be beyond the pale – for example, seeking generally to disclose everything in the public domain, or anything available in any register in any part of the world. Such broad disclosures are not really telling the buyer anything about the Target or the business but are instead seeking to create 'after the event' defences for the seller in the event of a warranty claim.

(c) Specific disclosures

The majority of the disclosure letter will take the form of specific disclosures, which are far more useful (from the buyer's point of view at least) in the context of the role of the warranties in eliciting disclosure. Specific disclosures are usually made by reference to each numbered paragraph in the warranty schedule, and set out the details of any facts, matters or circumstances which constitute (or may constitute) a breach of that warranty. The disclosure is supported by reference to attached copies of any relevant documents. For example, against a warranty that there are no claims under Target's insurances policies, the seller(s) should disclose details of any actual claims including their current status, whether the insurers are accepting the liability, and the size and nature of the claim – and may then make reference to any relevant policy wording or correspondence with the insurers, which would be attached to the letter or included in a separate bundle.

Precisely what is said, and in how much detail, depends in part on the wording of the precise warranty, and in part on the adverbial hurdle which must be overcome for the disclosure to be valid. It is for this reason that the precise wording of key warranties, and the definition of 'fair disclosure' (or whatever other concept is agreed), are so keenly negotiated. The buyer will want to elicit as much information as possible from the disclosure exercise, in order to understand the relevance of any disclosed matters to the business, and the likely quantum of any liability. Seller(s) will be more cautious, in that they will want to ensure that the disclosure will satisfy the relevant adverbial hurdle, but will not want to alarm the buyer unduly, or to make any statement that could be viewed to be misleading or which may prove to be inaccurate.

One issue that can arise in the context of disclosure is the question of whether the specific disclosures should qualify more than just the specific warranty by reference to which they are made. The seller(s) will be anxious not to have to repeat the same disclosure against multiple warranties where it may be relevant, for fear of missing one and allow a claim to be made for a matter already disclosed against another warranty. The buyer will not want all the specific disclosures simply to become, in effect, general disclosures, and may be concerned that the relevance of a disclosure made against one warranty may not be as clear or obvious in the context of another. A compromise wording is usually found to the effect that a specific disclosure made against a specified warranty also qualifies any other warranty in respect of which it constitutes a fair (or whatever other hurdle is used) disclosure.

4 Competition matters

4.1 Introduction

As with any acquisition of a business, the main competition issue to be considered in a private equity transaction is whether merger control legislation applies. Such legislation typically provides for:

(a) a procedure for the notification of a merger to a competition authority and the suspension of completion until approval has been given; the notification and suspension obligation is voluntary in the UK, but is often mandatory in other countries;

(b) the investigation of the merger by a competition authority which will seek to establish whether it may have a harmful effect on competition in any market;

(c) a short 'phase 1' period for approval in straightforward cases (typically, between four and eight weeks) and a longer 'phase 2' period for cases which raise substantive issues (typically, around six months);
(d) the prohibition of anti-competitive mergers;
(e) penalties for failing to notify and 'gun-jumping' before approval is granted (again, where notification and suspension is mandatory).

Not all mergers are subject to such control. Merger control legislation will have a series of jurisdictional tests and so typically will apply only where:

- one party acquires control or influence over another party (the 'control test'); and
- the relevant jurisdictional or size tests are met (the 'threshold tests').

There are now over seventy countries worldwide with merger control legislation each with their own set of control and threshold tests, often based on the turnover or market share of the parties. In the vast majority of these countries, where the jurisdictional test is met notification is mandatory, although, again, the vast majority of notified mergers are cleared as they do not raise a substantive competition or market issue.[18]

4.2 Typical issues for private equity transactions

Private equity transactions will often not raise any substantive competition concerns but, because of the way in which the control and threshold tests operate in practice, many transactions may be caught. Some of the issues that arise are the following:

(a) 'Control' is not a Companies Act concept, and can arise even on the acquisition of a minority interest where the acquirer will have a sufficient level of *influence* (see further below).
(b) The turnover of the acquirer for the purposes of the threshold tests is the turnover not just of the acquiring private equity vehicle but also that of the group to which it belongs and that of all portfolio companies controlled by the group. This will often greatly increase not just the level of the turnover but also its geographic spread.
(c) In assessing whether there are any substantive issues, it is necessary to take account of the activities of all portfolio companies.

In most jurisdictions, as referred to in section 2.5 above, contracts can be exchanged conditionally on clearance being granted but the delays and complexities caused will still be of concern to the parties. For that reason, sellers will often require competing buyers to confirm the likelihood of any such

18 In some countries (for example, within Europe, Germany, Ireland and Norway), the threshold tests are very low triggering a need for mandatory local competition clearance where the Target and the private equity investor (or more likely its other investee companies) have relatively low sales.

clearance being necessary at an early stage in the process. Accordingly, the competition review, including the identification of all relevant turnover of portfolio companies, the geographic location of sales and whether there are any overlaps between portfolio companies and the Target, must be conducted early.

4.3 Which rules apply?

In the European Economic Area (EEA), large transactions require prior notification to, and clearance by, the European Commission. In this case, the merger control rules of the individual EEA Member States do not apply (i.e. the transaction requires only one competition clearance in the EEA, as opposed to multiple national clearances in different EEA Member States: see section 4.6 below).

In the event that the transaction does not trigger the EU rules on merger control, parties to a proposed merger must look to see whether any relevant national merger control rules apply. The next section describes the main substantive and procedural elements of the system for reviewing and investigating mergers in the UK.

4.4 UK merger control legislation

The UK merger control rules are contained in Part 3 of the Enterprise Act 2002 (EA02). EA02 applies to transactions that lead to a 'relevant merger situation'. A relevant merger situation arises where:

(a) two or more enterprises (companies or businesses, or parts of businesses) *cease to be distinct*; and
(b) either a turnover or market share threshold test is met.[19]

(a) Ceasing to be distinct (control)

Broadly, two or more enterprises cease to be distinct when they are brought under common ownership or control. Enterprises are brought under common ownership or control through the acquisition in another enterprise of:

(a) a controlling interest (legal control, e.g. more than 50 per cent of the voting rights); or
(b) the ability to control its policy (*de facto* control); or
(c) the ability materially to influence its policy (e.g. acquiring 25 per cent or more of the voting rights enabling that shareholder to block special resolutions, or a lesser holding which gives the acquirer influence).[20]

19 Section 23 of the Enterprise Act 2002.
20 Section 26 of the Enterprise Act 2002.

Control can, therefore, be acquired where a private equity buyer acquires a minority stake in a business. The Office of Fair Trading (OFT) will consider stakes as low as 15 per cent as potentially conferring material influence particularly when combined with board representation and, invariably, when combined with veto rights over strategic commercial decisions (e.g. approval of budgets or business plans).[21]

(b) Threshold tests

For EA02 to apply, the transaction must also meet at least one of these two alternative size thresholds, namely, either:

(a) where the value of the turnover in the UK of the enterprise being acquired exceeds £70 million; or
(b) where, as a result of the merger, at least 25 per cent of any goods (or services) supplied (or acquired) in the UK (or a substantial part of the UK) are supplied (or acquired) by one and the same person.

For the 25 per cent share of supply test to be met, both parties must supply (or acquire) the relevant goods (or services) before the merger. For a private equity investor, this means evaluating whether any of the portfolio companies over which it or its group has material influence is active in the same market as Target.[22]

4.5 Notification: voluntary system

The UK merger rules operate a voluntary scheme of notification; there is no obligation in UK law to notify a relevant merger situation to the OFT for prior competition clearance. In practice, in private equity transactions, unless the acquirer's group has an interest in an existing portfolio company which is active in the same market as Target (or upstream or downstream), notifications are rare.

There are two principal ways to ask the OFT to reach a decision on a relevant merger situation:

(a) statutory voluntary pre-notification (by way of a so-called 'Merger Notice'); or
(b) informal submission.

When an anticipated (i.e. uncompleted) merger is in the public domain, a party to the merger may submit a statutory pre-notification of the merger

21 See generally OFT, *Mergers: Jurisdiction and Procedural Guidance* (June 2009), chapter 3.
22 See, for example, Case ME/1591–05, *Completed acquisition by the Blackstone Group of UGC Cinema Holdings Ltd*, OFT decision dated 28 April 2005, illustrated in Figure 4.1.

Blackstone Group's acquisition of UGC cinemas

The Blackstone Group acquired the Cineworld cinema chain in October 2004. The Cineworld acquisition did not raise any competition issues. Two months later in December 2004, it acquired the UGC cinema chain. The OFT investigated the acquisition post completion. The OFT took the following steps:

- it accepted hold separate undertakings from Blackstone LR Associates (Cayman) IV Ltd and Cineworld UK Limited to ensure that Cineworld and UGC were not integrated and that UGC was maintained as a going concern while the OFT could conduct an investigation;
- it conducted a phase I investigation of the merger and concluded that the merger may be expected to result in a substantial lessening of competition in 6 locations (where there were both UGC and Cineworld cinemas);
- it accepted undertakings in lieu of a reference from Blackstone LR Associates (Cayman) IV Ltd and Cineworld UK Limited to divest one cinema in each of the identified locations to a purchaser approved by the OFT.

Figure 4.1 An example of a non-notified investment: Blackstone Group's acquisition of UGC cinemas

to the OFT using a Merger Notice. On submission of a Merger Notice, the OFT is subject to strict time limits for reaching a decision. The OFT must decide, within twenty working days of receipt of a completed notification, whether to refer it to the Competition Commission (CC) (see below). The OFT may extend the period for decision-making by a maximum of ten working days.[23]

The parties may prefer to ask the OFT to review the transaction by way of informal submission. The advantage of this route is to give time to resolve any competition concerns, for example by giving undertakings in lieu of a reference. The OFT's administrative guidelines set forty working days as the normal time limit for reaching a decision where parties notify the OFT by way of informal submission.[24] The informal submission can be used for both anticipated and completed mergers. See Figure 4.1.

If the parties do not notify a relevant merger situation, the OFT has the power to investigate (before or after completion) whether the transaction raises competition concerns and, if it does, to refer it to the CC for an

23 Sections 96–102 of the Enterprise Act 2002; and Enterprise Act 2002 (Mergers Prenotification) Regulations 2003 (SI 2003/1369).

24 See OFT, *Mergers: Jurisdiction and Procedural Guidance* (June 2009), chapter 4, paragraphs 4.63–4.70.

in-depth investigation. The OFT must do this within four months of completion or of the transaction becoming public knowledge.[25] Where there are market overlaps, the OFT (and CC) has the power under EA02 to require the acquirer to 'hold separate' the acquired business until approval has been given.[26]

The OFT is under an obligation to refer a relevant merger situation to the CC for an in-depth investigation where it believes that the transaction may result (anticipated mergers) or has resulted (completed mergers) in a 'substantial lessening of competition' in any market in the UK for goods or services (the 'SLC test').[27] The OFT does not have to make a reference to the CC where the market is of insufficient importance (or *de minimis*) or where there are relevant customer benefits which outweigh the SLC.[28] There are provisions which allow the OFT to accept an undertaking in lieu of a reference where the parties offer commitments to remedy the SLC identified by the OFT.[29]

The CC must report on its determination within twenty-four weeks of the reference. This period may be extended by eight weeks.[30] The CC also applies the SLC test in coming to its conclusion. The CC may clear the transaction or may take remedial action to resolve any competition concerns, including clearing the transaction only subject to conditions, prohibiting it and/or ordering divestiture.[31]

The Competition Appeal Tribunal (CAT) hears appeals in respect of any merger decisions taken by the OFT or the CC (and exceptionally the Secretary of State).[32] The CAT is able to review the detail of the OFT's (and the CC's) investigation and supporting material in order to ascertain whether the OFT/CC's decisions are reasonable and demonstrate sufficient grounds for the conclusions reached.

4.6 EC merger control legislation

The EC merger control rules are set out in Council Regulation (EC) No. 139/2004 of 20 January 2004 on the control of concentrations between undertakings

25 Section 24 of the Enterprise Act 2002.
26 Sections 71 and 72 of the Enterprise Act 2002.
27 Sections 22 and 33 of the Enterprise Act 2002; and, as to the nature of the duty, see the Court of Appeal's judgment in *OFT* v. *IBA Health* [2004] EWCA Civ 142.
28 Sections 22(2) and 33(2) of the Enterprise Act 2002. For *de minimis* mergers, see OFT, *Exception to the Duty to Refer: Markets of Insufficient Importance* (OFT516b, November 2007); and, for 'relevant customer benefits', see section 23 of the Enterprise Act 2002.
29 Section 73 of the Enterprise Act 2002.
30 Section 51 of the Enterprise Act 2002.
31 Section 82 of, and Schedule 8 to, the Enterprise Act 2002; and Competition Commission, *Merger Remedies: Competition Commission Guidelines* (November 2008).
32 Section 120 of the Enterprise Act 2002.

(also known as the ECMR or the Merger Regulation).[33] It is enforced by the Directorate-General for Competition of the European Commission in Brussels (DG COMP). It applies to all countries comprising the European Economic Area (EEA), that is, the twenty-seven EU Member States, together with Iceland, Liechtenstein and Norway.

The ECMR is based on the principle of the 'one-stop shop'; once a transaction falls within the jurisdiction of the ECMR, the national authorities of the Member States are precluded from applying their own merger control laws to the transaction in question (except in certain limited circumstances).

A transaction will fall within the ECMR if it amounts to a 'concentration with a Community dimension'.[34]

(a) What is a concentration?

Broadly, a concentration occurs where the transaction brings about a lasting change in control in the companies concerned, whether by the acquisition of sole control, the acquisition of joint control or a change from joint control to sole control. It covers a merger of two or more previously independent companies (where two previously independent companies cease to exist as such), the acquisition of direct or indirect control of another company, and certain types of joint venture.[35]

The following should be noted and are often relevant in private equity transactions:

(a) 'Control' means having the possibility of exercising *decisive influence* over a company or undertaking on a lasting basis. This includes the acquisition of a majority of the equity of an undertaking or the acquisition of a minority shareholding to which special voting rights are attached which allow the minority shareholder to determine the strategic behaviour of Target. The right to block decisions on management appointments, budget or business plan would also typically confer (negative) control.

(b) A concentration may also arise where two or more companies have the possibility of exercising decisive influence jointly over another company. Joint control generally arises where two (or more) shareholders are able to veto strategic proposals (for example, through equal voting rights or special decision-making rights attaching to a minority shareholding), ensuring that there is joint agreement on a company's commercial policy.

33 OJ L24, 29.1.2004, p. 1.

34 Article 1(1) ECMR.

35 Article 3 ECMR; and, generally, the Commission Consolidated Jurisdictional Notice under Council Regulation (EC) No. 139/2004 on the control of concentrations between undertakings ('Commission Jurisdictional Notice'), Part B.

The EU merger control rules apply to concentrations where:

EITHER (1)

- the combined worldwide turnover of all parties exceeds €5 billion, *and*
- the turnover in the EU/EEA of each of at least 2 of the parties exceeds €250 million,

unless

- two-thirds of the EU/EEA turnover of each of the parties is in one and the same Member State

OR (2)

- the combined worldwide turnover of all parties exceeds €2.5 billion, *and*
- the turnover in the EU/EEA of each of at least two of the parties exceeds €100 million, *and*
- in each of at least three Member States, the combined turnover of all parties exceeds €100 million, *and*
- in those three Member States, the turnover of each of at least two parties exceeds €25 million,

unless

- two-thirds of the EU/EEA turnover of each of the parties is in one and the same Member State.

Figure 4.2 EU merger control thresholds

(c) A concentration can arise not only where control of legal entities is acquired through share purchases, but also where the assets comprising a business or some of the assets of a legal entity are acquired (for example, brands or licences), provided that market turnover can be attributed to such assets.

(b) A Community dimension: the turnover threshold

Whether there is a Community dimension depends on the respective turnovers of the parties concerned. In applying the turnover tests, it is irrelevant whether or not the parties are domiciled in the EEA or the transaction will be implemented in the EEA. The turnover thresholds are set out in Figure 4.2.[36]

36 Articles 1(2) and 1(3) ECMR.

4.7 Relevant turnover

So far as Target is concerned, the relevant turnover is generally that attributable to what is being acquired.[37] Calculating the turnover of the acquirer can, however, be a complex matter in the context of a private equity investment. Generally, the first question is who is acquiring control over Target?

This will often be a question of a case-by-case analysis. It is straightforward when the acquirer is a trade buyer in the form of a limited company. However, it can be more difficult with private equity structures. For example, for private equity funds set up in the form of limited partnerships, investors participating as limited partners normally do not exercise control (either individually or collectively); while the fund might acquire the shares and voting rights which give it control over Target, it is generally the investment company which has set up the fund that exercises that control. That control is exercised either because the investment company is the general partner, or through a management contract (or a combination of the two). In such circumstances, the investment company will be regarded as having acquired control over Target.[38]

The second question is what is the relevant turnover of the acquirer? Under the ECMR, it is usual to take the turnover of the acquiring entity and all of the group to which that entity belongs (a 'group' is defined in the ECMR[39]). In the context of a private equity acquirer that again can be complicated. For example:

(a) if the acquirer is an investment company then its turnover is likely to include:
   (i) its own turnover (generally, fee income); and
   (ii) the turnover (i.e. sales) of all portfolio companies controlled by the funds set up and managed by the investment company.[40]

(b) if the acquirer is the *captive* arm of a larger financial institution (e.g. a bank) then its turnover may well include:
   (i) its own turnover (generally, fee income);
   (ii) the turnover of the wider banking group;[41] and
   (iii) the turnover (i.e. sales) of all portfolio companies controlled by the captive investor.

The issue can be further complicated where the transaction is a co-investment by two or more private equity investors. Where the investors have the ability to exercise joint control (for example, where the co-investors each have a veto right over the Business Plan and budgets: see above), each jointly controlling

37 Article 5(2) ECMR.

38 See Commission Jurisdictional Notice, paragraph 15.

39 Article 5(4) ECMR.

40 See Commission Jurisdictional Notice, paragraphs 189–191.

41 There are special rules for the calculation of the turnover for credit and other financial institutions: see Article 5(3) ECMR.

investor will be regarded as an acquirer[42] and the relevant turnover will be that of each acquirer and its group (plus that of Target). This increases the risk that the relevant ECMR turnover thresholds will be met.

4.8 Notification: mandatory system

Where a transaction amounts to a concentration with a Community dimension, it must be notified to the European Commission for investigation by completing the required Form CO.[43] The ECMR sets out when a concentration must or may be notified. The parties *may* notify if they can show a 'good faith intention' to conclude an agreement to merge or if they have made a public announcement of their intention to merge. Notification *must* be made once the parties have reached agreement, a public bid has been announced or a controlling interest acquired, and, in any event, prior to implementation.[44] Implementation of the transaction is automatically suspended until the Commission has completed its review.[45]

Once the transaction has been notified, the Commission must adhere to strict time periods to decide whether or not the deal raises competition concerns. However, these time periods commence only once there is *effective notification*, that is, when the Commission has received complete, accurate and up-to-date information in the Form CO.[46] The submission of incomplete, inaccurate or misleading information can delay merger clearance and therefore completion of the transaction. The (management) time and resources required to complete the Form CO should therefore not be underestimated.

A simplified procedure exists for the handling of routine transactions which do not raise significant competition concerns.[47] Although such transactions must be notified in advance to the Commission, the parties are able to complete a short-form Form CO. This procedure will often be appropriate for private equity investments (provided there is no overlap between existing portfolio companies and Target).

There are penalties (fines up to 10 per cent of turnover) for failing to notify a transaction or implementing a transaction in breach of the suspension provisions, and penalties (fines up to 1 per cent of turnover) for providing incomplete or misleading information.[48] The Commission also has wide-ranging powers

42 See Commission Jurisdictional Notice, paragraphs 139–141.

43 Form CO is in Annex I to the Commission Regulation of 21 April 2004 implementing Council Regulation (EC) No. 139/2004 on the control of concentrations between undertakings (OJ L133, 30.4.2004, p. 1).

44 Article 4(1) ECMR.

45 Article 7 ECMR.

46 Article 10(1) ECMR.

47 Commission Notice on a simplified procedure for treatment of certain concentrations under Council Regulation (EC) No. 139/2004 (OJ C56, 5.3.2005, p. 32).

48 Articles 14 and 15 ECMR. For example, in June 2009, the Commission fined Electrabel €20 million for acquiring control of a competing electricity producer, CNR, without notifying the

of investigation, including powers to request information, conduct interviews and carry out on-the-spot investigations by entering and sealing premises, taking documents and seeking explanations. The Commission may exercise these 'dawn raid' powers at any time prior to notification as well as during its investigation.[49]

(a) Phase 1 investigation

On receipt of a complete Form CO, the Commission carries out an initial, Phase 1, investigation. Within twenty-five working days[50] from receipt of the complete Form CO, the Commission must either:

(a) clear the transaction (either outright or subject to conditions); or
(b) launch an in-depth Phase 2 investigation (*initiate proceedings*).

(b) Phase 2 investigation

The Commission will enter a Phase 2 investigation if it has serious doubts about the compatibility of the transaction with the common market. The Commission must reach a final decision within ninety working days following the initiation of proceedings. This period may be extended by no more than a total of twenty working days.[51]

(c) Substantive test

Under Article 2(3) of the ECMR, the EU Commission must prohibit concentrations with a Community dimension that would 'significantly impede effective competition' in the EU (the 'SIEC test'). The Commission has the power to accept undertakings (*commitments*) from the parties to remedy any competition concerns in order to prevent a prohibition by the Commission. Such undertakings can be given in either Phase 1 or Phase 2.[52]

4.9 Appeals and jurisdiction

Decisions of the Commission may be the subject of appeal to the Court of First Instance (CFI) by way of application for annulment under Article 230 of the EC Treaty. Such an application may be brought by the addressee of the decision or by any other person for whom the decision is of direct and individual concern. From the CFI, points of law may be appealed to the European Court of Justice.

acquisition and waiting for Commission approval. Electrabel has acquired just under 50 per cent of CNR which the Commission concluded gave it decisive influence over CNR given the wide dispersion of the remaining shareholders. Following notification, the Commission cleared the acquisition as it did not raise any competition concerns.

49 Articles 11–13 ECMR.
50 Article 10(1) ECMR.
51 Article 10(3) ECMR.
52 Articles 6(2) and 8(3) ECMR.

Although as a general rule concentrations with a Community dimension fall within the exclusive jurisdiction of the Commission and those without a Community dimension fall to be considered under relevant Member State national laws, the ECMR contains a number of exceptions where jurisdiction can be transferred back to a Member State or from Member States to the Commission for decision. Where these exceptions apply and are used, there can be an adverse impact on the timetable for review as they can involve, in addition to the actual notification, written submissions either by the parties and/or by Member States as part of the process of determining which competition authority will review the transaction. However, in appropriate cases, they can reduce the number of filings needed to be made on a transaction.[53]

A Member State may carry out a parallel investigation into a transaction falling within the ECMR if its *legitimate interests* are affected (for example, national security, the plurality of the media or prudential rules).[54]

5 Tax

5.1 Background

In a UK share sale transaction, it is almost invariably the case that a seller will be required to agree to pay to the buyer an amount equal to certain tax liabilities of Target. This is variously referred to as a 'tax indemnity', 'tax deed', 'tax covenant' or 'tax schedule', and such promise will be set out either in a schedule to the acquisition agreement or in a deed entered into pursuant to the agreement. Although the form of each such deed varies slightly, the basic obligation is the same: the seller promises to pay the buyer, on a pound-for-pound basis, an amount equal to any unexpected tax liabilities of Target. For ease of reference in this section, we refer to each such promise as a 'tax covenant'.

Initially, tax covenants were used to cover secondary liabilities; broadly speaking, tax liabilities of persons (other than the Target) which the Target became obliged to pay if the primary obligor failed to meet such liability. Such liabilities can typically arise where a company is a member of a group of companies and one of the other members fails to pay tax for which it is primarily liable. Such liabilities can also arise in certain circumstances where a shareholder of a company fails to meet its own tax liabilities. In such cases, it was considered that warranties, no matter how widely drafted, might not catch all such liabilities, and that in any event an indemnity basis of recovery was more appropriate for any such taxation liabilities. Over time, the scope of a tax covenant has therefore expanded away from this original purpose, and has became a more general underwriting of the tax affairs of the Target.

53 See Articles 4(4), 4(5), 9 and 22 ECMR; and Commission Notice on case referral in respect of concentrations (OJ C56, 5.3.2005, p. 2).

54 Article 21(4) ECMR.

5.2 Matters covered by tax covenant

Generally, the tax covenant will apply to all tax liabilities of Target arising as a result of an event occurring on or before completion of the share sale and, in very limited circumstances, to some liabilities arising as a result of a combination of events where some have occurred before completion, and some after completion. The tax covenant is given by reference to a set of accounts, with the seller not being liable to make a payment to the buyer in respect of any tax liability of Target to the extent provided for in such accounts. If the relevant accounts are not made up to completion (e.g. if the tax covenant is given by reference to the last set of audited accounts), then it would also be usual for the seller not to be liable to make any payment under the tax covenant in respect of any tax which arises in the ordinary course of business of Target between the date to which the accounts were made up and completion.

The tax covenant is given by the seller to the buyer rather than to Target. This arises as a result of case law during the 1980s (and in particular the case of *Zim Properties Ltd* v. *Proctor*)[55] which led to a concern that if Target receives a direct payment from the sellers this could be taxed as a capital gain within Target. This would have the consequence that the net amount received by Target (after paying tax on the receipt from the seller) would be insufficient to settle the liability for which it was paid. Buyers therefore usually required that the payment by the seller should be grossed up, that is to say, increased so that the net amount received and retained by Target (after taking account of any tax which Target suffered on the receipt) is equal to the amount required to meet the particular liability in question. Clearly, this was unattractive to sellers who risked having to pay more than the actual tax liability in Target in respect of which they had agreed to indemnify.

In 1988, HMRC published an extra-statutory concession (ESC D33) confirming that a payment between a seller and a buyer (but not a payment between a seller and Target) under a tax covenant will generally be treated for tax purposes as an adjustment to the purchase price rather than as a taxable receipt of the buyer. In view of this, it is now invariably the case that tax covenants are given by the seller to the buyer rather than to Target. On this basis, whilst a seller is still generally obliged to give a gross-up clause in favour of a buyer, it will be comparatively rare for circumstances to arise where the gross-up clause is called upon.

5.3 Limitations in the tax covenant

In relation to limitations:

(a) Usually, claims under the tax covenant will be subject to the overall cap on claims, i.e. that the seller is not liable to the buyer in respect of claims

55 [1985] BTC 42.

under the sale and purchase agreement to the extent that the aggregate liability under all claims exceeds the purchase price (or some lesser figure as may be agreed between the parties).

(b) There is no hard and fast rule as to whether threshold and *de minimis* financial limitations should apply to tax covenant claims. Some buyers take a purist view that a tax covenant is a pound-for-pound recovery mechanism and therefore that such limitations should not apply. However, there is no standard market position on this point.

(c) As noted in section 2.9 above, the usual time period for making tax covenant claims is seven years from completion, which is far longer than for commercial warranty claims. This period stemmed originally from the fact that HMRC generally had up to six years from the end of an accounting period to raise additional assessments to corporation tax or to enquire into tax returns. The statutory periods for raising enquiries have varied over the years and are due to change again on 1 April 2010. However, a seven-year window for tax covenant claims is very much the market standard position.

(d) There will be a raft of specific tax limitations designed to apportion risk (e.g. which party bears the change-of-law risk) and, from a seller's perspective, seek to limit liability for tax liabilities to the extent they are attributable to actions or omissions of the buyer or Target post-completion (e.g. failures to make appropriate tax claims and elections).

(e) It is extremely rare for disclosures in the disclosure letter (or for knowledge of the buyer prior to completion of potential tax covenant claims) to limit or prevent a buyer from making a claim under the tax covenant. Thus, if the seller wants to exclude liability under the tax covenant for known issues, it is necessary to incorporate a specific exclusion into the tax covenant.

Given the nature of the tax covenant, i.e. that it is based upon a pound-for-pound recovery rather than having to establish loss, a seller will wish to include provisions designed to ensure that a buyer is merely put in the position in which it would have been had the relevant accounts properly provided for tax. Thus, typically, there will be credit mechanisms for dealing with situations where the buyer or Target recovers any amount in respect of the tax liability from a third party, where the tax liability itself results in Target saving some other tax, and/or where the relevant accounts overprovide for certain taxes. In addition, there will also be provisions governing which party has responsibility for submitting and dealing with pre-completion tax returns and for conducting any dispute with HMRC.

5.4 Tax covenant on a private equity acquisition

In principle, there are no particular differences between the tax covenant in a buyout and the tax covenant in any other sale and purchase. Even if the seller runs the argument that the managers' role and knowledge mean that the seller should warrant less to a buyout vehicle than to a trade buyer, this argument is rarely successful in the context of the tax covenant – not least because the tax affairs of the Target (especially in a group where it was a subsidiary) are often undertaken at a level above the day-to-day running of the Target by the managers. It would be extremely rare for the disclosure letter or the knowledge of the buyer to qualify the seller's exposure under the tax covenant. Tax enjoys a special status in the negotiation of risk allocation.

6 Conclusion

In this chapter, we have considered the key aspects of the acquisition of a private company in the UK, and have focused, in particular, on the aspects which are of direct relevance where the buyer is backed by private equity. A key issue is the precise nature of the warranties to be given and the effect which the knowledge of the managers may have, first, to reduce the matters the sellers will warrant, and, secondly, to reduce the effectiveness of those warranties by providing a defence to the sellers for anything known by the managers when their knowledge is attributed to the buyer. We have also looked at some of the issues that can cause conditionality and delay to the transaction (in particular, competition law) and the consequences of this for the transaction, not least in the context of any material change in the business of Target between the signature of the agreement and completion.

Market practice in these areas has been affected in part by the bargaining power of the parties. Broadly speaking, as buyer vehicles in a buyout have become predominantly controlled by the investors (that is to say that the investors increasingly have a majority of the equity in the Newco), the practice in these areas for private-equity-backed buyers is aligning more closely to the practice of a trade buyer. Accordingly, private-equity-backed buyer vehicles are receiving broadly equivalent protection in terms of warranties and other cover as a trade buyer would receive notwithstanding the inside role of the managers in the transaction, which may otherwise be seen to differentiate the two potential buyers. Such trend is only likely to continue in the more buyer-friendly market in the UK following the credit crunch.

5 Equity documentation

1 Introduction

In this chapter, we will consider the principal equity documents that form part of a relatively standard buyout structure. Broadly similar documents would be used in other private equity transactions (for example, in a secondary or on a public-to-private transaction, tailored to reflect the particular differences inherent in such a deal). For this reason, the general overview set out in this chapter should also be considered in the context of those transactions.

This chapter will focus on the two key equity documents, namely the investment agreement and the articles of association of Newco. It will explain the reasons why there are two documents, and the key terms found in them in the context of the relationships between the different parties and the overall investment. It also includes comments on three key ancillary documents, being the equity offer letter or termsheet, the investment disclosure letter and the loan note instrument. The service agreements that govern the relationship between Newco and the managers in their capacity as employees are considered in chapter 7.

2 Equity offer letter

The equity offer letter (sometimes referred to as the equity termsheet) sets out, in a non-binding form, the key terms of the equity funding offer. It is usually written by the private equity investors to the managers and/or to Newco, and in effect provides a template for the drafting of the principal equity documents (in the same way that the heads of terms agreed with the seller(s) will provide a template for the acquisition agreement).

The offer letter will set out the amounts to be invested both by the private equity investors and by the managers, and also the form of those investments (by identifying the different classes of shares and loan notes that will be established in the Newco structure). It will also set out details of the fees and expenses payable to the investors for its investment and its ongoing monitoring. The offer letter will often then address other key commercial terms to be included within the equity documents as explained in more detail in this chapter, such as the yield on the loan notes, any liquidation or dividend preference on the investor shares, any ratchet, and drag and tag along rights. If the investors or the managers wish to see such matters resolved upfront, it may also go on to address other issues which often prove to be particularly sensitive in negotiation, such as the approach to cessation of employment and equity (i.e. good and bad leaver provisions and any vesting arrangement, as explained below), the nature of the investment warranties to be given by the managers and any key limitations that will apply, and the notice period and remuneration to be offered under each manager's service agreement.

Traditionally, the equity offer letter tended to be a short document, often providing the key financial details only without going into the more detailed legal areas of negotiation. However, the more recent trend is for more of the key equity terms to be agreed in advance by way of a detailed offer letter or termsheet. There are two main drivers for this. First, many investors are keen to see such matters resolved early (and perhaps outside the more adversarial context of the legal negotiation of detailed documents) as this can help ensure that the relationship between management and the investors is not soured, and that the equity documentation is completed more efficiently. Secondly, a more competitive market for deals has led to management teams wanting to explore deal terms in more detail before a preferred bidder is selected – even where the management team are not sellers themselves and so do not decide who the preferred buyer is, their views will in any event be very influential as it will have a significant impact on the deliverability of the transaction. In the buoyant market during the period leading up to the summer of 2007, it was not uncommon for the managers or their advisers to issue their own *pro forma* termsheet with some of the sections pre-completed, and others left blank, so that the key terms could be flushed out and the various bidders played off each other before exclusivity was granted.

Although equity offer letters are usually expressly stated to be non-binding and based on key assumptions (such as satisfactory due diligence, legal documentation being agreed, and so on), they will sometimes include a legally binding exclusivity clause (separate to the exclusivity arrangement agreed with the sellers) seeking to tie the management team to the relevant private equity house for a period of time. As explained in section 3.3 of chapter 2, such an agreement cannot impose a positive duty on the parties to negotiate but, in principle, it can bar them for a time from seeking funding elsewhere. How useful such a provision will be is debatable in the event of a breach. The measure of loss suffered could be construed to be the private equity investors' abortive costs, but there will always be some doubt if a deal to buy the business could have been concluded in any event on acceptable terms, even if the management team had honoured the exclusivity arrangement. The question also arises of whether the management team are of sufficient financial means to provide an effective remedy in the event of a breach. Nevertheless, tying management as well as sellers into an exclusivity arrangement should be considered, as this will usually have a deterrent effect. If the managers or their advisers have been playing one potential funder against another, it may be more reasonable for the successful party to seek formal exclusivity with some level of binding costs cover.

3 The investment agreement

3.1 Background and parties

The investment agreement (occasionally in the more traditional style referred to as the 'subscription and shareholders' agreement' or similar) is the principal contractual document regulating the terms and conditions upon which the private equity investors will invest in the ultimate parent Newco in which the investors and managers will hold shares (and, where relevant, any other subsidiary companies in the group structure[1]), and sets out other relevant matters for the ongoing operation of the group as an investee company in the portfolio of the private equity investors.

As a general rule, Newco itself and everybody who will become a shareholder of Newco as part of the initial completion process will be a party to the investment agreement, together with any subsidiary of Newco which is receiving a direct investment for loan notes. As explained in chapter 3,[2] in certain cases private equity investors will expect their shares (and sometimes loan notes) to be issued to and held in the name of a custodian or nominee. However, it will be usual for the fund itself to be a party to the agreement, rather than that custodian or nominee (although the custodian or nominee will usually be mentioned in the relevant operative provision).

Where there will be many employee shareholders with relatively small equity stakes, it would be unusual for such shareholders to have to sign up to the investment agreement. In these situations, it is particularly key that any provisions which are needed to bind these minority shareholders are reflected in the articles, as the articles bind all shareholders automatically by virtue of their membership of Newco.[3]

If anyone not already signed up to the investment agreement acquires shares at a later stage, whether as a result of a new allotment or by a transfer of shares, that person will be expected to join into the investment agreement (usually by way of a deed of adherence) as a condition to receiving those shares, unless the investors agree to the contrary. The deed of adherence is usually an agreed form document, often incorporated as a schedule to the investment agreement.

1 As explained in chapter 3, section 2.3, a buyout often requires a group structure with investors holding shares in the ultimate parent company, and investing by way of loan notes in a wholly owned subsidiary of that parent.
2 See chapter 3, section 3.3.
3 Section 33 of the Companies Act 2006.

It requires the new shareholder to be committed to the investment agreement and to be bound by the relevant obligations of the agreement as from the date upon which that shareholder becomes a member of Newco. Generally, the new shareholder will not be liable for any breach or non-observance of the investment agreement that occurred prior to the date of adherence. Similarly, the new shareholder would generally not be liable in respect of any breach of the warranties given in the investment agreement (even if he is otherwise joining as a manager or a permitted transferee of a manager).

It is important to note that the investment agreement is a private document. The articles, by contrast, are a public document required to be filed at Companies House. For this reason, the investment agreement is often the preferred document in which to place more confidential or otherwise sensitive arrangements. However, there are sometimes tax implications with the result that certain matters are better included in the articles; this must not be overlooked in determining the appropriate document for any particular provision.

3.2 Conditionality

The obligation of the private equity investors to make their subscriptions for shares and loan notes under the terms of the investment agreement is usually expressed to be conditional on a number of matters. Certain of these conditions flow naturally from the overall structure (for example, that the acquisition agreement and the banking documents have become unconditional). The private equity investors would not expect to be committed to investing in the structure if the deal is not actually going to proceed.

There is a tendency to use the list of conditions in an investment agreement to serve a checklist function – some of which can become fairly subjective, such as 'the investors receiving and being satisfied with the contents of the legal due diligence report'. There is no real need for this to be a condition, of course, as the private equity investors should be satisfied as to these matters before they sign. Many such requirements are now (more correctly) stated to be completion obligations instead and, accordingly, there is an increased tendency to include as conditions only those matters which cannot practically be satisfied at the time the private equity investors sign the investment agreement, and to deal with any checklist function elsewhere.

Conditionality becomes a more significant issue where there is a genuine reason for a delay between exchange and completion of the acquisition, for example due to a need to seek competition clearance to the transaction, or the approval by the seller's shareholders of the transaction where Target is a subsidiary of a listed company. In these cases, there will always be a desire for the seller(s) to achieve a 'certain funds' situation (or something close to it), for example the shareholders of a listed company who are required to approve a transaction may wish to have comfort that there is no real risk that the private equity investors can back out of the deal post-approval. More notably, certainty of funds is a key issue on a public-to-private transaction where the requirements of the Takeover Code apply (see chapter 10 below).[4]

A key issue on any transaction with genuine conditionality resulting in a delay between exchange and completion is the vexed area of material adverse change (MAC), mentioned already in the context of the acquisition agreement in chapter 4.[5] In this situation, the private equity investors will be entering into a commitment in the investment agreement to fund Newco at the time that Newco itself enters into the acquisition agreement (since Newco will need to be able to rely on that funding commitment, and the related bank funding, to finance the acquisition). There is, therefore, a legitimate concern on the part of Newco and its funders as to whether any material adverse change (whether such change occurs within Target's business only, or in its business sector, or in the economy generally) which occurs between exchange and completion should entitle Newco to be able to withdraw from the acquisition agreement (and accordingly not draw down the equity and bank funding) or, for example, whether a material warranty claim under the acquisition agreement that comes to light in that period of time should have the same consequence. Even if the funders do not simply withdraw, an appropriate right to rescind can assist any renegotiation in such a circumstance, whether of the price or of other terms. It should be noted that a trade buyer is in a similar situation if it seeks to buy Target using bank funding and there is a delay between exchange and completion; the situation is not peculiar to private-equity-backed deals.

In the context of a private-equity-backed deal, as for most private company acquisitions, some form of MAC provision is increasingly likely to be included if there is a genuine delay between exchange and completion under the acquisition agreement. As Newco has no other funding, it is important that all the funding commitments and the acquisition commitment are subject to the same conditions (in relation both to any adverse change and to the relevant transaction condition(s)). Sometimes, this is achieved by including a cross-referenced funding condition in the acquisition agreement itself (to the effect that the completion of the acquisition is conditional on stated funding still being available). This is clearly unattractive to a seller, and has the added complication that the seller needs to review the investment agreement and the bank facility agreement(s) in order to check the conditionality attached to the funding. It is generally easier if the MAC wording is on the face of the acquisition agreement, and the funding documents then effectively mirror this by being cross-conditional (that is, becoming unconditional simply upon the acquisition agreement itself becoming unconditional, as noted above). If the latter approach is adopted, the funders will of course be particularly interested in the precise detail of the relevant clause in the acquisition agreement which spells

4 Chapter 10, sections 4.1 and 4.2.

5 Chapter 4, section 2.6.

out its conditionality. However, it does at least reduce the need for a seller to understand or review the funding documents.

Whenever there is genuine conditionality in the investment agreement, it is important to bear in mind the factors listed in section 2.6 of chapter 4, including consideration of whether any party should be under an obligation to procure that any conditions are satisfied, and whether failure to satisfy any conditions should have any particular implications in terms of transaction costs. In the context of the investment agreement, as a general rule it is usual to see an obligation on Newco and the managers to use reasonable endeavours to procure satisfaction of the conditions specified in the investment agreement. It would be unusual, however, to have an express obligation in relation to costs if, in fact, the investment agreement does not become unconditional. This is because Newco itself is unlikely to be able to meet costs, and the managers will understandably be reluctant to do so out of their own funds. That is not to say the private equity investors would always bear their own costs if the deal does not complete. The question of abortive costs under the acquisition agreement (in the event of a breach of exclusivity, for example) is discussed in chapter 2.[6] The related issue of an inducement or break fee in a public-to-private transaction is discussed in chapter 10.[7]

3.3 Completion

The wording of the investment agreement completion clause is relatively mechanical in an investment agreement, so much so that the full detail is sometimes incorporated as a schedule. The equity investors and other subscribers (for example, the managers) will pay their subscription moneys, usually via the client account of the lawyers acting for Newco in the acquisition transaction. Newco (and, where relevant, other members of the group) will allot and issue shares and loan notes to the subscribers, enter their names in the relevant registers, and issue to them appropriate share or loan note certificates to evidence their holdings. As noted above, private equity investors (particularly where they are organised as a limited partnership, as is often the case) will often expect their shares (and sometimes also their loan notes) to be allotted into the name of, and held by, a custodian or nominee for the relevant investors.

The completion clause will also deal with the execution of other documents in the process, for example the execution of service agreements, banking and intercreditor documents, non-executive engagement letters (for a chairman, for example), and any other arrangements which the parties would expect to have in place at completion as part of the overall deal structure. Clearly, there will be a degree of overlap with the completion provisions under the facility documents and the acquisition agreement. It is important to ensure that the separate

6 Chapter 2, section 3.3.
7 Chapter 10, section 3.1.

completion arrangements in each document come together to form a smooth and effective overall completion process. Even if everything is covered 'on paper', there can be both legal and practical consequences if the steps under each document are not completed in the correct order, for example.

3.4 Investment agreement warranties

Virtually all investment agreements will require that the managers give warranties directly to the private equity investors. Sometimes, Newco itself also gives the same warranties, or its own separate warranties, in the investment agreement.

Typically, the warranties in an investment agreement relate to the personal history of the manager (for example, that he is contractually free to enter into the investment and his employment by Newco without breaching restrictive covenants, has a clean business history, and satisfies any particular regulatory requirements for the sector in which the business operates), the reasonableness of the preparation of the Business Plan and the projections and assumptions underlying it, and a confirmation from the managers that they are not aware of claims under the acquisition agreement or of any material inaccuracies or omissions in the commissioned due diligence reports.

It is quite common that the personal history warranty is dealt with by the managers completing and delivering a *pro forma* questionnaire (sometimes called a 'manager's declaration') to the private equity investors, on or before execution of the investment agreement. Such questionnaire is then backed up by a short warranty in the investment agreement on the accuracy and completeness of the delivered questionnaire. This mirrors the practice often used for directors of publicly traded companies. The questionnaire can sometimes cause problems if any of the questions prove to be sensitive – the most common issue being that such questionnaires often ask the managers to confirm their net worth (for reasons explained below).

Warranties are a standard feature of the acquisition agreement when acquiring a private company. In that context, as explained in chapter 4,[8] warranties are often said to have two objectives, namely, to allocate risk and to elicit disclosure. The warranties in an investment agreement are principally focused on eliciting disclosure – ensuring that the managers share what they know with the private equity investors, whether or not the sellers mention it in the acquisition process (or, indeed, whether or not the sellers are even aware of it). Special situations arise where the managers are also sellers (or some of the sellers), as would be the case in a secondary buyout. The interaction of the acquisition and investment warranties in this situation is considered in chapter 12.

Although the investment agreement warranties do allocate risk contractually, they usually provide a very limited remedy in this context, as there are a

8 See chapter 4, section 2.7.

number of reasons why a private equity investor is likely to choose not to bring a warranty claim against a manager under the investment agreement, even if there is a valid potential claim. These include the following:

(a) The reasons why private equity investments fail (or private equity investors suffer loss on an investment) rarely come from circumstances covered by the subject matter of the investment agreement warranties.
(b) The manager is unlikely to be good for a claim (i.e. able to pay it) if the loss is material. One of the principal reasons for private equity involvement in the transaction is to provide funding which the managers themselves cannot provide (as they do not have the personal resources). This particular aspect can be different in the context of a secondary buyout, where the managers have received cash out as part of the transaction.
(c) Reputational risk to the private equity investor. There can be adverse consequences for the investor if it becomes known that it is too readily prepared to bring a claim against managers (at least in the absence of fraud). Not only is there a risk that this would suggest that they had backed the wrong managers, but it may also make future management teams and their advisers more hesitant to deal with that particular private equity house (or, at least, to give warranties to it), and accordingly favour a less trigger-happy rival investor in negotiations on future deals. This would be the case, in particular, where there was a suspicion that the private equity investor was simply trying to recover its investment because the business had failed (as opposed to any fraud or similar gross impropriety surrounding the giving of the investment agreement warranties).
(d) The managers may still be valuable to the business. Unless the circumstances surrounding a warranty breach are so gross as to call into question the confidence which the private equity investors can place in the managers, the fact that there is a potential warranty claim against the managers does not, in itself, preclude the fact that the managers may still be of continuing value to the business. In an underperformance situation, for example, a relevant manager may still be the best person (or part of the best team) to turn around the investment. In that situation, bringing or threatening to bring a warranty claim against that valuable manager or management team would be a material disincentive, and could have an adverse effect on the present and future prospects of the investment itself as a result.

Accordingly, in the absence of fraud, private equity investors are unlikely to look to the investment agreement warranties as a principal remedy if something goes wrong in the investment. Instead, they will look first to the various mechanisms included in the documentation designed to assist them in an underperformance situation and, where appropriate, will seek to bring about a suitable change in management. Where relevant, they will look at the acquisition agreement warranties or other provisions in the acquisition documentation. This is not to say that the investment warranties do not really matter or should not be taken seriously – they are particularly important in ensuring that any information known to the managers which may be relevant to the investment decision is flushed out.

It is Newco that receives the investment. For this reason, as noted above, Newco will often give some or all of the warranties in addition to the managers. Generally, Newco would give the warranties relating to the due diligence, the Business Plan, and the 'back-to-back' warranty concerning breach of the acquisition agreement warranties.[9] For obvious reasons, it would be less common for Newco to give or to be liable in respect of the personal warranties given by a manager as to his own history and circumstances.

The likelihood of Newco being asked to give warranties varies as between particular private equity houses, and can also vary, inversely, by reference to the percentage of the equity which the private equity investors will own in Newco. In other words, the greater their percentage stake in Newco, the less likely it is that investors would seek to have a warranty claim against Newco (as such a claim diminishes even further the value of their investment, which is substantially owned by those investors anyway). The bank funder to the transaction is also often concerned to see that there is the potential for a warranty claim by the private equity investors against Newco itself, as this could cause some leakage of value to the private equity investors ahead of the agreed priority as between the funders. If the agreement does provide for Newco to give warranties, it will be usual for the intercreditor agreement to regulate the payment by Newco of any liability arising from a warranty claim, or the handling by the private equity investors of any monies received in respect of that warranty claim, in such a way as to preserve the relative priority of the bank in the overall funding structure. For these reasons, particularly in an institutionally led deal, it is quite common for the investors not to seek warranties from Newco at all. The bank would not expect direct warranties from the managers, so the bank does not generally have the same concern on warranties that the managers themselves give to the private equity investors. Indeed, the absence of such manager warranties would be regarded by a bank or its advisers as unusual.

3.5 Interaction between investment agreement warranties and acquisition agreement warranties

One issue which often arises in relation to investment agreement warranties is their interaction with the more historic and/or factual warranties about

9 See further section 3.5 below.

the business and affairs of Target and its group given by the seller(s) in the acquisition agreement. Although the investment agreement warranties will normally contain, for example, a warranty concerning the content of the due diligence reports (based on the knowledge of management), they are not principally focused on the history of Target and its business. As mentioned above, they principally look to address the personal circumstances and history of the manager, and the due preparation and reliability of the Business Plan and projections.

There may be two areas of overlap:

(a) Historic areas not covered by acquisition warranties. As noted in chapter 4, one area in which a management buyout differs from a more orthodox acquisition (for example, by a trade buyer) is the 'warranty risk', namely, that the seller may be reluctant to give warranties on matters which are within the particular knowledge of the managers themselves, and may well invite the buyer and its funders to seek comfort directly from the managers. Generally, this is resisted (see in particular the arguments in this respect in section 2.8 of chapter 4). However, if there are areas where this argument does not prevail in the negotiation of the acquisition agreement, it is possible that the private equity investors may, as a last resort, seek direct warranty comfort from the managers on these points in the investment agreement. This is a far less satisfactory position for the investors, not least because management do not provide an adequate remedy for all the reasons set out in section 3.4 above. However, particularly in a transaction where the private equity investors will have a minority stake in the new business, this is sometimes seen (and, in this situation, Newco will often give equivalent warranties).

(b) The private equity investor will often expect the managers to give a back-to-back warranty, standing behind the acquisition warranties. This warranty is usually given on a knowledge-qualified basis (often referred to in negotiations using the shorthand expression 'to knowledge'), that is to say that the managers warrant that they are not aware of anything that could give rise to a claim under the acquisition warranties (or, sometimes, under any provisions set out in the acquisition documentation). It is important to note that this is an awareness based warranty – the managers are not giving the same warranties that appear in the acquisition agreement (which are often not 'to knowledge'); they are merely confirming that they themselves do not know of any facts that might give rise to claims under those warranties.

The precise wording of the back-to-back warranty needs a little thought where the original acquisition warranty is itself a warranty to knowledge. By way of example, if in the acquisition agreement the seller gives a warranty that the seller is not aware of any breach of a particular contract to which Target is a party, the back-to-back warranty in the investment agreement can cover that particular issue in two different ways:

(a) It can ask the managers to warrant that they are not aware that the seller is aware of a breach of the contract in question. This is, in effect, asking the managers to confirm that they are not aware that there can be a claim under that warranty.
(b) It can ask the managers to say whether they (as opposed to the seller) are aware of any breach of Target's contract.

Of course, the private equity investor will usually be interested to know whether the managers themselves are aware of a breach of the contract, irrespective of whether the seller is aware of that breach. For this reason, the back-to-back warranty in the investment agreement is usually drafted to state that the managers are not aware of anything that would give rise to a claim under the acquisition warranties, assuming that no such warranties are qualified by reference to the knowledge or awareness of the seller(s) or of any other person. Where the managers have had an active role in the preparation of the acquisition agreement disclosure letter on behalf of the seller, this should of course make little real difference in practice.

3.6 Warranty limitations and defences

As the principal purpose of the investment agreement warranties is to elicit disclosure rather than to provide a post-completion contractual remedy for the private equity investors, the approach taken to limitations on those warranties in the context of the investment agreement is usually less strict (but also less comprehensive) than would be the case for limitations in respect of the warranties in the acquisition agreement.

Typically, the time period applicable to a warranty claim under the investment agreement will be between twelve and eighteen months (often tied to the delivery of a particular set of audited accounts for the Newco group, followed by a short period after their receipt for the private equity investors to consider those accounts). This is at the shorter end of what would be seen for the non-tax warranties in the acquisition agreement. As the investment agreement warranties do not normally cover the historic tax liabilities of Target, the longer seven-year period usually seen in the acquisition agreement for the tax warranties and covenant would not normally apply in an investment agreement.

Similarly, the maximum liability of the managers in respect of the investment agreement warranties is most usually expressed as a multiple of their salary (somewhere between one and three times initial salary is a typical outcome, with a fairly predictable compromise at two). Occasionally, it may be expressed in relation to the amount subscribed by the managers for their shares, or a multiple of that amount. Different considerations apply on the monetary limit where the transaction is a secondary buyout (see chapter 12[10]).

10 See chapter 12, section 3.4.

As a consequence of the market practice that has developed these established, salary-based, limits, the warranty cap is often set at a level which is substantially below the total amount invested by the private equity investors. This is a further reflection of the fact that these warranties are designed principally to produce disclosures (which can then go on to assist with the negotiation of the acquisition agreement, passing the pain to the seller(s) rather than management), rather than any meaningful allocation of risk towards the managers themselves. It is often expressed that the managers should face enough potential liability to focus their minds on taking the due diligence and disclosure exercise seriously, without the potential liability being so large that the risk is seen as unmanageable by the managers, however careful they are, or may keep them awake at night after completion (at a time when they ought to be focusing on growing the investment for the benefit of all the parties concerned).

This desire to ensure that the managers have a sufficient amount at stake in the warranties to take the disclosure exercise seriously often makes private equity investors particularly sensitive to any hold harmless or similar arrangements (for example, if warranty insurance is standing behind any risk that the managers might face). Usually, a warranty is sought that no such arrangements are in place. Such desire is also the reason for investors enquiring as to each manager's net worth – so that the impact of the usual, salary-based cap can be assessed for each particular individual.

There are structural differences between the relationship between the seller(s) and the buyer in a share acquisition (where usually the seller(s) will have no continuing involvement in Target, and the buyer will have day-to-day control), and the relationship between the private equity investors and the managers (where the managers will usually continue to be involved in the business, and will themselves have day-to-day control of the company). Accordingly, some of the limitations which are customarily included in the context of acquisition warranties do not necessarily apply in the same way to investment agreement warranties. It is not uncommon for the first version of the investment agreement to contain a set of warranty limitations designed to protect the managers already inserted by the lawyers acting for the private equity investors. The hope in this is that the debate around limitations can then take place in the context of those specific clauses (for example, the precise monetary and time limits) rather than leaving the managers' lawyers to produce a long-form limitation schedule, which is usually more appropriate for an acquisition agreement. Many of such limitations (for example, the limitations covering third party actions or conduct of claims typically found in an acquisition agreement) are often seen as irrelevant in a context where the warrantors (i.e. the managers) are continuing to run the business, and the warranties are limited to their personal circumstances, the Business Plan, and knowledge-based warranties concerning the due diligence reports and Target's business. As noted in section 2, the extent of such limitations (including the time and monetary limits that apply on managers' warranties) may also be agreed upfront as part of the equity offer letter process.

Since the principal purpose of the warranties is to elicit disclosure, most, if not all, of the investment agreement warranties may well be qualified by knowledge to a greater extent than would be the case for acquisition agreement warranties. Further, certain warranties will be given only by particular managers. For example, it is usual that the personal warranties about a particular manager's history and freedom to contract will be given separately, each manager speaking only for himself and his own position. As a general rule, the other warranties are given on a joint and several basis so that the private equity investor need only show that one of the managers was aware of the relevant matter to have a claim against any of them. Bargaining power can affect exactly how this operates, as in any transaction. However, the monetary limits are personal – i.e. each manager is capped by his own limit. An individual manager would not normally be expected to be liable for an aggregate amount across all the managers with the right (however valueless) thereafter to seek a contribution from his fellow managers.

One unusual aspect of the warranties in the investment agreement (by comparison to the situation more usually seen where multiple sellers are selling in the same acquisition agreement) is the desire on the part of the private equity house to be able to proceed against one manager without having to proceed against all of them (or, for example, to be able to compromise or release a claim against one manager without affecting any claims against the others). Similarly, there can be a resistance to any indemnity arrangements or other similar contribution arrangements between the managers which would have the effect of enabling any one manager who is pursued for a breach of warranty to seek to push some or all of his liability onto the other managers, or to seek a contribution from them towards his liability. This is not because the private equity investors particularly want to proceed against a specific manager. It is a reflection, in part, of the commercial context (discussed in section 3.4 above) that it can be a significant disincentive to have to bring a claim against a manager who is still of ongoing value to the business (whether that claim would be a direct claim against the valuable manager by the private equity investor, or the risk of consequential claim by a fellow manager against whom the private equity investors are bringing a principal claim). As much as anything, this might be viewed as the investors seeking to strengthen the hand of Newco in the event of a particular manager leaving Newco during the life of the investment. The fact that there may be potential claims against that manager is sometimes a factor to take into account in agreeing the terms upon which the manager will leave the business and the amount, if any, of compensation he may receive in respect of his former directorship or employment, or the consideration he may receive for his shareholding.[11] Conversely, releasing that manager from warranty risk can be an attractive term of the overall compromise package for his departure. The weight of this bargaining chip

11 See further chapter 11, section 5, regarding parting company with a manager.

would be diminished if the departing manager could call the bluff of the private equity investor, knowing that it would be unlikely to proceed if it also had to proceed against (or risk the departing manager bringing some claim for contribution against) the continuing managers. Similar considerations would not normally arise in the mind of the buyer in relation to potential claims against multiple sellers under the acquisition agreement, assuming such sellers are no longer within the business.

It is a standard provision of an investment agreement that, if a claim is made by the private equity investors under the warranties, the manager will not seek any contribution from Newco, or from any of its group companies, employees or officers, or bring any claim against them as a consequence. It would be materially disadvantageous to the private equity investor if a warranty claim by it against a particular manager could, in turn, diminish the value of its investment further through some form of third party claim or counterclaim by the relevant manager against Newco, Target or its group or employees. This is similar to the position that a buyer would seek from a seller in the acquisition agreement.

In any situation where Newco does give warranties, it would usually be subject to the same time limit in respect of claims as the managers giving warranties under the investment agreement have negotiated for themselves. However, the monetary limit would usually be set at the total amount invested by the private equity investors. There is a reasonable case to be made for limiting the liability to the amount which the investors are investing for their equity shares. The argument is that, if the loan notes are repaid together with relevant interest, then there is no loss in respect of them in any event. If the loss giving rise to the warranty claim is sufficient to prevent full repayment of the loan notes and interest, then the private equity investor has as much remedy as it needs by seeking to pursue its right as a creditor to receive that money (subject to the intercreditor and other applicable rules), and does not need an additional or substitute remedy under the warranties for any diminution in value of the loan notes. If Newco cannot repay the loan notes, it is also unlikely to be able to pay up on any claim for their loss resulting from a breach of warranty in the investment agreement. Having said that, this argument does not usually prevail and, where Newco does give warranties, it remains usual to set that limit at the total amount invested.

One final issue which can arise in relation to the ability of investors to claim under the investment agreement warranties is the question of whether the investors have knowledge of any circumstances that may give rise to a claim. It is common for the investment agreement to include a provision which states that, save for any matters that are disclosed in the disclosure letter, no knowledge of the investors (whether actual, implied or constructive knowledge) shall preclude the investors from making a claim. This mirrors the issue already explored in chapter 4 as to whether Newco should be able to claim in respect of matters of which either the management team or the investors are aware under the acquisition agreement.[12]

12 See chapter 4, section 2.8.

Legal advisers to management may seek to delete this clause on the basis that the investors should not be able to seek a remedy where the common law would prevent such recovery based on the investors' knowledge, or may go even further than this and suggest that the investors should provide a confirmation that they are not aware of any matters that may give rise to a claim under the investment agreement warranties. Both of such amendments would usually be resisted by the investors. As the purpose of the investment agreement warranties is principally to elicit disclosure, investors would argue that such amendments create a far more significant risk that the disclosure exercise will not be conducted with appropriate diligence. It may also be argued that the subject matter of the warranties – relating principally to the managers' personal circumstances, their own knowledge of matters relating to Target, and the Business Plan which the managers are responsible for – are issues on which only the managers can offer a true perspective, and as such the knowledge of the investors is not relevant.

3.7 Restrictive covenants

The investment agreement will include restrictive covenants from the managers in favour of the private equity investors and usually, though not invariably, in favour of Newco also. This is in addition to the restrictive covenants that a manager would normally be expected to provide in his service agreement to Newco (or whichever other company in the group will be his employer). In a secondary buyout, where a manager is often also a seller, that manager will usually provide a third set of restrictive covenants to the buyer in the acquisition agreement in his capacity as a seller.

Subject to the comments which follow, the format of the restrictive covenants in an investment agreement is broadly the same as in a typical acquisition agreement. It will preclude direct competition with the Newco group and the solicitation of key employees, customers or suppliers as is appropriate to protect the underlying business, and will contain a prohibition against the use of specific trade names or marks of the group's business as it exists at the time of the cessation of employment. It will also usually have an acknowledgment of the reasonableness of those covenants on the part of the manager, and typical 'blue pencil' wording (so that, if the court did find the covenants as a whole to be unreasonably restrictive, it may be willing to enforce them by deleting the offending part or otherwise reducing their scope).[13]

Two or, in some cases, three sets of restrictive covenants may often appear excessive, and this can give rise to some protracted negotiation. However, it is important to note that the restrictive covenants are given in different capacities,

13 Generally speaking, courts are more likely to delete an offending part of a covenant (provided the restriction following such deletion makes sense and is not unreasonable) than to amend wording, but in any event it is preferable to ensure the covenant is reasonable from the outset rather than to rely on the 'blue pencil' clause.

in favour of different parties, and to protect different goodwill. By way of example (and assuming for this purpose the manager is also a seller, and therefore providing three different sets of restrictive covenants):

(a) In the *acquisition agreement*, the manager is providing restrictive covenants in his capacity as the seller of an asset. The time period for the restriction will run from the date of completion of the acquisition, and the goodwill to be protected and geographic extent of the covenants will be judged by their reasonableness in the context of that share sale, and the goodwill of the Target group at the time of that sale. Accordingly, where the manager remains in the business and that business in turn develops and changes after the sale, it would be unusual (and probably unenforceable) to seek to protect that new or enlarged goodwill under the acquisition agreement. All restrictive covenants under English law are *prima facie* void save and to the extent to which they are reasonable as between the parties and in the public interest. The argument here is that the reasonableness of the acquisition agreement restrictive covenants should be judged as between a share seller and a buyer (on an arm's length basis), and in the context of the general public interest in enabling sensible restrictive covenants to be given (without which no seller could extract any meaningful value for the goodwill associated with what is sold, creating little incentive to generate that goodwill in the first place). In the same way that the buyer could seek to enforce a restrictive covenant (so far as it is reasonable) from a seller who takes his proceeds and moves on, the buyer can seek the same restrictive covenant from a seller staying on in the business as a director and/or shareholder in the buyer group.
(b) In the *service agreement*, the manager is entering into the transaction as an employee, albeit usually a senior one. Accordingly, the courts will look at the restrictive covenant by reference to what is reasonable in the context of a senior employee who has a similar role, and similar interaction with customers, suppliers and employees. However, this covenant will generally be written to protect the goodwill existing at the time the employment ends. To that extent, although it is subject to the generally shorter periods and higher standard of reasonableness expected in an employment situation, the service agreement covenants have the advantage that they can protect the goodwill as it evolves following the buyout and up to the time when the employment ceases.
(c) In the *investment agreement*, as in the service agreement, this covenant is designed to protect not just the goodwill at the time of the acquisition, but also the goodwill as it evolves and develops from that date until the date of cessation of employment (or in some cases, the date on which the manager ceases to be a shareholder). It is usually argued that the investment represents a form of joint venture between co-owners (more

> similar, say, to a partnership) than the transaction between an employer and employee, and therefore the courts should allow a more onerous set of covenants than would be acceptable simply in an employment situation. This is reinforced by the fact that often (although not always) there may be a share transfer at the time the manager ceases to be employed, reinforcing the argument that this relationship is more akin to that of co-owners, and therefore any assessment by the courts as to what is reasonable should be closer to that which would be applied in the context of the acquisition agreement restrictive covenants, rather than in the context of the service agreement.

One interesting area of overlap is the general rule of law that a party who is in repudiatory breach of contract cannot also seek to hold the other party to the terms of that contract (at least where the party not in breach has accepted the repudiatory breach).[14] As is explored further in chapters 7 and 11,[15] the ending of a senior manager's employment often occurs in situations where it is not practicable to comply with the terms of the service agreement, or with employment legislation. It is not, therefore, uncommon to find that the employer company is in repudiatory breach of the service agreement, even where there may be sound commercial reasons why the employment of a manager must end (from the point of view of the private equity investors and the rest of the Newco board). In particular, there is often a compelling business need to do so quickly to avoid the risk that a recalcitrant manager may seek to influence others (whether inside or outside the company), or to harm the business in some way during a protracted disciplinary or consultation process. For this reason, a restrictive covenant in the service agreement is often of little practical use at the very time when a private equity investor would most want to use it. Having a separate set of restrictive covenants in the investment agreement, to back up the employment restrictions and protect the goodwill of the group at the time of the cessation of employment, is therefore of particular advantage. Whilst it is not necessarily clear that the courts will fully uphold the argument that they are separate arrangements, and that a repudiatory breach of the service agreement should not be taken into account in determining the validity of the obligations in the investment agreement, it is clearly a better position to be in than having to rely solely on restrictive covenants in the service agreement. Similarly, unless management is in a very strong position, it would be unusual for the investors to agree to express contractual cross-default (i.e. for a provision to be included in the investment agreement stating that the restrictive covenant in that document cannot be relied on where the manager has been wrongfully dismissed under that manager's service agreement). To accept such a cross-default would significantly damage the value of the separate restrictive covenant in the investment agreement.

14 See *General Billposting Company Ltd* v. *Atkinson* [1909] AC 118.

15 See, in particular, chapter 7, section 2.4, and chapter 11, section 5.

Another area of overlap is the subject of garden leave.[16] It is generally accepted that, if a manager is placed on garden leave (so that he remains employed but is not required to do any work, and is usually excluded from the company's premises, personnel and facilities), then the time spent on garden leave should be offset not only against the restrictive covenant that may otherwise arise in the service agreement, but also against any time limits on the restrictive covenant in the investment agreement. If such a provision is not included, then the courts are arguably less likely to consider that the restrictive covenant is enforceable. In *Credit Suisse Asset Management Ltd* v. *Armstrong*,[17] the Court of Appeal stated that there was no automatic principle that the periods should be offset, but that the existence of a garden leave clause would be a factor taken into account in determining the validity of a restrictive covenant, and, as a result, an express provision offsetting the two has emerged as market practice in both the service agreement and the investment agreement.

The precise terms of the restrictive covenant in the investment agreement do need to be considered in the context of particular managers. There may well be certain managers who are particularly key to the business, or whose ability to damage the goodwill is greater, such that a longer or otherwise more restrictive covenant can be justified. As a general rule, a chief executive or sales director is usually more able to damage the goodwill than a finance director. The reasonableness and the validity of any restrictive covenant will vary from transaction to transaction, and from individual to individual.

3.8 Confidentiality obligations

The investment agreement will also contain confidentiality obligations, drafted so as to apply for so long as the relevant information of the group is confidential, with customary carve-outs for any disclosure which must be made by law or under the requirements of regulatory bodies. This confidentiality obligation will be expected from each of the managers. In contrast, the private equity investors themselves will usually be reluctant to give express contractual confidentiality obligations, and may ask the managers to rely on common law obligations of confidentiality. If the investors do accept an obligation (and some will not as a matter of policy), it will inevitably be subject to specific exceptions to permit communication between different investors, between any investor directors or the chairman and the investors, and between the investors and the banks or any other funders or potential funders to the business. Disclosure to a potential buyer is also often negotiated as a specific carve-out to any express confidentiality obligation on the part of the investors.

16 On garden leave generally, see chapter 7, section 2.3.
17 [1996] IRLR 450.

3.9 Board composition

The investment agreement will often contain provisions as to the composition of the board, although, as noted in section 4.14 below, these will often be supplemented by similar provisions in the articles. Notwithstanding the fact that in many situations the private equity investors have a majority equity interest, it is still usual to find express provisions in the investment agreement dealing with the ability of the investors to appoint and remove directors.

The private equity investors will usually have the right to appoint a particular number of investor directors (two is most common, although sometimes only one may be appointed). Occasionally, there will be some restriction as to who may be appointed as investor director (for example, that the investor director should be either an employee of the private equity investor, or should be approved by the board of directors). Usually, however, the ability to appoint and remove investor directors is entirely a matter for the private equity investors themselves without any such restrictions. It should be noted that not all private equity investors will exercise this power to appoint investor directors as a matter of course. Many prefer to keep it in reserve, not least given the extensive duties which any directors owe to a company under common law and statute.[18] Any fee payable for the investor directors is usually paid directly to the private equity investors (or, more specifically, to the manager of the relevant funds), rather than to the individuals concerned.

The clause may also deal with the appointment of the chairman. This is often subject to some obligation on the part of the private equity investors to consult with the board (or perhaps manager shareholders), although in practice the private equity investors will usually have the final say on the identity of the chairman. Private equity investors are very keen to find a chairman who can be of genuine value to the business, and who will be seen by the executive directors as bringing desirable qualities to the board. Most chairman appointments are non-executive, and the chairman is not usually an employee of the private equity investors (although investors have formal or informal panels of chairmen whom they look to for appointments, often on a sectoral basis). A chairman will usually be expected to take an equity shareholding in the company. This may simply be sweet equity, or more unusually might include a small strip of shares and loan notes on the same terms as the investors, and a further strip of shares on the same sweet equity terms as the managers.[19] The chairman may also be expected to sign up to the investment agreement, although if this is the case he would not normally have any liability under the warranties. Practice in relation to the restrictive covenants will also vary, as most

18 See, in particular, sections 171–179 of the Companies Act 2006. Private equity investors need to bear in mind that their actions may also subject them to such responsibilities as a shadow director, if the board is inclined to behave in accordance with the instructions of a particular individual. For more on these duties, see chapter 11, section 6.

19 For the meaning of 'sweet equity', see chapter 3, section 2.2(c).

chairmen would not wish to accept the full extent of the restrictions set out for executive managers in a typical investment agreement. The chairman will usually be entitled to a fee payable by Newco directly to him, or sometimes to a consultancy company which is providing his services. It is usually desirable for the first chairman to be appointed at the time of completion, although this is not always possible in practice.

Although the investment agreement may specify which of the managers will be on the board of Newco at completion and their executive roles, it is unusual for there to be a hard right for the managers to appoint a director or a particular number of directors to the board, particularly if the investors have voting control of the company. Private equity investors (particularly in a majority position) would seek to resist any provisions in the investment agreement or in the articles which could be seen to give a hard right to management, or to any particular manager, to have a board position. If any such provisions are conceded in negotiation (which is unlikely without strong commercial justification, perhaps on a secondary transaction), there will usually be a carve-out which reduces or removes them in certain underperformance situations so that, in practice, they will not be able to prevent the private equity investors being in the ultimate position to take any action they believe necessary to rescue the investment or to make changes to the board composition in those circumstances.

Similarly, where the private equity investors are in a majority equity position, the investors will often request an express right to appoint and remove any person as a director of the company (and not just their own appointees). As a matter of general company law, as shareholders with a majority of the votes available at general meeting, they would have the power to do this in any event. However, the investment agreement and/or the articles will usually contain express provisions to reinforce this power, not least because the time period required to remove a director under the statutory procedures in the Companies Act 2006 (which can be twenty-eight days or longer)[20] can be seen as unhelpful if a swift decision needs to be made. This power for controlling shareholders to appoint or remove directors immediately is not peculiar to private equity. A similar provision will often appear in the articles of subsidiary companies within groups, so as to enable holding companies to have the same power of immediate appointment or removal without notice at that level. The position varies more widely where the private equity investors have a minority stake. Some investors will insist on a hard right to appoint or remove directors being granted in favour of the investors, or at least the remuneration committee.[21] Other investors might accept that a majority of the shareholders or directors

20 Section 168(2) of the Companies Act 2006 requires special notice of any resolution to remove a director, defined in section 312 to require notification to the company at least twenty-eight days before the meeting at which it is moved.

21 For committees, see section 3.10 below.

are required for any board changes in the ordinary course, and then take a hard right only in circumstances of underperformance.[22]

Often, the investment agreement will enable the private equity investors to appoint an observer. If so, the investment agreement provides that the observer is not a member of the board and cannot vote at board meetings. He will, however, be entitled to receive copies of all papers and to attend and (usually) speak at the board meeting. This ability is helpful for certain private equity investors who wish to have a close connection to board meetings without their appointee taking on the full statutory and fiduciary responsibilities of being a legal director of the company. For this reason, the power to appoint an observer is sometimes expressed to exist only whilst there is no investor director in office. However, practice does vary, so an observer may be entitled to attend board meetings irrespective of whether there are investor directors in office.

An investor director faces a clear potential conflict of interest in his role in that, in addition to his duties to Newco, he may well also be an employee or even a director of the private equity investor, and a director of other companies in which that private equity investor has invested. The interests of Newco and of the private equity investor do not always align, particularly if there is a need to rescue the transaction. Chapter 11 sets out a more detailed analysis of directors' duties generally (which include the duties of any investor director), and also highlights certain provisions which are now often included in the articles to seek to regulate the conflicts that may otherwise arise, particularly in the context of the new statutory duty to avoid conflicts under section 175 of the Companies Act 2006.[23]

3.10 Board committees

It is usual for the investment agreement to provide that there will be a remuneration committee, similar to that found in a listed company. The remuneration committee will usually comprise the chairman, the investor directors and the chief executive (although members of the committee are usually precluded from taking part in any vote in relation to their own remuneration). The remuneration committee will have the effective say in relation to salary and other benefits of the managers (and, sometimes, other senior employees). In many cases, it will also have the power to exercise other provisions in the service agreement, for example the power to suspend or dismiss the manager as an employee.

Many investments will also feature an audit committee, usually comprising the chairman and the investor directors. The finance director will usually attend meetings of the audit committee but will not normally vote. The role of

22 For a further analysis of enhanced investor rights on underperformance, see section 4.3 below.

23 See further chapter 11, section 6.

the audit committee will again be similar to that in a listed company, including reviewing the work of the auditors and the internal accounting systems of the group.

3.11 Information

The investment agreement will contain provisions requiring Newco to provide regular management information to the private equity investors, including monthly management accounts in a format approved by them, statutory accounts within a given period, and draft budgets for approval in advance of each financial year. There will usually also be a provision requiring Newco to provide such other information in relation to the business and affairs of its group as the investors may specify. Investors may have more detailed requirements as a matter of house style (for example, to be informed of material litigation or disputes), or to reflect the sector in which the investee company trades (for example, weekly sales data in a retail business).

These information obligations are usually reinforced by an express right for the private equity investors, at the expense of Newco, to send in their own accountants to obtain the information if there is any material delay or default in compliance.[24]

3.12 Investor consents

The investment agreement will normally contain a comprehensive list of matters requiring prior approval from the investors (or, sometimes, an investor director) before any such transactions or dealings are entered into by the group. The precise list of veto matters varies based on the preferences of investors, although a relatively standardised list of 'must haves' has emerged. Typical examples of investor consents include:

- any change to the share capital of Newco, including the granting of any options or warrants, or any share reduction or own share purchase;
- any change to the constitution of Newco or any other group company;
- any exercise by the board of rights set out in the articles (for example, in relation to share transfers);
- material capital expenditure;
- material litigation;
- appointment and removal of directors (other than the investor directors or the chairman) or any change to or termination of their service agreement or other terms of appointment;[25]
- any transaction or arrangement between the group and any manager (or any connected person), or any variation or termination of the same;

24 See further chapter 11, section 2.3.

25 Note that, even where the investors have no hard right to appoint or remove a director, they would still expect a veto on any appointments or removals.

- any material departure from the Business Plan or agreed annual budget;
- any material acquisition or disposal by the group;
- any proposal for the listing or sale of a member of the group;
- any change of auditors or accounting policies, practices or standards (beyond those required generally by a change of law or to ensure compliance with generally accepted accounting practices); and
- any change to the bankers or other funders of the business.

The purpose of these business covenants is to ensure that any material matter outside the ordinary course of the business of the group, or which may materially and adversely affect it in the context of the ultimate exit, are brought to the attention of the private equity investors and approved by them. There is a sensible balance to be struck between, on the one hand, imposing such a restrictive regime upon the company that the managers are not able to carry on the day-to-day operation of the business without pestering the private equity investors constantly for consents and, on the other hand, having such limited control over the business that the investors are not sufficiently informed of material issues on a timely basis, or able to exercise the proper controls that they would wish to in respect of their investment.

Certain of these restrictions may be subject to specific monetary thresholds or other carve-outs. Similarly, particularly where a decision needs to be reached in a hurry, there may well be a procedure to enable the investor director to give certain consents at board meetings or by way of e-mail. Sometimes, managers will ask for a time period to be built around consents, perhaps reinforced by a provision that the private equity investors are deemed to give consent if they do not object within a particular period. However, such mechanisms are usually resisted by the private equity investors to ensure there is absolute clarity in practice (in other words, to ensure that, until an express consent is given, there is no consent, to avoid any doubt). Investors prefer to ensure the consents only cover the fundamental or material concerns, such that (once agreed) there is no fetter on the exercise of such veto rights. They would not generally agree to have to be 'reasonable' in the exercise of a discretion, for example.

The investment agreement will often provide that, where any such consent is given subject to conditions, it will be a breach of the agreement if the matter in question is implemented without complying with such conditions. The investment agreement will also usually require Newco to meet any out-of-pocket expenses incurred by the private equity investors in considering any application for consent, whether or not that consent is given. This is in addition to any monitoring or similar fees (see section 3.13 below).

Traditionally, many of these consent rights were supplemented by express provisions in the articles seeking to provide that it would be a breach of the class rights attached to the private equity investors' shares in Newco if the relevant matter occurred without the necessary consent. This list of specific class rights in the company's articles is nowadays generally much reduced, and most investors instead rely on their majority equity control (where relevant), and on the more substantial list of consents set out in the investment agreement. Whilst a comprehensive list of matters requiring class consent in the articles has the advantage of attaching the veto protection for the investors to the shares, there is a significant disadvantage to the restrictions on the company's capacity to transact (which may be sensitive) being included in a document in the public domain. For further details of those veto rights which are still often reserved for investors in the articles, see section 4.16 below.

3.13 Investor fees and expenses

The investment agreement will set out details of the fees payable by Newco to the investors. The precise terms may vary, but typically these include:

(a) An arrangement fee payable to the private equity house (somewhere around 2–3 per cent of the total sum invested by the private equity house under the investment agreement would be typical).
(b) An annual monitoring fee payable to the private equity house in respect of the ongoing monitoring of the Newco group. Practice in respect of the charging of monitoring fees varies. Some investors will appoint their own investor directors, for whom fees will be payable (to the relevant private equity investor) for so long as they are in office, but do not charge a monitoring fee. Others may reserve the right to appoint investor directors without the charging of investor director fees, but charge a contractual monitoring fee whether the investor directors are in office or not. Sometimes, a contractual monitoring fee is stated to apply only if there are no investor directors in office, such that the investors are thus compensated if investor director fees are not being paid. The amount is often index-linked, i.e. increased annually by reference to the increase during the preceding twelve months in the retail price index.

These two fees are an important part of the cash flow and funding of the management company that manages the private equity investor's funds, and will be payable regardless of the performance of Newco or its profits, subject only to any regulation by the terms of the intercreditor arrangements with the senior lenders. As indicated in section 3.12 above, any extra out-of-pocket expenses incurred (for example, in considering any request for an investor consent) are usually also chargeable to Newco.

These fees are usually excluded from any ratchet or other mechanism which measures the investors' returns as part of the equity incentivisation of management. In effect, they are usually treated as a running cost of the business, rather than as a yield or benefit to the private equity investors.[26]

26 See further section 4.6 below.

4 Articles of association

4.1 Background

All private-equity-backed businesses will have bespoke articles of association, which are adopted before the private equity investors' subscription for shares in Newco is completed. The form of these articles will be negotiated alongside the investment agreement.

Traditionally, articles of association are designated as 'short form' or 'long form'. 'Short form' means that the relevant default provisions which apply to all companies (the relevant version of Table A in the case of a company incorporated before 1 October 2009, and the relevant model articles for companies incorporated after that date) form part of the articles of the company, save and to the extent to which the articles explicitly disapply or are inconsistent with these default provisions. Long form articles exclude the default provisions, and set out in one document all the provisions of the articles of association of the company. Traditionally, short form articles would usually be shorter than long form, because they can rely upon the relevant default provisions, and only need to address those matters where the shareholders want other particular provisions to apply to the company.

The articles of private equity companies are generally short form. This means that any person seeking to understand the provisions of the articles needs to read not only the form of articles filed at Companies House, but also the default provisions (whether Table A or model articles) that supplement those articles. The fact that private equity articles are short form does not, however, necessarily mean that they are short. Private equity articles are often among the most complex form of articles of association that you would see in any UK company (although, on balance, they have tended to shorten and be simplified in the last ten years, particularly as more transactions have featured investors with a significant majority stake).

In addition, the changes that have been, and continue to be, introduced to company law under the Companies Act 2006 (and its related commencement orders) are having an effect upon the articles of all UK companies, including those backed by private equity. In particular, the change as from 1 October 2009 of the default provisions applicable to new companies resulting from the introduction of the model articles may cause significant changes to the documents filed at Companies House for investee companies incorporated after that date. Many of the issues and solutions will be similar, but the 2006 Act does introduce new opportunities and challenges that have to be addressed; see, for example, the issues that have resulted from the statutory notification of directors' conflicts of interest in the context of section 175 of the Companies Act 2006.[27] This is a changing area. Accordingly, it is possible that some of the

27 For further discussion, see chapter 11, section 6.7.

provisions discussed in this chapter may become increasingly uncommon in the future, and new areas of concern or opportunity may arise. However, having regard to the fundamental tensions inherent in the private equity structure, the positions of the relevant parties in relation to those tensions, and the typical solutions proposed, it is likely that the practical issues confronted will remain much the same for the foreseeable future.

As explained in chapter 9, the taxation consequences arising for any holder of shares, and in particular shares received by managers by virtue of their employment, also affect the specific rights (for example, on income or return of capital) which will be included in the articles for private-equity-backed companies. This can both complicate and limit the scope and detail of the provisions in the articles.

Changes in UK company law and taxation law and practice, and the increasing tendency of private equity investors to constitute the majority (sometimes the overwhelming majority) in value of the equity shares, have all over time combined to cause significant changes to the detail of articles of private-equity-backed companies over recent years. This trend seems likely to continue, given the increased political and regulatory scrutiny of the sector already referred to in this book.

4.2 Share structure and core share rights

One of the main purposes of the articles is to set out the share rights attached to the classes of shares in Newco. The number of classes, and the rights attached to each, will depend to a large extent on the particular share structure used (see further chapter 3 in relation to transaction structures). However, as a minimum, it is usual to find two classes of equity shares, one designed to be held by the private equity investors (investor shares), and the other to be held by the managers (manager shares). The main reason for two separate classes is to allow for differentiated rights in relation to transferability, good and bad leaver, and drag and tag along rights (to mention but a few of the differences), the detail of which is explored in this chapter. If the particular transaction structure also requires different dividend or capital rights for the two groups, then the need for separate classes is made even clearer. Where there is a ratchet which impacts different management shareholders in different ways, a second-tier management group that needs to be motivated by a small shareholding or share options, the deal is a secondary, or there are otherwise additional natural 'groups' of shareholders, then there may well be more than two equity classes.

Traditionally, the labels attached to the different classes of shares tended to be descriptive of their underlying class rights (especially when preference share classes were more common in deal structures). For example, you would often find cumulative convertible participating preferred ordinary shares (perhaps abbreviated as CCRPO shares), or convertible redeemable preference shares

(CRPS shares), and so on. These fairly cumbersome descriptive tags are now far less common, with the preference being to identify the different classes of share alphabetically, for example A shares (or maybe A ordinary shares) for the private equity investors, B shares for managers, and so on. Matching letters can be used to identify any loan notes or preference shares so that the different instruments held by each class of shareholder are effectively badged together; this can be particularly helpful on a secondary buyout where the investors and the managers are both likely to hold different instruments (and, in the case of any rolling managers, possibly more than one class of share to distinguish the institutional strip equity from the sweet equity).[28]

4.3 Voting

As a general rule, the investor shares and the manager shares will have voting rights; that is to say, their shares will entitle the holder to receive notice of any general meeting and to attend and vote at it or, as the case may be, to receive and sign any written resolution which it is proposed should be signed by the members of Newco.[29] Very occasionally (and typically only on very large, institution-led deals), the manager shares will be non-voting.

It is usual for one vote to be attached to each equity share, so that (as explained in chapter 3) each private equity investor and each manager will pay the same price for each equity share, entitling them to voting rights *pro rata* to their equity shareholding. In many cases, however, the investor shares may have enhanced voting rights (known as swamping rights) or, as another way of achieving a similar result, the manager shares may be disenfranchised (that is, have their voting rights suspended), in the event of certain underperformance circumstances arising. This is particularly likely in a situation where the investor shares are not otherwise such a large proportion of the total shares that an equal treatment, share for share, gives them overwhelming voting control. Whether enhancement or disenfranchisement is used, the intention is to ensure that the voting rights attached to the manager shares cannot block any urgent action, such as a refinancing, that may be required to protect the investment.

The events that typically trigger this enhanced voting position for the investors include:

(a) any arrears or non-payment of any monies due (whether interest or capital) in respect of any loan notes or preference shares (as the case may be) held by the investors;
(b) any arrears or non-payment of any dividends due (whether or not Newco can lawfully pay the same), where the same accrue, in respect of any equity shares held by the investors;

28 See further chapter 3, section 3.5, and chapter 12.
29 The procedure for the passing of written resolutions is now governed by section 288 of the Companies Act 2006.

(c) a breach of certain, or sometimes any, of the obligations contained in the investment agreement or articles of association of Newco by any other party;
(d) an actual or potential breach of the terms of Newco's banking facilities (including any covenants set out in such facilities);
(e) material financial underperformance, such as a failure by Newco to achieve a particular percentage of the budgeted EBITDA (or a similar profit measure) as envisaged in the Business Plan or in subsequent annual budgets. Such percentage is often fixed at a level which is higher than that proposed for the profit-based banking covenant, so that (in theory at least) the enhanced voting rights might be triggered before a banking default.

Different private equity firms have different approaches to the circumstances in which they would wish to trigger an enhanced voting position. Whilst almost all investors who enhance their votes on underperformance would expect non-payment of amounts due to them to constitute a default, the approach that investors take to breaches of the banking facilities or the measurement of profit achieved against Business Plan will differ. In respect of bank covenants, some investors require that it is not just an actual breach which triggers enhanced voting, but that a 'look forward' type test should also apply; that is to say that, if the investors believe there will in the future be a financial default, then their voting rights will be enhanced. The subjective nature of such a provision is an obvious point of contention, and it is usual for management's lawyers to try to argue for its removal altogether, or at the very least to introduce some concept of reasonableness. Whilst some investors might ultimately settle for a factual breach, rather than an anticipation that there will be a breach, there are many investors who will insist that some kind of look forward test is required.

There are some common safeguards that can be negotiated on behalf of management teams to mitigate against the potential for abuse of these enhanced voting rights. For example:

(a) Allowing a 'grace period' for the payment of any outstanding monies, or the rectification of breaches of any documentation. A time period of seven to fourteen days is typical here.
(b) It would be usual for the rights not to be triggered automatically, but instead for the investors to be obliged to serve a notice to enhance their rights if the relevant circumstances occur. This obviously creates a degree of certainty as to whether the voting rights have been enhanced or not. This is also often an important protection for the investors, many of whom may not wish to take a higher level of voting control without making a conscious decision to do so, as there may well be accounting and/or tax implications for the investors to consider.
(c) A general provision is usually included to state that, once a relevant default has been remedied, the enhanced voting rights cease to apply and the original voting position is reinstated.

(d) Investors may agree that enhanced voting rights triggered by breaches of documentation (such as the investment agreement and the articles, or the banking documents) should only apply in the event that certain provisions in such documents are breached, or possibly if such breach might reasonably be considered to be material.

The keenness with which these provisions are negotiated varies in proportion to the underlying voting rights in a normal situation: where the private equity investors do not otherwise have a majority voting position, the managers are likely to have more bargaining power in determining the precise parameters in which (whether through swamping or disenfranchisement) the private equity investors would gain voting control of Newco.

In addition to underperformance, the articles may also provide that the voting rights of the shares of a particular member are suspended in other circumstances. For example, if a manager becomes a leaver under the articles, the voting rights are often suspended until such time as the shares are transferred to another person or the pre-emption mechanism is exhausted. Sometimes, if a leaver is allowed to keep shares after he has become a leaver, their voting rights are suspended or they are converted to a separate non-voting class. This is designed to enable the leaver to retain the economic benefit of the shareholding, but without the risk of delay in any urgent matter that might arise if the leaver retains shareholder votes.[30]

If there are other classes of shares in the transaction structure (for example, preference shares), they will normally be non-voting. In some situations, preference shares may be entitled to vote (for example, if their own class rights are affected or, sometimes, as an underperformance or late dividend remedy). However, as private equity investors often already enjoy voting control by virtue of their equity shareholding, or can obtain it through one of the swamping or disenfranchisement mechanisms referred to above, preference shares are most usually non-voting in all situations.

The actions which investors are likely to take in practice in the event that underperformance circumstances do arise are considered in more detail in chapter 11.[31]

4.4 Dividends

Where there are two classes of equity share, they normally rank equally for any dividends paid, but without a right on the part of any shareholder to receive a particular level or rate of dividend. That is to say that, if the board does declare a dividend, each shareholder will receive the same amount share for share, but the shareholder has no fixed right to any particular level of dividend in any accounting period, or to require that a dividend be declared by the directors.

30 For leavers, see section 4.11 below.

31 See chapter 11, section 4.

Usually, either through board control or through a specific class right or investment agreement veto, the private equity investors will have to give a separate or additional consent before the board approves the payment of any dividend in these situations. This is because the private equity investors will normally not wish any dividend to be paid on the equity shares, but would prefer to focus all members on realising value by capital gains growth and achieving an exit. For tax reasons, managers will typically prefer to receive any growth in the form of capital gain at exit rather than by dividend as well. The additional hurdle of consent also helps to protect the directors from a claim that they ought to pay a dividend; it may otherwise arguably be a breach of their duty not to do so.

If any class of shares is to have a fixed right to receive a dividend, this will be expressed in the articles. Usually, such a dividend will be made 'self-declaring', so that, if Newco is legally able to pay a dividend of that amount, there will be a hard right to receive it as a debt. This is to reduce the risk that the board may otherwise choose to exercise a discretion to prevent, reduce or delay the payment of the dividend.

In some deals, particularly where the private equity investors were in a minority equity position, it was customary to have a priority dividend (referred to as a participating dividend), calculated as a percentage of EBITDA or pre-tax profit. Sometimes, this percentage was stepped so that the rate increased year by year (after, say, year three), so as to increase the cost of private equity money to the business after that time, and thereby encourage all shareholders to find an exit. Also, a dividend was a useful barometer of underperformance: if the company was unable to pay the dividend, then some other measure would be triggered (such as enhanced voting rights, as noted in section 4.3 above).

The use of such dividends to police performance and provide a yield became less fashionable as investors moved towards the bulk of the private equity investment being provided in the form of loan notes rather than preference shares (as discussed in chapter 3).[32] The underperformance measures by reference to bank covenant breach, or a profit shortfall against Business Plan, are also generally considered to be a more useful test of when to take enhanced control than the late payment of a dividend. The trend away from dividend yields can also be explained, in part, by the trend away from minority deals (where the investors may have little ability to influence the exit without making its funding more expensive) and towards majority deals. If the market moves towards private equity stakes being increasingly in share form (whether equity or preference shares) rather than loan notes, or there is an increased number of minority, development-capital-style transactions rather than institution-led majority buyouts, it is quite possible that some of these traditional dividend yield mechanisms may come back into fashion.

32 See chapter 3, section 2.2(b).

In any event, it is important to bear in mind that the intercreditor arrangements forming part of the banking documentation will normally limit or preclude any dividend, or will prescribe certain tests that have to be satisfied before a dividend can be paid. The precise interaction between the banking documents and any dividend rights needs therefore to be clearly considered and factored into the arrangements. Where there is a dividend payable to the investors as of right, such as a participating dividend, the bank would usually allow the dividend to continue to accrue, but prohibit payment to the extent this results in any breach of the covenant tests in the facility agreement.

4.5 Return of capital and allocation of sale proceeds

The articles will set out the respective rights attached to the different classes of shares in relation to return of capital and the allocation of sale proceeds. Where there are only two classes of equity shares, they are often expressed to rank *pari passu*, that is to say that whatever is available by way of return of capital or on a sale will be allocated on an equal basis, share for share. In some situations, there will be a liquidation preference in favour of the private equity investors, so that any amounts available on a return of capital or a sale will be applied first in repaying to the private equity investors the amount paid on the investor shares (usually at face value, although sometimes, for riskier, venture capital investments, there may be a multiple), and thereafter in paying a catch-up amount to the manager shares (returning both classes to equality), before allocating any remaining sum on an equal share-for-share basis. This is just one example of a liquidation preference, and variations are sometimes seen. Clearly, the precise allocation of capital and sale proceeds will depend upon the particular transaction structure, and where a ratchet is included in a transaction[33] care is needed to ensure that the provisions providing for a return of capital on liquidation are not inconsistent with those arrangements. There may be tax implications for some private equity investors if a liquidation preference is included in respect of their equity shares, so the requirements of the particular investors must always be checked.

Where there are further classes of shares in addition to the straightforward manager and investor classes, their respective rights on a return of capital or in respect of sale proceeds will also be specified in the articles. This is normally a fairly straightforward exercise, with the allocation being determined by reference to the nature of the shares, and their priority, in the context of the deal structure as a whole. For example, a class of preference shares will normally be entitled to a fixed prior amount ahead of any classes of equity shares, but nothing further beyond that point. Where preference shares are created which are redeemable (as an alternative, or in addition, to investor loan notes[34]), the articles will specify the precise redemption rights, including the redemption

33 See further section 4.6 below.

34 See chapter 3, section 2.2(b).

price and process to be followed. They will also deal with the consequences of any partial or late redemption. As is the case for any accruing dividends, the intercreditor arrangements would regulate any cash outflow to the investors or to the managers under any redemption or similar mechanism, so the interaction of these provisions should again be carefully considered.

4.6 Ratchet

The nature of a ratchet was explained, in outline, in chapter 3.[35] In essence, a ratchet is an incentive mechanism which entitles the managers to receive a higher proportion of the exit proceeds if an exit is achieved beyond a particular 'hurdle' return rate for the investors. The hurdle rate is usually determined by reference to the internal rate of return (IRR) achieved by the investors as a result of the exit.[36]

Not all private equity deals involve a ratchet. However, where a ratchet is part of the transaction, the appropriate mechanism to calculate and deliver the effect of the ratchet will generally be set out in the articles. In simple terms, there are two ways of reallocating equity value through the ratchet:

(a) changing the equity ratios between the investors and the managers; or
(b) leaving the equity ratios as they are, but including provisions in the articles which apportion the price in favour of one class at the expense of the other class.

The commercial effect of each approach is the same, namely, to change how the equity proceeds are divided when compared to that which would have been the case but for the operation of the ratchet.

The traditional way of achieving the reallocation of value in a ratchet is to change the ratio between the two equity classes. For example, suppose that in a particular transaction the investor shares represent 75 per cent of the total equity shares (say 75,000 shares), and the manager shares represent 25 per cent (25,000 shares). If the ratchet is achieved, it will be necessary to reallocate the value between these classes. Suppose that, to reallocate the overall proceeds in the way envisaged by the ratchet mechanism (based on the actual exit value and the total return achieved by the investors) it is necessary that the equity proceeds are allocated in the ratio 50:50 rather than 75:25. To achieve this, the traditional method would be to leave those shareholders whose proportion of the proceeds is to be enlarged (i.e. the manager shares) as is, at 25,000 shares. The number of investor shares would then be adjusted so that, after adjustment, they stand in the correct ratio to the manager shares (by reducing their shareholding to 25,000 shares to achieve the 50:50 ratio). The 50,000 equity shares in the total issued share capital after such adjustment would then be sold at the same price per share.

35 See chapter 3, section 3.2.
36 For the meaning of IRR, see chapter 1, section 3.4.

There are two legal methods for achieving this reduction in the number of investor shares. One is to use a *redemption ratchet*: that is to say that the 50,000 investor shares that are to be removed from play are redeemed (usually at the original subscription price), leaving behind the desired 25,000 investor shares (or 50 per cent of the total equity when aggregated with the manager shares). This mechanism is more complex in that it requires the investor equity shares to be created as a redeemable class of shares from the outset, and also requires Target to have available distributable profits at the time of the exit to facilitate the redemption of the 'unwanted' investor shares. There can also be tax consequences of such a redemption ratchet, depending upon the precise tax affairs of the investors.

Accordingly, it has become more common to structure this form of ratchet as a *conversion ratchet*. Under this mechanism, the 50,000 'unwanted' investor shares are converted into a class of worthless deferred shares, leaving behind only 25,000 valuable investor shares. The worthless deferred shares are sold for a very low consideration at the time of the sale, and all other equity shares (i.e. the original 25,000 manager shares, and the remaining 25,000 investor shares) are sold at the same price share for share, having the desired result of 50 per cent of the equity proceeds being paid to the investors and 50 per cent to the managers.

More modern ratchet structures may achieve the ratchet reallocation not by altering the number of shares or the ratio between the two share classes, but instead by increasing the share of the exit proceeds that the favoured class will receive beyond a *pro rata* basis, with the proceeds payable to the other class reducing accordingly. This is often referred to as a *proceeds ratchet*. Typically, this is achieved by amending the return of capital and exit proceeds provisions referred to in section 4.5 above so that all the proceeds of sale are required to be paid into a communal bank account and then distributed between the two classes in whatever proportions the ratchet requires. So, on the example above, the relevant article would state that total proceeds of the sale are paid 50 per cent to the manager class and 50 per cent to the investor class irrespective of the number of shares in issue in each class. This has the same result as the redemption or conversion ratchets, but there is no need to change the number of shares as part of the exit mechanism; the managers simply sell their smaller number of shares at a higher price per share.

The taxation implications of the structuring of a ratchet must always be considered carefully. For example, as noted in chapter 3, for tax reasons ratchets are sometimes structured as a reverse ratchet – so that the managers' proportion of the proceeds reduces if the relevant hurdle is not met, rather than it being enhanced if the hurdle is met – in which case a proceeds ratchet is often considered to be a more straightforward way of achieving this. The taxation implications of ratchet mechanisms are considered further in chapter 9.[37] It

37 See chapter 9, section 4.4.

should also be borne in mind that a *proceeds ratchet* is not, in itself, a suitable mechanism to use where the ratchet is triggered on a listing, as it operates on the premise that the two (or more) different classes of equity share will have a different price. Typically, articles which use a proceeds ratchet on a sale or return of capital will also include an obligation that the share capital be reorganised at the time of a listing so that the shares stand in the correct ratios.

Whilst the legal mechanism that is used in the articles to give effect to a ratchet can be understood relatively easily (whether by redemption, conversion or allocation of proceeds), the drafting of a ratchet can often be complex. This is largely because the legal definitions required to determine how the IRR achieved on exit is measured can be quite cumbersome. It requires not only an explanation of what the IRR actually is, but also of the value which is to be attributed to the equity shares on exit (which is simple enough in the event of a sale of Newco for cash, but more complex where the exit involves deferred, contingent or non-cash consideration), and of the cash flows received by the investors during the life of the investment which should be included, or excluded, when calculating the IRR. A worked example is often helpful; whilst it should not replace comprehensive drafting in the articles, it can help to illustrate the impact which an IRR-based ratchet will have for the management proceeds on exit, and to check that the drafting which has been included in the articles will achieve the desired result.

4.7 Share transfer: background

The articles will invariably set out detailed provisions relating to the transfer of shares. It should be remembered that fully paid shares are freely transferable unless the articles restrict their transfer.

In the context of a private-equity-backed company, it is unlikely that shares will be freely transferable without any form of restriction. The precise arrangements found vary between private equity firms, and will also be affected by the relative size of the investment, and the proportion of the company's share capital which is held by the private equity investors. Details of the common features encountered in a private equity context are set out in the following sections.

4.8 Permitted transfers

The articles will usually specify certain transfers that may be made without pre-emption in favour of the remaining shareholders. These are generally known as 'permitted transfers' (or as transfers to 'permitted transferees'). The types of permitted transfer may vary according to the class of shares.

Where the class of shares is held by private equity investors, there will usually be a permitted transfer provision allowing transfers within the relevant private equity fund, and also (although not invariably) as between two or more separate funds managed by the same private equity manager. These mechanisms are often closely reviewed to ensure that the permitted transferees for the private equity shares do not allow what is, in effect, a sale to be achieved (by permitting transfers outside the relevant investor's controlled funds) without the managers having a right to tag along.[38] Where an investor is a company, rather than a limited partnership fund, it is common for a permitted transfer provision to allow transfers of shares to other members of that company's group (with a clawback provision requiring such shares to be transferred back to the original transferor, or another member of the transferor's group, if the transferee leaves the group).

Traditionally, the permitted transferees for manager shares have been their family members (the definition of which tends to include the manager's spouse, civil partner or issue) and family trusts. Although these provisions are quite often included, actual transfers to family members are less common in practice than had previously been the case, principally for tax reasons. Where transfers are permitted, it is not uncommon to have a limit on the total proportion of the manager's original stake that may be transferred in this way (typically, 50 per cent) to ensure a majority of the management shares remain in the hands of managers themselves. If the family relationship ceases (for example, on divorce), there is usually a mechanism which requires that the shares are transferred back to the manager (or to somebody who remains a permitted transferee of that manager) to ensure shares remain with individuals who continue to have a sufficiently close relationship with the manager in question.

One key point to bear in mind on transfers to family members is that it is highly undesirable for shares to be registered in the name of any person under the age of eighteen. This could cause considerable problems at the time of a sale, not least in the context of warranties (even in relation to the most basic warranties as to title to shares sold). If, for tax or other reasons, a manager wishes a family member under eighteen to have shares, this is better done behind a trust.

Transfers to family trusts may also be permitted by the articles. Where a family trust is involved for any reason, it is not uncommon for the private equity investors to reserve the right to see the trust deed, and approve the identity of the trustees. Their purpose in doing so is to check that the beneficiaries fall within the permitted transferees and, more importantly, to check that the trustees will be in a position to give warranties and other contractual comfort to a buyer as may be necessary at the time of an exit. As explained in chapter 13, it is usual for a manager giving warranties on the exit to seek to limit his liability to, at the very most, the consideration which he receives. Where some of that value in fact passes to family members or to family trusts, it is important that the value received on exit for the shares transferred remains available to support the warranties given; particularly given that the investors will usually

38 See section 4.13 below concerning tag along rights.

not provide any warranties other than as to title to their shares, which in itself significantly reduces the warranty cover available to the buyer on exit.[39]

If there is any employee benefit trust envisaged to provide incentives to second-tier managers or for the purpose of warehousing,[40] there will usually be further permitted transfer provisions to enable not only transfers to the trust, but also transfers on a change of trustee, transfers to equivalent trusts, and transfers to beneficiaries under the trust.

In respect of both the investor shares and the manager shares, there is usually a provision which enables any transfer to be made without pre-emption, provided that the holders of a particular majority of shares (or sometimes a particular majority of each class of equity shares) consents to the transfer. Where one group of shareholders can allow this outside transfer unilaterally (for example, the private equity investors) the interaction with the tag right needs to be carefully considered. A tag right is of limited use if the right can be effectively circumvented by way of a permitted transfer.[41]

There is also often a carve-out to permit a transfer to the company itself on a purchase of own shares without pre-emption (although, in this case, if the private equity investors do not in any event have enough voting strength to block a purchase of own shares at the shareholder level, they will be given a specific class right or investment agreement veto to prevent any such own share purchase without their prior approval).

4.9 Voluntary transfers

The articles will set out detailed pre-emption provisions which are to apply in the case of voluntary transfers (that is, transfers which do not fall within one of the permitted transfer categories applicable to the relevant shares). In practice, voluntary transfers are rare (except in certain private company structures which have an internal market, and, even then, separate bespoke mechanisms are usually included in the articles). Furthermore, the private equity investors may require any manager shareholders to seek their consent before they may offer their shares, in effect creating a 'lock-in' until such time as an exit arises, or that manager ceases to be an employee (and thereby triggers the compulsory transfer mechanism outlined in section 4.11 below). The main reason, therefore, for the voluntary transfer mechanisms in the articles is so that the subsequent provisions dealing with compulsory share transfers (as outlined below) can be applied using the same mechanism, with certain changes as are necessary to give them the desired commercial effect for those circumstances.

A typical voluntary transfer mechanism will require any shareholder who wishes to transfer his shares (in practice, it is only likely to be a manager or one of his permitted transferees) to notify Newco of his intention to transfer the

39 See further chapter 13, section 3.3.

40 On warehousing, see further section 4.12 below.

41 For tag rights, see section 4.13 below.

shares, the price at which he wishes to transfer the shares, and any identified transferee(s). Where a consent is required from the investors as outlined above, this must usually be sought before the notice is served.

Usually, there is a mechanism to enable the board (again, acting with investor consent) to agree the price at which the shares will be offered for sale with the transferor or, where such agreement cannot be reached, to refer the matter to an independent firm of accountants for valuation. The independent valuation will generally look to ascribe a fair value to the shares, as defined in the articles. That definition must be studied carefully; in general, this simply means a fair value that would be paid by a willing buyer to a willing seller for the shares but, notably, such valuation is often determined without applying a discount for any minority shareholding. Where the matter is referred to an independent valuation, a voluntary transferor is normally given the right to withdraw the transfer notice if he does not like the price determined. In the event that the voluntary transferor does elect to withdraw the transfer notice following receipt of the valuation, he will often be expected to pay some or all of the valuation costs.

The transferor is often entitled to impose a total transfer condition when serving a transfer notice. This means that the transferor is entitled to withdraw all the shares from the offer process, unless buyers are found for all the shares on offer. It should be noted that the withdrawal of a transfer notice and the imposition of a total transfer condition are generally not permitted on any application of the compulsory transfer mechanisms described in sections 4.10 and 4.11 below.

Once the price has been agreed or determined, and provided that the voluntary transferor has not withdrawn the transfer notice, Newco, as agent, will then offer the shares to those members who are entitled to pre-emption on the transfer under the terms of the articles. Usually, this is done so that the shares are first offered to holders of the same class of shares, and then to holders of other classes. In some cases, however, any shares offered on a voluntary transfer are offered *pro rata* amongst all shareholders irrespective of the class held. Since the shares in question are most likely to be manager shares, this second structure is more favourable to private equity investors than class-by-class pre-emption. Sometimes, there is only one offer, but a class-by-class approach nevertheless dictates how the shares should be allocated if the total number of shares applied for in response to the offer exceeds the number offered. It is therefore important to review pre-emption provisions with great care; but it is most usual to find that the allocation will be class-by-class and *pro rata* amongst holders of the relevant class of shares, with a proviso that no individual buyer should be allocated more shares than he has applied for.

The pre-emption provisions will set out the timescales in which offers must be made and accepted, and during which completion will occur following the pre-emption process being exhausted, as well as the documents to be provided and mechanics for delivery of the purchase price on completion. Usually, an irrevocable power of attorney is included in the articles to enable the transfer to be executed if, at that time, the transferor is for some reason unwilling or unable to complete the transfer documentation. This power of attorney is very important in a compulsory transfer situation.

One question which arises at the end of the pre-emption process is whether the transferor is then free to transfer any shares not taken to some other person (i.e. to an outsider). Usually, the articles will prevent this, or make it subject to the prior approval of the transferee by the investors (or by the board with investor consent). The remaining shareholders may well be unwilling to see an outsider holding shares in the company.

It is important when considering any transfer mechanism (and, in particular, a compulsory transfer mechanism) to remember that shares are transferable except and to the extent to which that right is restricted in the articles (or other relevant documents). Accordingly, the mechanism must be both tightly defined and clear. Any ambiguity will generally be interpreted in favour of freedom of transfer (which is usually not the result that the other shareholders, and in particular the private equity investors, would wish for).[42]

4.10 Compulsory transfer

Almost all articles adopted by a private-equity-backed company will contain a compulsory transfer mechanism. To be more precise, the mechanism is usually in fact a compulsory offer rather than a compulsory transfer; that is to say that in certain circumstances a member is required to offer up his shares in accordance with the relevant pre-emption process. It is unusual for there to be any contractual obligation on any other shareholder, or on Newco, actually to have to purchase the shares offered. In practice, there will of course be a strong desire to keep the shares within the existing shareholder groups (or to ensure they are available for incoming managers or employees) and, accordingly, one or more buyers are usually found for shares offered under a compulsory transfer mechanism, particularly where the transfer price is below market value; however, the party which is subject to the mechanism does not have a guarantee of that fact.

The most common situation that gives rise to a compulsory transfer is the termination of the employment of a manager, which is discussed in more detail in the next section. Other examples of compulsory transfer events include: shares held by a family member or family trust which are not offered back when required under the articles; shares held by a transferee group company of a member, if that transferee ceases to be a member of the group without transferring the shares back to the continuing group; and shares held by a member who dies, or who becomes bankrupt or subject to some other insolvency process. In all these cases, the mechanism usually provides that the board with investor

42 See *Greenhalgh* v. *Mallard* [1943] 2 All ER 234.

consent (or, in some cases, the private equity investors themselves) may serve a notice at any time within a particular period after the occurrence of the event requiring the member to offer up his shares following the pre-emption process described in section 4.9. In these situations, the price is most usually a fair value for the shares agreed or determined in accordance with the relevant provisions in the articles. In common with all compulsory transfer situations, the transferor is not allowed to withdraw the transfer notice if he does not agree to an independent valuation, and a total transfer condition is not permitted. Often, those shares which are the subject of a compulsory transfer notice are disenfranchised during the relevant pre-emption process.

4.11 Compulsory transfer on cessation of employment ('leavers')

As noted above, the compulsory transfer situation which is most frequently encountered in practice is that on the cessation of employment of a manager. Almost invariably, the articles contain a mechanism entitling either the board (with investor consent), the private equity investors themselves, or an investor director to require any manager who has ceased to be employed to offer his shares in accordance with the pre-emption provisions as described above. It is important to check the drafting surrounding the event which triggers the mechanism carefully. In some cases, giving or receiving notice to terminate employment is enough to trigger the power; in other cases, it arises only once the employment actually ends.

As in the other examples of compulsory transfer, the transferor is not permitted to withdraw his transfer notice if he does not agree with the independent valuation, and a total transfer condition is generally not permitted. The obligation to offer up shares generally also extends to any other shareholder who has received shares from that manager as a permitted transferee, such as family members and family trusts. For convenience, in the summary which follows, we will focus on the obligations of the manager himself, but it is important to bear in mind that these other members who received shares from him will also be subject to the same mechanism if that manager ceases to be employed.

Except in the case of a secondary buyout (where at least some of the manager's shares may not be subject to the compulsory transfer process),[43] the manager is generally expected to offer up all of his shares. The key question, therefore, is the price at which the shares should be offered. In the UK, two different approaches have historically been adopted in this area; namely

(a) conduct; and
(b) vesting.

It should be noted from the outset that the two approaches are not mutually exclusive, and accordingly a leaver mechanism may well include both conduct and vesting elements.

43 See further chapter 12, section 3.2.

(a) Conduct

'Conduct' for these purposes means that the circumstances in which the employment has ended are taken into account, under provisions in the articles usually described as Good Leaver/Bad Leaver provisions. The general principle is that a Good Leaver is required to offer his shares at fair value, whereas a Bad Leaver is required to offer his shares at the lower of the initial subscription cost paid for the shares and fair value. This means, in effect, that a Bad Leaver will get no upside on his investment. Clearly, the critical issue is therefore the precise definitions of the circumstances in which an individual will be treated as a Good Leaver or Bad Leaver.

In a simple structure where there are only two categories of leaver, it is customary to define one category (usually Good Leaver, perhaps unsurprisingly given that the articles are usually drafted in the first instance by the investors' lawyers), and then to define the other category as any leaver who is not in that defined category. This has the advantage that no situation can fall between the definitions. Good Leaver will normally include death, retirement at an agreed retirement age, serious disability and ill-health. Other examples often found include wrongful dismissal or unfair dismissal (although this latter definition in particular can be a difficult area for private equity situations for the reasons outlined in chapter 7[44]), and also any circumstances where employment ceases because the part of the business in which the manager is employed leaves the group (for example, if the manager is employed in a particular subsidiary or division, and that is sold off by the group and the manager goes with it).

In some situations Bad Leaver is defined. In those cases, it would generally include dismissal for material breach of service agreement (and sometimes also of the investment agreement), dismissal for gross misconduct, and other circumstances giving rise to a summary dismissal[45] right on the part of Newco (or the relevant group company employing the manager). A resignation on the part of the manager typically falls within the definition of Bad Leaver as well; investors are generally unsympathetic to any manager looking to walk away before the ultimate exit.

(b) Vesting

The other approach adopted to determine how the compulsory transfer mechanism will apply on cessation of employment is vesting. Under a vesting approach, the value of the shares vests over time; typically a period of three to five years from the date of the original investment (or the date of commencement of employment of the manager, if later).

Where vesting is applied in the UK context, this generally means that the 'vested' proportion of the shares are offered back on cessation of employment

44 See chapter 7, section 3.2.
45 See chapter 7, section 3.4, on summary dismissal.

at fair value (an equivalent treatment to Good Leaver status), and the remainder are offered at the lower of cost and fair value (equivalent treatment to a Bad Leaver). The precise structure of the vesting varies: often it is in annual stages (and not always in a straight line), but at the other extreme vesting may arise proportionately on a day-to-day basis. Vesting is seen as attractive because it removes some of the acrimony from the Good Leaver/Bad Leaver distinction, and it also means that a manager is rewarded for the time which he has spent in the business. Vesting can have a positive motivational effect by giving the manager a real sense of share value accruing, regardless of when or how his employment may later come to an end.

As noted above, these two approaches are often combined. Often, there will be a three-tier structure: Good Leaver (very narrowly defined); Bad Leaver (very narrowly defined); and Intermediate Leaver (defined as a leaver who is neither a Good Leaver nor a Bad Leaver). The idea here is that, at the extremes (for example, death for a Good Leaver and dismissal for gross misconduct for a Bad Leaver), conduct is taken into account. However, where the circumstances of the cessation of employment fall within the intermediate category (most obviously, dismissals in circumstances other than those justifying summary termination), a time vesting approach is applied. This compromise can be attractive both to Newco and the private equity investors on the one hand, and to the departing manager on the other. Often, the circumstances surrounding the cessation of employment do not clearly fall at either extreme. For example, the evolution of the business may mean that a particular manager no longer has the ideal skill set to carry out his role, although he is able to perform to a standard such that any dismissal would not clearly fall within the category justifying a summary dismissal. Also, personal or other issues may arise between managers themselves, or between the private equity investors and a particular manager, which means that it is in the best interests of the investment as a whole that the manager leaves in circumstances which do not justify a summary dismissal.[46]

The whole debate around compulsory transfer provisions, and particularly the Good Leaver/Bad Leaver definitions and any vesting timescale, will invariably be among the more emotive issues in the negotiation between the managers and the private equity investors. Investors often wish (or will be required) to set out their policy on this point at an early stage, as part of their equity offer letter or termsheet. Whilst it may be easy to portray the issue as a 'them and us' argument between the two classes of members, it is important to bear in mind that the dismissal of the entire management team at the same time is extremely unlikely. In practice, any cessation of employment is far more likely to apply only to one manager at any time. Further, particularly where there is a right of pre-emption applying on any shares clawed back which favours other

46 For more commentary on the circumstances in which a manager may be dismissed, and the implications that arise, see chapter 11, section 5.

holders of share in the relevant class, the remaining managers can actually benefit from the shares that come back either directly (in that they will have the chance to buy them) or indirectly (in that the shares may instead be available to motivate a successor to the departing manager). This latter point is an advantage to all shareholders in that, if the leaver's shares were not made available, all existing holders would otherwise have to be diluted by any new shares issued to motivate a replacement manager. This more pragmatic approach can often help in the negotiation of leaver provisions; that may appear to be a classic 'divide and conquer' strategy, but it also reflects the commercial reality if a departure becomes necessary for whatever reason.

4.12 Warehousing

A warehousing mechanism is often included in the articles to deal with the need for at least some of the shares to be available to motivate a successor to the departing manager. If the shares clawed back are not used (but simply pass on pre-emption, say to the continuing managers) then either all shareholders will be diluted by a new allotment of fresh shares to the successor, or the salary and other benefits package for that manager will need to be enhanced to compensate for the lack of equity, depressing the value of the shares already in issue. The form of warehouse mechanism used will vary but may include any of the following.

(a) A purchase of own shares by Newco, or 'buyback'. Such a mechanism can work, subject to Newco having sufficient distributable reserves at the time of departure. The shares bought back are cancelled (enhancing the equity stake of each of the other shareholders *pro rata*) at the time of departure, and are then, in effect, reissued as needed to the successor (diluting the other shareholders back down towards their original stake). This mechanism does have problems, however. An underperforming company may not legally be able to purchase the shares if it does not have distributable reserves (which is often the situation in which a compulsory transfer arises). A buyback also requires a payment of cash by Newco to the exiting shareholder, and the bank is likely to have a veto on such payment under the banking documents, particularly in an underperformance situation. Buybacks may also distort the proceeds that should be payable to each class of shareholder under any ratchet arrangement. Despite these limitations, the possibility of a buyback is often included as a potential warehouse mechanism, although it is usually supplemented by at least one other warehouse mechanism in case it cannot be used in practice.

(b) A direct transfer of shares by the leaver to the successor. This effectively avoids the need for a warehouse. Its use is also limited, however, because:

   (i) the successor may not have been identified, or may not as yet be ready to buy the shares;

(ii) it may not be intended that the successor gets all the shares on offer; and

(iii) the price payable to the departing manager may well not be the price at which the shares are to be made available to the successor, either in a Bad Leaver situation (because the lower cost price is too generous an offer to the new manager) or a Good Leaver situation (because the fair value paid in order to agree a compromise package with the departing manager is prohibitively expensive to the incoming replacement).

The use of a direct transfer is more likely on planned departures; i.e. where there is a period of time between the departure being agreed and its being implemented, during which succession planning can take place. In cases of dismissal, of course, such outcome is highly unlikely. Direct transfers may also be seen in underperformance situations, where the manager's shares are so clearly 'underwater' that a compromise deal can be agreed for the replacement to acquire the shares in a relatively short timescale. Where a direct transfer is possible, it is particularly important to ensure that any leaver's shares can be disenfranchised during the period from the date on which the manager first receives or serves notice to the date on which the replacement manager acquires the shares.

(c) A transfer to the private equity investors as a warehouse. This solution can cause some concern on the part of other managers as to whether the equity will actually be made available to a successor, and not just retained by the investors. It can also be a problem for the private equity investors, who may well be unable to fund the amount involved, or may be unable to acquire a higher proportion of the equity shares due to the accounting or taxation implications that arise if they do so. In practice, it is often a warehouse of last resort, especially if Newco cannot fund a purchase or the bank will not consent to Newco or an employee benefit trust being used.

(d) An employee benefit trust (EBT) is a common solution to the shortcomings of these other mechanisms. By ensuring that a leaver's shares are offered to an EBT, the shares can be made available for transfer to employees or future employees, or options may be granted over such shares, as becomes appropriate over time. The EBT needs to be funded to acquire the shares, usually by Newco either directly funding that amount by way of loan or capital contribution, or perhaps by Newco guaranteeing external borrowings by the EBT. There may be some legal and fiduciary duties for the directors to consider in relation to such funding, especially in an underperformance situation, and the question of whether consent is required from the bank may also be relevant. In many cases, however, the EBT can be an effective warehouse, and in practice it is the one most often seen, especially if there is a material price to be paid for the shares clawed back.

All of these warehouse mechanisms (apart from direct transfers to successors) also raise the question of what should happen to any clawed-back equity that is not used for a successor, perhaps because not all is needed for that purpose, or possibly because an exit occurs more quickly than was envisaged. If the shares are being warehoused by the private equity investors, there may be an arrangement that they will be transferred to the other managers (typically, at acquisition cost, plus an interest charge to reflect the carrying cost), in effect replicating the position that would have applied had the pre-emption provisions been applied on a class-by-class basis. Where the EBT is to act as the warehouse vehicle, the question of how any unallocated value in the trust should be distributed is a matter for the trustees, although management at least have the comfort that such proceeds may only be applied to the benefit of employees and not the investors. If a buyback is used, no adjustment is usually made if not all the shares are reissued, such that any advantage that arises from this is, in effect, shared *pro rata* by all existing equity holders.

4.13 Drag and tag

Private equity articles will usually include 'drag and tag' provisions (also referred to as 'drag along' and 'tag along').

(a) Drag rights

A 'drag' is a mechanism whereby, if a particular group of shareholders (often defined as a majority in value of the equity shareholders, or perhaps simply as the private equity investors) wish to sell their shares to a third party, all other shareholders can be compelled to sell on the same terms per share. This drag along right is supported by a power of attorney to ensure that the relevant share transfers can be delivered. A drag mechanism is very important to private equity investors and will be common to most transactions, with the exception only that it is not seen in situations where the private equity investors have a very small minority position (and therefore cannot exert enough influence to demand that a right is included). Even in those minority cases, investors may still insist on such a right being included on a postponed or conditional basis, for example a right that is only triggered after a period of time, or on an under-performance. Since the mid-1990s, there are very few private equity investors in the market who would agree to being locked into a Newco with no hard right to exit at some point in the future. Sometimes, other tactics are used to drive exit (an increasing, stepped dividend in favour of the private equity investors as outlined in section 4.4 above, for example); but a mechanism to focus the minds of other shareholders on the need for an exit is a key factor for most private equity investors.

Sometimes, whilst accepting the general principle of a drag, the managers will seek to fetter or limit it in some way, for example by proposing that the drag should not be available before a particular time period has elapsed (to enable the management team time for the Business Plan to be rolled out to a stage where a higher valuation may be expected). In other situations, they will seek to limit the drag so that it must pay in cash (so that the managers cannot be dragged into a non-cash consideration sale, for example receiving shares in a public limited company buyer). They may also seek to provide that the person acquiring Newco under the drag mechanism must be independent of the private equity investors, and that the offer must be *bona fide*. This final point is usually acceptable to investors, and indeed similar wording often appears in the first draft document issued by the investors' lawyers. There is often resistance, however, to the other provisions, which are generally viewed by investors as limiting a legitimate ability for the private equity investors to realise their investment. It is a question of bargaining power.

If any time or similar fetter is accepted on the drag, it would be usual to draft it so that the drag can be applied without such fetter if a particular proportion of the managers agree (this has the advantage of stopping any one manager blocking a sale, even if his colleagues wish to accept it), or in an underperformance situation (where the private equity investors will want the unfettered right to act and, if necessary, to drag all the shares into a sale). Assuming that the circumstances triggering underperformance rights[47] are defined in a way that marks a serious diminution in performance compared to the forecast in the Business Plan, or is linked to some other significant adverse event such as a breach of bank covenant, this latter point should not be objectionable to managers. If the business is underperforming to that extent, for all practical purposes the game is over, and it is unlikely that the managers would have any legitimate reason to wish to avoid a drag because it denies them realistic upside. The value of their shares in that situation is likely to have already substantially diminished, if not completely collapsed.

One issue sometimes raised by the managers is that they should have a right to match, whereby, if the private equity investor is willing to sell on particular terms, the managers have the right to be offered the chance to buy the shares from the private equity investors at that valuation (if they can), rather than being required themselves to exit the investment (for example, if the managers believe that a higher value can be achieved if they run the business to a later date). Of course, in practical terms, it is often unlikely that the managers would be able to fund the purchase of the private equity stake from their own resources. Accordingly, if a right to match is accepted, there would need to be a reasonable period of time to enable the managers to find alternative funding and for the new funders to carry out any due diligence into the business and the new Business Plan. The right-to-match deal would, in effect, be a secondary buyout.

47 See section 4.3 above.

Private equity investors generally do not like rights to match, for two reasons. The first is that it may distract the managers from the main sale process at the time of an exit (as would happen, of course, in any secondary transaction, but, if there is no hard right agreed upfront, the private equity investors can take a decision at the time as to whether they would wish to encourage the managers to pursue such an opportunity). The second, and in many ways the greater concern, is that the existence of a right to match may discourage other potential buyers from negotiating to acquire the business. They may believe they are simply a stalking horse, or may not be willing to wait for the right to match to elapse before their offer can be accepted and closed. The potential distraction of management time, and the likelihood that the managers are looking to pursue their own interests rather than facilitating the sale process, will also be of concern. If the management team is in a position where they are able to make an offer, they are always free to do so (subject, of course, to agreeing the necessary dispensation from their service agreements to enable them to pursue the opportunity). Therefore, the private equity investors would argue that no formal right to match is needed; if the managers at the time are able to make the best offer (whether best is determined in terms of price or deliverability), it is unlikely that the private equity investors would choose to accept an offer from a party whose offer is less attractive. For all of these reasons, a right to match is usually strongly resisted, and rarely given.

It is important that, if a drag right is agreed, the drafting catches what are often described as 'after-acquired shares'. For example, if the manager (or any other person for that matter) has any subscription or call options, or other right which means that he may acquire shares in Newco at the time of the sale or even afterwards, the buyer will also wish to have the right to acquire these shares. In other words, a future buyer will not allow any options to continue to subsist once they have acquired the company, and the private equity investors will want to ensure that the interests of any option holders are effectively delivered on sale. In practice, the person who has the right to subscribe for the shares is often paid a cash cancellation payment not to exercise the right. However, it is important that the drag provision is drafted in a way to catch any such after-acquired shares, not least if a cash cancellation agreement cannot be reached at the time of the exit.

(b) Tag rights

In many ways, a tag right is as important to the managers as the drag right is to the investors. A 'tag right' is the right for a minority shareholder to tag along with any exit by the other shareholders. The idea is that one or more shareholders should not be able to exit his or their investment(s) (demanding a premium for the sale of a significant or controlling stake), whilst the other minority shareholders are left as shareholders in the investment, and do not share in the value realised.

Historically, tag rights were common features of transactions where the private equity investors were minority shareholders, granted in favour of all minority holders including those investors. They have survived in favour of management as the trend has shifted towards investor-led and investor-controlled deals for various reasons, including:

(a) fairness and alignment of interests;
(b) management expectation based on market practice;
(c) arguably, there is no real detriment to the investor (see below); and
(d) the inclusion of tag rights is often seen as the mirroring trade-off to the managers accepting the drag rights that the investors will usually insist on.

In practical terms, there is little detriment to private equity investors in conceding a tag right, as any genuine sale to a third party is most likely to be designed to sell 100 per cent of the equity in any event. A buyer rarely wishes to acquire a majority controlling stake alongside other shareholders, particularly where those shareholders are managers who may otherwise feel aggrieved by the transaction. If the investors merely wish to complete internal transfers, so as to change the proportions of the equity held by their own funds for example, this is usually possible under the permitted transfer provisions,[48] provided that the transfers contemplated are between existing investors, or amongst funds managed by the same private equity house or syndicate.

There are some additional issues that can cause practical and technical problems on both drag and tag mechanisms without careful drafting.

(c) Threshold

The first issue is the setting of a suitable threshold for each mechanism, i.e. what proportion of the equity share capital of Newco must be sold before the drag or tag rights arise. On the drag, the relevant threshold is often a controlling interest (commonly defined as shares which together have over half the voting rights). Where the investors are in a minority, however, the threshold will usually be defined simply as an offer which is acceptable to all of the investors or, at worst, a majority of the equity shareholders of which the investors form part. It would be unusual for investors to accept a position where they themselves can be dragged, unless they have a particularly insignificant minority stake, and very little influence, for historical reasons.

This same logic is sometimes also applied to the tag right, and the apparent symmetry between the drag and the tag right aids this outcome. However, it is not that uncommon to find a lower proportion (say, 25 or 30 per cent) of the equity shares triggers tag rights, so that a significant minority sale would offer the other shareholders protection. In that event, the protection may be offered on a proportionate basis, such that, where investors wish to transfer shares

48 See section 4.8 above.

amounting to, say, 40 per cent of their holding, the other shareholders are able to join in and sell the same proportion of their equity shares on like terms. This proposition is occasionally accepted in negotiation, although it is not too common in mid-market deals where the reality is that investors are most likely to exit entirely, or not at all.

(d) Interaction with pre-emption rights

It is also important to check the interaction between the drag and tag rights and the pre-emption rights arising on any normal voluntary transfer. In the case of the drag, the articles should be drafted so that service of a drag notice (or any other exercise of the drag right) has the effect that no other right of pre-emption arises on a share transfer to the intended buyer (whether by the shareholders exercising the drag, or the shareholders being dragged). To apply normal pre-emption in a drag situation would, in effect, provide the dragged shareholders with a right to match.

Tag rights that bite at the same level as the drag right are normally worded so that no tag arises if the drag is exercised (which means that the pre-emption rights on a voluntary transfer normally fall away on the same basis). If for some reason the drag is not exercised (even though available), or if the tag arises on transfers at a threshold below the level at which a drag right can be exercised, then it is not as usual to disapply pre-emption. This means that the other shareholders get not only a tag right, but also a right to buy under the normal voluntary transfer mechanism. If this scenario is considered likely, then both the managers and the investors should consider carefully whether this is what they would want; in practice, however, such tag offers are unlikely to arise.

(e) Treatment of non-cash consideration

A further issue on drag and tag rights arises if the consideration offered on any sale of shares includes anything other than simply cash. Where, for example, the consideration includes shares or loan notes to be issued by the buyer, or involves a choice as to the form of consideration, then complications can arise. One possibility, more likely in situations where the private equity investor is a minority shareholder, is that the private equity investors may look to obtain priority for the cash element, leaving the managers with the less liquid forms of consideration. Beyond the practical difficulties of defining 'an equal price per share' if the investors get cash and the managers receive, say, consideration shares in the capital of the buyer, such a position will most likely be viewed by the managers as unfair.

Even if such a priority claim for cash consideration arguably has some merit to protect a minority private equity investor (who is less likely to drive the exit negotiations), this is much harder to argue where the private equity investor is in a controlling position and leads the sale negotiation. In those cases, managers may look to argue that they themselves would not wish to be dragged into some form of illiquid consideration – especially if there is investment or credit risk in the shares or loan notes, and no ready market in which to sell them – and seek priority on the cash consideration for their own shares.

Inevitably, the usual compromise is that each form of consideration will be split and shared amongst the sellers *pro rata* to their respective shareholdings. However, the final outcome on the apportionment of any non-cash consideration may be a function of the bargaining power of the parties, as well as their respective shareholdings.

4.14 Directors: appointment, removal and conflicts

The articles will usually set out more detailed provisions relating to the rights of the private equity investors to appoint investor directors and the chairman, as described in section 3.9 above. Similarly, if the private equity investors have a hard right to appoint or remove any director, this provision is often found in the articles. There are advantages to placing this mechanism in the articles, as the articles can confer a constitutional right upon the relevant member or members to exercise the power; if the member serves the relevant notice, then the appointment or removal takes effect automatically assuming the right is drafted correctly. For the reasons noted in chapter 11, it is preferable that a right of removal in particular is included within the articles should the investors wish to remove a director.[49]

Chapter 11 also describes the new statutory duties of directors in some detail, including the new statutory duty on all directors (including any investor director) not to allow himself to be in a situation where he has a duty or interest which conflicts or may possibly conflict with his duties to the company. As described in that chapter, many private equity investors have adopted the practice of including wording in the articles to approve, in advance, the situational conflict which can arise where a private equity director is also interested in, or has a duty to, the private equity investor or one of its other investee companies.[50]

4.15 Quorum

The articles will normally contain express quorum requirements for general meetings and for board meetings. The precise terms may vary, but typical provisions would be that a general meeting is not quorate unless a private equity investor is present by corporate representative or by proxy, and that (if there is an investor director in office) a board meeting is not quorate unless the investor director is present or agrees to it taking place in his absence. In deals where the private investors are in control or have a material minority stake, this is normally not viewed to be controversial. More challenging is the suggestion

49 See chapter 11, section 5.3.
50 See chapter 11, section 6.7.

sometimes made that a manager shareholder (or a manager as director) must be present as part of the quorum at the relevant meeting. This is normally strongly and successfully resisted by the private equity investors, principally because they do not wish the meeting to be delayed or its business frustrated by manager non-attendance. This is particularly sensitive if urgent action is needed, or some disagreement exists or is anticipated between the private equity investors and the managers.

4.16 Class rights for investors

As mentioned in section 3.12 above, the traditionally long list of class vetoes has been shortened in more recent transactions, mainly reflecting the shift from minority investments to institutionally controlled buyouts. However, it is still usual to see a brief list of class vetoes in the articles. Such provisions will usually state that the class rights attached to each class of shares may not be varied or abrogated without the consent of the holders of a particular majority (typically, 75 per cent) of that class, and will then state that for these purposes the rights attached to the investor class of shares are deemed to be varied or abrogated if certain matters are transacted without their consent. This has the effect of enshrining within the articles a list of fundamental matters that should not be transacted without investor consent.

A typical list of explicit class rights includes:

(a) changes to the authorised share capital of Newco or to its issued share capital (including consolidation, sub-division, redemption or buyback);
(b) reduction or return of capital;
(c) allotment of shares, or the granting of share options or share conversion rights;
(d) any change to the memorandum or articles of association of Newco;
(e) re-registration of Newco as a public limited company, or as unlimited; and
(f) registering any transfer of shares not permitted by the articles.

Such rights are often included within the separate list of investor consents included in the investment agreement as described in section 3.12; however, it is quite common to see the 'belt and braces' approach of these more fundamental concerns being included as a separate class consent as well, to provide an additional level of protection for the investors.

The question sometimes arises of whether any specific class rights should be given in respect of the manager shares. This will normally be resisted by the private equity investors, particularly if the investment is institutionally controlled. It is perhaps more likely that managers will be able to negotiate some explicit class rights in the context of a secondary buyout – due both to the increased bargaining power of the rolling managers, and to the more compelling need for the managers to protect their rolled investment. If any class rights are agreed to, there will usually be a mechanism to reduce or cancel these rights in a distress or underperformance situation.

5 Investment disclosure letter

A more detailed explanation of the role of the disclosure letter in the acquisition agreement as a defence to warranty liability is set out in section 3.1 of chapter 4. Those general comments apply also to the investment disclosure letter written by the managers to the private equity investors in respect of the warranties in the investment agreement. However, it is important to realise that, in practice, the investment disclosure letter is generally a much shorter document than its equivalent in the acquisition process. In some transactions, there may be no investment disclosure letter at all.

To understand the reasons for this, it is helpful to consider the typical warranties in the investment agreement (already highlighted in section 3.4 of this chapter):

(a) Warranties about the manager and his personal and business history. Depending upon how these are worded, it is often the case that no actual disclosure is necessary. Assuming the manager has a relatively clean history, nothing may need to be said. The former practice of asking detailed questions of the managers as part of the warranties (which would require detailed disclosure of matters such as employment history or previous directorships) has been superseded by the completion of a manager's questionnaire or declaration containing that factual information, with a straightforward warranty that the content of such document is true.

(b) Warranties on the preparation and reliability of the Business Plan. Some disclosure may be needed here but, generally speaking, if something has changed or come to light since the draft Plan was first prepared, most private equity investors would rather that the Plan itself was altered to be in a form that matches the warranty by the time the investment agreement is signed. Indeed, some private equity firms will not accept any disclosure against the Business Plan warranty for exactly this reason.

(c) Warranties on the accountants' report and other commissioned due diligence reports. Some disclosure may be needed here. Again, the private equity investors would rather that the managers fed any comments to the accountants or other reporters on the various drafts of the reports so that, by the time the final versions of the reports are issued, they can be covered by the warranty without the need for disclosures. However, if there is a difference of view (the managers believe one thing and the accountants or other reporters another), or if there is a time pressure which prevents the reports being completely updated, some disclosures will usually be accepted.

(d) A back-to-back warranty confirming the acquisition agreement warranties. Again, some disclosure may be needed here. However, if the managers are also involved in the preparation of the acquisition agreement disclosure letter, that letter should contain details of all relevant matters within their knowledge, and as a result there should be no need for separate disclosure in respect of the back-to-back warranty in the investment agreement.

Occasionally (as highlighted in section 3.5(a) of this chapter), the private equity investors will be persuaded to rely only on warranties from management in relation to certain historic matters relating to Target that the seller is not prepared to warrant in the acquisition agreement. In these cases, it is more likely that additional disclosures will need to be made in the investment disclosure letter on those matters. If this is the case, the disclosures against those warranties are clearly more likely to resemble the disclosures that would usually be found in the acquisition disclosure letter. Similarly, in those circumstances, the managers are more likely to seek more extensive and protective limitations in the investment agreement than they would seek on the more typical investment agreement warranties. This extends to seeking more extensive general disclosures in the investment disclosure letter akin to those found in the acquisition disclosure letter. In the absence of such warranties, however, the general disclosures contained in the investment disclosure letter will be far more limited, again to reflect the reduced need to qualify warranties of the nature described in paragraphs (a) to (d) above.

6 Loan note instrument

As outlined in chapter 3, most modern private equity transactions involve the investors subscribing for loan notes rather than preference shares, in addition to equity shares.[51] There are several different forms of loan note used by different investors and the tax, regulatory and banking issues that arise in respect of those different loan notes can create bespoke, and complex, drafting.[52] However, there are also some common features and issues that arise irrespective of the type of loan note used.

It is important to bear in mind that the terms of the banking documentation, in particular the intercreditor agreement, will regulate the ability of a private equity investor to exercise any of the rights in the loan note instrument, or the ability of the issuing company to honour it. As described in chapter 6, the investors are often not entitled to receive any payments until both the senior debt and any mezzanine debt has been repaid in full without the lenders' consent.[53]

51 See chapter 3, section 2.2(b).

52 See chapter 9, section 2.2, for details of certain types of loan note, and their respective tax treatments.

53 See further chapter 6, section 4.3.

6.1 Form of instrument/loan notes

The loan note instrument is usually a deed poll executed by the issuer which confers rights on the note holders for the time being, but does not require a note holder to be a party to it. The loan notes will usually be in registered form, that is to say that the issuer will maintain a register of note holders, and legal title is proved by entries in the register. The instrument will set out the relevant provisions for such registration. Once the relevant holder is entered in the loan note register the terms of the loan are prescribed by the loan note instrument, in much the same way as the rights of a shareholder are set out in the articles of association upon that shareholder being entered in the register of members.

6.2 Yield and repayment

The instrument will set out the rate of interest that is payable on the notes, how it is calculated, when it is paid (or compounded), and what happens if it is not paid. As noted above, whilst it is possible that loan note interest will be paid on the notes, it is more common for the intercreditor agreement to prohibit the payment of any cash interest (or at least a substantial proportion of it) until any prior-ranking bank debt has been repaid in full. In those cases, as outlined in chapter 9, interest payments may instead be satisfied by the issue of Payment In Kind notes ('PIK Notes'). These are simply loan notes, usually in the same form as the existing notes, which are issued to the existing note holders for an amount equal to the amount of accrued interest.

The loan note instrument will also set out details of when the loan notes are repayable and the terms and mechanics for this. Usually, there will be a bullet or single repayment of the loan notes scheduled for a future date which is at least twelve months following the date on which all prior-ranking bank debt has been repaid.

6.3 Events of default

The loan note instrument will include details of the circumstances in which note holders are able to demand repayment of the loan notes ahead of the normal due date. The precise terms will vary, but typical events include:

- late payment of interest (after a grace period);
- other breaches of the loan notes instrument;
- other breaches of the investment agreement or the articles (if included, this may be limited to breaches of certain clauses, and subject to a grace period to remedy first);
- cross-default in the event that any senior term debt becomes repayable early;
- insolvency or administration affecting the issuer (or sometimes other key members of the group); and
- a sale, listing, winding up or other exit event.

Whilst on the face of the instrument the principal sum outstanding under the loan notes may become repayable in particular circumstances, the intercreditor agreement will usually prohibit the investors from enforcing any rights to demand such repayment, at the very least until a standstill time period (typically, between 90 and 180 days) has expired, or more often until all prior-ranking debt has been repaid.

6.4 Transfer of notes

Loan notes are usually transferred simply by the completion of a stock transfer form for the securities, as for shares. A transferee of the loan notes may be required to adhere to the investment agreement, and will almost invariably be required to adhere to the intercreditor agreement with the bank funders.

Loan notes are freely transferable unless the instrument or some other agreement restricts or prohibits transfer. In a private equity context, the transfer of loan notes is often limited by the instrument. A typical restriction would be that the holder may only transfer notes to someone to whom it could transfer investor shares as a permitted transfer without pre-emption rights applying under the articles of association of Newco.

Formal stapling is sometimes also seen, so that the loan notes may only be transferred alongside the accompanying shares, and in the same overall proportions. However, this can lead to adverse tax consequences, as it can result in the interest on the loan notes being treated as a distribution for tax purposes, and therefore not tax deductible for the issuer of the note.[54] It is partly to overcome this issue that it is common to have more than one Newco in the deal structure. This then allows the investor loan notes to be stapled to shares in a company which is different to the company which issues the loan notes, as it is widely considered that such stapling does not result in the interest being treated as a distribution for tax purposes.

6.5 Changes to the loan note instrument and consents

Where the consent of the note holders is required to a particular matter under the instrument, a threshold will normally be set based on a proportion of the principal amount of loan notes in issue (usually 75 per cent), such that a consent at or above that threshold will bind all note holders. Typically, this requires a written consent at the relevant level, or consent being obtained from such proportion of the note holders by way of votes at a meeting of the note holders. If a meeting is contemplated, the instrument will normally set out the notice, quorum and voting requirements for such a note holder meeting, which are largely similar to the provisions typically included in a company's articles of association for shareholder meetings.

54 See section 209(2)(e)(vi) of the Income and Corporation Taxes Act 1988.

The most common reason for a consent to be sought is for a change in the terms of the instrument, for example to agree to a rescheduling of the principal sum or the reduction or deferral of interest payments as part of a restructuring in the event of underperformance.

7 Conclusion

We have seen in this chapter that the investment agreement and the articles set out the principal contractual relations between the investors on the one hand, and Newco and the managers on the other. Clearly, other documents are also relevant (most obviously the loan note instrument and related intercreditor documents, and the service agreements entered into by the managers), but these two documents set out the core terms agreed between the shareholders, and are designed to regulate in advance some of the situations which experience shows will often arise during the life of an investment. These documents also anticipate likely exit scenarios for the investment, and seek to provide appropriate protections and mechanisms to deal with them. Chapters 11 and 13 touch upon how the provisions in the investment agreement and the articles can impact on the issues encountered during the life of the investment and on exit, respectively.

It is worth bearing in mind, however, that there are limits on how effectively these contractual arrangements can protect private equity investors and other interested parties in every likely scenario. For example, the arrangements around cessation of employment will often protect Newco and the investors to a large extent if one or two of the managers leave (or are required to leave), but may be of little use if there is a complete breakdown in the working relationship between the investors and the management team as a whole. Similarly, although warranties can be important for bringing out information (in particular in relation to the affairs of Target) and enabling Newco, backed by private equity, to maximise its negotiating position and contractual protections against the seller(s), the investment agreement warranties will not provide an effective remedy if there is a material problem in the future with the investment.

The drag provides a useful mechanism to force an exit (and, in particular, to prevent a single or small number of shareholders blocking the ability to realise a 100 per cent exit), but the ability to drive the entire management class into the sale is unlikely to produce a good overall financial return for the investors if, in practice, the managers do not co-operate with the sale process or give warranties. Equally, the drag mechanism is of no practical use on an IPO or similar public market exit. The absence of active co-operation from all directors (executive and non-executive) in an IPO is show-stopping; unless, of course, the board composition can be changed to remove any reluctant directors.

The contractual documentation can provide a sensible degree of protection but, first and foremost, private equity is a relationship between the private equity investors and the managers. The ability of the documentation to protect the position of the private equity investors if they have backed the wrong business (or the wrong team) is, in the last resort, very limited; the importance of backing the right business, and the right team, remains critical.

6

Debt funding

1 Introduction

In this chapter, we turn to look in more detail at the debt financing aspects that need to be considered in the context of the acquisition of Target. We have already seen in earlier chapters that private equity investors will, in all but a small minority of situations, look to the debt finance markets for a significant proportion of the funding required to meet the purchase price of Target, and to supply the necessary working capital facilities that will support Target's operations post-acquisition.

The nature and extent of debt finance packages supporting private-equity-backed acquisitions has evolved rapidly in recent times and, it would be fair to say, since the turn of the millennium we have already seen debt financing structures go more than full circle in terms of quantum, leverage, pricing and gearing. This has been the result of a period of sustained growth in the private equity and leveraged finance markets followed by a rather abrupt retrenchment in the marketplace sparked by the widely reported credit crunch. As a result (and to ensure the reader has a full understanding of what has and will shape the nature of debt funding packages in the future), in this chapter we seek to provide a brief overview of market trends in this financing sector since the early part of the new millennium, together with a short analysis of how these trends were affected by the credit crunch which ensued in the latter part of 2007. That analysis and overview then sets the tone for (a) a more general consideration of how the third party debt funding package may look in the post-credit-crunch marketplace; (b) how investors might go about structuring their debt funding requirements; (c) how the approach to banks and financial institutions might be made; and (d) what the core terms and conditions of the debt facilities may look like.

To reiterate an observation that is made in chapter 3, funding structures (and therefore transaction structures) can vary depending upon the size and/or complexity of the transaction in question. As in the rest of this book, we have concentrated on the typical funding structures that would be employed in connection with the acquisition of a medium-sized domestic UK

Target[1] as the primary basis for discussion and analysis. However, brief details of the alternative funding structures used during the boom period to facilitate larger transactions is also included in section 6 below.

2 Debt finance in private equity transactions: an overview of recent history

In the second half of 2007 and throughout 2008, the UK banking sector (and, more generally, the global banking community) found itself in the midst of one of the worst financial crises in recent memory sparked by (although it would be unfair to say it was entirely as a result of) the collapse of the sub-prime lending market in America. To put that into context, in August 2007 we saw the first run on a major UK financial institution (Northern Rock plc) for approximately 140 years leading to its nationalisation; to date we have seen the UK government provide tens of billions of pounds in financial support to bolster the balance sheets of the big UK high street banks, and Lloyds TSB Bank plc (now the Lloyds Banking Group plc) and the Royal Bank of Scotland plc have been substantially nationalised through significant injections of government equity funding.

This book will not examine in detail the backdrop to or the reasons for this credit crunch, although many readers will no doubt be familiar with the genesis of the credit crunch and its effect on the global financial services sector through other works or the press. However, in the circumstances, it would be difficult to launch into a meaningful examination of the debt finance options available in the context of private equity transactions without at least providing:

(a) a brief overview of what the debt finance structures for equivalent transactions looked like in the early part of the new millennium;
(b) a quick synopsis of how high levels of liquidity and an increase in borrower power led to significant changes in the way transactions were financed; and
(c) a short commentary on the prognosis for debt funding in the future, as financial institutions and corporates work their way through the credit crunch, its aftermath and (perhaps) the resulting revised approach to leveraged debt financing that will prevail for the foreseeable future.

2.1 Why seek debt finance?

Debt finance has been and will continue to be a central feature of the vast majority of private-equity-backed acquisitions for several reasons:

(a) by introducing leverage into an acquisition structure, the absolute equity cash element required to be funded by the investors is kept to a minimum;

1 Say, with an enterprise value in the region of £50 million to £300 million.

(b) minimising the amount of the equity investment for each transaction enables the investors to engage in more transactions and therefore increase, diversify and balance their portfolio (with the core aim being to maximise the ultimate value of the portfolio);
(c) greater leverage helps investors to maximise the internal rate of return[2] on the equity funds invested when a successful exit (by sale or flotation) is achieved; and
(d) (although perhaps not at the forefront of the active considerations when looking to make an investment but nonetheless a benefit) minimising the amount of the equity investment in a particular transaction reduces the potential loss to the private equity firm (and its funds) in the event that the Target fails or is ultimately divested at a lower value than that at which it was purchased due to poor performance, to other external circumstances affecting the sector in which the Target operates, or to the macro-economic environment.

2.2 What was the benchmark funding package in the early part of the new millennium?

In the early part of the new millennium, debt finance packages for mid-market acquisitions in the UK had become quasi-standardised. Although there would inevitably be the usual level of negotiation around specific commercial and legal terms on a deal-by-deal basis, the basic parameters of what the debt financing would look like were broadly identifiable and would typically include the following:

(a) *Senior term debt.* Except perhaps in smaller transactions with a debt requirement below approximately £30 million, this would commonly be split into three sub-tranches (tranches A, B and C, roughly in the ratio 60:20:20) with seven-, eight- and nine-year maturities, respectively. Tranche A would amortise (i.e. be repayable in instalments) over the term; tranche B would be payable in two equal lump sum instalments after seven-and-a-half and eight years; and tranche C would be payable in one lump sum at the end of year nine. The cost of financing would be calculated by reference to a margin over LIBOR[3] (or, for debt denominated in euros, EURIBOR[4]) with the margins typically ranging from 2.25 per cent to 3.5 per cent across the three tranches of senior debt, with tranche A being the lowest-priced tranche.

2 For the meaning of internal rate of return (IRR), see chapter 1, section 3.4.
3 The British Bankers Association interest settlement rate, being a reference rate based on the interest rates at which banks can borrow unsecured funds in the London interbank market, as displayed on Reuters.
4 The Euro interbank offered rate, being a reference rate based on the averaged interest rates at which banks can borrow unsecured funds in the eurozone interbank market, as displayed on Reuters.

(b) *Senior working capital debt.* This would be available for a seven-year period on a revolving basis to provide the ongoing working capital funding for Target operations.

For mid-market transactions where the full debt funding requirement could not be met by sufficient senior debt appetite, the structure would also typically include:

(c) *Mezzanine term debt.* A tranche of term debt that is junior to the senior term debt and senior working capital debt, with a maturity extending one year beyond the final maturity date of the senior term debt. It would be repayable in one lump sum instalment after all the senior term and senior working capital debt had been repaid and discharged in full. The cost of mezzanine financing would also be calculated by reference to a margin over LIBOR (or, for debt denominated in euros, EURIBOR) with the margins typically ranging from 8 per cent to 12 per cent.

2.3 Growth market, increased liquidity and rising borrower power?

As outlined already in chapter 1, during the period from 2003 to early 2007 activity in the debt finance, corporate acquisition and private equity markets boomed. Private equity investors were able to raise larger funds, debt liquidity increased with new types of funder and financial product entering the marketplace (e.g. CDOs and CLOs,[5] hedge funds), competition among private equity houses for target businesses became fierce and competition among financial institutions to win mandates to arrange, underwrite and provide the debt financing packages supporting leveraged acquisitions was strong.

As a consequence:

(a) Sellers were able to demand premium prices for target businesses due to competition among private equity and, occasionally, trade bidders.
(b) Increased purchase prices were accommodated due to a greater availability of funding in a highly liquid debt market. Multiples of total debt to Target earnings ('leverage') moved gradually from a range of three to five times to a range of anything from five to (at least in 2006 and 2007) potentially ten or eleven times (and, in some well-publicised cases, even more).
(c) Larger debt finance requirements were met by increased appetite among funders for traditional senior and mezzanine products. In addition, new entrants to the funding market increased appetite for: (a) the longer maturity non-amortising tranches of senior term debt (which started

5 Collateralised debt obligation funds and collateralised loan obligation funds. These are funds established for the purposes of investing in a broad portfolio of collateralised debt with a view to taking a passive investment on a term basis but seeking to take advantage of superior rates of return achievable on the underlying loan asset.

to form a larger part of the senior term debt package[6]); (b) alternative forms of debt funding such as 'second lien debt' or 'stretch senior debt';[7] and (c) various additional types of junior mezzanine debt (for example, 'pay if you can' mezzanine, 'pay if you want' mezzanine or 'payment in kind' (PIK) mezzanine[8]). These instruments helped to plug the funding gap between the committed equity investment and the higher purchase prices being demanded. They also afforded bidders a greater opportunity to tailor their debt packages to help reduce the burden of expensive debt service on immediate Target cash flow generation post-acquisition. The increased risk associated with these types of debt instrument was offset by higher interest rate margins above cost of funding. However, confidence was high that a swift exit in a buoyant market would bring about a full redemption together with the associated commensurate rate of return.

(d) An ability to access greater debt funding meant that debt-to-equity ratios ('gearing') increased, with investors able to keep the size of their equity investment per deal relatively small (therefore increasing internal rates of return on investments upon successful exits).

(e) The increasing competition over time coupled with buoyant equity markets meant that investors were confident that successful exits from their investments could be achieved. In addition to the traditional avenues of exit (i.e. flotation or sale to a trade buyer), exits were also possible through secondary and (in some cases) tertiary buyouts of Target by other investors who saw opportunities to make equity returns by accessing larger and cheaper debt packages and growing Target revenues and profits. They, in turn, shared a similar confidence in achieving an eventual successful exit due to the same buoyant equity markets.

(f) Significant returns could be made relatively quickly by investors on investments. In some cases, this could be done pursuing a strategy of effective refinancing and re-gearing, taking advantage of increasingly favourable funding terms; in others, by exiting early through secondary buyout and taking advantage of the increasing competition among buyers. To a degree (although not always or as a general rule), these strategies could be pursued to achieve superior returns alongside or, in some

6 With the split between tranches A, B and C of the senior term debt moving gradually from 60:20:20 to, in some cases, 33⅓:33⅓:33⅓.

7 A tier of debt designed to sit in terms of priority between traditional senior and traditional mezzanine indebtedness. This concept originated in the US market and migrated across to the UK market around 2005.

8 These types of junior mezzanine are deeply subordinated tranches of indebtedness customarily providing for: (i) accrued interest to be (in some cases at the option of the borrower) rolled up and added to the principal amount of the loan; and (ii) a maturity for the principal plus accrued interest falling six months beyond the final repayment of the traditional mezzanine facility.

cases, in preference to the more traditional methods of creating value highlighted in chapter 1, such as seeking cost savings, increasing market share through investment or adopting buy-and-build strategies to create business synergies.[9]

2.4 The crunch point

Arguably, a funding boom in a discrete sector was always going to burst. As it turned out, it was a funding boom in a sector other than the mergers and acquisitions sector which brought about the onset of the credit crunch in August/September 2007. The collapse of the American sub-prime mortgage market was the first domino to fall.

Things moved quickly in a global banking sector that is based on a high degree of trust in the stability of other financial institutions in the marketplace. The collapse of the American sub-prime mortgage market led to a loss of trust among financial institutions. Financial institutions were not prepared to lend to other financial institutions as they had no immediate visibility on their level of exposure to irrecoverable sub-prime debts and therefore, more generally, on their financial stability. As a consequence, the interbank market that funds and essentially underpins global lending activity ground to a halt.

As the events unfolded over the fifteen months following September 2007, the full extent of the severity of the financial crisis became known. During that period, the most immediate consequences on the leveraged acquisitions market were:

(a) *Rapidly contracting liquidity.* Banks were not prepared to lend to each other, and, within themselves, financial institutions were counting the cost of their exposures, the level of their write-downs and the corresponding impact on their own capital pool and ability to lend. Consequently, overall levels of funding availability became very limited.
(b) *Withdrawal of certain funders from the market.* The credit crunch and its immediate financial consequences caused certain key players (such as the main Icelandic banks, who had been very active lenders in the UK buyout market) to withdraw from the market due to their own financial condition.
(c) *Financial institutions began to re-assess risk in the context of every transaction.* They either began to shy away from funding highly leveraged (and therefore technically higher risk) transactions, or demanded higher pricing on the debt packages they were prepared to offer in order to more appropriately price the risk.
(d) *The debt syndication markets contracted.* Even to the extent that a funder was prepared to countenance funding a particular transaction they were no longer prepared to underwrite the full amount of funding required.

9 See chapter 1, section 3.4.

The turmoil in the debt markets meant that they could no longer be confident of reducing their exposure and transaction risk through a successful post-completion syndication of the debt to other market participants.

(e) The appetite for some of the higher risk alternative financing products dwindled:[10] these products had become prevalent between 2003 and early 2007, but, after then, their popularity dwindled and funders retrenched to the more traditional products.

In summary, lack of liquidity forced higher pricing, lower leverage multiples, lower gearing and a need for investors (except for the smallest deals that could be funded on a bilateral basis by one senior lender) to form 'clubs' of banks in order to reach their desired debt funding quantum. This in turn led to more protracted transaction processes, a longer and more difficult negotiation to agree terms, and a higher risk of failure if one or more of the banks in the club could not get the requisite credit approval.

2.5 So, what now?

Since 2008, the UK has been in the midst of a recession that some commentators have forecast may last for at least twenty-four months, and possibly longer. There will no doubt be activity during this recession, but it will be muted and at a slower pace than before with a general flight to quality. Investors will most likely refocus on seeking investment opportunities where value can be clearly created using the traditional methods of streamlining, lowering cost bases, driving business synergies or perhaps adopting slower-burn buy-and-build strategies (as well as the management of their existing investments during such difficult times).

As for the availability of debt finance, immediate indications seem to be that: (a) there will be a medium-term readjustment in approach to leverage multiples and gearing; (b) pricing of debt packages will be increased to levels that more appropriately reflect the risk associated with a leveraged credit; and (c) there will be a retrenchment towards the more traditional forms of debt structuring.

The pricing that will attach to the senior and mezzanine debt tranches in future is very much dependent upon the amount of debt that is being provided, the financial strength of the Target group, the appetite among the senior and mezzanine finance markets to invest in the particular transaction, and the prevailing market and sector conditions.

Given the challenging nature of the market conditions that have prevailed since the credit crunch, it is difficult to provide meaningful guidance as to the pricing that may be achieved in respect of senior and mezzanine debt. The small number of mid-market transactions that have taken place in the early

10 For example, second lien debt, junior mezzanine debt, high-yield bonds and securitisations, as mentioned in section 2.3.

part of 2009 suggest that debt providers are looking for a margin of between 3 per cent and 5 per cent over cost of funds in the case of senior debt, and a margin upwards of 15 per cent over cost of funds in the case of mezzanine debt. These figures are necessarily only a guide, and the actual margins that may be negotiated in the context of a particular deal will be dependent upon many factors.

3 Overview of debt funding

3.1 Debt structures

In chapter 3, we considered the various corporate structures that are typically employed in a mid-market leveraged buyout of a UK Target. We will use those structures as the basis for our analysis of the potential debt funding package that may ultimately be put in place. The level of debt funding that can be obtained for a particular transaction will necessarily be a function of the size of the acquisition, the perceived credit profile and financial prospects of the Target, the results of the financial modelling that is prepared by the investors, prevailing market conditions and, more generally, appetite among the bank lending community.

As discussed in chapter 3, the deal structure for a smaller acquisition where the bank funding comprises only senior debt can be kept relatively straightforward and the debt funding will likely be provided directly to the bid vehicle.[11] In situations where multiple layers of third party debt funding are required (including mezzanine finance) it may be necessary to employ a more complex acquisition structure so as to achieve the structural separation of the different tiers of indebtedness.[12] To allow for the possibility of multiple Newcos in the structure, this chapter will again adopt the Topco, Midco and Bidco terminology used in Figure 3.4 in chapter 3 where relevant.

3.2 Scoping the debt funding requirement

First and foremost, it will be necessary to give full consideration to the type and extent of the debt financing that will be required both to fund the acquisition and to provide for the ongoing operational needs of the Target. This will include some or all of the following:

(a) *Term funding.* Sufficient term debt will need to be available to Bidco in order to: (a) meet the purchase consideration that is due and payable in cash to the seller(s); (b) to pay all costs and expenses that will be incurred by Bidco, any Midcos that feature in the eventual corporate structure and Topco in connection with the making of the acquisition; and (c) to enable

11 See Figure 3.1 in chapter 3.
12 See Figure 3.4 in chapter 3.

Bidco to repay and discharge any existing indebtedness of Target so that it is acquired on a debt-free basis. Debt providers will almost invariably insist that Target is taken debt-free since they will wish to avoid having to spend time and money negotiating potentially complex intercreditor arrangements with the incumbent financial creditors. In addition, they will want to ensure that the assets of Target are free from encumbrances which may have been given in favour of such creditors so that the new debt funding package takes the benefit of full first-ranking security over the assets of Target. The term funding will be made available either by way of senior facilities in its entirety, or as a combination of senior facilities and mezzanine facilities.

(b) *Working capital funding.* Following completion of the acquisition, Target will most likely need access to working capital to facilitate ongoing business operations. Thought will need to be given to the currencies in which working capital may be needed and the potential requirement for one or more members of the wider Target group to accede to the debt facility documentation as borrowers, so that they can directly draw on any working capital provision. The working capital facilities will be made available under the terms of the senior facilities agreement and will usually comprise revolving credit facilities for drawing in cash. They may also afford Target the ability to call for the provision of bank guarantees and letters of credit in place of cash drawings in the event that such financial instruments are required to be issued in favour of contract counterparties in the ordinary course of business.

(c) *Other ancillary facilities.* Other types of facility may be required. These may comprise overdraft facilities, guarantee facilities, bonding facilities, BACS facilities, credit card facilities and/or foreign exchange facilities. The determination as to any ancillary facilities that may be required will, by necessity, be made on a deal-by-deal basis.

(d) *Capital expenditure facilities.* It might be the case that Target is engaged in a business requiring significant immediate or short-to-medium-term capital expenditure investment. Alternatively, the Business Plan may involve a degree of capital expenditure investment in order to improve operations, update or acquire and fit out premises, increase production capacity, and so on. To that end, the debt funding may need to include specific provision for facilities to fund capital expenditure over the first two or possibly three years following completion of the acquisition.

(e) *Future acquisition facilities.* Creation of value in the Target post-acquisition may be premised upon a buy-and-build strategy or an ability to purchase other smaller complementary businesses that have been identified in order to achieve business synergies. As a result, it may be necessary to consider how those potential acquisitions will be funded and whether a specific debt funding line for future acquisitions should be negotiated.

3.3 The financing process

It is difficult to separate the debt financing process from other aspects of the transaction. Often, work streams will cross over each other as, to some degree, the outcome of one work stream may impact upon others and therefore it will be an evolving process. However, once the nature and scope of the preferred debt financing package has been formulated, the next step will be for the investors to approach potential funders to assess their appetite to provide financing at the required levels and to obtain indications as to pricing and terms.

To obtain these initial soundings from funders, the investors (or, possibly, the seller(s), who increasingly look to secure debt funding as part of an auction process) will prepare and circulate, against signature by the funder of a confidentiality letter, a short heads of terms together with an information memorandum which describes the proposed transaction, gives some background information about the financial performance of Target, and sets out details as to the Business Plan base case. The funders would then be requested to submit termsheets setting out in detail the indicative terms and conditions on which they would be prepared to provide the debt funding. Those termsheets would be negotiated, and ultimately the funder(s) offering the most attractive terms would be selected.

During the period of boom prior to the credit crunch, a different practice developed. Due to competition among funders being high, to some degree the investors could dictate the terms on which they required the funding to be provided. Consequently, in place of asking the funders to submit termsheets, long-form detailed termsheets were prepared and submitted to the potential funders setting out the optimum terms, conditions, pricing, covenant package and so on required by the investors. The funders would then be invited to mark up those provisions that they could not accept. Again, the termsheet would be negotiated with each funder, and ultimately the funder(s) offering the most attractive terms would be selected.

As noted in the commentary at the start of this chapter, current market conditions and liquidity constraints mean that the balance of negotiation power is highly likely in the short to medium term to rest with the banks.

3.4 Finance: bilateral, arrange-and-underwrite, or club?

Depending upon the amount of the desired debt financing, it may be that one funder is prepared to provide the debt financing on a bilateral basis. Consequently, for smaller mid-market acquisition transactions, it is quite often the case that the full quantum of the debt funding requirement will be provided on a senior secured debt basis by one funding bank. However, this would typically only be the case in situations where the total debt requirement does not exceed, say, £15 million or £20 million (or possibly, in some cases, up to £30 million), representing the levels at which banks operating in the UK mid-market are comfortable taking and holding a debt position on their balance sheet in relation to any given mid-market leveraged buyout.

For larger mid-market transactions, where the financing requirement may be significantly in excess of these sums, the preferred practice for the investors would be for one or two financial institutions to arrange-and-underwrite the financing package. In other words, pursuant to the competitive tender process described above, each potential funder would be asked to set out the terms on which it would be willing to provide the full amount of the debt with a view to syndicating the debt among a wider group of lenders following completion of the acquisition. From the perspective of the investors, this approach has the advantage that, once the preferred sole or joint arranger(s) and underwriter(s) have been selected, there would be only one or two counterparties to negotiate with in order to agree and finalise the funding terms and documentation – leading to greater speed of process.

Historically, financial institutions have been willing to assume arrange-and-underwrite positions since they had a high degree of confidence that the debt could ultimately be syndicated, provided they had concluded the financing on terms that fell within sensible market parameters. Successful syndication would reduce their exposure to a more acceptable level that they are prepared to take and hold on their balance sheet in relation to any one transaction. Clearly, this level of confidence will depend to a significant degree on the prevailing appetite among financial institutions to purchase the debt and the general levels of liquidity in the marketplace.

As we have already noted, one of the effects of the credit crunch has been a period of contracting liquidity and therefore contracting syndication markets. Some of the financial institutions that assumed arrange-and-underwrite positions on deals shortly before September 2007 found that they could not ultimately sell the debt and were left with large balance sheet exposures to individual transactions. The result has been an increasing move towards club financing deals, that is to say, a situation where a club of banks is formed at the outset whose aggregate take-and-hold positions meet the full financing requirement for the transaction. For example, if an investor is looking for £100 million of debt finance, it might need to form a club of between four and six banks, each funding between £15 million and £25 million. Generally, this has led to more difficult negotiations and more protracted funding processes, as all members of the club become involved in the detail of the negotiation and documentation of the final financing terms.

It would be fair to comment that, since the credit crunch, financial institutions remain wary of arrange-and-underwrite positions, particularly on larger mid-market transactions. This will not be eased to the extent that recession bites and general liquidity remains tight. Consequently, we can expect to see a higher proportion of syndicated financings done on a club basis throughout the period of recession being experienced in the UK since the credit crunch.

3.5 Due diligence on the Target

The due diligence process will typically be conducted alongside the financing process. However, in some cases (particularly given the prevailing challenging market conditions), the investors may wish to be comfortable that they have taken initial soundings from potential funders which suggest there is funding appetite before incurring significant expenditure on detailed diligence.

The debt providers to Bidco will be very interested in the results of the pre-acquisition due diligence since they will be (a) looking to the cash flows and financial standing of the Target as their only source of repayment of indebtedness, and (b) reliant upon the assets of the Target as their only security for the repayment of their debt. One must also remember that the debt funding will often form the larger part of the overall (debt plus equity) funding being provided to Bidco. Consequently, the debt providers need to be able to satisfy themselves that their investment is prudent.

As a result, the private equity investor (both from its own investment perspective and from the perspective of achieving the optimum debt financing package) needs to ensure that all major risks have been highlighted as part of the due diligence process and appropriately dealt with – perhaps by being factored into the purchase price for the Target (possibly by means of purchase price retentions or staged payments), or otherwise adequately allocated between Bidco and the seller in the legal documentation (through warranties and indemnities).[13]

4 Financing documentation

The negotiation of the financing documentation will reflect, among other things, the terms and conditions set out in the funding termsheets and the results of the due diligence review. Set out below is an overview of the principal provisions of the core financing documents.

4.1 Senior Facilities Agreement

The Senior Facilities Agreement (SFA) will set out the terms and conditions attaching to the provision of the senior debt facilities required for the transaction. This will invariably be the principal (and, in some cases, the only) form of debt finance in a UK mid-market acquisition transaction. The agreement will customarily be prepared using the Loan Market Association precedent for leveraged finance transactions.

The SFA will include the following provisions:

(a) Facilities available

The facilities provided to Bidco will normally include:

(a) Term facilities, the proceeds of which will be used to pay the acquisition consideration, discharge the acquisition costs incurred by Bidco,

13 For an overview of due diligence, see chapter 2, section 4.

any Midcos and Topco, and discharge all existing indebtedness within the Target group. In many cases, the term facilities will be split into more than one tranche, with each tranche attracting different terms and conditions principally as to repayment maturity and interest rate.

(b) Revolving credit facilities to fund the ongoing working capital requirements of the Target group. The SFA will contain provisions allowing the revolving credit facilities to be drawn by way of cash advances, letters or credit or bank guarantees, and also by way of other ancillary facilities (as described in section 3.2 above).

(c) Possibly, capital expenditure facilities and future acquisitions facilities to the extent required or desirable in the context of the transaction (and also as described in section 3.2 above).

Bidco will be the principal borrowing party under the SFA since it is the vehicle that needs the term facilities to fund the acquisition. There will also be provisions allowing members of the Target group to accede to the SFA post-acquisition as borrowers. This will facilitate a direct ability on their part to access the working capital facilities that have been made available.

(b) Drawdown period(s)

Based on the different purposes for which each of the facilities is to be used, the facilities will be available for drawdown over differing periods (referred to as the 'Availability Period' in each case):

(a) The term facilities will be available for drawdown for a relatively short period since they will be used in full immediately upon the completion of the acquisition. In the case of acquisitions of private companies, it is not unusual to have the SFA executed on the day on which the acquisition is due to complete, or shortly before. As a result, the Availability Period for the term facilities may be as short as five days or even less. Where a private acquisition contemplates a split exchange and completion (for example, because of competition clearance issues), the period for which the term facilities are available for drawdown by Bidco will need to be negotiated accordingly. This is because the SFA will generally be executed at exchange to ensure the necessary funding is available when the sale and purchase agreement is signed, but the funds will not be needed until completion. In this context, it should be noted that the debt providers will not want to have the commitment risk for the term debt on their balance sheet for a longer period of time than is absolutely necessary due to their risk-weighted capital regulatory requirements. The investors can therefore expect funders to require any periods between exchange and completion to be kept to the minimum possible. Different requirements as to Availability Periods arise in relation to acquisitions of public companies and these are looked at in more detail in chapter 10.[14]

14 See chapter 10, section 4.2.

(b) The revolving credit facilities will be available for a longer period (typically, co-extensive with the term of the senior term facilities) as they represent the ongoing working capital funding that is supporting the costs incurred in connection with the ongoing operations of the Target group.

(c) Any capital expenditure facilities or future acquisitions facilities will most likely be made available for a period of one to three years. This is because they are principally being used to ensure that identified capital expenditure investment and/or other identified acquisition targets (where a buy-and-build strategy is being pursued) can be made and/or purchased (as the case may be) within a sensible period following the acquisition.

(c) Repayment and interest terms

The repayment profiles of the different facilities will vary. As a result, the interest costs attaching to each of the facilities will also vary commensurate with the overall risk analysis and rate of return profile modelled by the debt providers:

(a) Depending upon continued market appetite for tranches of longer maturity, non-amortising senior debt instruments, and depending upon the total quantum of term debt required by Bidco, the senior term debt may well be split into two or three tranches. In contrast to the position prior to the credit crunch (as described in section 2.2 of this chapter), indications in the first half of 2009 are that appetite for the tranche B and tranche C facilities of old[15] will be scarce. As a result, the senior term facilities being offered are predominantly single tranche amortising facilities with a term of no more than five years. There are, however, some signs that dual tranche structures may be contemplated whereby a second tranche of non-amortising debt with a tenure of six years is also offered. The shape of the senior term debt package will no doubt evolve and change as financial institutions look to structure their financing packages most appropriately as the economic climate and deal activity improves.

(b) The revolving credit facilities will be drawn and repayable over shorter periods of time (commonly three or six months and set in line with the time periods used to calculate the interest payable in respect of those loans). However, Bidco (or such other member of the Target group that is the borrower) will have the ability (subject to there being no subsisting event of default under the SFA) to *roll over* each loan on its repayment date into a new loan. This avoids the physical repayment and redrawing of cash advances that continue to be required to fund the business.

15 See the description of these tranches in section 2.2 above.

(c) Capital expenditure and future acquisitions facilities will probably amortise in line with the senior term debt. However, in each case, the amortisation will only commence once the Availability Period for each such facility has expired (potentially, two or three years after completion of the acquisition). Since the total amount that will actually be drawndown under those facilities may not be certain when the SFA is signed, it may well be the case that the SFA provides for a straight-line amortisation of the actual drawn debt under each facility from year two (or three) on the same semi-annual repayment dates as those applicable to tranche A. It should be noted that securing these types of facility has become more difficult. The prevailing economic climate since the credit crunch has led to financial institutions being more alert to how and where they tie up their capital base. Whilst it may still be possible to secure these types of facilities where there is a clear and imminent intention to fund capital expenditure or pursue strategic and clearly identified acquisition opportunities, investors will likely struggle to secure these types of committed facilities where plans are less certain and the aim is more to achieve funding flexibility for opportunities that may (but are not certain to) arise in the future.

In all cases, interest will be payable at a specified margin over LIBOR (or possibly EURIBOR in relation to drawings in euros) and some commentary as to likely levels of pricing is set out in section 2.5 above.

(d) Mandatory prepayments

The SFA will set out provisions indicating those circumstances where Bidco is required to procure the mandatory prepayment of the facilities prior to their scheduled maturity. Customarily, these circumstances will include the following:

(a) *Sale, change of control and listing.* The funders have agreed to provide specific financing for the acquisition of the Target group by a certain private equity firm that they are prepared to support against the agreed base case model in the Business Plan. To the extent that the Target group (or indeed Bidco or Topco) is sold by the private equity firm to a third party, the debt providers will want to ensure that their facilities are prepaid and discharged in full. The same is true where, as opposed to a complete divestment of the group, there is a partial divestment or co-investment which results in a change in control of the group (most obviously, where a private equity firm's funds cease to hold sufficient shares to control a Target which it previously controlled). The rationale is that the new owners or new controlling shareholders may have different plans for the business. They will likely have different funding requirements and may want to pursue a growth and development strategy that is different to the one that was originally presented to the funders and that underpinned their financial analysis, their risk assessment and, overall, their willingness to invest in the transaction by providing the debt funding.

(b) *Sales of assets.* The undertakings given by Bidco in the SFA (discussed below) will limit the circumstances in which members of the group can sell their assets. The reasoning is quite clear: the assets will form a core part of the value of the group and be required for operational purposes. As noted earlier in this chapter, the debt providers are reliant upon the operational revenues and assets to support and provide collateral for the funding they have made available to Bidco. They will therefore be conscious not to allow valuable assets or assets that are important to the operations of the business (and therefore the generation of revenues) to be sold. That said, there will be certain negotiated and agreed exceptions to this general prohibition which will permit certain categories of assets to be sold to third parties (for example, assets that are required to be sold in the ordinary course of trade, obsolete and redundant assets, assets connected with or related to non-core businesses etc.). Even where certain types of assets are permitted to be sold, the debt providers will seek to have the proceeds of sale reinvested in replacement assets or other assets useful to the business. To the extent that proceeds are not so reinvested or perhaps exceed a certain agreed material value, the debt funders will expect those proceeds to be applied in prepayment of the debt rather than used for other general corporate purposes within the business or to repay the investors.

(c) *Insurance proceeds.* For equivalent reasons to those set out in paragraph (b) above, insurance proceeds received by the group in connection with the loss or destruction of, or damage to, assets will be required to be used in prepayment of the debt facilities unless they are applied in reinstatement of the relevant assets or in the purchase of replacement assets. It will be necessary for the investors to consider whether certain types of insurance proceeds should be excluded from the prepayment provisions. For example, those proceeds that are required to be paid across to third parties under public liability insurance and those proceeds that are intended to compensate the group for loss of earnings or business interruption.

(d) *Proceeds of claims against the sellers of the Target group.* Although it is preferable to identify potential problems through the diligence process, Bidco will typically have the benefit of certain indemnities and warranties in the sale and purchase documentation as described in chapter 4. Claims under those indemnities and warranties will, to a large degree, represent compensation to Bidco for issues that have resulted in a loss of value in the Target group. Since the quantum of the debt funding will have been premised upon an analysis of that value, the debt providers will look for the proceeds of any claims against the seller(s) to be passed back to them in the form of a mandatory prepayment of the debt. Investors will need to consider carefully whether to negotiate certain materiality limits (below which no prepayment is required) or indeed whether certain types of claim (for example, claims for unpaid tax liabilities from prior years) offset liabilities to third parties and must therefore be excluded from the prepayment obligation.

(e) *Excess cash flow.* In the context of leveraged acquisitions, the debt providers will be very keen to see the risk de-leverage quickly. As a result, they will usually look to ensure that, where the group generates excess cash flow in a given financial year, a proportion of that excess cash flow is used to retire (i.e. prepay) the debt. Negotiating the exact percentage of excess cash flow that is required to be applied in prepayment will be dependent on how highly leveraged the transaction is at the outset. It may be possible to negotiate that the percentage threshold reduces as the transaction de-levers and certain reduced leverage multiples are achieved.

(e) Representations and warranties

Each member of the group that is a borrower and/or guarantor of the debt will be required to give certain representations and warranties for the benefit of the debt providers in relation to itself and each of its subsidiaries. Figure 6.1 lists the matters that customary representations and warranties would seek to address in respect of the borrower and its group.

Clearly, the full language of the actual representation or warranty will be negotiated based on the facts and the results of due diligence. In the context of a particular transaction, additional representations may be included to deal with specific matters relating to that transaction, specific circumstances affecting the Target group or the type of business in which it is engaged. All of the representations and warranties will be deemed to be made on the day on which the SFA is signed, and (if different) the day on which the acquisition completes and the facilities are first drawndown.

A smaller sub-set of the representations and warranties (typically, being those that relate to matters that are not adequately covered by the positive and negative undertakings set out in the SFA: see below) will be deemed to be repeated on the date of each other drawdown of the facilities, and on the periodic dates throughout the term of the facilities upon which payments of interest are due. The aim of these representations and warranties is really to provide an early warning system for the debt providers. A breach of representation or warranty will permit the acceleration and/or cancellation of the facilities in

- it is duly incorporated and validly existing
- its obligations under the SFA and other financing and transaction documents are legal, valid and binding
- entering into the financing documents will not conflict with other obligations binding upon it
- it has the power and authority to enter into the financing documents and the other transaction documents
- the law chosen to govern the financing documents is valid and the documents will be admissible in evidence
- it is not insolvent
- no stamp duty or filing taxes will be payable in connection with execution of the financing documents
- none of the information it has provided in relation to the transaction is misleading
- its financial statements give a 'true and fair' view of (if audited) or 'fairly represent' (if unaudited) its financial position for the period to which they relate
- no material litigation or proceeding is pending or threatened against it
- all taxes due have been paid
- it has good title to all its assets
- it legally and beneficially owns all shares in Target (or will upon completion of the acquisition)
- all material intellectual property is beneficially owned and not infringed
- the documents recording the terms of the acquisition that have been supplied to the debt providers are true and complete and record all terms of the acquisition
- Topco and Bidco are holding companies only and have not engaged in any activity other than the acquisition of the Target group
- all pensions are fully funded or operated and maintained in accordance with all applicable laws (including statutory funding objectives and minimum funding requirements)
- no security or financial indebtedness is in place other than as permitted under the SFA

Figure 6.1 Representations and warranties

certain circumstances. As a result, the negotiation of the terms of the representations and warranties is a good opportunity to flush out any potential issues with the Target group or business that may not have come to light through other means.

(f) Positive and negative undertakings

The various members of the group will also be required to adhere to certain positive and negative undertakings. The essence of the undertakings

- obtain and maintain all authorisations required for business
- comply with all applicable laws and regulations
- ensure its obligations to the debt providers rank at least pari passu with its obligations to all other creditors
- maintain adequate insurance
- maintain material intellectual property
- maintain its accounts with approved banks and implement agreed cash management processes
- pension schemes to be fully funded or, in case of defined benefit schemes, to be operated and maintained in accordance with applicable laws
- allow lenders access to books and records following defaults
- enforce its rights under the acquisition documents
- pay all taxes when due

Figure 6.2 Positive undertakings

ensures that the business is maintained and operated lawfully and within certain agreed parameters so as to prevent any leakage or diminution of value, or any activity that could be considered to be prejudicial to the position of the debt providers. The exact nature and extent of the undertakings will be subject to considerable negotiation between the debt providers and the investors.

The right balance needs to be struck between preventing actions that could be considered to be prejudicial to the position of the debt providers, and allowing sufficient operational flexibility on a day-to-day basis. Figures 6.2 and 6.3 list the main positive and negative undertakings that would typically be included. As with the representations, the nature and extent of the undertakings may be expanded to deal with specific matters relating to the transaction or specific circumstances affecting the Target group or the type of business in which it is engaged.

(g) Financial covenants

Whilst the positive and negative undertakings will monitor operational performance, financial covenants will be included in the SFA to monitor the financial performance of the business. The role of the financial covenants can be summarised as:

- not to create security over any of its assets except as permitted or arising by operation of law
- not to dispose of any assets except as permitted
- not to incur financial indebtedness except as permitted
- not to make acquisitions, or enter into joint ventures or mergers, except as permitted
- not to change the nature of its business
- not to grant loans or give guarantees in favour of third parties
- not to pay or make dividends or make any payment in relation to any mezzanine debt or investor loan notes except as permitted
- not to enter into any transactions other than on arm's length terms
- not to amend the acquisition documentation
- not to enter into treasury or derivative transactions except as permitted

Figure 6.3 Negative undertakings

- ensuring financial discipline within the group;
- monitoring the financial strength of the group;
- ensuring that the financial performance of the group remains acceptable and grows in line with the expectations of the debt providers and the projected growth set out in the base case model in the Business Plan;
- in the case of a breach of covenant, giving the debt providers an ability to accelerate the debt, cancel their commitments and/or put the facilities on demand at an appropriate stage before the value in the group has been significantly eroded due to underperformance.

Typically, the following financial covenants will be sought by funders:

(a) *Leverage*, being the ratio of total debt to earnings of the group. The funders will expect the group to de-lever over time as debt is amortised/prepaid and earnings grow.
(b) *Interest cover*, being the ratio of earnings of the group to debt service costs. This will test whether the group can generate sufficient earnings to more than cover its interest payments and other finance charges.
(c) *Cash flow cover*, being the ratio of cash flow to total debt payments. Whilst the interest cover covenant will measure business performance, the cash flow cover test will measure whether the group has enough

actual cash to meet all payments that are due in respect of its debt (including interest, fees and scheduled principal repayments).

Each of the above covenants will be measured at the end of every financial quarter on a rolling twelve-month basis by reference to the financial performance of the group over the prior four quarters. Special provision will usually be made for the first three quarters following completion of the acquisition in order accurately to test early performance. This may take the form of: (a) taking into account pre-acquisition performance to achieve a full twelve-month testing period; (b) testing at the end of each quarter on a 'last quarter annualised' basis; or (c) testing against the actual results achieved over the actual period elapsed since the completion of the acquisition.

In addition to the above, the debt providers may also wish to place certain annual limits on the amount of capital expenditure that can be made by the group in each financial year. This could be tested by reference to actual monetary limits or a limit set at a percentage of the projected capital expenditure set out in the base case model in the Business Plan (e.g. 110 per cent).

Financial covenants are very carefully negotiated. History shows that they are often the first covenants to be breached in a transaction. Consequently, far from being standard, the actual detail of the covenants and the way in which they are calculated will be deal-specific and will need to be tailored to reflect the basis on which the group draws up its accounts, and the assumptions and criteria on which the Business Plan has been prepared. The ratio levels for the leverage and interest cover covenants will usually be set at a certain headroom to the ratios that are projected to be achieved in the base case model in the Business Plan (typically, 20 per cent). The cash flow cover covenant will typically be set at a constant level of 1.1:1 or 1:1.

In recent years, investors looked to secure mechanisms that would allow them to remedy financial covenant breaches so as to avoid funders cancelling the funding commitments and accelerating their loans for temporary periods of underperformance that are not representative of an ongoing downward performance trend. These so-called 'equity cure' provisions effectively allow the investors to put in additional equity capital (or subordinated loans) which would be treated (depending upon the mechanisms that are negotiated and agreed) as bolstering earnings or cash flow or perhaps notionally reducing debt by, in effect but not in reality, treating the new cash as having been used to prepay debt. Once the cash is injected, the covenants would then be recalculated, and if the relevant ratios are met following the recalculation the breach will be treated as having been cured.

Where these cure provisions are agreed, the investor would have a limited period of time following the occurrence of the financial covenant breach to opt to put in additional capital. In addition, the debt providers would also place limitations on the number of times (typically, two or three) that the cure provisions may be invoked, and prohibit the use of the cure on two consecutive covenant test dates. The rationale for that is that a need to cure more frequently suggests a more general downward performance trend within the business.

Given the current market circumstances, and the fact that banks are likely to be more rigorous in their funding terms going forward, it is questionable whether they will continue to agree to the inclusion of equity cure provisions in mid-market transactions.

(h) Events of default

Certain specified triggers will be included in the SFA which will lead to an ability on the part of the funders to accelerate and demand repayment of their debt: these are referred to as 'events of default'. These will relate to situations where the group breaches the terms on which the debt has been provided or situations that materially impact on the viability of the business, its value or the legal efficacy of the transaction. Figure 6.4 sets out brief details of the events of default that will customarily be included in the SFA.

The private equity house will be concerned to avoid hair-triggers leading to a withdrawal of the debt funding. Consequently, cure rights (where defaults can be cured) allowing the group to take immediate steps within a specified period of time to reverse the breach and other materiality thresholds will be negotiated.

4.2 Mezzanine facility documents

(a) Mezzanine Facility Agreement

Mezzanine finance is a secondary source of finance for Bidco in the context of an acquisition. As has already been outlined, the advent of mezzanine originally came about to provide investors with a source of finance that would bridge the gap between (a) the purchase price and acquisition costs and (b) the aggregate of the amount of funding that the investor is prepared to commit and the amount of senior debt that can be raised in the market.

The Mezzanine Facility Agreement (MFA) will set out the terms and conditions attaching to the provision of the mezzanine debt. It will be based upon and follow very closely the terms and conditions set out in the SFA, and will usually be prepared once the SFA negotiation is well progressed. The key differences between the MFA and the SFA can be summarised as follows:

(a) Mezzanine debt will comprise only a term loan to be utilised in conjunction with the senior term loan to meet the purchase price and acquisition costs. Working capital facilities and ancillary facilities will not be provided on a mezzanine basis.

- failure to pay sums when due
- breach of positive or negative undertakings
- breach of financial covenants
- representations or warranties found to be untrue or misleading when made or deemed repeated
- cross default with other indebtedness (subject to de minimis thresholds)
- material adverse change in the business
- insolvency and related events
- unlawfulness, invalidity or rescinding of the financing documents or the acquisition documents
- material audit qualification to the group's accounts
- failure to comply with the terms of the intercreditor agreement
- material litigation
- expropriation of assets
- default under the mezzanine facility agreement (if applicable)
- change of ownership

Figure 6.4 Events of default

(b) Mezzanine debt will be junior to the senior debt. In other words, it will rank in right of repayment at all times behind the senior debt and will usually take the benefit of a second-ranking interest in the security package taken by the senior debt providers. Consequently, whilst the provisions relating to mandatory prepayment in the SFA will be mirrored in the MFA, they will be disapplied until the senior debt facilities have been prepaid and discharged in full.

(c) The MFA will frequently contain prepayment penalties in the first one or two years of the loan.

(d) The financial covenants set out in the MFA will mirror those set out in the SFA but the testing ratios will be set at a level which provides additional headroom (typically, 10 per cent) over the testing ratios set out in the SFA.

(e) Due to the junior nature of mezzanine debt, and consequently the greater risk to the mezzanine debt providers of ensuring repayment in full, mezzanine debt will command a higher rate of return than senior debt. As outlined in chapter 3, this higher rate of return would typically be achieved through:

- a higher interest rate on the debt which may be split into a rate of cash pay interest (interest that must be paid on a quarterly or six-monthly basis by Bidco) and non-cash pay interest (interest that is calculated on the outstanding debt on a quarterly or six-monthly basis, but is rolled up and only payable at the end of the term when the principal is repaid). This is referred to as payment in kind (PIK) interest; and
- possibly, an 'equity kicker'. This refers to the issue of warrants by Topco to the mezzanine debt providers which will allow them to subscribe for shares in Topco at the time, for example, of a sale or listing of Topco. These warrants are aimed at providing (it is hoped) an enhanced performance-related return for the mezzanine providers over and above the cash pay interest and the PIK (see section (b) below).

Investors are generally opposed to the equity kicker because it has the effect of diluting the share capital owned by the investors at the time of the sale or listing of Topco, and ultimately reduces the rate of return on their equity investment. However, this view is not universal as there can be a tangible relationship, and other benefits, by ensuring that the mezzanine provider has an equity interest in the business.

Prior to August 2007, the market saw a growing trend in warrantless mezzanine with the mezzanine providers receiving only cash pay interest and PIK. This move was principally driven by investors to avoid the dilution issue but, whilst not necessarily welcomed by the traditional mezzanine houses, the certainty of return on warrantless mezzanine appealed as an investment to the increasingly prevalent CDO and CLO funds that became more active in the leveraged funding market. Current market circumstances will most likely see a return of warrants into typical funding structures.

(b) Mezzanine warrants

A warrant instrument will be entered into, enabling Topco to grant an option to the mezzanine funder(s) to subscribe for new shares in Topco. In appearance it is similar to a loan note instrument, in that it entitles Topco to issue certificates to the relevant funder(s) who are entered into a register of warrant holders, and with effect from such registration the holders are bound by the general terms set out in the instrument. The exercise price of the warrants is normally par, so that it entitles the mezzanine funder to low-cost equity in order to provide the kicker referred to above.

The following commercial issues arise when drafting or negotiating a mezzanine warrant:

(a) *How many warrant shares?* This is not as straightforward a question as it may seem. Mezzanine funder termsheets will typically say that warrants are to be granted over a percentage of the fully diluted share capital of Topco (e.g. warrants representing 3 per cent of the fully diluted share capital). However, what is often unclear is whether the warrant will be over a fixed number of shares that represent that proportion of the equity as at the execution of the warrant instrument, or whether the warrant will be over such number of shares as represents that percentage of the equity upon it being exercised. For example, in the event of future funding rounds by way of share issue, a warrant holder entitled to 3 per cent of the equity as at the exercise of the warrant would effectively get a 'free ride' on that future funding round (i.e. it would remain entitled to 3 per cent of the enhanced equity even though it has not put any money in at the time of the further funding round). Similarly, in the event of any shares being bought back by Topco in the future, a mezzanine funder entitled to receive a fixed percentage of the share capital would receive fewer shares upon the warrant being exercised (i.e. its overall stake is not increased *pro rata* by virtue of the buyback being completed, which it would be if it were a shareholder). A mezzanine funder's starting-point will often be that it wants the fixed number of shares, or (if greater) that number of shares which entitles them to the relevant percentage stake – but this can be negotiated, for example by stating that dilution should apply if warrant holders choose not to participate in the funding round on a *pro rata* basis (see also below).

(b) *When can the warrants be exercised?* As a warrant holder typically holds a warrant in order to participate in the exit, it follows that a mezzanine warrant should in practice only be exercisable conditionally upon an exit occurring. Notwithstanding this, many mezzanine funders start negotiations by requesting that their warrant should be exercisable at any time (in order that they could exercise their discretion to become a shareholder before an exit actually arises), although the investors and management shareholders may well resist this. Where a warrant is to be exercised at any time, provision should nevertheless be included for the warrant to be exercised conditionally upon an exit occurring in order that a mezzanine funder can elect to serve a notice that it will be entitled to the warrant shares only upon an exit arising should that become necessary. Consideration should also be given as to whether the warrant can be exercised in whole and once only, or whether it can be exercised in part and on a number of different occasions. The shareholders will prefer a warrant holder only to be entitled to exercise its warrant once in respect of all of the relevant shares to avoid inconvenience, and in practice most mezzanine funders would have no objection to this.

(c) *Who can the warrants be transferred to?* A mezzanine funder will typically start from the perspective that their warrants should be freely transferable. However, in theory, this could allow external warrant holders of whom the other shareholders do not approve – and accordingly it is usual to include restrictions such that the mezzanine warrants can only be transferred (a) to persons to whom the mezzanine facilities themselves are transferred (which will usually be prescribed by the MFA) or (b) to such other persons as they would be entitled to transfer the underlying warrant shares if they had exercised their warrants (effectively ensuring that the mezzanine shares are subject to the same pre-emption rights and any other restrictions on transfer as any issued shares). It is important to ensure that any such transfer restrictions do not operate in any way which may hinder the ability of all of the shareholders, and the mezzanine funder, to achieve the relevant exit. Equally, provisions should be included to ensure that a sale of the entire issued share capital can be completed (and that the warrant will lapse if not exercised), provided the mezzanine funder has been given an opportunity to exercise any warrants and participate in the exit.

(d) *Should the warrant holder be entitled to board representation?* Warrant holders may request the right to appoint a representative director to the board, although this would usually be resisted by the investors. An observer might be an acceptable compromise, or agreement could be reached that any such party may attend board meetings only if there is a default under the MFA.

(e) *Anti-dilution protection.* In the event of any future funding rounds involving the issue of shares, the mezzanine funder will typically require protection that no new shares can be created without the consent of the warrant holder(s), unless such new shares created are either offered to the warrant holder(s) *pro rata* as if it were already a shareholder, or alternatively are taken into account when determining the overall proportion of the equity which the warrant entitles the holder to obtain (in the event that the warrant is over a fixed percentage of the share capital, rather than a fixed number of shares). It is also possible that future *bona fide* reorganisations could affect the position of the warrant holder (for example, bonus issues, or a consolidation of share capital). Accordingly, provisions should be included for an adjustment to the number of warrant shares and/or the exercise price in order to ensure that the warrant holder's position is not affected by any such restructuring. This will typically be subject to independent verification (if required) to be undertaken by the group's auditors, or by an independent accountant.

(f) *Should the warrant holders have any other protections?* For example, a prohibition on the payment of dividends or excessive remuneration to management without the warrant holder's consent is often required (as paying such dividends would effectively dilute the value of the underlying business and hence the warrant). The warrant will also usually include rights to receive financial information (at least the audited and management accounts). Provisions are also usually included for the warrant holder to be kept informed of the progress of any exits, and with a time period for notification of that exit to the warrant holders prior to such exit being transacted (e.g. no exit may arise unless the warrant holder has had ten business days' prior notice), during which period the warrant holder may exercise its rights to participate in the exit.

4.3 Intercreditor Agreement

Given the different levels of debt being provided to Bidco on different risk/ rate of return profiles, it is essential that the respective rights and rankings of each type of creditor throughout the term of the financing are regulated. As discussed in chapter 3,[16] the rights of the various creditors can be regulated in two ways:

(a) *contractual subordination*: a position where the competing rights of creditors against the same corporate entities within a group are regulated by contract; and
(b) *structural subordination*: a position where the rights of creditors are regulated in their priority by principles of company and insolvency law, with the result that the closer a creditor is to the operating/current assets or cash flows the more it will be structurally senior in right of payment.

Figure 3.3 in chapter 3 sets out a diagrammatic representation of how true structural subordination may be achieved, although it is probably fair to say that most transactions will incorporate an element of both structural and contractual subordination.

This would particularly be the case where a transaction contains both senior secured and mezzanine secured indebtedness. In this situation, whilst the senior debt may be funded directly to Bidco, the mezzanine debt to Midco and the investor debt to Topco (giving the appearance of structural subordination of the mezzanine debt and the investor debt), it would be usual for both the senior and mezzanine facilities to be guaranteed by and secured against the assets of the whole group (including the Target group) (see Figure 6.5). This effectively creates competing rights of the senior and mezzanine creditors at every level of the corporate group structure, and competing rights of the senior and mezzanine creditors and the investors at the Topco level. Ultimately, therefore, this will lead to a need for the priority of those competing claims to be regulated by contract.

Typically, the intercreditor agreement will be signed by Topco, Midco, Bidco, the members of the Target group and all debt (senior, mezzanine and investor) providers.

Intercreditor agreements by their very nature are heavily scrutinised by each group of debt providers and will invariably be heavily negotiated. A brief

16 See chapter 3, section 2.3(b).

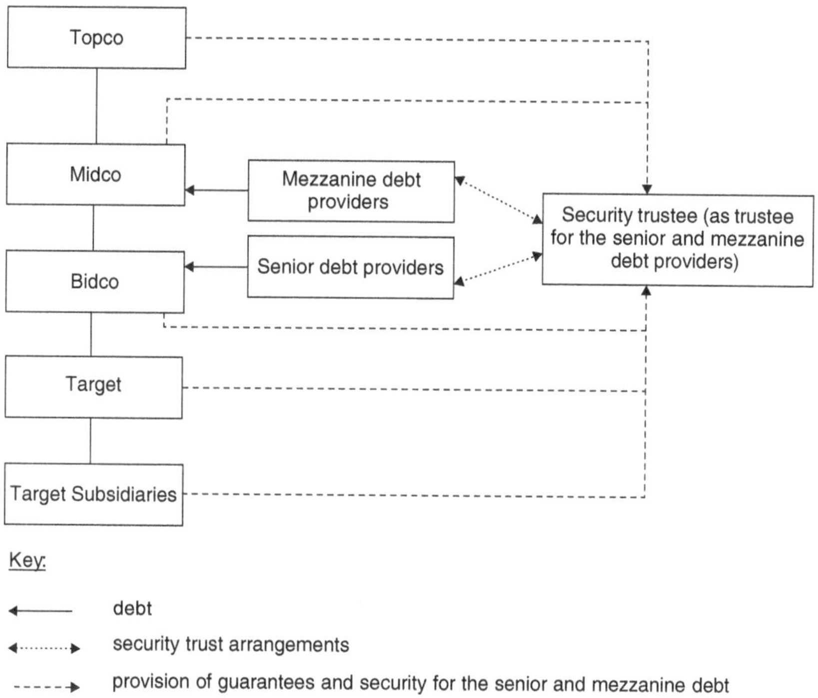

Figure 6.5 Security structure

summary of the key matters that will be covered in an intercreditor agreement is set out below.

(a) The rights of the investors in respect of any loan notes will be deeply subordinated to the rights of the senior and mezzanine debt providers. This essentially means they will not be entitled to receive any payments until both the senior and mezzanine debt are repaid in full. In some cases, there may be negotiated exceptions which might allow for a running yield to be paid on the loan notes. If this is accommodated by the senior and mezzanine debt providers, it would usually be subject to conditions around financial covenant compliance (both on a look forward and look back basis), and no default having occurred or subsisting under the senior and/or mezzanine facilities.

(b) Mezzanine debt providers will be subject to certain payment restrictions. The previous section of this chapter explained that the terms of the mezzanine debt will usually have the debt principal repayable in one bullet repayment, scheduled to occur twelve months following the contractual term of the senior debt. On top of that, the servicing by Bidco of periodic cash pay interest obligations on the mezzanine debt will generally be subject to restrictions should an event of default in respect of the senior debt occur. Such payment blockage would typically remain in place until the senior event of default is cured.

(c) Provisions will be included as to how monies are to be applied in the event that Bidco is unable to service its debt and, accordingly, the security package is enforced. In keeping with the intended priorities of senior and mezzanine debt, once all costs of enforcement have been met, the remainder of the proceeds of enforcement will be applied, first, to meet outstanding obligations in respect of the senior debt and, secondly, to meet outstanding obligations in respect of the mezzanine debt.

(d) Certain restrictions will be placed on the ability of the mezzanine funders to take any of the following actions in circumstances where Bidco is in default under the terms of the MFA:
  (i) exercising any right to enforce any security;
  (ii) suing or instituting any other creditors' process against any member of the group;
  (iii) petitioning for or taking any steps to initiate any insolvency, liquidation or dissolution proceedings against any member of the group; or
  (iv) accelerating and calling for immediate repayment of any of the mezzanine debt or otherwise putting the mezzanine debt due and payable on demand.

These restrictions are generally designed to ensure that the senior debt providers retain as much control as possible over the destiny of the group in a default scenario, since they would typically have the most to lose. Rather than being a strict prohibition, these restrictions are usually coupled with a concept of standstill. Standstill puts a maximum time limit on the inability of the mezzanine debt providers to take action following an event of default under the MFA (usually between 90 and 180 days).

This standstill period affords the senior debt providers a period of time in which to work out a strategy to deal with the default, but gives the mezzanine funders comfort that they can ultimately take action at the expiry of the standstill period if a suitable strategy for maintaining the facilities has not been agreed and the event of default under the mezzanine debt continues to subsist.

As the loan notes held by the investors are usually deeply subordinated to the senior debt and any mezzanine debt as referred to above, the loan note holders are generally prohibited from taking any of the actions in paragraphs (i) to (iv) in respect of amounts due under the loan notes without the consent of both the senior and mezzanine lenders.

5 Security requirements of funders

The debt providers will require the legal due diligence on the Target group to include a detailed analysis of its existing indebtedness, and an appraisal of the existing security interests that subsist over its property and assets. The results of this analysis will be material to the debt providers (both senior and mezzanine) since they will be reliant upon recourse to those assets to protect their debt investment. It will also, with few exceptions, be a condition to the provision of funding that all existing financing arrangements of the Target group are discharged in full, and all associated security for those arrangements released.

An example of how a security package may be structured is set out in Figure 6.5. Essentially:

- All the companies within the group will provide guarantees of the senior and mezzanine debt. This will be achieved by the accession of the members of the group to the guarantee provisions that are included in each of the SFA and the MFA. In the case of Bidco, this will still be a requirement notwithstanding that it is the main borrower. This is essentially because other companies within the group may become borrowers under the senior working capital facilities and incur a portion of the debt funding themselves.
- Under the terms of the intercreditor agreement, each of the senior debt providers and the mezzanine debt providers will appoint a common institution to act as their security trustee. The trustee will then take the benefit of all the security interests granted by the members of the group and hold them on trust for the debt providers. The intercreditor agreement will contain detailed provisions as to how the security is to be held, what the security trustee can do, whose instructions it must act upon and how proceeds of the security (in circumstances of enforcement) are to be allocated among the debt providers, in each case in line with the agreed priority between the senior and mezzanine debt providers.
- The security will comprise: (i) full fixed and floating charges over all the assets of each member of the group (including the shares in their subsidiaries); (ii) an assignment by way of security of rights in respect of material contracts (including the acquisition documents, any hedging agreements and potentially certain material customer contracts); and (iii) an assignment of any keyman insurance policies put in place by the group in respect of key members of management.

Until recently, English law prohibited companies from giving financial assistance for the purchase of their own shares or the shares in their parent company. Looking at the security structure set out in Figure 6.5, the giving of guarantees and security by members of the Target group to support the debt incurred by Bidco to acquire the shares of Target would historically have constituted prohibited financial assistance. Notwithstanding the prohibition, in the case of private companies the assistance could be given if the company went through a procedure (known as the 'whitewash' procedure) specified under the Companies Act 1985.[17] Depending upon the size of the Target group, this process could be very cumbersome and costly, and was a key feature of leveraged acquisitions. To the relief of many, with effect from 1 October 2008 the prohibition on the giving of financial assistance by UK private companies was abolished, although the prohibition still remains in the case of public companies and subsidiaries of public companies (see further chapter 10[18]), and the situation must also be checked for any overseas subsidiaries. However, each of the relevant directors will still need to be mindful of their fiduciary duties to every company of which they are a director that is granting security, and must therefore be satisfied (by way of example) that there is a corporate benefit of doing so for each such company, and that this will not result in any unlawful distribution.

6 Alternative financing structures for larger transactions

6.1 Background

In the context of larger transactions, prior to the credit crunch there was an increasing trend for funding to be drawn from a combination of senior debt finance and high-yield debt, with the high-yield debt being utilised in favour of mezzanine debt. This alternative was only really available in the context of larger deals since, in general terms, the minimum size of offering worth pursuing in the high-yield bond market is about £150 million.

In such larger deals, the utilisation by Bidco of the capital markets to raise finance by issuing medium-to-long-term debt instruments presented an attractive source of financing for the following reasons:

(a) the term of high-yield bonds usually ran to between ten and twelve years, which is longer than the term usually seen in mezzanine finance agreements;
(b) high-yield bonds generally attracted a lower rate of return than mezzanine finance; whilst the interest payable on high-yield bonds would all be cash pay (i.e. no deferred PIK), high-yield bond holders did not require the provision of warrants;
(c) high-yield bonds typically did not benefit from security;
(d) high-yield bonds did not have the same strict package of maintenance covenants and undertakings as would otherwise be included in the SFA or MFA; and

17 See sections 151–157 of the Companies Act 1985 (now repealed by virtue of the Companies Act 2006). Essentially, the procedure involved all the directors of a company intending to give financial assistance swearing certain statutory declarations as to solvency that were reported on by the auditors.
18 See chapter 10, section 4.2.

(e) in transactions that utilised a combination of senior debt and high-yield debt, it has historically been possible to achieve higher leverage ratios. In other words, Bidco was able to raise higher levels of debt, thereby increasing the debt-to-equity ratio and consequently facilitating higher rates of return for the private equity investors on a successful exit.

Recently, given the downturn experienced in confidence in the capital markets, the use of high-yield bonds has been almost non-existent. However, the market will no doubt return and this type of finance will again be considered in the context of acquisition finance structuring.

One of the key problems with using high-yield debt funding in the context of an acquisition is the logistical issue of ensuring that Bidco has access to sufficient funding on the day that the acquisition is due to close in accordance with the terms of the acquisition agreement (and, in the case of a public-to-private transaction, the requirements as to certain funding, discussed in chapter 10,[19] are satisfied). Given the nature of raising finance in the capital markets it is unlikely that this certainty would be afforded, and consequently 'bridge financing' techniques are utilised to deal with this.

6.2 Bridge debt

The use of bridge funding ensures that Bidco has committed bank facilities in an amount sufficient to pay the purchase price for Target and meet all acquisition costs on the date on which it is obliged to do so. However, due to the perceived benefits and the cheaper cost of high-yield debt, the full intention of Bidco and its investors is to have this bridge funding refinanced very quickly following the completion of the acquisition with high-yield debt.

Given the nature of bridge lending, there are two particular features of this type of finance that should be noted.

(a) Interest rates are typically subject to a ratchet. Essentially, the longer it takes before the high-yield take-out offering is completed and the bridge debt repaid, the higher is the rate of interest on the bridge debt. The frequency of the ratchet and the amount of each increase in interest rate will be negotiated on a deal-by-deal basis, but they are intended to be painful since the underlying rationale is to incentivise a refinancing of the bridge debt as soon as possible.

(b) Cramdown. This term refers to a situation where, if the proposed high-yield take-out has not occurred within a specified period of time, then the bridge lenders can arrange a high-yield offering on the terms that they feel are required in order to ensure that such offering is successful, and require the private equity investors to accept such terms and proceed with such offering.

19 See chapter 10, section 4.

6.3 Structural subordination

One further financial structuring issue that needs to be borne in mind for such larger deals is the potential requirement for true structural subordination. It was noted in section 5 above that the relative priorities and rankings of senior and mezzanine debt were ordinarily likely to be policed and regulated by the terms of an intercreditor agreement between the financing parties and Bidco. In other words, they were policed by contract. Senior lenders are often more tolerant of such contractual subordination arrangements in mezzanine deals, since the mezzanine market has historically comprised fewer participants and these are well known to the senior lenders in the UK and Europe (and whose behaviour in the context of an insolvency situation may be predicted).

In contrast, the high-yield market would invariably comprise a diverse, global, anonymous community of bond holders that changes frequently. Consequently, senior lenders are for more likely to insist that any high-yield bond debt must be structurally subordinated to the senior debt funding.

7 Conclusion

There is no doubt that investors and financial institutions face interesting times. In the wake of the credit crunch, financial institutions are re-pricing risk, unwilling to offer high leverage multiples (anything above three times EBITDA is proving more difficult to achieve), demanding lower gearing and seeking to keep a tighter control on the businesses to which they lend money.

It has only been possible in this chapter to provide an overview of the historical context that has shaped the current market, and to offer some thoughts through experience about how the debt financing of an investor acquisition may look moving forwards and beyond 2009. There will be activity in the mid-market in the UK, but it will likely be muted in the short term. It will be more difficult for investors to identify opportunities that are attractive to them as lower leverage, lower gearing and higher priced debt funding impact their ability to meet their return hurdles (or at least meet them quickly).

The prevailing view is that mid-market activity is set to return more quickly than activity in the high-value leveraged acquisitions market – good deals can still be done, and debt funding is available. It is just going to take a little longer to broker deals on terms that are acceptable to all involved.

7

Employment-related issues

1 Introduction

In this chapter, we consider the key employment terms of the managers that will need to be negotiated alongside the other transaction documents. Issues concerning remuneration, notice periods, grounds for dismissal and the like will often be emotive, and the negotiation of the managers' service agreements in the (often adversarial) context of the wider deal can accentuate this further. Of course, it is important to the managers that their legal adviser fights their corner in negotiating a fair position. However, it is also true that a manager needs to be mindful of the fact that generous terms negotiated for the benefit of that manager and his or her colleagues may come back to bite, should one of those managers fail to deliver and need to be replaced. Like the negotiation of the other equity documents discussed in chapter 5, the key is to ensure that each manager balances his or her position as a director and shareholder of Newco with their requirements as an employee.

We will also consider the interaction of the termination of employment provisions in a service agreement with the equity position of the manager. There is usually significant overlap, such that an employment lawyer negotiating these terms needs to be familiar with the issues being discussed and negotiated in the investment agreement and articles of association, and *vice versa*. Common approaches to 'Good Leaver' and 'Bad Leaver' definitions, highlighted in chapter 5,[1] will therefore be considered again in the context of the termination of a manager's employment. In this chapter, we also address the issues that arise on the termination of the employment of a manager, including the manager's potential contractual and statutory claims, and the common terms of any settlement agreement.

Finally, we briefly consider the ways in which employees who fall outside the senior management team may be offered incentives linking their own remuneration to the performance of the business. Many private equity investments rely on a significant contribution being made by the so-called 'second tier'

1 See chapter 5, section 4.11.

within the management structure, and it is therefore common to see an incentive scheme put in place to motivate those individuals towards the achievement of a successful exit. Whilst the terms of such incentives may be less generous than for the senior team, the rewards made available to such employees in the event of an exit may nevertheless be significant.

Throughout this chapter, we refer to Newco on the assumption that Newco is the company employing the manager. This is usually, although not invariably, the case, and therefore should be clarified for any particular transaction. Where a multiple Newco structure is adopted,[2] the Topco would usually (but, again, not always) be the employer company.

2 Employment terms

2.1 Introduction

Whilst the equity terms are likely to be of primary importance to the manager, there are certain employment terms that are also material, and therefore likely to be the subject of negotiation. It is often sensible for these terms to be highlighted in any initial equity termsheet or questionnaire, so that the position may be flushed out or agreed at the outset of the deal, particularly from the management team's perspective if there is a competitive process which may enable a more favourable position to be negotiated than if such terms are left until the formal legal process when the service agreements are documented.

These key terms may also have a direct impact on the manager's equity position, by virtue of the interaction of the relevant provisions and definitions between the service agreement and the investment agreement and articles of association. Care is needed to ensure that documentation is consistent, and that such interaction does not inadvertently lead to an undesirable or otherwise incorrect commercial outcome.

2.2 Notice

The notice period has a significant bearing on the negotiation of any severance package should a manager be dismissed. In practice, once the investors and/or the other directors have decided that a manager should leave the business, it would be rare for that manager to work during their notice period. Instead, it is more likely that the manager will be placed on 'garden leave' (see section 2.3 below), or that they will be paid in lieu of notice (see section 2.4 below). It is therefore important that both of these options are covered in the drafting of the manager's service agreement. Subject to that, the notice period will directly influence the quantum of any severance payment in the event that the employer

2 See further chapter 3, section 2.3.

makes a payment in lieu of notice, or the quantum of any damages claim in the event that the employer dismisses without giving due notice.

It would be usual for the service agreement to include a notice period that is consistent whether the manager or Newco decides to terminate the relationship, although in some cases unequal notice periods are agreed, with the longer period invariably required from Newco. A notice period of six months *each way* is common for senior managers, with a period of three months *each way* being an alternative for less significant junior managers. Periods of nine months or twelve months may arise for particularly senior, experienced managers who are considered essential to the group's success (from the employer's perspective), or who are able to negotiate a more favourable package (from the employee's perspective), but most investors will resist periods in excess of six months other than in exceptional circumstances. Occasionally, there are circumstances where an initial fixed term is seen, for example on a secondary buyout where the commitment of a rolling manager for a reasonable handover period is considered important.

The notice period may also have an impact on the manager's equity vesting,[3] if it is included for the purpose of determining whether shares have vested or not. As vesting periods are generally stated to expire when employment is terminated, it might appear obvious that any notice period served would count towards determining whether shares are vested. However, many articles of association are drafted so as to define the termination date for these purposes as the date on which any notice is served, rather than the date on which any notice expires (or would be deemed to expire, but for a payment in lieu of notice provision being exercised). This should always be a point for explicit instructions in the event that a time-based vesting approach is agreed.

2.3 Garden leave

Any employer would generally be advised to ensure that it has the express right to place the manager on garden leave during any period of notice.[4] Accordingly, most investors would include this as a standard requirement in their service agreements. As noted above, it would be unusual for a manager to be dismissed in circumstances where he would be required to continue to work for his full notice period in a private-equity-backed company.

As is discussed in more detail in chapter 11, the rights of a manager as a director must be considered on the termination of any employment, in addition to the rights of the manager as an employee. To ensure that such rights do not hinder the ability of Newco to exclude a manager from the business, investors will generally ensure that Newco can require the manager to resign any

3 See chapter 5, section 4.11.

4 It is advisable to include an express right to place an employee on garden leave in order to make it clear that the employee does not have an implied right to work which precludes garden leave: see *William Hill Organisation Ltd* v. *Tucker* [1998] IRLR 313.

directorships during the garden leave period. If this right is not included, the manager may have a continuing right to be a director and, as such, have the right to attend board meetings and to see board papers. The right to require the manager to resign any directorships is often supported by an express power of attorney enabling any director of Newco to serve notice terminating such directorship on his behalf, and provisions in the articles of association enabling the investors to remove any director on notice in any event.[5]

The employer should also insert an express obligation of good faith and exclusive service during any period of garden leave.[6] In the absence of such a provision, the employee may argue that he is permitted to take up new employment during the garden leave period.

If Newco places the manager on garden leave without the express right to do so, and/or refuses a manager who is a director access to board meetings without the express right to do so, this may amount to a repudiatory breach of the employment contract which, if accepted by the employee, brings the employment to an immediate end and releases the employee from his own obligations under his service agreement (including, most notably, any post-termination restrictive covenants in the service agreement).

A manager will wish to ensure that the right to place that manager on garden leave only applies once notice has been served, and that it will not be applied for more than six months (in the event that the notice period is longer than six months). The latter point is consistent with the current approach of the courts.

2.4 Payment in lieu of notice

As mentioned in section 2.3, a party in repudiatory breach cannot rely on post-termination restraints if the repudiatory breach is accepted by the employee.[7] It was for this reason that employers originally began to include payment in lieu of notice (PILON) clauses in employment contracts, which enable employers to lawfully terminate the employment before the expiry of the notice period. Therefore, in order to preserve any restrictive covenants in the service agreement (which will be in addition to any restrictions under the investment agreement which apply to the managers by virtue of their equity participation[8]), the investors will want to ensure that a PILON clause is included in the service agreement.

Although the employer may ordinarily wish to terminate the employment contract lawfully by giving full notice or making a PILON, it may in some cases

5 For further discussion on the drafting and enforceability of such provisions, see chapter 11, section 5.3.

6 Following on from *Symbian* v. *Christensen* [2001] IRLR 77 (CA), it is recommended that this right is expressly set out in the employment contract.

7 *General Billposting Company Ltd* v. *Atkinson* [1909] AC 118.

8 See chapter 5, section 3.7.

choose to breach the employment contract by failing to give due notice and not making a PILON. In these circumstances, the manager would have a claim for damages, reflecting their loss of salary and benefits for the relevant notice period. However, the manager would have a duty to mitigate (i.e. take reasonable steps to secure new employment and thereby reduce their loss of earnings and the value of their damages claim). If the employer is not concerned about losing the restrictive covenants in the employment contract (possibly because it can rely on restrictions contained in the shareholders agreement that bind the manager), it may choose to breach the employment contract on the basis that it believes the manager will secure new employment relatively quickly, with the result that the employer's liability for damages is less costly than making a PILON. A manager may seek to avoid this outcome by either making the PILON non-discretionary (i.e. providing that, if Newco fails to give due notice and does not have grounds for summary dismissal, it is contractually obliged to make the PILON), or by including a separate liquidated damages clause that sets out a pre-agreed sum which is payable in the event that Newco fails to give due notice.

There is a risk that, if the pre-agreed sum under a liquidated damages clause is excessive and unconscionable, it will be void as a penalty.[9] The central question is whether, at the time the contract was negotiated, the main purpose of the clause was to deter the employer from breaching the contract or to compensate the employee for the breach. The former indicates an unenforceable penalty. With these principles in mind, a discount has traditionally been applied of, say, 10 per cent to any liquidated damages calculation so that it is easier to argue that the pre-agreed sum reflects possible mitigation and is a genuine estimate of loss. However, based on more recent case law,[10] it appears that it is now easier to enforce liquidated damages with little or no discount in the employment field.

It is common to find that the PILON is limited to salary only. The manager can argue that this does not fully compensate them for the notice period. However, the employer can argue that the salary is unmitigated (i.e. it is not reduced if the manager secures new employment relatively quickly) and is paid upfront (giving the advantage of accelerated receipt), and that this represents a fair compromise. In a private equity context where the main value of the manager's appointment is contained in his equity participation, the manager may be less concerned about whether the PILON is limited to salary and more concerned as to the definition of 'Good Leaver' and 'Bad Leaver' in cases of dismissal, and specifically in this context whether the notice period is taken into account in determining whether shares have vested.[11]

9 This follows from the principles in *Dunlop Pneumatic Tyre Co. Ltd* v. *New Garage & Motor Co. Ltd* [1915] AC 79.

10 *Murray* v. *Leisureplay plc* [2005] EWCA Civ 963.

11 See further section 2.2 above, section 4 below, and chapter 5, section 4.11.

If a PILON clause is triggered, then the payment is viewed as a contractual debt so that an obligation on the part of the employee to mitigate his or her losses does not apply. However, employers are increasingly including mitigation within the drafting of the PILON. Whilst not strictly relevant in a private equity context, applying mitigation also reflects corporate governance best practice for listed companies, and the recommendations of the Combined Code 2008. Whilst including mitigation in the PILON will be attractive to the employer, a manager may argue that this is inappropriate, for example by:

(a) referring to the origins of PILON clauses, i.e. they benefit the employer by enabling it to terminate early without breaching the contract, so that it can still enforce the restrictive covenants;
(b) arguing that the *quid pro quo* for protecting the covenants is that the PILON is payable in full;
(c) pointing out that a PILON does not entail a breach of contract, and therefore the application of mitigation is misconceived; and
(d) if the PILON is salary only, pointing out that the omission of any payment in respect of other benefits (such as bonus, pension and insurance benefits) means that a substantial discount has already been applied to the PILON.

From the manager's viewpoint, applying mitigation to a PILON is particularly objectionable if it is a salary-only PILON. To apply mitigation in such cases means that the manager is worse off than under a general damages claim where mitigation is applied against his full contractual remuneration package.

2.5 Grounds for summary dismissal

Most service agreements include a summary dismissal clause, whereby an employer will have the contractual right to dismiss an employee without any period of notice in certain circumstances. This right will be implied into the contract where, for example, the employee has committed gross misconduct or is grossly incompetent. These implied rights are construed narrowly by the courts, however, and as a result most investors will require that Newco has an express right to summarily dismiss an employee on the basis of broader grounds under the terms of the manager's service agreement.

As discussed in more detail in section 3.4 below, depending on the definition of 'Good Leaver' and 'Bad Leaver', a summary dismissal may have a substantial impact on the manager's equity vesting. In addition, the drafting of the grounds for summary dismissal will impact upon the manager's financial package on termination, in that it will negate the need for the employer to place the manager concerned on paid garden leave for a period or to make a PILON.

The express grounds for summary termination are largely similar to those found in service agreements for senior directors outside private equity. For example, the service agreement may provide that the manager can be summarily dismissed if he or she:

(a) is guilty of gross misconduct, gross incompetence or any wilful neglect in the discharge of their duties;
(b) commits any material or persistent breach of their service agreement;
(c) fails to perform their duties to a reasonable standard (usually based on the opinion of the board);
(d) is guilty of fraud or dishonesty, is guilty of a criminal offence (other than a minor traffic offence), or otherwise brings the group into disrepute;
(e) is disqualified from holding office as a director under the Company Directors Disqualification Act 1986;
(f) is admitted for treatment under any mental health legislation.

Whilst such provisions are always subject to a degree of sense check and negotiation, particularly where there is any requirement for the board to reach a conclusion on the conduct of the individual, they can prove particularly contentious in private equity transactions. Rightly or wrongly, managers are often more wary of private equity investors than they would be of their fellow directors or shareholders in a family owned company or even a public company. The fact that a leaver who is subject to summary dismissal proceedings is often defined as a Bad Leaver, with the resulting capped valuation of the individual's equity, means that there can be significant amounts at stake over and above the PILON payment or damages claim that would be lost by falling within the summary dismissal circumstances.

A particular provision that investors and their advisers may look to include in a private equity transaction is a clause enabling summary dismissal in the event that a manager commits any breach of the investment agreement or articles of association. Such clauses are often strongly resisted by management teams and their lawyers on the basis that such breaches may arise inadvertently, or may not be material, given the extensive nature of the consents, information rights and so on in the investment documentation.[12] It is often argued that the remedy of damages for a breach of those provisions is sufficient protection for the investors, and that the significant financial impact that can flow from a right to summarily dismiss is disproportionate to the wrongdoing attached to such a breach. Nevertheless, such a right undoubtedly gives the constitutional documents more legal teeth, and investors are often unsympathetic to arguments that suggest a breach of the investment documentation may arise. A common compromise is for such a clause to be worded in terms of material or persistent breaches of the relevant documents, perhaps limiting the right to breaches of specific obligations of importance, or carving out those matters that are seen as less significant.

12 See chapter 5 for more detail on the content of investment documents.

2.6 Restrictive covenants

In addition to any restrictive covenants applying to the managers in the investment agreement (see chapter 5[13]), the investors are likely to want to see restrictions included in the service agreement in favour of Newco. The covenants take various forms and may prohibit the manager from being engaged or employed in or having an interest in a competing business, soliciting or dealing with clients or customers, soliciting or employing employees of the business or interfering with suppliers.

It is beyond the scope of this book to set out a detailed analysis of the drafting and enforceability of restrictive covenants; however, the general principles and background in chapter 5 provide helpful guidance for the purposes of drafting or negotiating the covenants in the service agreement. The underlying principle is that the covenants will only be enforced to the extent that they are reasonable and necessary to protect the legitimate interests of the employer, meaning that they must be limited in their scope and duration. As we have seen, whilst the courts may be prepared to strike out those parts of the covenants that are unreasonable, they will not generally be prepared to rewrite the covenants. For example, if the period of restriction is unreasonable, the court will not impose a shorter period, and instead the covenants will be unenforceable. For this reason, as highlighted already in chapter 5, it is common to offset any period of garden leave against the period of the restrictive covenants; i.e. the period of the restrictive covenant is more likely to appear reasonable (and therefore enforceable) if credit is given for any period during which the manager is excluded from the market whilst on garden leave.

In general terms, the covenants in the service agreement will usually be of more limited scope than those in the investment documentation. It is usually accepted that it is more reasonable for the investors, and possibly Newco, to expect such protections in the context of their relationship with the individual as a shareholder, than it is for Newco to seek such protection in the context of an employee. As a consequence, whilst the language of the two documents will usually be similar in defining what constitutes a competing business, or a material customer, supplier or employee, the covenants in the service agreement will often be of shorter duration.

2.7 Remuneration and benefits

The service agreement will set out details of the salary and other benefits to be received by the manager. These will often be discussed and agreed between the managers and the investors directly, or with input from financial advisers, such that the lawyer is presented with a schedule of the benefits to be included in the draft contract. Details may also have been included in any equity termsheet or questionnaire at the outset of the deal, to avoid difficult

13 See chapter 5, section 3.7.

discussions at a later stage. In any event, the investors will wish to ensure that full provision for all such benefits has been included in the Business Plan, and will use the due diligence exercise to verify the suitability of the remuneration package, and a comparison of such proposed remuneration against that earned by the directors concerned before the buyout.

One area where private equity investors can differ in their approach (both when compared with other types of shareholder, and indeed amongst themselves) is on the question of bonus schemes or payments for the senior directors. Often, the management team from a buyout will be used to participating in a bonus scheme under the previous ownership regime, and they may therefore expect such participation to continue. However, investors will want to see managers move away from a mindset of employment to one of ownership, and therefore may challenge whether a bonus scheme is appropriate at historic levels, or indeed at all. Depending on the particular circumstances, and the particular investor(s), it is possible that a bonus scheme may be less generous to the senior directors going forward, or be removed altogether, on the basis that managers will be substantially rewarded for their performance through the life of the investment should a successful exit be achieved. Managing the expectations of the investors and the managers is key in this area, ideally by including full details of all remuneration (including performance bonuses) in the Business Plan from the beginning.

Where a bonus scheme is agreed, the managers and their advisers may wish to have the contractual comfort that comes from such arrangements being clearly documented in the service agreement. At its most comprehensive, this may involve agreeing complex definitions of profit-triggers and the setting of year-on-year targets aligned with the Plan. However, given the unpredictability of the performance of the investment, and how an unexpected outcome in one particular year can render such incentives as redundant in that year and future years, investors often prefer to leave the detail of any such arrangements (including the setting of suitable targets) to the discretion of the remuneration committee, on a more flexible and ongoing basis.

The sensitivity of negotiations concerning remuneration and benefits should not be underestimated. Whilst managers will be expected to show some shift in mindset from employee to shareholder, this cannot be expected overnight, and in any event must be kept in check to ensure that a manager is remunerated fairly. Sometimes, those benefits that might be viewed as relatively insignificant in the context of the deal as a whole, such as the make and model of company car or standard of business travel, can prove to be the most emotive issues for management.

2.8 Other terms

The service agreement will include other provisions typical for a senior director. For completeness, these include:

(a) scope of role and duties, including job title, time commitment and working hours, and geographical location;

(b) holiday entitlement;
(c) sickness absence provisions;
(d) provisions to protect confidential information and company documents;
(e) express provisions to confirm that any inventions or other intellectual property will be the property of the group; and
(f) disciplinary and grievance procedures and policies.

3 The interaction of service agreements and leaver provisions

3.1 General

An underlying premise in any buyout is that the managers have an ongoing and integral role in the running of the business. However, the management team is likely to evolve over time as managers depart (voluntarily or involuntarily) and are replaced. Given that the purpose of equity participation for the managers is to incentivise them, a departing manager will usually forfeit some or all of his equity interest, and it will be redistributed to his replacement or amongst the remaining managers.

As we have seen in chapter 5,[14] the articles of association will therefore include 'Good Leaver' and 'Bad Leaver' provisions which set out the detail of what happens to the equity interest of a manager who leaves the business. It is worthwhile briefly revisiting this issue, however, now that the content of a service agreement is more fully understood, and the employment context in which a dismissal takes place can therefore be appreciated.

Where a manager is a 'Bad Leaver', any shares held by the manager will be compulsorily purchased, usually at a price which is the lower of the original subscription price and the market price for the shares. There are a range of approaches that can be adopted when drafting leaver provisions, but invariably these will explicitly link the context in which the termination of employment arises to the equity position of the manager on departure.

Where a manager voluntarily resigns, the position is fairly straightforward: he will almost certainly be treated as a 'Bad Leaver', unless there were particular circumstances where an early resignation was envisaged (such as the resignation of a founder manager after a handover period on a secondary buy-out: see further chapter 12[15]). If the manager is dismissed, however, the position is more complex and will depend on the circumstances of the dismissal. Often, the investors' preferred approach (or starting-point, at least) is to define 'Good Leaver' by reference to a limited number of defined categories (such as termination of employment due to death, normal retirement, ill-health and redundancy) and to provide that all others are Bad unless a discretion is exercised to treat them as Good. In those cases, and assuming the categories are drafted

14 See chapter 5, section 4.11.
15 See chapter 12, section 3.2.

fairly, this would mean that the manager will be a 'Bad Leaver' if, for example, he is dismissed because he is seen as having generally underperformed.

However, where such an approach is resisted or negotiated, it may be necessary to consider whether a manager has been unfairly dismissed or wrongfully dismissed in order to ascertain how a leaver is to be treated. The question of whether a manager can be summarily dismissed, or has been constructively dismissed, may also be relevant.

3.2 Unfair dismissal

It is quite common to see the concept of unfair dismissal introduced when negotiating the definitions of 'Good Leaver' and 'Bad Leaver'. If such a concept is accepted, the precise drafting will be key in determining what this means in practice.

The right of an employee not to be unfairly dismissed is a statutory right. In essence, in order for a dismissal to be fair, the employer must show that it has a fair reason for dismissal (such as redundancy, conduct or capability) and that it has followed a fair procedure. For example, if an employer dismisses an employee due to redundancy, a fair procedure would require the employer to show that it had fairly selected the employee for redundancy, consulted the employee about the proposed redundancy (including considering alternative employment opportunities in the group) before confirming the decision to dismiss, and then given the employee a right of appeal against the dismissal. For a capability dismissal, unless the employee is grossly incompetent, a fair procedure will usually require a series of warnings before any dismissal, with each warning identifying the employee's performance failings, setting objectives for the employee to achieve over an identified timeframe, and making it clear that if those objectives are not achieved a further warning (and ultimately a dismissal) may follow.

It is therefore possible for an employer to have a fair and proper reason for dismissing an employee, but for the dismissal to be unfair because the employer has not followed a fair procedure. However, it is relatively common for employers not to follow a full and fair procedure when dismissing senior managers. If the investors and/or fellow directors of a manager have lost confidence in a manager, the prospect of following a protracted performance management process with a series of written warnings is unlikely to be attractive. The dismissal is therefore often effected with little or no procedure being followed. Given that the maximum compensation for unfair dismissal is capped (at approximately £77,600[16]), this is often seen as a price worth paying to remove an executive who is perceived not to be performing to the required standard. However, if 'Good Leaver' status follows from a dismissal that is procedurally unfair, the

16 This figure includes a compensatory award for loss of earnings of up to £66,200 and a basic award based on length of service and age of up to £11,400, with such figures being revised annually in February. This is the correct figure as at October 2009.

equity implications of removing the manager without following a fair procedure can be substantially greater than an employment claim for unfair dismissal. In addition, the investors will be concerned that a relatively minor failure in a dismissal procedure may result in a finding of unfair dismissal.

In light of the above, the investors will want to ensure that procedural unfairness in relation to a dismissal does not trigger 'Good Leaver' status. This can be achieved by making it clear that only a substantively unfair dismissal, and not procedural unfairness, will result in 'Good Leaver' status. The extensive set of circumstances in which a dismissal may be considered unfair, and a general assumption that an employment tribunal may be more predisposed towards the employee than an employer, means that some investors resist the concept in any event.

3.3 Wrongful dismissal

An employer *wrongfully dismisses* an employee if it terminates in breach of the employment contract, i.e. it fails to give due notice without having grounds for summary dismissal (such as gross misconduct) and, if applicable, fails to make a payment under a contractual PILON clause.

In most cases, the fact that the employer has failed to give due notice will not be seen as relevant to 'Good Leaver' status, and will instead be viewed as a separate employment matter. An employee who is wrongfully dismissed is entitled to bring a claim for damages reflecting the loss he has suffered as a result of the breach, i.e. a sum reflecting salary and contractual benefits for the notice period but subject to the employee's duty to mitigate his losses (i.e. take reasonable steps to secure new employment and thereby reduce their loss of earnings and the value of their damages claim).

As a result, the concept of wrongful dismissal is far clearer, and more under the control of the investors and the other directors, than unfair dismissal. As a consequence, the fact that an individual who is wrongfully dismissed will be treated as a 'Good Leaver' may offer little meaningful comfort to a manager, and on that basis might not be considered to be an appropriate test for determining whether a leaver should be treated as a 'Good Leaver' or 'Bad Leaver' at all. Nevertheless, it is not unusual for articles of association to include individuals who are wrongfully dismissed within the 'Good Leaver' definition. This usually serves only to reassure the manager that his contractual position will be adhered to, and does not in itself provide a manager with the protection that there must be particular grounds supporting the decision for an individual to be treated as a 'Bad Leaver'.

3.4 Summary dismissal[17]

An individual who is dismissed summarily will almost invariably be categorised as a 'Bad Leaver'. However, whether this is accepted as a given, or indeed

17 See further section 2.5 above.

might provide a basis on which the distinction between a 'Good Leaver' and a 'Bad Leaver' might be determined, will depend upon how the grounds for summary dismissal are defined in the service agreement.

For example, the service agreement may provide that the manager can be summarily dismissed if:

(a) he refuses or fails to comply with any instruction of the board;
(b) he fails (in the opinion of the board) to perform his duties to a satisfactory standard; or
(c) he commits any act which (in the opinion of the board) brings or could bring himself or the employer into disrepute.

The above grounds are substantially broader than gross misconduct, and give the board a discretion to determine whether the circumstances fall within the relevant criteria. Whilst an employer must exercise such discretion in good faith and must not act capriciously, the manager's position is relatively weak under the above drafting. Whilst a manager will not necessarily oppose linking 'Good Leaver' and 'Bad Leaver' status to summary dismissal grounds, management's advisers should try to ensure that the grounds for summary dismissal are defined as narrowly as possible.

Taking the three grounds referred to above, a manager's adviser may begin by looking to replace them with a simple reference to gross misconduct and gross incompetence. However, if the investor refuses such a narrow approach, a compromise may result so that, for example, summary dismissal only applies if the individual:

(a) 'Wilfully refuses to comply with any reasonable and lawful instruction of the board.' This requires that the manager has *wilfully* refused to comply with an instruction rather than simply *failed* to comply. It also requires that the instruction is both reasonable and lawful.
(b) 'Materially fails to perform their duties to a satisfactory standard provided the manager has first been given written notice of such failure, specifying the reasonable steps they must take to remedy such failure within a reasonable period, and they have failed to do so.' This requires a material failure to perform and, by removing the reference to the board, it means that the failure to perform must be assessed on an objective basis. It also ensures that the employer must have notified the manager of their failure to perform and given the manager the opportunity to improve before summarily dismissing them.
(c) 'Commits any act which brings them or the employer into disrepute provided always that if such breach is capable of remedy, the manager shall first have been given written notice of the breach requiring them to remedy the same within a reasonable period and shall have failed to do so.' In this example, we have again removed the reference to the board so that whether the manager has brought him or herself or the employer

into disrepute is objectively assessed. The wording also requires that the manager has in fact brought him or herself or the employer into disrepute rather than simply requiring conduct that *could* bring them into disrepute. Finally, the revised wording requires that the manager is given the opportunity to remedy the breach in the event that it is capable of remedy.

From this brief example, it can be seen that the merits of linking summary dismissal to 'Good Leaver' and 'Bad Leaver' status depends on the detailed drafting of those grounds. Such definition does not usually, in itself, provide a satisfactory means for determining all the circumstances in which a dismissal should result in an individual being treated as a 'Bad Leaver'; however, this illustration of the typical negotiation that can arise on a summary termination clause does serve to emphasise how the drafting of both the equity and the employment documentation must be understood in detail for the full commercial position to be appreciated. If an automatic 'Bad Leaver' status is accepted in cases of summary termination, more expansive drafting in the service agreement can result, as it will have far more significant commercial implications for the manager than was originally envisaged.

3.5 Constructive dismissal

Generally, if a manager voluntarily resigns from their employment, such manager will be a 'Bad Leaver' and forfeit their equity. However, if the resignation is in response to a fundamental breach of the employment contract by the employer, the termination may, as a matter of law, be deemed to be a constructive dismissal. Depending on how dismissals are treated under the leaver provisions, this could therefore result in 'Good Leaver' status even if the documentation is silent as to constructive dismissals. In any event, management may look to negotiate that constructive dismissal is expressly treated as a 'Good Leaver' situation.

If the concept of constructive dismissal is introduced in the articles, this can be broadened or narrowed by expressly providing that a resignation for 'good reason' will trigger 'Good Leaver' status, and going on to define 'good reason', rather than relying on the common law test for constructive dismissal, which requires that the employee resigns in response to a fundamental breach by the employer. A range of approaches can then be adopted in relation to the drafting of 'good reason'. A narrow approach might be to confine 'good reason' to a very limited set of circumstances, such as the manager's removal as a member of the board. A broader approach might be to add particular matters to the common law test, for example specific assurances that have been given to the employee, such as their reporting line and/or responsibilities.

In general terms, it is difficult for investors to argue that an individual who is constructively dismissed should be treated simply as a resignation (and therefore as a 'Bad Leaver'), rather than as a dismissal (which may result in

'Good Leaver' status, depending on the treatment of dismissals in the articles). The introduction of more expansive concepts of constructive dismissal will usually be resisted by investors, however. Most will wish to hold a firm line that no individual can hand in their notice before exit and expect a return, irrespective of the circumstances. However, the concept can still merit exploration where there are particular sensitivities on the part of one or more of the managers.

4 Employment issues on termination

4.1 Types of claim

In chapter 11, we will consider in some detail the issues faced by investors when considering the removal of a manager during the lifetime of the investment. The rights of the manager as a director, a shareholder and an employee must all be considered. As has already been seen in this chapter, a service agreement can only be drafted and negotiated with the eventuality of termination in mind. It is therefore convenient briefly to consider the claims that an individual may have as employee, and how those claims might be compromised.

A manager has two different types of employment rights: contractual and statutory. In the event that a manager is dismissed, the parties will need to assess the potential claims under both headings.

We have already referred in section 2 to the possibility of contractual claims following the dismissal of a manager under that manager's service agreement. Where the terms set out in the contract are not adhered to, this may result in the employer being in repudiatory breach. If such breach is accepted by the manager, this may result in the employer being unable to enforce the provisions in the service agreement (most notably, the restrictive covenants) post-termination. Where summary rights to dismiss are invoked, whether express or implied, particular care is required to ensure that the circumstances in question do entitle Newco to dismiss such individual without notice. In addition to the question of whether the manager should have been entitled to notice in circumstances where he has been summarily dismissed (with the result that the manager is entitled to a claim for damages, possibly liquidated), a wrongful dismissal may also have the consequence of a manager being treated as a 'Good Leaver' rather than a 'Bad Leaver'.

In relation to statutory claims, we have already recognised the manager's right not to be unfairly dismissed.[18] The manager will have a range of other statutory rights. It is beyond the scope of this book to list all of the manager's statutory rights in all circumstances; however, two particular areas are highlighted in sections 4.2 and 4.3 below by way of illustration. The first area, discrimination claims, highlights how statute may provide a right to claim

18 See section 3.2 above.

compensation in addition to any claims for unfair dismissal or contractual claims. The second, whistleblowing, highlights how particular legislation can impose an assumption that a dismissal should in certain circumstances automatically be considered unfair (but with more far-reaching consequences than other unfair dismissals).

As is explained in more detail in chapter 11, a termination will often lead to a 'kitchen sink' approach to negotiation, with all possible arguments in the context of the individual's dismissal being tabled to maximise that individual's compromise package. Other statutory claims might include, by way of example, claims in respect of equal pay, holiday pay or deductions made from wages.

4.2 Discrimination claims

If the manager is dismissed or subjected to a detriment on the grounds of sex, race, disability, age, sexual orientation, religion or belief and this treatment cannot be justified, the employer will be liable for unlawful discrimination. Unlike unfair dismissal, there is no cap on the compensation that can be awarded for loss of earnings resulting from a discriminatory dismissal. This is particularly relevant if a discriminatory dismissal leads to 'Bad Leaver' status in relation to the manager's equity as, in those circumstances, the potential compensatory award could reflect the loss of equity as well as loss of salary and contractual benefits.

In addition to compensation, if the manager brings a successful discrimination claim, he or she will also receive an 'injury to feelings' award. The level of these awards fall into three bands:

(a) £600 to £6,000: less serious cases, for example one-off incidents or isolated events;
(b) £6,000 to £18,000: more serious than the first band, but not meriting an award under the third band;
(c) £18,000 to £30,000: the most serious category which would apply, for example if there has been a lengthy period of harassment.

Only in exceptional cases will the injury to feelings award exceed £30,000.

4.3 Whistleblowing

If the manager is subjected to a detriment (such as dismissal) because they have made a 'protected disclosure', they may have a claim under the Public Interest Disclosure Act 1998. This protection is limited to disclosures relating to criminal offences, breaches of legal obligations, miscarriages of justice, dangers to health and safety, damage to the environment and the deliberate concealing of information about any of the foregoing.

It should be noted that this legislation can cover a wide range of disclosures. For example, a breach of a legal obligation could include a breach by the employer of a contract with a supplier, employee or customer.

If an employee is dismissed because he has made a protected disclosure, the dismissal will automatically be unfair, and the employee will be entitled to compensation for the dismissal. However, the usual cap on unfair dismissal compensation does not apply and therefore, as with a discrimination claim, the compensation could be substantial if the dismissal led to 'Bad Leaver' status and forfeiture of the manager's equity.

4.4 Compromise agreements

In the event that the manager may have claims relating to the termination of his employment, the employer may wish to consider asking the manager to enter into a compromise agreement. This is an agreement preventing the manager from issuing or continuing any statutory or contractual claims. A compromise agreement usually forms the core of any negotiated termination package where a manager is dismissed from a private equity investment.

Whilst contractual claims can be settled in a simple settlement agreement, in order to settle statutory employment claims (such as discrimination or unfair dismissal), the settlement terms must either be negotiated and concluded with the involvement of ACAS conciliation, or they must be confirmed in the terms of a formal compromise agreement. In order to be binding, the following conditions must be satisfied for a compromise agreement:

(a) it must be in writing;
(b) it must relate to particular complaints or proceedings;
(c) the manager must have received advice from a relevant independent adviser (such as a qualified lawyer or fellow of the Institute of Legal Executives) on the terms and effect of the proposed agreement and its effect on their ability to pursue their rights before an employment tribunal;
(d) the adviser must be covered (at the time they advise the manager) by a contract of insurance or an indemnity covering the risk of a claim by the manager in respect of any loss arising in consequence of that advice;
(e) the agreement must identify the adviser; and
(f) the agreement must state that the conditions regulating compromise agreements under the relevant employment legislation are satisfied.

The advantage of concluding a compromise agreement satisfying these strict criteria is that it will provide the employer with certainty that the manager is not able to pursue any employment claims. However, a potential disadvantage is that the manager will need to take legal advice in order to conclude a binding compromise agreement (thereby increasing his awareness of any potential claims), and the employer may therefore need to offer an inducement to persuade the manager to sign the agreement. For this reason, in situations where a parting is relatively amicable, but the investors or other directors are concerned that such independent legal advice may lead to a more protracted negotiation, a less formal agreement or document setting out the basis on which the position has been settled may be entered into. This does not give Newco any legally binding comfort in respect of statutory employment claims; however, investors may prefer to take this risk to avoid the more cumbersome process.

There is a range of terms that can form part of any settlement, whether in a compromise agreement or a simpler form of agreement. For example, the employer and the manager may be concerned about the impact of the manager's departure on their respective reputations. Common provisions forming part of the settlement include the following:

(a) Agreeing to a form of announcement, on the understanding that neither party will make any further announcements. The employer should be wary of agreeing onerous restrictions on what it can and cannot say under the terms of any settlement. It may need to be able to deal with questions from colleagues, suppliers and customers, and to be in a position to respond to press reports. It may be preferable to settle the form of a basic statement, and to agree that any further statements will be consistent with the tenor of that statement. This provides more flexibility than, for example, committing Newco to pre-agree all statements with the manager.

(b) Imposing a specific obligation prohibiting the manager from making any damaging or disparaging remarks about the group or its officers, employees, suppliers, customers or clients. The employee may seek a reciprocal undertaking from Newco. Newco should be wary of agreeing to procure that none of its employees will make a disparaging remark about the manager, given that Newco is unlikely to have this level of control over its employees, and the circumstances of departure may mean that such remarks are a realistic possibility in practice. Newco might instead consider agreeing to issue a written instruction to a list of named employees, requiring them not to disparage the manager, which is at least a requirement within Newco's control.

(c) Agreeing a form of reference that will be provided by Newco. Newco should bear in mind that it has a duty to any new employer to provide a fair, accurate and balanced reference. If Newco breaches this duty, the new employer may bring a claim for damages against Newco reflecting the loss suffered by the new employer as a result of it relying on the inaccurate and/or unbalanced reference. It is advisable to include a disclaimer in any reference stating that, whilst it is given in confidence and in good faith, this is on the understanding that Newco accepts no responsibility for any errors, omissions or inaccuracy in the information or for any loss or damage that may result from reliance being placed on the reference. However, the effectiveness of such a waiver is unclear,[19]

19 The effectiveness of this waiver is subject to its satisfying the requirement of reasonableness under section 2(2) of the Unfair Contract Terms Act 1977.

and, if Newco has concerns about conduct and/or performance, it is better to agree only to provide a basic reference confirming details such as job title and employment dates.

As we will see in chapter 11, the negotiation of an exit package can be a complex area, with the rights and claims of the manager as employee, director and shareholder all having to be taken into account. As such situations are often far from amicable in practice, it is essential to ensure that all of such aspects are documented at once; the signing of a compromise agreement may result in Newco and its shareholders losing the bargaining power to agree the terms on which the equity is to be clawed back from the departing manager, and *vice versa*.

5 Employee incentives

5.1 Introduction and purpose

It has become increasingly common for private-equity-backed companies to motivate those key employees who do not form part of the senior management team (and who will therefore not be a party to the investment agreement or, usually, have an equity stake) so as to align their interests with the interests of the management and investor shareholders in focusing on an exit event.

Giving employees a financial stake in their employing company should (or so the theory goes) motivate them to help promote and grow the business. Growing the business will enhance the value of the business, which, over time and in turn, will benefit those same employees as they receive greater rewards either by exercising their share awards or receiving bigger cash bonuses – a virtuous circle. Other advantages of giving employees a financial stake in their business are retention (the embedded value of their share awards may mean that their consequent loss does not warrant moving jobs) and recruitment (the potential for greater financial reward can be an attractive recruitment tool). In addition, in some circumstances, it may be possible to implement tax-efficient share incentives that benefit from being subject to capital gains tax (CGT, taxed at 18 per cent as at the time of writing) rather than as income.

In a private equity context, incentive schemes tend to focus on a small group of key *second-tier* management below board level. There is little use of *all-employee* share arrangements in private-equity-backed companies, as the scarcity of equity means that the level of reward would be marginal across all employees. However, allocating a pot of, say, 5–10 per cent of the share capital to such key managers is likely to deliver sizeable rewards on an exit. Such incentives offer a very clear line of sight for participants: stay with the company, and grow the business in order to assist in delivering an exit for the private equity funders and the senior managers, and you will share in the ultimate proceeds. Equity incentives are therefore a very efficient incentive and reward mechanism; in some cases, this can be contrasted with listed companies, where

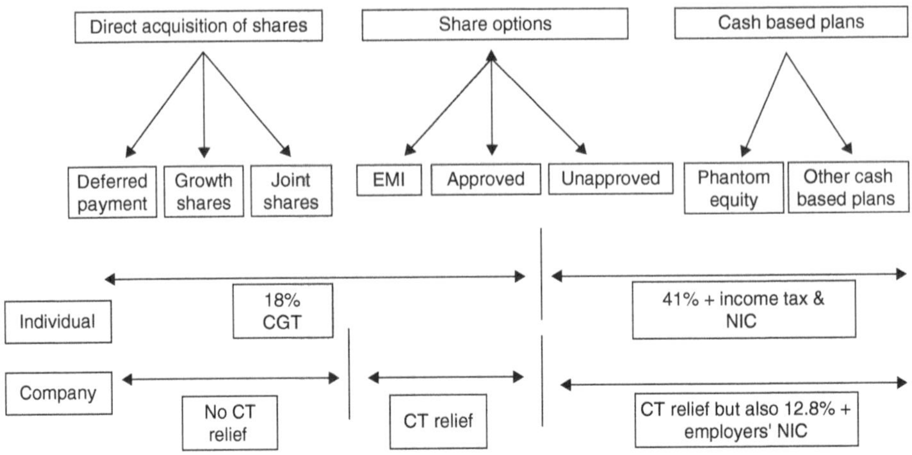

Figure 7.1 Equity incentives: an overview

the ultimate gain is subject to the vagaries of the market, and there is often little or no feeling of being able to influence the eventual outcome.

In almost all cases, the ability of employees to realise value from share options or awards is linked to an exit event, either a sale of the company or a listing. In addition, the number of shares or options that *vest* (i.e. to which any participant becomes entitled) may be dependent on certain financial objectives. These financial objectives, or performance conditions, are designed to align the financial performance of the business and the objectives of the shareholders with the financial rewards of the employee; for example, options or awards may only vest when certain predetermined profit margins, profit levels, exit returns or IRRs[20] for the investors are achieved.

5.2 Possible structures: an overview

Incentive arrangements could comprise one or more of the following alternatives. Figure 7.1 illustrates the key features, and taxation implications, of each by way of summary.

(a) Share option arrangements

Under these schemes, an employee is granted an option to acquire shares in Newco at some future time or on the occurrence of a future event. On exercise of the option, the employee must pay for the shares, and the incentive is the prospect of an increase in the value of the shares between the date when the option is granted and the date when the employee exercises it.

The UK government has helped encourage employee share ownership by creating tax-efficient methods to grant employees share options in the

20 For the meaning of IRR, see chapter 1, section 3.4.

companies they work for. These are usually referred to as HMRC-approved share plans.

In relation to private-equity-backed companies, there are two share plans which may be appropriate: Enterprise Management Incentives (EMI) and Company Share Option Plans (CSOPs). Both plans are share option plans which enable employees (if certain conditions are met) to exercise their options subject to CGT at 18 per cent and free of income tax and national insurance contributions. Such tax treatment makes the use of some share-based incentive arrangements much more attractive from a tax perspective than the use of cash.

An EMI plan allows an employee to hold an option over up to £120,000 worth of shares in a company. The rules governing who can grant EMI options and who can receive them are complex. However, broadly speaking, in order to qualify the employee must work at least twenty-five hours a week for the company (or a subsidiary) or, if less, for at least 75 per cent of the time he spends on remunerative employment and self-employment, and he cannot hold a material interest in the company (broadly 30 per cent of the voting rights). In addition, the company must be an independent trading company with (group) gross assets of no more than £30 million, and must not be carrying on an excluded trade. An additional condition that was imposed in 2008 is that a group cannot qualify if it employs more than 250 employees; this is quite limiting. A condition that can cause problems for many private-equity-backed companies is that of independence. The company whose shares are to be placed under option must not be under the control of another company. The structuring of private equity investments is quite often such that the company will be under the control of the private equity provider for these purposes, and therefore will not qualify under the EMI rules.

A CSOP is less generous, in that the market value of shares under option is limited to £30,000 and the options must, in most cases, be held for three years in order to obtain maximum tax advantages. One of the main problems with a CSOP is that the shares used must not be subject to certain restrictions. Often, in private-equity-backed companies, it is not desirable to grant options over unrestricted shares and therefore not always possible to comply with the CSOP legislation.

However a share option scheme is to be structured, care is needed in the implementation. The investment documentation will typically require the consent of the investors before any scheme can be put in place, or options awarded. This enables the investors to ensure that the shares are allocated in a way that provides an effective incentive to the correct individuals, whilst not resulting in excessive dilution of their own returns. Where a percentage pool is agreed at the time of completion of the buyout for allocation post-deal (as is quite often the case, with all parties preferring to focus their efforts on the main transaction before finalising all the detail of the share incentives), the allocation of options may fall outside the usual investor consent regime, provided that the individuals to be rewarded and terms of the scheme have been approved by the remuneration committee, and the agreed pool of shares has not been exceeded.

Care is also needed to ensure that the departure of an individual is properly dealt with. The rights of any leaver will usually be set out in the scheme rules and/or in each individual's option agreement, and are generally less favourable than the leaver terms negotiated with senior management in relation to their equity. The employee concerned will usually forfeit his or her options on departure unless there are unusual circumstances such as death or ill-health.

Any share options will usually be exercisable only upon the relevant exit event occurring. In practice, the cost of exercise is often deducted from the sale proceeds payable on the relevant shares upon the exit event occurring, with the individual employees receiving the net balance.

(b) Share award plans

Under these types of plans, an employee is allocated with a number of shares which are issued to that employee upfront. Two of the arrangements most suited to private-equity-backed companies are 'deferred shares' and 'growth shares'. These arrangements are often implemented in conjunction with an employee benefit trust, which is used to buy shares back from departing employees, and to warehouse the shares until they can be allocated to a new manager in due course.

A 'deferred share plan' is an arrangement under which employees acquire shares from the outset, but all or part of the consideration payable for them is deferred to a later date, for example an exit event. This method can be used where the shares have significant value at the time of acquisition, which the employee may be unable to fund upfront. The outstanding consideration is treated as a beneficial loan for tax purposes.

On departure, the treatment of leavers is similar to the provisions for senior managers, in that, where an employee is a 'Good Leaver', he will get market value when he sells the shares. However, where the employee is a 'Bad Leaver', he will only get back what he paid for the shares (or their market value, if less). However, as for share options, the definitions of 'Good Leaver' and 'Bad Leaver' are often less favourable to the employee for the second tier.[21]

One advantage of a deferred share arrangement is that its implementation typically only requires minor changes to be made to the articles of association, together with some relatively straightforward share plan rules and related agreements. The participant would need to fund the acquisition (or be at risk for the deferred amount), which in some cases can help align the interests of employees and shareholders, but in other cases may lead to the incentive scheme not being particularly viable. Generally speaking, this approach is

21 See further section 5.4 below.

most helpful in situations where the equity does not already have significant value; where there is substantial value already created for shareholders, the risk attached to such a scheme and the substantial contribution required (even on deferred terms) may make it unattractive.

'Growth share' schemes look to address those situations where the equity already has substantial value. Under such a scheme, employees are given a new class of share which only entitles the holders to future growth in the value of Newco. This requires a valuation of Newco to be carried out, and the creation of a new class of shares (with accompanying rights in the articles of association) such that holders will only be entitled to the proceeds from exit above that valuation. Employees subscribe for the new class of share at a more modest price (as the shares will deliver a return only if the current valuation is exceeded on exit), and as a result the difficulty of participants having to find substantial sums to invest is avoided, but the exposure to participants of a fall in value is limited to this initial subscription amount (unlike a deferred share arrangement).

In the cases of both deferred shares and growth shares, an important aim is to ensure that the participant will be subject to CGT (18 per cent at the time of writing) on the growth in value of his shares, and not to income tax and national insurance contributions. It is important that the shares are valued for tax purposes, and that both the employing company and the employees enter into section 431 elections within the necessary period post-acquisition, to ensure such tax treatment.[22]

(c) Cash-based arrangements

Alternatively, a bonus plan may be put in place that does not involve the employee receiving any shares. Instead, the bonus scheme is designed in such a way that it entitles the manager to a cash benefit by reference to the value of a company's shares, or some other key measure, on exit. For example, a 'phantom share option plan' does not involve the granting of any share options at all, but will produce a cash bonus equal to the increase in the value of a company's shares between the date of 'grant' of the phantom option and the date on which it is 'exercised'.

Such arrangements are very flexible, and have a significant advantage in their simplicity (creating clarity for the participant, which can be more effective in motivating the employee than more complex share option or ownership plans). The quantum of benefit for participants can easily be calculated upfront and, if desired, capped. Payout does not necessarily need to be linked to the value of the company and can, instead, be focused on specific outcomes or actions.

The downside of such arrangements, however, is that they do not engender the feeling of being a shareholder (although phantom equity may make the

22 See further chapter 9, section 4.3.

employee feel like a quasi-shareholder), and a cash outflow from the business, which is not usually attractive to the other shareholders on exit. More notably, such cash payment will be subject to income tax (currently payable at a far less attractive rate than capital gains tax) and national insurance contributions. With careful drafting, such bonus payments should be deductible for corporation tax purposes in the hands of Newco, although any buyer would need to be satisfied on this point if the benefit of such deduction is to be factored into the price received by the selling shareholders on any exit transaction.

5.3 Key issues to consider with all incentive arrangements

As highlighted already in the context of share options, it is necessary to consider what happens to share options or awards in the event that the participant leaves employment. Generally, it is accepted that 'Good Leavers' will be defined more narrowly than for the manager shareholders, such that it is often limited to those employees who leave for reasons such as death or ill-health, or perhaps redundancy or retirement at normal retirement age, or otherwise at the discretion of the remuneration committee. It is extremely unlikely that a 'Bad Leaver' (and, in the ordinary course of events, therefore, most leavers) would be entitled to retain his option or award following departure, so forfeiture provisions will apply such that the employee loses the option or award if he leaves at any time before exit.

It is always necessary to consider the types of shares that are to be used in incentive arrangements. Should employees have voting rights or rights to receive dividends, for example? It is again usual for the terms offered to the second-tier managers to be less generous than those offered to management shareholders, and most share incentive schemes are flexible enough to deal with these issues. For example, it is common for the shares which are the subject of such a scheme not to have voting rights at all, or for any options granted to be exercisable only on exit, such that the voting position never alters at any time during the life of the investment.

One issue that is often of significance for a private company is whether or not there is a market for the shares to be acquired under an incentive scheme, as otherwise there would be little perceived value of the incentive. Again, this is not usually such an issue for private-equity-backed companies, as share options or awards generally vest only in the event of a sale or listing of Newco.

The following key commercial requirements should also be considered:

(a) an incentive scheme should be transparent and easily understood by the employees who will participate in it;
(b) employees must 'buy in' to the arrangements, which generally means they must be able to see a clear attractive benefit;
(c) the costs incurred in implementing the plan should be affordable to Newco, and should not outweigh the potential benefits;

(d) the plan should enable Newco to offer sufficiently attractive payouts to ensure that the total reward is competitive within the marketplace, and creates an appropriate incentive to drive the business forward; and
(e) the arrangements should fit with the other components of the employees' remuneration package.

5.4 Issues on exit

On the sale of Newco, a key issue to be addressed is that any potential buyer will want to ensure that it can obtain 100 per cent of the share capital. The smaller number of employees who typically participate in an incentive scheme in a private equity context means that the logistics for the delivery of any option shares (in return for the net proceeds from sale) is often relatively straightforward. Nevertheless, it is important to ensure that drag along provisions are carefully drafted so as to capture any shares that may be issued pursuant to pre-existing options.[23] As options are a right to acquire shares, any potential buyer on a sale will consider them with great care. The risks of not adequately dealing with options are at best poor employee relations, and at worst unexpected minority shareholders. This should not be an issue for incentive plans where employees already hold shares at the time of exit.

Any option documentation entered into by participants should allow all options to become exercisable on a sale of Newco. In addition, specific provisions in the option documentation may be included whereby the option holders are given the opportunity to exchange their existing options for options over shares in the acquiring company.

When a company lists, it is usual for new incentive arrangements to be put in place to motivate and retain employees following the listing. These must comply with regulatory requirements, and address institutional investors' concerns. It may be that consideration is given to rolling over existing awards (i.e. awards granted prior to listing) into a new plan, although this is unusual.

Given the fact that equity incentives are now fairly commonplace, they should not, if properly implemented, cause any issues to the buyer on an exit, or to the broker on a listing. However, care is needed at the time of implementation to ensure that a successful exit will not be hindered, and that the participants in the scheme will not have a disproportionate level of influence at the time of exit.

6 Conclusion

The negotiation of the service agreements for management will often be an emotive and difficult area, but it is essential that adequate protection is provided both to the managers and to Newco. The complexities of employment

23 See further chapter 5, section 4.13.

law mean that specialist input must always be sought; however, it is not the case that the service agreements can be negotiated in isolation from the other investment documents. Even if the key commercial terms are reasonably clear, minor nuances in the drafting can have significant implications for the overall balance of power, or the commercial outcome on any departure. The lawyer drafting the investment agreement and articles of association must work closely with the employment specialist to ensure that the documents sit neatly together. As we will see in chapter 11, they must also work closely together in the event that a decision is ultimately reached to dismiss a manager.

Share-based incentives also have a key role to play in the private equity arena. The challenge is to implement creative arrangements to ensure that the competing interests of the investors, the senior managers and the participants are effectively aligned, such that the participants have a clear line of sight on growing the business through to an exit event. When implementing incentive arrangements for individuals outside the senior management team, the tax treatment of any particular proposal will be key, and care is needed to ensure that potential pitfalls on departure of a manager or ultimate exit are avoided.

A properly structured incentive scheme, combined with comprehensive and carefully documented employment terms, can bring significant value to bear for the benefit of all parties at the time of exit. It is essential, however, to ensure that oversight on the part of any of the lawyers will not result in any particular individual having an inappropriate reward or bargaining position; in that respect, the interests of the lawyers representing the investors and the management team respectively are often more aligned than first appears.

8 Pensions

1 Introduction

In this chapter, we look at the complexities that arise where a transaction involves a UK pension scheme. The chapter begins by explaining some basic concepts and terminology relating to UK pension schemes. For practitioners who do not encounter issues surrounding pension schemes often, the different types of scheme and regulatory framework can be intimidating, but they must be appreciated so that the issues that arise where a pension scheme is involved can be properly understood and addressed with the minimum impact on cost and timetable.

The 'moral hazard' legislation is also explained in some detail, as this is frequently encountered and has significant implications in the private equity arena. The chapter concludes with an overview of the specific issues that arise in the context of private equity deals on acquisition, during ownership and on exit.

2 Key issues and principles

2.1 Types of pension scheme

There are two basic types of pension scheme:

(a) 'Defined contribution' schemes, where the contributions to be paid to the scheme by both the members (employees) and the employers are defined (typically, as a percentage of salary). A notional member's account is maintained for each member. The benefits provided are those which can be purchased (usually from an insurance company) with the member's account at the time the pension becomes payable. The member takes all of the risks, for example in relation to investment performance, inflation and annuity rates.

(b) 'Defined benefit' schemes, where the benefits to be provided to members are defined. These are typically 'final salary' schemes where the benefits are calculated by reference to pensionable salary at or shortly before retirement (or earlier leaving date), e.g. one-sixtieth of pensionable salary for each year of scheme membership. The member knows what the benefits will be because they are defined; however, the costs of securing those benefits are unknown. Usually, defined benefit schemes are 'balance of cost' schemes. This means that members contribute at a fixed rate (sometimes nil), and the employers pay the balance of the costs. This means the employers take all of the risks on investment performance, annuity rates, and so on. Sometimes, these schemes are 'shared cost', where the members and the employers share the costs in a fixed proportion, typically 60 per cent employer, 40 per cent members.

There are some hybrid benefit designs. The most common are:

(a) 'career average revalued earnings' (often referred to as CARE), where each year's benefits are based on salary during that year; and
(b) 'cash balance': this looks more like a defined contribution scheme. However, it is a risk-sharing arrangement because the employer promises a particular cash balance at normal retirement date which is then used to purchase an annuity. The employer bears the investment risks. The members bear the annuity rate risks.

The most material risks for private equity investors relate to defined benefit schemes. The issues discussed in this chapter, therefore, primarily relate to these schemes.

2.2 Pension scheme funding

There are a number of different ways that the funding of defined benefit pension schemes can be measured. This often causes confusion. The different methods and their usual application are as follows:

(a) *IAS19 (or FRS17/IFRS) basis.* This is the accounting basis which companies are required to adopt to account for their pension schemes in their accounts. It is mandatory for accounts in respect of accounting periods commencing on or after 1 January 2005 (listed companies must use IAS19; unlisted companies can choose between FRS17 and IAS19). Prior to that, during a transitional period, the funding level on an IFRS basis was mentioned in the notes to the accounts, but did not flow into the balance sheet. For the purpose of this measure, regardless of the assets in which the scheme is invested, the liabilities of the scheme are discounted by reference to AA corporate bonds. This can lead to some anomalous results. For example, in March 2004, the AA corporate bond rate was particularly low. As a result, many companies had significant accounting deficits even though the scheme was well funded on a scheme-specific funding basis (see (b) below). In contrast, in December 2008, AA corporate bond rates were particularly high because of the difficulty of companies, particularly financial institutions, obtaining debt. As a result, in many cases the accounting position will not have been as bleak as the funding position. The accounting funding measure has no relevance for the actual funding of a scheme.

(b) *Scheme specific funding basis.* This is the basis used to determine the contributions that are payable to a defined benefit pension scheme. It is based on actuarial methods and assumptions adopted for the scheme in accordance with the Pensions Act 2004. The assumptions used vary from one scheme to another and from one actuarial valuation to another which, together with the scheme and investment experience in the intervening period, can mean that the funding level can vary greatly from one valuation date to another. Although the scheme specific funding basis arises under the Pensions Act 2004, how it applies in relation to individual schemes depends on the scheme's rules. Usually, the methods and assumptions are chosen by the trustees with the agreement of the employer, but this can vary. It is essential to review a scheme's rules to understand a scheme's balance of power. If the trustees have unilateral power to fix the contribution rate, negotiations with them on all matters will be very different than for schemes where the power is balanced between the employer and the trustees. The process for setting the contribution date is described in more detail below.

(c) *Buyout basis.* This is the cost of securing the benefits with an insurance company by purchasing annuities and deferred annuities. This generally leads to a much greater deficit for a scheme than any other basis. This basis is used when liabilities are actually being bought out, and for calculating 'section 75 debts'.[1] It also may be relevant if the Pensions Regulator is considering a clearance application where there is corporate activity which may cause material detriment to the scheme, or where it is more uncertain that the employer will continue as a going concern.[2]

(d) *PPF buyout basis.* This is a concept introduced by the Pensions Act 2004. It is a buyout basis but only for those benefits that are covered by the UK Pension Protection Fund (PPF) (see further section 3.1 below). This measure is used to determine the PPF levy which a scheme has to pay. It may also be relevant if the Pensions Regulator is considering a clearance application.[3]

The trustees of a defined benefit scheme are required to obtain actuarial valuations of their scheme annually, or tri-annually if actuarial reports are obtained for the intervening years.[4] Typically, valuations are carried out tri-annually, although trustees often have power to carry them out more often should they decide to do so. The results of the actuarial valuation are then used to determine the employer's contribution obligations.

It is a key piece of due diligence[5] to establish who has power to set the contribution rate. If the trustees have a unilateral power, then they may seek to increase

1 See section 2.3 below.
2 See 'moral hazard' in section 3 below.
3 See 'moral hazard' in section 3 below.
4 Section 224 of the Pensions Act 2004.
5 For due diligence generally, see chapter 2, section 4.

Trust Deed and Rules	Taking account of the Pensions Act 2004
Unilateral trustee power, with no power for the employer to suspend or vary contributions	Unilateral trustee power but the trustees must consult the employer
Unilateral trustee power, with power for the employer to suspend or vary contributions	Joint trustee/ employer power
Actuary power	Joint trustee/ employer power, but the actuary must certify that the agreed amounts are not less than what he would have specified

Figure 8.1 Power to set contributions

and/or accelerate employer contribution obligations following a purchase by a private equity house, particularly if the purchase is highly leveraged. The scheme's trust deed and rules govern who has power to set employer contributions, but this is subject to overriding provisions of the Pension Act 2004.[6] Individual scheme requirements vary widely, but, typically, the power may be vested as shown in Figure 8.1 (which shows the implications of the overriding provisions).

Where it is a joint power, the actual bargaining position between the trustees and the employer will be influenced by a number of factors, including what other powers the trustees have under the trust deed and rules. Key powers under a trust deed and rules include the investment power (trustees typically have a wide investment power[7]) and the power to wind up the scheme (trustees sometimes have a unilateral power). When a scheme winding up is commenced, a statutory debt will be triggered equal to the buyout deficit of the scheme (see further section 2.3 below). Although it would be a draconian step for trustees to trigger a winding up, if they have power to do so it can have a significant influence on the bargaining position in funding discussions.

Under the Pensions Act 2004, the trustees (having consulted the employer or with the consent of the employer, depending on the scheme provisions, as summarised above) must:

6 Sections 38–57 of the Pensions Act 2004.

7 This is given to trustees under most trust deeds and also under section 35 of the Pensions Act 1995, subject to express restrictions in the trust deed which are relatively unusual.

(a) decide on the methods and assumptions used to calculate the scheme's 'technical provisions'[8] (technical provisions, essentially, means the value of the scheme's liabilities);
(b) prepare a 'statement of funding principles',[9] which is a document that sets out those methods and assumptions, and the period within which any deficit is to be remedied;
(c) prepare a 'recovery plan',[10] which is the document that sets out how any deficit is to be remedied; and
(d) prepare a 'schedule of contributions',[11] which is the document setting out the contributions the employer is required to pay, including those covered by the recovery plan and those required to meet future service benefits.

All of these must be in place within fifteen months of the effective date of the actuarial valuation, although the Pensions Regulator has power to extend this (and does so in practice where the trustees must reach agreement with the employer, and it seems that this will be obtained if further time is available). If the trustees fail to put these documents in place within the required timescale (typically, because they have been unable to obtain employer agreement, or if the actuary cannot give any certification which he is required to give), the Pensions Regulator has wide power to impose contribution rates and other matters. The Pensions Regulator has been clear in its guidance that it does not expect this to occur often.

The Pensions Regulator has issued guidance to assist trustees and employers to implement the statutory funding regime. It places significant emphasis on the *strength of the employer covenant*, which is defined as the ability and willingness of an employer to meet its funding obligations under the scheme.

Trustees are very likely to take the view that a highly leveraged purchase will materially weaken the strength of the employer covenant, because the employer is arguably both less able and less willing to meet its obligations. With any proposed transaction, it is essential to engage with trustees early on in the process to reassure them where possible, and to obtain a clear understanding of whether they are likely to take steps that could lead to increased or accelerated funding requirements.

2.3 Section 75 debts

A statutory debt is triggered under section 75 of the Pensions Act 1995 (commonly referred to as a 'section 75 debt'):

(a) when a scheme winds up (as referred to in the context of trustee powers above), in which case a debt is payable by the employer (or a proportion of

8 Section 222 of the Pensions Act 2004.
9 Section 223 of the Pensions Act 2004.
10 Section 226 of the Pensions Act 2004.
11 Section 227 of the Pensions Act 2004.

the debt by each of the employers, if there is more than one) equal to the scheme deficit calculated on a buyout basis;[12] and

(b) where the scheme is a multi-employer scheme, if one of those employers ceases to have any employees who are active members of the scheme at a time when there are still active members of the scheme employed by other employers (called "an employer cessation event"), in which case a debt is triggered on the exiting employer (called the 'cessation employer') equal to a proportion of the deficit of the whole scheme, again calculated on a buyout basis, on the exit date. This is often of relevance in private equity transactions, as a section 75 debt is often triggered on the separation of a non-core business from its parent group.

There are regulations which set out further details in relation to the calculation of the debt on a 'cessation employer'. With effect from 6 April 2008, these regulations were materially amended, in particular to include a statutory mechanism whereby the amount of the debt payable by an exiting employer may be reduced. As issues can still relate to events which took place before 6 April 2008, both regimes are discussed below. In respect of any transactions being negotiated now, clearly only the post 6 April 2008 regime will be relevant.

(a) Pre 6 April 2008

If an employer cessation event occurred before 6 April 2008, then the Occupational Pension Schemes (Employer Debt) Regulations 2005[13] (the '2005 Regulations') will apply, regardless of when any action may be taken to deal with the debt.

Under the 2005 Regulations, there are two ways that the debt payable by the exiting employer can be reduced:

(a) *Apportionment under the scheme provisions.*[14] A scheme can have a rule allowing a section 75 debt to be apportioned in a way that is different from the statutory formula. However:

   (i) the introduction of a new apportionment rule will usually be a 'Type A event' and therefore a potential trigger for the Pensions Regulator's moral hazard powers (see further section 3 below); and
   (ii) any use of an apportionment power to reallocate a debt after the date that the employer cessation event occurred is automatically a Type A event. It will also often be regarded as a 'compromise agreement', whereby the trustees are regarded as having agreed to compromise a section 75 debt owing to the scheme, which again can be a trigger for

12 For the meaning of 'buyout basis', see section 2.2(c) above.

13 SI 2005/678.

14 Regulation 6 of the Occupational Pension Schemes (Employer Debt) Regulations 2005 (SI 2005/678) provides that the employer's 'share of the difference' (which is the debt due) can be the amount due under a scheme provision.

the Pensions Regulator's moral hazard powers. Further, the scheme may cease to be eligible for the Pension Protection Fund (see section 3.1 below). As a result of these implications, it would be very difficult indeed for the trustees to agree to apportion a section 75 debt which was triggered by a cessation event before 6 April 2008.

(b) *Approved withdrawal arrangement (AWA).*[15] Under an AWA, the debt payable by the cessation employer is reduced and the balance is guaranteed (the guarantor can be another scheme employer, or a person connected with the cessation employer or with another employer). An AWA must be approved by the Pensions Regulator, which approval can only be given where the debt is more likely to be paid if the AWA is approved. In practice, this can make it difficult for an AWA to be implemented, unless circumstances are such that the cessation employer is in fact unable to pay the debt and was unable to do so on the date it ceased participating.

(b) Post 6 April 2008

If an employer cessation event occurs on or after 6 April 2008, the 2005 Regulations as amended by the Occupational Pension Schemes (Employer Debt and Miscellaneous Amendments) Regulations 2008 (the '2008 Regulations')[16] will apply. Under the 2008 Regulations, there are now four ways that a section 75 debt payable by a cessation employer can be reduced. These are:

(a) a scheme apportionment arrangement;
(b) a regulated apportionment arrangement;
(c) a withdrawal arrangement; or
(d) an approved withdrawal arrangement.

Prior to April 2008, the lack of a meaningful statutory mechanism for reducing the amount of a section 75 debt payable by a cessation employer often acted as a roadblock on transactions where a section 75 debt would have been triggered. Particularly given that section 75 debts are calculated on a buyout basis, payment of the full debt was often not commercially viable. Although all of the new statutory mechanisms require trustees' consent, in practice the existence of these arrangements should mean it is possible, in some circumstances, to make arrangements whereby a reduced section 75 debt is payable to facilitate transactions.

(i) **Scheme apportionment arrangements** A scheme apportionment arrangement is an arrangement under the scheme rules whereby the cessation employer pays a lower share of the deficit than would (in the absence of the arrangement) have been the case, and whereby all or part of the amount which would have

15 Regulations 7, 7A and 7B of, and Schedule 1A to, the Occupational Pension Schemes (Employer Debt) Regulations 2005 (SI 2005/678).
16 SI 2008/731.

been the cessation employer's share of the deficit is apportioned between one or more of the remaining employers. There is no requirement for the reapportioned share actually to be paid by a particular date. The key restriction on scheme apportionment arrangements is that the trustees must agree to the arrangements, and can only do so if the 'funding test' is met.

Broadly, the funding test requires the trustees to be reasonably satisfied that:

(a) the remaining employers will be able to meet the payments which are due under the scheme's schedule of contributions (taking into account any changes required under the scheme apportionment arrangement); and
(b) the effect of the scheme apportionment arrangement will not be to affect adversely the security of scheme benefits as a result of any:
    - material change in legal, demographic or economic circumstances (as described in scheme funding legislation) that would justify a change to the method or assumptions used for the scheme's 'technical provisions' used for assessing scheme funding (see further section 2.2 above); or
    - material revision to any existing recovery plan under which a scheme's deficit is being paid off.

The introduction or use of an apportionment rule would be a potential Type A event triggering the Pensions Regulator's moral hazard powers (see section 3 below).

(ii) **Regulated apportionment arrangements** Regulated apportionment arrangements are only relevant in the case of schemes that are likely to enter the Pension Protection Fund[17] as a result of the scheme employer's insolvency.

There is no funding test for a regulated apportionment arrangement, but instead there is a requirement that it must be approved by the Pensions Regulator, and that the board of the Pension Protection Fund must not object to the arrangement.

(iii) **Withdrawal arrangements** A withdrawal arrangement under the 2008 Regulations is similar to an approved withdrawal arrangement under the 2005 Regulations (see above), in that it is an agreement between the scheme trustees, the exiting employer and a guarantor. However, with a withdrawal arrangement under the 2008 Regulations, the amount of the section 75 debt payable by the cessation employer is determined by reference to the deficit calculated on the scheme specific funding basis, rather than on a buyout basis.[18] Therefore, the amount of the debt should be much less. It may be paid in instalments.

The guarantor must provide a guarantee to pay an amount described as 'amount B'. There are two alternative methods which may be used for calculating amount B. The first is the section 75 debt which would have been payable had the cessation employer's debt been triggered at the 'guarantee time' (see

17 For more on the Pension Protection Fund, see section 3.1 below.

18 The Occupational Pension Scheme (Employer Debt) Regulations, Regulation 6C and Schedule 1A. For the meaning of 'scheme specific funding basis', see section 2.2 above.

below) rather than at the time of the employer cessation event. The second is for amount B to be (broadly) the difference between the debt triggered under the withdrawal arrangement and the debt which would have been triggered had there been no withdrawal arrangement.

Amount B will be treated as a debt due by the guarantor at the 'guarantee time' (broadly, the time of the scheme winding up, the occurrence of an employer insolvency event, or an earlier date on which it has been agreed that the guarantor will make payment).

Trustees may only enter into a withdrawal arrangement if they are satisfied that the guarantor would be able to pay the likely amount B were amount B to be calculated at the date of the withdrawal arrangement. The trustees must also be satisfied that the 'funding test' is met. This is the same as the funding test set out in relation to scheme apportionment arrangements above, except that the trustees need consider only the first limb of the test (continued ability to make payments under the scheme's schedule of contributions), not the second limb (effect on security of scheme benefits). Therefore, the funding test is technically less onerous for a withdrawal arrangement than for a scheme apportionment arrangement. This is because under a withdrawal arrangement the cessation employer pays a prescribed minimum amount (i.e. the amount of the deficit calculated on the scheme specific funding basis).

(iv) **Approved withdrawal arrangements** An 'approved withdrawal arrangement' is broadly the same as a withdrawal arrangement, but the amount paid by the cessation employer can be less (potentially nil). An approved withdrawal arrangement, as the name suggests, is approved by the Pensions Regulator.

As with a non-approved withdrawal arrangement, the cessation employer pays a lower amount than would have been due as a debt in the absence of the arrangement, and a guarantor guarantees to pay amount B in specified circumstances. However, there are the following key differences:

(a) in addition to the events which may trigger an obligation for the guarantor to make payment under the guarantee for (non-approved) withdrawal arrangements, the Pensions Regulator has the power to trigger an obligation to make payment under the guarantee; and
(b) the Pensions Regulator may release the guarantor from its obligation if payment has not yet fallen due and the Regulator considers that the approved withdrawal arrangement is no longer required.

The Regulator may approve a withdrawal arrangement if satisfied that it is reasonable to do so, and the trustees have notified it that the funding test (see 'withdrawal arrangements' above) is met. The 2008 Regulations contain a (non-exhaustive) list of factors to which the Regulator may have regard for this purpose; for example, this includes the effect of the arrangement on security of scheme benefits.

	Scheme Apportionment Arrangement	Withdrawal Arrangement	Approved Withdrawal Arrangement
Minimum initial payment	None	Deficit on: • scheme specific funding basis or • PPF buy-out basis	Expenses
Guarantor required	No but apportionment to a participating employer	Yes	Yes
Regulator approval required?	No	Yes	Yes

Figure 8.2 Section 75 arrangements

The post 6 April 2008 mechanisms which might be applied in the context of a purchase or exit are summarised in Figure 8.2.

Where a private equity firm is purchasing a participating employer, it may be possible to put a scheme apportionment arrangement in place if there is another participating employer that is suitably strong. Alternatively, the seller could look at putting a withdrawal arrangement in place. A withdrawal arrangement is unlikely to be an attractive solution for a private equity exit, however, as a private equity investor is unlikely to be willing or able to provide or procure the necessary guarantee. These possibilities are considered further in section 4 below.

3 The Pensions Regulator and 'moral hazard'

3.1 The Pensions Regulator and the Pension Protection Fund

The Pensions Regulator is a statutory body established by the Pensions Act 2004.[19] Its objectives are to:

(a) reduce the risk of claims on the Pensions Protection Fund;

19 Section 1 of the Pensions Act 2004.

(b) protect the benefits of members of occupational pension schemes; and
(c) promote, and improve the understanding of, the good administration of work-based pensions.[20]

The Pension Protection Fund (PPF) is a fund, also established by the 2004 Act, that provides protection to beneficiaries of underfunded defined benefit pension schemes whose employers become insolvent. The PPF is funded by a levy paid by all defined benefit schemes. The amount of levy a scheme pays depends on a number of factors, including the strength of the sponsoring employer (currently determined by a Dunn & Bradstreet score which attempts to measure the likelihood of company failure), and the funding level of the scheme on the PPF buyout basis.[21]

There are a number of criteria a scheme must satisfy in order to be eligible for the PPF. One of these is that the trustees must not have entered into a 'compromise agreement', for example by agreeing to compromise a section 75 debt in a manner other than those set out in section 2.3 above. Therefore, scheme trustees have to be careful not to exercise their powers in relation to scheme funding or section 75 debts in a way that would prejudice eligibility.

The Pensions Regulator has a number of statutory powers. The most significant for the purpose of the issues discussed in this chapter are those in relation to scheme funding already outlined, and the so-called 'moral hazard' powers, which allow the Pensions Regulator to impose accelerated funding on scheme employers, or even to pierce the corporate veil (in other words, look beyond the employer to third parties). For obvious reasons, this further aspect is of particular significance in a private equity context, with private equity firms being concerned to ensure that no liability attaches to those firms or their managed funds as a consequence of any actions taken.

The Pensions Regulator's moral hazard powers consist of powers to issue a 'contribution notice' or a 'financial support direction' on a scheme employer, or a person who is 'connected' with or an 'associate' of an employer participating in a defined benefit pension scheme. Both powers are considered in the following sections, as well as the meanings of 'connected' persons and 'associates' for these purposes.

3.2 Contribution notices

The Pensions Regulator can issue a contribution notice to a person, requiring that person to pay a specified sum equal to all or part of the deficit of the scheme (calculated on a buyout basis) to the trustees of the scheme.[22] A contribution notice can be issued in respect of acts or omissions which took place on

20 Section 5 of the Pensions Act 2004.
21 For the meaning of 'PPF buyout basis', see section 2.2(d) above.
22 Section 38 of the Pensions Act 2004.

or after 27 April 2004, and can be issued for up to six years after the date of the relevant act or omission.

The Pensions Act 2008 includes various amendments to the circumstances in which a contribution notice can be issued. The most substantive changes were retrospective to 14 April 2008, the date on which they were first announced. Therefore, the position for acts or omissions occurring before or after that date will differ.

(a) Pre 14 April 2008

In respect of an act or omission before 14 April 2008, the Pensions Regulator can issue a contribution notice to a person where the Pensions Regulator is of the opinion that the person was a party to a deliberate act or omission, which first occurred on or after 27 April 2004, and the Pensions Regulator is of the opinion that the 'main purpose' (or one of the main purposes) of the act or omission was:

(a) to prevent the recovery in whole or in part of a section 75 debt; or
(b) other than in good faith, to prevent a section 75 debt from becoming due, to compromise or otherwise settle a section 75 debt, or reduce the amount of a section 75 debt that will become due.[23]

The persons who can be issued with a contribution notice are:

(a) a scheme employer; or
(b) any person who is an associate of or connected with[24] a scheme employer (including individual directors), although a contribution notice cannot be issued to an insolvency practitioner.

There has been uncertainty as to what would be required to satisfy the 'main purpose' test. Would the Pensions Regulator need evidence to show that there was a conscious intent, or would it be enough that the person was aware that the pension scheme would be affected even though that was not actually the primary purpose of the act or omission? In most commercial transactions, any negative impact on the pension scheme will not be the primary purpose of the transaction, even though this may well be a known (and perhaps even desirable) result. As a result of this uncertainty, the Department of Work and Pensions confirmed on 14 April 2008 that the power to issue a contribution notice would be amended.

(b) Post 14 April 2008

For acts and omissions from 14 April 2008 onwards, the Pensions Regulator has a power to issue a contribution notice on any person who is a party to an act or omission (or series of acts or omissions) where: (a) the Pensions Regulator is of the opinion that the act or omission has detrimentally affected in a material way

23 Section 38 of the Pensions Act 2004.
24 See section 3.5 below.

the likelihood of accrued scheme benefits being received[25] (referred to as the 'material detriment' test); or (b) the Pensions Regulator is of the opinion that the main purpose or one of the main purposes of the act or omission was to prevent recovery in whole or in part of a section 75 debt or to prevent a section 75 debt from becoming due to compromise or otherwise settle such a debt or reduce such a debt.[26] The more extensive nature of the Regulator's powers, and in particular the introduction of the material detriment test, has led to widespread concern that these powers might be exercised in an increasingly wide set of circumstances.

In deciding whether the material detriment test is met, the Pensions Regulator must have regard to such matters as it considers relevant, including:

(a) the value of the assets and liabilities of the scheme;
(b) the effect of the act or omission on the value of those assets or liabilities;
(c) the obligations of any person to support the scheme;
(d) the effect of the act or omission on any of those obligations (including where the act or omission would result in those obligations being enforceable in a different country);
(e) the extent to which any person is likely to be able to discharge any obligations to support the scheme;
(f) the extent to which the act or omission has affected or might affect the extent to which any person is likely to be able to discharge its obligations to support the scheme; and
(g) such other matters as may be prescribed.[27]

There will be a statutory defence[28] where:

(a) before becoming a party to the act or failure, the person gave due consideration to the extent to which the act or failure might detrimentally affect in a material way the likelihood of accrued scheme benefits being received; this requires the person to have made the enquiries, and carried out the other acts, that a reasonably diligent person would have made and carried out in the circumstances; and
(b) either:

- where, as a result of that consideration, the person considered that the act or failure might have such an effect, the person took all reasonable steps to eliminate or minimise the potential detrimental effects that the act or failure might have on the likelihood of accrued scheme benefits being received; or
- having regard to all relevant circumstances (of which the person was aware or ought reasonably to have been aware) prevailing at the time at which the act occurred or the failure to act first occurred at the relevant

25 Section 38A of the Pensions Act 2004.
26 This second limb is the same as the pre 14 April 2008 except that 'otherwise than in good faith' has been removed.
27 Section 38A(4) of the Pensions Act 2004.
28 Under section 38B of the Pensions Act 2004.

time, it was reasonable for the person to conclude that the act or failure would not detrimentally affect in a material way the likelihood of accrued scheme benefits being received.

A more subtle change to the test with effect from 14 April 2008 was to clarify that the powers apply to a series of acts and/or omissions, and not only single acts or omissions. The Pensions Regulator's powers have also been extended where there is a transfer from one scheme (the initial scheme) to another scheme (the transferee scheme). If the Pensions Regulator would have had power to issue a contribution notice to a person in respect of the initial scheme, the power is extended to enable a notice to be issued to such person in respect of the transferee scheme, even though that person may not be a scheme employer of the transferee scheme or connected to or an associate of such a scheme employer.

For acts or omissions from 14 April 2008 to 6 April 2009 (the date on which the wider powers came into effect) the Regulator issued a statement to the effect that it will not operate the wider powers unless one of the actions or situations below is the subject of the proposed use of the power:

(a) moving the employer or pension scheme to another jurisdiction;
(b) splitting the operating company from the pension scheme without appropriate mitigation for the pension scheme;
(c) splitting the assets from the operating company without appropriate mitigation for the pension scheme;
(d) transferring scheme assets and liabilities to another scheme which did not have adequate support from an employer;
(e) running a scheme for profit without adequate account being taken of member interests; or
(f) business models in which risk is predominantly borne by scheme members, but high investment returns would benefit investors.

The Pensions Act 2004 (as modified by the Pensions Act 2008) offers some guidance on the factors which the Pensions Regulator will take into account in deciding whether to issue a contribution notice. A contribution notice will be issued only if the Pensions Regulator is of the opinion that it is reasonable to impose liability on the person[29] to pay the sum specified in the notice, having regard to the extent to which, in all the circumstances, it was reasonable for the person to act, or fail to act, in the way that the person did,[30] and such other matters as the Regulator considers relevant, including:[31]

(a) the degree of involvement of the person in the act or omission;

29 Section 38(3)(d) of the Pensions Act 2004.
30 For acts or omissions on or after 14 April 2008 only. See section 38(3)(d) of the Pensions Act 2004 which was replaced with effect from 26 November 2008 by the Pensions Act 2008.
31 Section 38(7) of the Pensions Act 2004.

(b) the relationship which the person has or has had with the scheme employer (including whether the person has or has had control of the scheme employer);
(c) any connection or involvement which the person has or has had with the scheme;
(d) if the act or failure to act was a notifiable event for the purposes of section 69 of the Pensions Act 2004 (which is a duty to notify the Regulator of certain events), a failure by the person to notify the Regulator of that event;
(e) all the purposes of the act or failure to act (including whether a purpose of the act or failure was to prevent or limit loss of employment);
(f) the financial circumstances of the person; and
(g) for acts or omissions on or after 14 April 2008:[32]

- the value of any benefits which directly or indirectly the person receives, or is entitled to receive, from the scheme employer or under the scheme;
- the likelihood of creditors of the scheme employers and any other persons with liabilities to support the scheme being paid, and the extent to which they are likely to be paid.

3.3 Financial support directions

The Pensions Regulator can issue a financial support direction on a person where a scheme employer is a *service company* or is *insufficiently resourced*.[33] A financial support direction requires the person or persons to whom it is issued to ensure that:

(a) financial support is put in place within a specified period;
(b) financial support is then maintained for so long as the scheme exists; and
(c) the Pensions Regulator is notified of prescribed events in respect of the financial support.[34]

The 'prescribed events' for these purposes are:

(a) if any person to whom a financial support direction has been issued has a duty to notify the Regulator of a notifiable event (under section 69 of the Pensions Act 2004, which is a duty to notify the Regulator of certain events[35]), a failure by that person to do so;

32 Section 38(7)(ea) and (eb), inserted with effect from 26 November 2008 by the Pensions Act 2008.
33 Section 43(2) of the Pensions Act 2004.
34 Section 43 of the Pensions Act 2004.
35 Notifiable events include a decision for a scheme employer to cease to carry on business, a breach by a scheme employer of banking covenants and a decision to sell a scheme employer.

(b) any insolvency event[36] in relation to a person to whom a financial support direction has been issued; or
(c) any failure to abide by the terms of the financial support that was put in place.[37]

A scheme employer is a 'service company' if it is a company within the meaning given by section 735(1) of the Companies Act 1985,[38] it is a member of a group of companies, and its turnover as shown in the latest accounts prepared for the purposes of its statutory accounts is solely or principally derived from amounts charged for the provision of the services of its employees to other members of that group.[39]

The test as to whether or not a scheme employer is 'insufficiently resourced' is more complex. In essence, it is satisfied where:

(a) the value of the resources of the scheme employer is less than a prescribed percentage, currently 50 per cent,[40] of the estimated section 75 debt of the scheme; and
(b) there is a person or there are two or more persons connected or associated with each other[41] (but not an individual) who is associated with or connected to the scheme employer, and the value of the resources of that person is not less than an amount equal to the difference between the estimated section 75 debt of the scheme and the value of the resources of the insufficiently resourced employer (i.e. there is an associated or connected person or persons which is capable of making up the shortfall).

Working out the value of the resources of a scheme employer for these purposes can be complicated.[42] The first step is to look at the net assets, being the aggregate of the employer's assets less the aggregate of the liabilities (including all liabilities reflected in the employer's accounts).[43] For these purposes,

36 An insolvency event is defined in section 121(2) of the Pensions Act 2004 and paragraph 5 of the Pension Protection Fund (Entry Rules) Regulations 2005, and includes administration, creditors' voluntary arrangements and administrative receivership.
37 Regulation 4 of the Pensions Regulator (Financial Support Directions etc.) Regulations 2005 (SI 2005/2188).
38 To be replaced from 1 October 2009 by Schedule 1, Part 1, to the Companies Act 2006 and replaced by section 1 of the Companies Act 2006, although section 44 of the Pensions Act 2004 has not been amended accordingly.
39 Section 44 of the Pensions Act 2004.
40 Regulation 6 of the Pensions Regulator (Financial Support Directions etc.) Regulations 2005 (SI 2005/2188).
41 As amended by the Pensions Act 2008, which removed an anomaly to the effect that the Pensions Regulator could not have issued a financial support direction where a group consisted of a number of relatively small companies, none of which could individually meet the shortfall, but which could do so collectively.
42 See Regulations 7–12 of the Pensions Regulator (Financial Support Directions etc.) Regulations 2005 (SI 2005/2188).
43 Regulation 9(4) of the Pensions Regulator (Financial Support Directions etc.) Regulations 2005 (SI 2005/2188).

any pension scheme surplus or deficit is not taken into account to avoid effective double counting. The second step is to apply any 'fair value difference', meaning that any difference between the market value of the employer's assets and the value reflected on the balance sheet is to be taken into account. The final step is then to add the 'entity value difference' to such amount, being the value of resources after the fair value adjustment. If the value of the resources of the employer, after any of these steps, is less than 50 per cent of the estimated section 75 debt of the scheme, then the employer is insufficiently resourced.

It is possible to apply to the Pensions Regulator to ask for confirmation that an employer is not insufficiently resourced.[44] However, if the value of the employer and the amount of the scheme deficit are such that this seems necessary, any confirmation from the Pensions Regulator will probably be of relatively little value, given that the test can be undertaken at any point in time. Therefore, the position could change; the employer could become insufficiently resourced shortly after such a confirmation is given.

The Pensions Regulator can issue a financial support direction on any person who is an associate of or connected with a scheme employer (see section 3.5 below). Where the scheme employer is a company, a financial support direction cannot be issued on an individual. This means that, unlike contribution notices, financial support directions cannot be issued on individual directors. A financial support direction can be issued up to two years after a person ceases to be associated with a scheme employer.[45] This was increased from one year on 6 April 2009. There is a transitional period until April 2010, where the relevant period is reduced by the number of complete months remaining until April 2010.

As with contribution notices, the Regulator can only issue a financial support direction where the Regulator is of the opinion that it is reasonable to impose the requirements of the direction on that person.[46] The matters which the Regulator must take into account, where relevant, are similar. They are:[47]

(a) the relationship which the person has or has had with the scheme employer (including whether the person has or has had control of the scheme employer);
(b) the value of any benefits received directly or indirectly by that person from the scheme employer;
(c) any connection or involvement which the person has or has had with the scheme; and

44 See Regulations 9(2) and 10 of the Pensions Regulator (Financial Support Directions etc.) Regulations 2005 (SI 2005/2188).
45 Section 43(9) of the Pensions Act 2004, and Regulation 5 of the Pensions Regulator (Financial Support Directions etc.) Regulations 2005 (SI 2005/2188).
46 Section 43(5) of the Pensions Act 2004.
47 Section 43(7) of the Pensions Act 2004.

(d) the financial circumstances of the person.

A financial support direction requires the person on whom it is issued to put financial support in place for the scheme. This may consist of:[48]

(a) an arrangement whereby all of the companies in the group are jointly and severally liable for the scheme liabilities;
(b) an arrangement whereby the ultimate holding company of the employer's group is liable for the whole or part of the employer's liabilities in relation to the scheme;
(c) an arrangement which meets prescribed requirements whereby additional financial resources are provided; or
(d) other arrangements as may be prescribed.

As the power to issue a financial support direction relies on objective tests and, in particular, has never required the Pensions Regulator to show any fault, this power has been of greater concern to private equity buyers who are concerned about the possibility of being required to provide support for a pension scheme of one of its investee companies.

At the time of writing, only one financial support direction has been issued, on 18 June 2007. It was issued against Sea Containers Limited, a Bermuda-based passenger transport and marine leasing company. It required Sea Containers Limited to provide financial support for two pension schemes of its UK subsidiary, Sea Containers Services Limited, a service company. The financial support direction was upheld by the American bankruptcy court in September 2008. This has curbed speculation that contribution notices and financial support directions issued by the Pensions Regulator may not be enforced abroad, particularly outside the European Union, although there is still some uncertainty on this point depending on the particular situation and jurisdiction.

In the autumn of 2008, it was widely reported that Duke Street Capital paid £8 million into the pension scheme of Focus DIY, a company that it had sold almost twelve months previously. Although no information was made publicly available, there was widespread speculation in the media that this payment was made as a result of threats by the Pensions Regulator to issue a financial support direction to Duke Street. As there has only been one financial support direction issued, there is no precedent for the arrangements that might be put in place in response to the issue of a financial support direction. In practice, the Pensions Regulator encourages companies to provide resources for their schemes, such that the actual enforcement of its moral hazard powers is unnecessary.

48 Section 45 of the Pensions Act 2004.

Contribution Notices	Financial Support Directions
Can be issued up to 6 years after an act or omission	Can be issued 2 years after parties cease to be associated or connected
Fault based – there must be an act or omission	No fault – based only on financial strength
Can be issued on individuals (including directors)	Can only be issued on companies where the scheme employer is a company
Requires an immediate contribution (up to the buy-out deficit)	Requires financial support

Figure 8.3 Key features of contribution notices and financial support directions

Figure 8.3 contrasts the key characteristics and tests in respect of the two moral hazard powers.

3.4 Clearance

There is a clearance procedure under the Pensions Act 2004 whereby a person can apply to the Pensions Regulator for confirmation that the Pensions Regulator will not issue a contribution notice or, in theory at least, a financial support direction on the applicant in respect of particular facts and circumstances which are notified to the Pensions Regulator in the clearance application. Where it is considered that there is or may be what is described as a 'Type A event', thought should be given to seeking clearance from the Pensions Regulator.

The Pensions Regulator issued clearance guidance in April 2005, shortly after the moral hazard powers came into force on 5 April 2005. It was clear from this guidance, and is also clear from the Pensions Regulator's behaviour, that the Pensions Regulator interpreted its moral hazard powers very widely. The 2005 guidance categorised events into: (a) 'Type A events', being events which are or may be financially detrimental and of which the Pensions Regulator would like to be notified, and in relation to which consideration should be given to seeking clearance; (b) 'Type B events', which do not affect the scheme and where clearance would not be appropriate; and (c) 'Type C events', where the position is less clear.

The term 'Type A event' has now been widely adopted to describe any event which will or may be prejudicial to a pension scheme. Type B events and Type C events, on the other hand, are not used in practice; the Pensions Regulator is only generally contacted in circumstances where there may be a Type A event.

Although expressed to be illustrative only, the 2005 guidance set out concrete examples of events that the Pensions Regulator would regard as detrimental. In summary, these were:

(a) *Change in priority.* A change in the level of security given to creditors where the scheme might receive a reduced dividend on insolvency. The granting of security other than in respect of new money would be regarded as detrimental if it affected more than 25 per cent of the assets of the group or of the employer. Although there was effectively a 'tickbox' checklist of when the test would be satisfied, in practice it was often difficult to assess whether there was a Type A event under this test in respect of a group.
(b) *Return of capital.* A reduction in the overall assets of the employer available to the scheme. A return of capital would be regarded as detrimental where a payment was made to an entity which could not be the recipient of a contribution notice or a financial support direction and the amount involved was more than two times the average return over the past three years, or where it would reduce dividend cover to less than 1.25 times (retained after tax profit, divided by the return of capital over the period).
(c) *Change in the control structure.* Where a scheme employer is sold or there is a change in the persons against whom a contribution notice or financial support direction could be issued which was *material.* Such a change would be material where it negatively affects the scheme employer's credit rating.

Under the 2005 guidance, an event was only a Type A event if the pension scheme had a 'relevant deficit'. In normal circumstances, the relevant deficit was taken to be the greater of the IAS19/FRS17 deficit or the PPF buyout basis deficit. This was a pragmatic approach, as schemes had generally not yet carried out their first scheme specific funding valuation, and there was no other consistent measure that would have been suitable. Where a scheme had completed its first scheme specific funding valuation, the deficit on that measure would be the relevant deficit if greater. This meant that companies which agreed prudent assumptions with their trustees for funding purposes could be prejudiced if they later sought clearance. Also, in the event that there was any concern that the employer was not viable as a going concern, then the buyout deficit would be the relevant deficit.[49]

In the period following the issue of the 2005 guidance, the illustrations in the guidance came to be regarded by many as a comprehensive checklist of the circumstances in which the moral hazard powers could apply. Further, where it was commercially viable, some took the approach of ensuring their scheme did not have a relevant deficit by paying additional contributions into a scheme before embarking on a particular transaction which would have been a Type A event had there been a relevant deficit.

49 For more on valuation methods and approaches, see section 2.2 above.

Revised guidance has subsequently been issued which is much less prescriptive about what is a Type A event, and how the relevant deficit should be calculated. Under the new guidance, the first question is whether or not there is a 'detrimental event'. This is essentially an event which:

(a) prevents recovery of all or part of a section 75 debt;
(b) prevents a section 75 debt from becoming due;
(c) reduces a section 75 debt; or
(d) weakens the strength of the employer covenant.

It should be reasonably clear whether any of the first three will be taking place. In general terms (although the position is not always clear), the employer covenant will be weakened if there will be an adverse impact on the employer's ability or willingness to meet its obligations to fund the scheme on an ongoing basis, or there is a reduction in the amount that would be available to the scheme on insolvency.

If there is a weakening of the strength of the employer covenant, there will only be a Type A event if it is material, i.e. materially detrimental to the ability of the scheme to meet its liabilities. Relevant factors which go towards determining if a weakening of the employer covenant is material are:

(a) the amount by which the covenant is weakened (where this can be quantified);
(b) the size of the employer after the event;
(c) the size of the scheme; and
(d) the amount of the relevant deficit.

This can be slightly circular, because the appropriate measure for the relevant deficit depends on the degree of the detriment. Usually, the appropriate measure for the relevant deficit will be the highest of the deficits calculated on either (a) the FRS17/IAS19 basis, (b) the PPF buyout basis, or (c) the scheme specific funding basis. However, a higher basis may also be relevant where the event is significantly material or, as before, if there is concern that the employer may not continue as a going concern. In the latter case, it seems likely that buyout will be the appropriate measure for the relevant deficit. Similarly, it is possible that in cases of extreme detriment, which might include highly leveraged purchases by private equity buyers, an appropriate measure might be *self-sufficiency*. This is similar to buyout, but effectively excludes the insurance company profit from the calculations. It assumes the investments are all in low-risk, fixed-return products, so that the scheme can be continued indefinitely with no requirement for further funding from the employer. Trustees and employers will often not agree how the relevant deficit should be measured, and even where they do there is a wide range that can be calculated under each method. Particularly where the detriment is material (or the trustees perceive it to be so), agreeing what the relevant deficit is can take some time. In short, it can be very difficult to ascertain what the correct measure is for the purposes of determining whether there is material detriment. As the guidance is quite new, there is relatively little precedent to assist with this question.

Clearance is a voluntary procedure under which the Pensions Regulator confirms to the applicant that it will not issue a contribution notice or, sometimes, a financial support direction[50] in respect of a particular act or omission (or series of acts or omissions). Clearance is given on the basis of the information provided to the Pensions Regulator with the application. Detailed information must be provided. The timetable for any proposal or transaction therefore needs to include sufficient time to put this information together for both the trustees (who must generally be involved in any clearance application) and the Pensions Regulator. Usually, the trustees are asked to enter into confidentiality agreements before being provided with confidential details about a transaction and its financing. A buyer will usually obtain consent from the seller before engaging directly with the trustees of a seller's scheme, although this is by no means always the case. If there is a material inaccuracy or omission in the information provided to the Pensions Regulator, the clearance will be worthless.

Ideally, the trustees should negotiate the terms of any clearance and support the application. The Pensions Regulator suggests that the trustees should behave like bankers, and normally expects the trustees to take independent financial advice. The Regulator regularly emphasises that it wants to be a referee, and not a player, in clearance negotiations. In practice, however, the Regulator often adopts a much more active role than this suggests. Occasionally, clearance is granted where the trustees (perhaps unreasonably) refuse to support the application. More often, the Regulator will require more mitigation in exchange for granting clearance than the trustees have negotiated.

3.5 Associates and connected persons

The test to determine whether a particular person or entity is connected with or an associate of a scheme employer can be quite complicated, and may have far-reaching consequences for private equity transactions. For example, it includes not only a holding company, but extends to cover any shareholder with one-third or more of the voting power at a general meeting of the scheme employer. It could also catch an investor with a smaller equity stake, if the board of directors of the scheme employer is accustomed to acting on the direction of that person. Further, having a common director makes companies connected for these purposes.

50 As noted in section 3.3, generally this will not be possible since financial support directions are not fault-based but depend on the resources of employers and their associates at any point

The terms 'associated' and 'connected' have the meanings given to them in the Insolvency Act 1986. In simple terms, a person is 'connected' with a company:

(a) where the person is a company, it is a director or shadow director of the company or an associate of such a director or shadow director;
(b) where the person is a limited liability partnership (LLP), it is a member or shadow member of the LLP or an associate of such a member or shadow member; or
(c) if the person is an associate of the company.[51]

The definition of 'associate' in the Insolvency Act 1986 is extensive,[52] and covers a range of situations between individuals and companies. A person is an 'associate' of an individual if that person is:

(a) the individual's husband or wife or civil partner,
(b) a relative of:
    (i) the individual; or
    (ii) the individual's husband or wife or civil partner; or
(c) the husband or wife or civil partner of a relative of:
    (i) the individual; or
    (ii) the individual's husband or wife or civil partner.

A person is an associate of any person with whom he is in partnership, and of the husband or wife or civil partner or a relative of any individual with whom he is in partnership; and a Scottish firm is an associate of any person who is a member of the firm. A person is also an associate of any person whom he employs or by whom he is employed.

A company is an associate of another company:

(a) if the same person has control of both, or a person has control of one and persons who are his associates, or he and persons who are his associates, have control of the other, or
(b) if a group of two or more persons has control of each company, and the groups either consist of the same persons or could be regarded as consisting of the same persons by treating (in one or more cases) a member of either group as replaced by a person of whom he is an associate.

Finally, a company is an associate of another person if that person has control of it or if that person and persons who are his associates together have control of it.

in time. There was a 'squash court clearance' process, which allowed for a clearance in respect of financial support directions, provided that certain conditions were met before any dividend was paid, but this proved difficult in practice and was not widely used.

51 Section 249 of the Insolvency Act 1986.

52 Section 435 of the Insolvency Act 1986.

For these purposes, a person has control of a company if:

(a) the directors of the company (or another company which has control of it, or any of them) are accustomed to act in accordance with his directions or instructions; or
(b) he is entitled to exercise, or control the exercise of, one-third or more of the voting power at any general meeting of the company (or of another company which has control of it).

Therefore, a private equity firm may be connected with a scheme employer, depending on the particular structure of the firm's funds and the investment by those funds. For example, even where steps have been taken to ensure that the shareholding of an investor is less than 50 per cent of the share capital of an investee company (as often occurs to avoid the investee company being a subsidiary of such investor), such investor may nevertheless be an associate of or connected with it. Similarly, where funds have been established using a limited partnership structure as typically encountered in the UK, the general partner may well be associated or connected with the employer depending on the shareholding of each fund, the overall fund structure, and the relationships between different funds.

4 Private equity transactions

4.1 Introduction

We have already made reference to a number of situations where the issues concerning the triggering of a section 75 debt, or the moral hazard legislation, can have implications for private equity firms. With the substantial body of legislation now surrounding pension schemes, and the uncertainty created by some of the broader provisions, it can be difficult for practitioners to identify exactly which issues will apply to any particular situation in practice. In this section, we will briefly outline the key issues typically encountered in the private equity arena. It is beyond the scope of this book to provide comprehensive details on all of the issues that might be faced; however, it is intended that this section, combined with the background information that preceded it, will provide the reader with a useful starting-point for tackling this complex area.

The pensions issues that arise on the initial acquisition will vary depending on whether the acquisition is to be structured as a share purchase or an asset purchase. Where the acquisition will involve a purchase of shares in Target (as is more usual, although the existence of a scheme may in itself be a factor in deciding that the deal should be structured by way of asset purchase instead), it is essential to establish whether Target is the principal employer of a pension scheme, in which case the pension scheme will be acquired along with the Target unless steps are taken to change the principal employer to a group company retained by the seller, or alternatively whether Target is a participating employer in the seller's group pension scheme.

We will begin by explaining the issues in the case where Target is a participating employer, and the initial transaction is a share acquisition, as this is most frequently encountered. We will then look at the issues faced where Target is the principal employer, and then the issues on an asset rather than a share purchase, before concluding with a summary of the issues faced if Target continues to offer final salary benefits during the lifetime of the investment and on exit.

4.2 Issues when acquiring a Target which is a participating employer

If Target participates in a seller group pension scheme, the most likely impact of the transaction is that Target will cease to participate in the scheme from completion, in which case a section 75 debt will become payable by Target.

The issues for the buyer are:

- What is the estimated section 75 debt that will be triggered?
- Will steps be taken to seek to obtain the agreement of the trustees (and, where appropriate, the Pensions Regulator) to reduce the section 75 debt?
- Who will actually pay the section 75 debt and, if it is not the Target, how will the Target receive an effective discharge of its liability?
- Are there any other provisions which may impose liability on Target, in particular under the scheme rules?
- Are there any moral hazard issues?
- What future service benefits will be provided and how?
- Will the buyer accept liability for past service by allowing for past service transfers?

(a) The section 75 debt

Unless action is taken to change the position, a section 75 debt will be payable by Target when it ceases to participate in the scheme on its acquisition by the private-equity-backed Newco. There are various options for dealing with this including reaching agreement with the trustees that the amount due will be a reduced amount (possibly nil), and/or that the debt will be payable by a different party, using the statutory provisions described in section 2.3 above. Another key issue will be whether any payment made to the scheme is eligible for tax relief.

Where a section 75 debt will be triggered, the most common outcomes are as set out below.

(i) **Target pays the section 75 debt in full** A complexity with this approach is the fact that the actual amount of the section 75 debt will not be known for some time after completion, when the section 75 debt has been certified by the scheme actuary and demanded by the trustees. It is therefore difficult to estimate with any accuracy the appropriate price reduction before completion.

Where this approach is adopted, the price adjustment is usually made after completion, when the actual amount of the debt is known.

An amount equal to an estimate of the section 75 debt is sometimes held in a retention account.[53] When the section 75 debt is calculated, the amount needed to pay the section 75 debt can then be released to the Target (or to the buyer, who must procure that the Target pays the section 75 debt), with any balance remaining being released to the seller, or any shortfall being made good by the seller, as applicable. It must be Target and not the buyer that pays the section 75 debt in order for tax relief to be available. An adjustment is then made to the purchase price to reflect the payment by Target.

(ii) **Seller pays or procures payment of the section 75 debt in full** This can be more straightforward, as there is no need to reduce the purchase price. The seller will seek to ensure that tax relief is available, whilst the buyer will want to ensure that the liability of Target is discharged, as quickly as possible. The seller could make the payment as the Target's agent, although this needs to be documented carefully.

A withdrawal arrangement[54] can be used to transfer the liability from Target to the seller group company that will make the payment. The trustees should not have difficulty in agreeing such a withdrawal arrangement that involves payment of the section 75 debt in full.

(iii) **Target pays the section 75 debt in part** A withdrawal arrangement can be entered into whereby a reduced section 75 debt is paid by Target, with the balance being guaranteed by an appropriate seller group company. This requires the agreement of the trustees, the Target and the guarantor. Unless the arrangement is approved by the Regulator, the reduced debt payable by Target must be at least equal to Target's 'share' of the deficit calculated on the scheme-specific funding basis. The actual debt that will be paid by Target will need to be factored into the purchase price (in advance if possible, or as a price adjustment if not). The time needed to secure the trustees' agreement must be factored into the transaction timetable.

The trustees must be satisfied that the guarantors[55] would be able to pay the estimated guaranteed amount, and the 'funding test' is met, before they have the power to agree.

An alternative would be to enter into a scheme apportionment arrangement whereby a reduced section 75 debt (potentially nil) is paid by Target with the balance being apportioned to one or more other participating (seller group) employers. The trustees, Target and the employers taking an additional liability all must agree. This can be attractive to companies, as a separate formal guarantee is not required, but will only work if there is an appropriate

53 See chapter 4, section 2.4, concerning retention accounts generally.

54 See section 2.3 above.

55 See section 2.3 above.

company that is participating. In appropriate circumstances, a company can become a participating employer to facilitate this approach.

A material factor for the trustees in deciding whether to agree to a scheme apportionment arrangement will be the proposed use by the seller of the sale proceeds from the transaction. If they are to be retained within the seller group which sponsors the pension scheme, they may be more likely to agree. If there is to be a dividend to a parent company which has no formal obligation to fund the scheme, or to ultimate shareholders, the trustees may be less likely to do so, or may in that situation insist that a proportion of the section 75 debt is paid by Target.

As any such arrangement reduces the amount of a section 75 debt that will be payable by the exiting company, the parties should also consider whether it is a Type A event and whether clearance should be sought. A private equity buyer will be particularly concerned about any risk of liability being imposed on Target which has not been reflected in the purchase price. If the seller is sufficiently strong, that risk may be able to be addressed with an indemnity alone. However, it is more prudent (and therefore more likely) that clearance to the proposal will be sought from the Regulator, or alternatively that a regulated withdrawal arrangement will be used (see further section (c) below).

(iv) **Target continues to participate in the seller group scheme after completion** This approach avoids triggering a section 75 debt at the time of completion. However, it is often unattractive for a number of reasons, including:

- The section 75 debt is merely delayed until Target in fact ceases to employ scheme members. Protection against this liability, which will not arise until an unknown time in the future, is difficult to achieve. An indemnity might be sought for such liability, but that of course relies on the continued strength of the person providing the indemnity.
- Target will be required to continue to pay contributions to the scheme, but will most likely have no input into how those contributions are set. Contribution caps and indemnities can be negotiated, but, as there is a direct liability from Target to the scheme, these will again only be effective if the seller group remains of sufficient financial strength.
- The whole buyer group will be connected to Target, which remains a scheme employer for the purposes of the moral hazard legislation, and as a result will be exposed to the Regulator's moral hazard powers.

It is therefore unusual for this solution to be adopted, although it should not be overlooked altogether. For example, it may be appropriate if the seller group is strong and the number of affected employees is small.

(b) Other provisions imposing liability

A crucial part of the due diligence process will be the review of the scheme's governing documents, to assess whether there are any provisions under which liability can be imposed on Target. For example, scheme rules may include provisions requiring contributions on exit which are similar to section 75 debts. They are relatively unusual, but must be dealt with at the same time as the section 75 debt when they exist.

(c) Moral hazard issues

Another key issue on the acquisition of a Target which is a participating employer is the question of whether there are any moral hazard risks associated with the transaction. If the section 75 debt is paid in full, then it seems unlikely that there should be any moral hazard risks for the Target in respect of the seller's scheme. Nevertheless, it is not unusual (and generally considered reasonable) for the buyer to request indemnity protection from the seller. A contribution notice could technically be imposed for up to six years if the Target was involved in a relevant act or omission prior to completion. A financial support direction could be imposed for up to two years after completion if any scheme employer is 'insufficiently resourced' during that time (or is a service company).

The Pensions Regulator can only impose liability on a person if it forms the opinion that it is reasonable to do so. It is difficult to see how this conclusion could be reached if Target paid its section 75 debt in full. Nevertheless, it is usual to find indemnity protection, or at the very least robust warranty cover, even when a section 75 debt is to be paid in full. If the seller group is not strong, this risk should be considered further; if the seller group were to fail, the Regulator may regard a strong Target backed by private equity funders as an attractive party to pursue.

If a section 75 debt is not to be paid in full, the buyer will need to consider very carefully the associated moral hazard risks and how they are to be addressed. As noted above, a withdrawal arrangement or scheme apportionment arrangement which reduces a section 75 debt is potentially a Type A event. The simplest option would again be an indemnity from the seller, which is usually not resisted (since it would be unreasonable to expect Target or the buyer to make a payment into the seller's scheme which has not been factored into the purchase price). If the buyer is not comfortable relying on the seller's indemnity, particularly for a larger exposure where the seller's group ongoing covenant is more questionable, then an alternative solution will be required.

One option would be a regulated withdrawal arrangement. Although this is different from clearance, it is difficult to see how the Regulator could form the view that it is reasonable to impose liability on Target in circumstances where the Regulator approved the agreement whereby the section 75 debt payable by Target was reduced. This could lead to parties seeking approved withdrawal arrangements even where a scheme apportionment arrangement or an (unapproved) withdrawal arrangement would have been possible.

The other alternative is to seek clearance. This has typically been the approach adopted, although it can be an expensive option as the Regulator has, until recently, usually required the deficit (calculated on a scheme-specific funding basis, accounting basis or PPF buyout basis, whichever creates the greatest deficit) to be fully funded, usually over a short period of say three to five years, in exchange for granting clearance. Recently, in part in response to the more challenging economic times, the Regulator has in appropriate circumstances indicated a willingness to be more flexible, for example by accepting non-cash mitigation rather than insisting on the full deficit being paid in cash. Such mitigation might include guarantees or liability-reduction exercises,[56] which combined with a smaller cash contribution can eliminate the deficit.

If any guarantee were given as part of such a package, it should ideally not exceed the expected period of ownership. Guarantees also add extra complexity on exit; they may need either to continue or to be replaced. In any event, private equity funds are unlikely to be willing or able to provide such guarantees themselves.

The seller may have its own moral hazard concerns. This will be the case if there are any proposed Type A events associated with the sale, such as the payment of a dividend, or if the sale of one subsidiary could impact on the strength of covenant of the remaining group (for example, if the companies supply goods to one another, have common customers, or have inter-company debt to be taken into account).

If the seller or the buyer wants to make the obtaining of clearance a condition precedent to the transaction, this can cause delays and, possibly, prevent the transaction from completing.[57] It is therefore important to identify at the outset whether this is an issue and involve the trustees and the Regulator so that they are ready to respond quickly where necessary.

(d) What future service benefits will be provided?

Assuming the Target ceases to participate in the seller group scheme, alternative arrangements will need to be made for future service pension benefits for affected employees.

Considerations are:

(a) Do employees have a contractual right to any particular type of benefits? Often, employees (senior executives in particular) may have express contractual provisions entitling them to be a member of a defined benefit scheme, possibly with a pre-determined level of benefits. Usually, care is taken to ensure that the right to be a member of a pension scheme is subject to the scheme's trust deed, and rules which confer powers to amend or terminate the scheme. Employees from privatised industries or who were outsourced from the public sector often have such statutory or contractual rights.

56 Liability-reduction exercises are steps to reduce scheme liabilities through transfer or buy-outs. See further section 4.5 below.

57 On conditions precedent generally, see chapter 4, section 2.5.

(b) Will there be an adverse reaction from employees if less generous future service benefits are provided? In difficult economic times, this may be less likely, as employees will be protective of their jobs, but in prosperous times this can be a significant concern.
(c) In 2012, legislation is expected to be introduced requiring employers to provide a minimum level of pension benefits (e.g. for a defined contribution scheme, minimum employer contributions of 3 per cent).

If there is a contractual right to particular benefits, the buyer will need to consider what steps to take to mitigate the risks of employees disputing a unilateral change to their contracts of employment, for example by obtaining individual consents to the new terms. If there is no right to particular benefits, Target can provide whatever pension benefits it likes, subject to compliance by Target with its duty of mutual trust and confidence to its employees and, if they are introduced from 2012, the new minimum requirements.

In this regard, it is helpful if a meaningful consultation is undertaken with employees. There is an obligation under the Pensions Act 2004[58] to consult with employees for a minimum period of sixty days over changes to future service pension benefits. Historically, there was no clear sanction for breach and, in particular, a breach does not invalidate the change itself – although, from April 2009, changes to this legislation mean that a breach could lead to a £50,000 fine. It is also not clear from the legislation whether the obligation to consult applies in the context of changes made as a result of corporate transactions, rather than in the ordinary course of business without any change of ownership. In practice, a shorter consultation is often carried out in the case of transactions because of time constraints, or consultation is carried out post-completion with the changes then being backdated.

Of course, a private equity buyer may consider that the acquisition is an opportunity to reduce staff benefit costs. However, the removal of a pension benefit may often constitute a significant reduction to the remuneration package of employees. To avoid unnecessary adverse impact on morale, or claims that the change is a breach of contract or the employer's duty of trust and confidence, it is prudent to approach any proposed change sensitively, consulting where possible.

(e) Past service transfers

Sellers may try to impose an obligation on buyers to accept liability for past service benefits, by a contractual commitment to allow transfers in respect of past service benefits to the buyer's new scheme. This would reduce the liabilities in the seller's scheme and, depending on how the amount of the transfer payment is calculated, may improve the funding position. This is often particularly attractive to sellers with large schemes, or where the Target employees represent

58 Sections 259–261 of the Pensions Act 2004.

a significant proportion of the active members of the scheme. Transferring past service liabilities may reduce the section 75 debt, and may assist in obtaining agreement from the trustees to a withdrawal arrangement (as a transfer would result in the same business continuing to back the same pension liabilities).

Transfers can be made without employee consent if the past service benefits offered by the buyer's scheme are broadly no less favourable than the benefits in the seller's scheme (which in practice usually means identical or close to it). If the benefits are to be different (most obviously, if the buyer's scheme is defined contribution), then individual employees' consents will be required. A transfer without consent will therefore only be appropriate if the buyer will provide a defined benefit scheme for Target employees. Private equity buyers generally resist such a proposal – having a defined benefit scheme will prove burdensome during the life of the investment, and cause the same issues on exit as those encountered by that buyer on purchase.

It may be attractive to allow employees to take past service transfers to a new defined contribution scheme on an enhanced basis. This allows the seller to rid its scheme of liabilities, and may well improve the funding position of the seller's scheme on both an accounting basis and a scheme specific funding basis (and almost inevitably will do so on a buyout basis) notwithstanding the enhancement. Although buyers may not be agreeable to accepting such transfers in all cases, it can help ensure that a transfer to a defined contribution scheme is received more positively by employees. Of course, the clean break offered to the seller by such a proposal can be reflected in price negotiations between the parties.

4.3 Target has its own pension scheme

Where Target is the principal employer, the pension scheme will effectively transfer to the buyer group, and therefore the position of the scheme will be even more central to the underlying transaction.

The areas that must be considered and negotiated are complex, necessitating detailed discussions and negotiations between all parties, with the benefit of actuarial advice where appropriate. The main issues to be considered are the following.

(a) Agreeing the implications for the price

Most fundamentally, an appropriate adjustment will be needed to the purchase price to reflect the scheme funding level. This will require actuarial advice, and is invariably an area of intense negotiation.

(b) Funding obligations of Target going forward

The trustees may seek to accelerate Target's contribution obligation if they have concerns over the viability or the ongoing ability and willingness of Target to fund the scheme following the transfer of ownership. In the context of a leveraged private equity deal, the trustees may very well take a more prudent approach towards funding after completion, as they will be concerned that there may be an impact on both ability to pay (because servicing acquisition debt will reduce available cash) and a willingness to pay (because of a perception that private equity owners will be more reticent about funding).

This would be consistent with Regulator guidance, which places significant emphasis on the importance of the strength of the employer covenant as a cornerstone for funding matters.[59] The buyer will have to undertake significant discussions and negotiations with the trustees in this respect.

(c) Additional due diligence

The focus of legal due diligence in recent years has often been around moral hazard risks and the extent of the section 75 debt where Target is a participating employer. Where Target is the principal employer, it is essential that due diligence also identifies any powers the trustees have which may be of ongoing concern. For example, they will typically have power to trigger a valuation (with the practical result that the trustees then use such valuation exercise to seek an increase to contributions), and power to switch to a more prudent investment strategy (which will ultimately increase costs). They may have unilateral power to fix employer contribution rates, or to trigger a winding up of the scheme (which would trigger a section 75 debt).

Further unfunded liabilities may also be identified by due diligence, for example if a scheme closure or reduction in benefits has not been validly adopted (as often arises if a scheme has attempted to reduce future service accrual or close without the drafting being closely scrutinised from this perspective) or if a scheme has benefits which are discriminatory (as between men and women, or on the grounds or age).

(d) Moral hazard

It will be necessary to consider whether clearance from the Pensions Regulator should be sought, and if so what the funding and timing implications are likely to be. This is particularly important for a private equity buyer as part of a highly leveraged transaction, as this will inevitably be regarded by the trustees and Pensions Regulator as detrimental as the scheme will transfer to a highly leveraged group where the ability and willingness of the employer to fund the scheme are very likely to be regarded as having been adversely affected.

4.4 Target is acquired as an asset purchase

Where the acquisition is structured by way of an asset purchase, there are no moral hazard risks for the buyer in connection with a seller group scheme (unless

59 See Regulator Codes of Practice on 'Funding defined benefits' and 'How the Pensions Regulator will regulate the funding of defined benefits'.

a buyer group company is connected with a seller group scheme employer, e.g. if there are common directors). The seller may have moral hazard concerns, for example if it proposes to distribute the sale proceeds. Similarly, if a seller group company will cease to participate in a seller group scheme as a result of the sale, a section 75 debt may be triggered. This will be a concern for the seller and not the buyer; a buyer of a business where the Target employees participate in a defined benefit scheme will only be concerned about these issues to the extent that they raise commercial issues (particularly as to timing) for the seller to the point that this has an impact on the transaction as a whole.

The buyer's other concern will relate to what future service benefits should be provided. The decision as to the future service benefits can be difficult for the would-be buyer in a competitive bid situation. Providing ungenerous benefits may be a disadvantage if the seller is paternalistic towards its employees, is concerned about the perception of retained employees, or if there is strong union involvement. Conversely, assuming more generous provision may result in the bid price seeming uncompetitive, if another bidder makes less provision for future service costs.

The obligations on the buyer of the business will be governed by the Pensions Act 2004 and the Transfer of Undertakings (Protection of Employment) Regulations 2004 (TUPE). Under the Pensions Act 2004, and regulations made thereunder,[60] the buyer must provide a minimum level of pension benefits for future service. The minimum benefits to be provided depend on whether the buyer's scheme is defined benefit or defined contribution. In summary, the minimum is:

(a) *defined contribution scheme*: employer contributions of up to 6 per cent to match the rate of contributions paid by the employee. This is limited to 6 per cent of 'basic pay'. Note that this applies even if the seller's scheme was less generous than this; or
(b) *defined benefit scheme*: a scheme which meets a qualitative test (broadly, a final salary scheme which provides one-eightieth of average qualifying earnings for each year of pensionable service), or which meets fairly ambiguous prescribed criteria (which broadly suggests the minimum employer contribution towards the benefits should be at least 6 per cent of pensionable pay).

It is possible for the employee and the buyer to agree to contract out of these obligations after completion.

If the transferring employees were formerly members of a defined benefit pension scheme, they may also have rights to redundancy or early retirement benefits which transfer under TUPE. Under TUPE, the rights and obligations relating to employees are generally transferred from the seller to the buyer

60 Sections 257 and 258 of the Pensions Act 2004, and the Transfer of Employment (Pension Protection) Regulations 2005.

on an asset sale. This means that an employment contract has effect after a transfer as if it had been originally made between the employee and the buyer. However, there is an exception for rights to old age, invalidity and survivors' benefits under an occupational pension scheme.[61] This means that an employee's rights to these benefits under an occupational pension scheme, whether the seller's scheme is defined benefit or defined contribution, will not transfer to the buyer.

However, whilst rights to old age, invalidity and survivor benefits under an occupational scheme do not transfer, any other benefits under an occupational pension scheme will transfer under TUPE. Obligations under an employment contract to make contributions to personal pension schemes transfer, as do obligations to provide life assurance benefits through schemes which are not occupational pension schemes. Two decisions of the European Court of Justice[62] are authority for redundancy benefits under pension schemes transferring under TUPE, along with other benefits payable before the scheme's normal retirement age, e.g. a right to retire early.

There are arguments that this principle will not apply in the private sector, since both of the cases referred to above involved public sector schemes where the redundancy/early retirement pension was a separate benefit from the pension at normal retirement age (i.e. the schemes did not simply put the old age pension into payment, and so this was arguably a separate contractual entitlement). However, these technical arguments have never been tested, and it is therefore common practice to address these potential liabilities in the asset purchase agreement. Such rights are often referred to as 'Beckmann rights', named after the first of the aforementioned European cases.

Unlike the minimum obligations under the 2004 Act, the employee and the buyer cannot contract out of these rights. It is therefore a key piece of due diligence to identify what Beckmann rights there are in a seller's scheme, and consider how to address them. Options for addressing such rights are:

(a) ignore them for the purposes of future pension provision (and seek to manage the risk of claims being brought);
(b) seek indemnity protection for past service benefits, and possibly also for future service costs (particularly where redundancies are envisaged in the short term);
(c) replicate the benefits for the future (in practice, this is relatively unusual, particularly for private equity buyers who will not usually have a scheme in place with which to replicate the benefits, and will not want to establish one);
(d) replicate the benefits for a period, and seek to change them at a later date in a way that is not associated with the TUPE transfer (again, this would

61 TUPE, Regulation 10.

62 *Beckmann* v. *Dynamco Whicheloe Macfarlane Ltd* [2000] PLR 269; and *Martin* v. *South Bank University* [2004] IRLR 74.

be unusual for a private equity buyer which did not already have a scheme in place);

(e) participate in the seller's scheme (this is very unusual because of the moral hazard risks and section 75 debt issues arising where a non-group company continues to participate in a scheme, as outlined in section 4.2 above).

The degree of risk as to whether Beckmann benefits may become payable will influence the approach taken to address the risk, and possibly the decision as to what future service benefits will be provided.

As for a share purchase where Target is only a participating employer, there is no obligation for a buyer to involve itself in past service benefits. However, offering to accept transfer payments in respect of past service benefits (see section 4.2 above) may again be helpful – and may result in a lower price being acceptable, as the seller will reduce its liability under its retained defined benefit scheme.

4.5 Issues during ownership and on exit

There will usually only be material pension issues for a private equity buyer during ownership, or on ultimate exit, if the Target is a principal employer, such that the buyer effectively acquires a defined benefit pension scheme. There are references above to situations where a buyer might establish a defined benefit pension scheme, but in practice this is extremely unusual.

Where a private equity buyer does find itself owning a company or group with a defined benefit pension scheme, for whatever reason, it will be important during the period of ownership:

(a) to ensure that the employer company does not pay contributions to the scheme which will not ultimately be reflected in the sale price on exit;

(b) to prevent the trustees (to the extent it is possible) from adopting more prudent assumptions, which could lead to a reduction in the sale price at the time of exit because of a deteriorated funding position; and

(c) to maintain a good working relationship with the trustees to ease any discussions that may be necessary in relation to any Type A events that may occur during ownership (e.g. payment of dividends), section 75 debts that may be triggered during ownership (if Target is a group of companies and there is a restructuring during ownership), or at the time of exit.

If any Type A events occur during ownership, consideration should be given to seeking clearance.

It may be preferable to pay amounts into the scheme during ownership (which should ultimately be reflected in the sale price), rather than waiting to pay amounts into the scheme after exit (which will not be reflected in the sale price). The Focus DIY case referred to above[63] highlights the possibility of a private equity firm being required to contribute to a scheme after exit if issues are not addressed during ownership.

With a view to maximising return on exit, and reducing the negative impact that a defined benefit scheme may have on how attractive Target may seem to potential buyers, an owner may wish to consider whether any liability management exercises should be pursued. These could involve:

(a) reducing future service benefits (to reduce the extent to which liabilities increase during ownership);
(b) closing the scheme to future accrual, to prevent further defined benefit liabilities from accruing;
(c) offering deferred pensioner members (enhanced) cash transfer values to reduce scheme liabilities;
(d) encouraging the trustees to buy out portions of the scheme liabilities with an insurance company if and when the market conditions are attractive;
(e) encouraging the trustees to follow a different investment strategy, if it is felt either that the trustees should:

    (i) invest more prudently to reduce volatility – an owner may wish to reduce the risk of scheme asset values dropping, which would increase the deficit and increase a price adjustment on exit (while accepting that the long-term expected returns will be lower); or
    (ii) invest less prudently to maximise return – an owner may prefer to see the trustees invest in assets with greater anticipated returns which, over the long term, could reduce costs.

These techniques should help to reduce any price reduction that is made in respect of the pension scheme at the time of exit.[64]

If Target has its own defined benefit pension scheme, then clearly the issues raised in the context of the original acquisition in the preceding sections will again apply on a subsequent sale. Such issues will also arise on a sale by Target of any subsidiaries, or underlying businesses or assets, by way of partial exit. A private equity buyer must always be mindful of how the issues on the original deal will return, in reverse, on exit if Target has a defined benefit scheme.

On any exit or partial exit, thought must be given to whether clearance should be sought in connection with the sale. If clearance is obtained, there is relative certainty of a clean exit, and that there will be no post-completion surprises. If the Target is highly leveraged immediately before sale, then it is perhaps less likely that the sale itself will be a Type A event – the position of the trustees, as unsecured creditor, may not be worse (or may even be better) after the sale when compared with before. However, where the acquisition debt

63 See section 3.3 above.

64 As outlined in section 4.2, such techniques can also reduce the cash contribution required to obtain clearance.

has been repaid or partially repaid, there may well be a Type A event, particularly if the sale is to a new leveraged buyer rather than a trade acquirer with a strong balance sheet.

As ever on exit, consideration must be given to the comfort that was obtained on the original transaction, in order that the comfort offered to the ultimate buyer on exit matches that protection. For example, where the Target was acquired by way of asset purchase rather than a share purchase, it will be important to seek to ensure that any warranties or indemnities for Beckmann liabilities[65] do not go wider than the warranties or indemnities that were given at the time of purchase.

5 Conclusion

Private equity investors often seek to avoid acquiring or investing in companies with defined benefit pension schemes. This is understandable, as the potential liabilities are often material and volatile, and the issues which need to be addressed are complex. However, there are steps that can be taken to reduce the impact of a defined benefit scheme, and private equity investors should not necessarily dismiss an otherwise attractive investment simply because of the existence of such a scheme. There are steps that can be taken to mitigate the risk and, with actuarial advice, the risks can also be factored into the price.

The attention to legislative developments in the press often focuses on the negative – the increased breadth of the Regulator's powers, for example. However, there have been helpful developments too, such as the new arrangements for dealing with section 75 debts, and there are indications that there may be further developments in this area, for example so that section 75 debts will not arise on internal restructuring. The more challenging economic conditions experienced in the UK since the credit crunch of 2007 have had an adverse impact (in terms of the impact of volatility in the markets on funding deficits), but have also equally led to the Regulator taking a more pragmatic approach to facilitate transactions which ultimately make sense for all of the relevant parties.

65 See section 4.4 above.

9

Tax on private equity transactions

1 Introduction

In this chapter, we will consider the tax issues for the private equity investor, Newco and the managers of the investee company in respect of a UK private equity transaction, and how such tax issues impact upon the structure of a private equity transaction including the form of debt finance. The tax issues of the different parties are dealt with in turn; however, in reality, many of the issues are overlapping. For example, if Newco is unable to obtain a tax deduction in respect of the coupon upon the investor debt, this will have an impact for both the investor and the managers, as it will result in a higher tax charge within Newco which will impact upon the value of their investment in Newco.

In chapter 3, there is a detailed analysis of transaction structures, including diagrams to demonstrate those structures most often encountered. This taxation chapter assumes a transaction structured in such typical fashion. As outlined in that chapter, it is increasingly common for a double (or more) Newco structure to be used, one reason for such a structure being the desire that the investor's equity funding should be provided to a different company than that to which the investor's debt funding is provided for the tax reasons outlined in section 3.2 below. Generally, where there is more than a double Newco structure, this is driven by the non-tax reasons (such as the desire to achieve structural subordination) discussed in chapter 3. For ease, references to 'Newco' in this chapter are, unless otherwise indicated, a reference to each of the Newcos in the structure.

2 Tax issues for the investor

2.1 Structure of the investor

It is beyond the scope of this book to consider in detail the different structures adopted by investors which invest in UK investee companies. However, such structures and the tax aims associated with them do impact upon how underlying investments are made in UK private equity transactions.

Typical structures range from UK limited partnerships,[1] foreign partnerships, UK companies, venture capital trusts, tax haven companies and companies, such as Luxembourg SICAVs, which are able to secure the benefit of double taxation agreements. The structure adopted will be influenced by a mixture of commercial factors (such as where the executives of the private equity investor are based) and tax implications. The minimum aim from a tax perspective will be to ensure that a person investing through an investor is in no worse a position than if it invested directly in an investee company. The type of structure used will vary significantly, depending primarily upon the tax residence and tax status of the underlying investors, the type of underlying investment being made by the investor, and the place in which such investments are to be made.

An investment in a UK investee company may generate a coupon on any debt provided, dividend returns and gains from realising the investment. Each of these is considered in turn below.

2.2 Returns from debt: withholding tax

Generally, when a UK company pays interest in respect of debt, it is required to withhold income tax from such payments[2] and to account for such tax to HM Revenue & Customs (HMRC); this is subject to a number of exceptions, the main one being referred to below. For the private equity firm (and its investors), tax withheld from interest payments will, at the very least, represent a cash flow cost, and in some cases it will represent an absolute cost (i.e. if the private equity firm (and its investors) is unable to recover the tax from HMRC, or if they do not have a UK tax liability against which to offset the withholding tax).

Save in limited circumstances, there is no requirement upon Newco to withhold tax from payments of interest made to another UK company or to non-UK companies which are liable to UK corporation tax in respect of such interest.[3] Thus, if the investor is a UK company, there should be no withholding tax obligation in respect of interest payments upon the investor debt.

Typically, most investors cannot rely upon the exception referred to above because they are not structured as UK corporation taxpaying entities. For such investors, one of three strategies is generally adopted to avoid any UK withholding tax upon the coupon on the investor debt, as follows:

(a) To make use of what is known as the 'Quoted Eurobond Exemption'.[4] Where this exemption is available, there is no requirement for tax to be withheld from payments of interest. The main condition which must be satisfied to obtain such treatment is that the debt instrument is listed on

1 For further details, see chapter 3, section 3.3.
2 Section 874 of the Income Tax Act 2007.
3 Sections 933 and 934 of the Income Tax Act 2007.
4 Section 882 of the Income Tax Act 2007.

a recognised stock exchange. For these purposes, a recognised stock exchange is the Official List of the London Stock Exchange and certain other exchanges designated as such by HMRC. One such exchange is the Channel Islands Stock Exchange, and this has been the exchange of choice for these purposes, mainly on account of the relatively low cost and ease of listing.

(b) To issue the debt as 'deep discount bonds'. These are debt instruments which generally do not carry interest, but which are issued at a price which represents a discount to the face value of the bonds (e.g. bonds with a face value of £100 are issued at a price of £90). Upon maturity of the bonds, the face value (i.e. £100) of the bond is paid. The amount of the discount paid is calculated to represent the interest which would be payable on a typical debt instrument. This strategy is adopted because there is no obligation to withhold tax from discount payments (as opposed to payments of interest).

(c) To establish the investor in a jurisdiction which has a double taxation agreement with the UK under which the requirement for the UK investee company to withhold tax is reduced or eliminated. A favoured location for such entities is Luxembourg.

2.3 Dividends from UK investee companies

There is no withholding tax in the UK in respect of dividends paid by a UK investee company to an investor regardless of the structure or residency of the investor. Accordingly, the receipt of any dividends from UK investee companies is not a significant factor when determining the structure of an investor, or the way in which it will make its investments in UK investee companies.

2.4 Gains on realising investments

Generally, non-UK tax residents will not be liable to UK taxation on any gains realised from selling an equity stake in a UK investee company. The two principle exceptions to this are:

(a) where the equity stake is held as an investment but the non-UK investor carries on a trade in the UK through a permanent establishment and the equity stake is used for the purposes of that trade or permanent establishment;[5] and

(b) where the equity stake is held as an asset of trade carried on in the UK rather than as an investment.[6]

This tax treatment has two main impacts in the context of private equity investors. First, the investment policies of most investors are established with a view

5 Section 10B of the Taxation of Chargeable Gains Act 1992.

6 Section 19 of the Corporation Tax Act 2009.

to maintaining that their activities amount to an investment activity rather than that of trading or dealing in equity stakes and securities. To the extent that there is any activity which might be construed as trading or dealing this is often carried out through a separate vehicle established by the investor for the purpose. It is beyond the scope of this chapter to provide a comprehensive analysis of the so-called 'badges of trade' which are used to indicate whether an activity is trading or investment in nature. However, one of the factors is the length of time the equity stakes and securities are held prior to a sale (the longer the stake is held, the more indicative it is likely to be of investment). Typically, the investment policies of investors indicate that stakes are likely to be realised in a three-to-five-year timescale, which is helpful in establishing that the activities of the investor are of an investment nature. In the recent past, when the private equity market was more buoyant, there were a number of investors which consistently realised their equity stakes on a much shorter timescale. There have been persistent rumours of HMRC scrutinising such investors' activities closely to determine whether they may amount to the carrying on of a trade in the UK rather than an investment activity. However, to date we are not aware of such an argument being actively pursued by HMRC in the context of a significant investor.

Secondly, this is the reason that most investors will be established either as non-UK tax resident vehicles (such as a tax haven company or a Luxembourg SICAV), or as tax transparent vehicles (such as a UK limited partnership). As mentioned in chapter 3, for investors investing solely in UK investee companies, the UK limited partnership is generally the preferred vehicle, as there is no UK tax at the level of the fund and each underlying investor in the fund is subject to UK tax on its share of the income and gains of the fund according to its own personal circumstances. Further, the UK tax rules do not generally impose any fetters on how the limited partnership can operate in the UK (this is to be compared, say, with a tax haven company, where to maintain its non-UK tax resident status it will be necessary for it to be managed and controlled outside the UK).

There are generally two classes of investors which are established as UK tax resident companies. The first are retail funds such as venture capital trusts or investment trusts, each of which are generally exempt from UK tax on gains realised from selling equity stakes held as an investment.[7] The second are the captive private equity arms of UK financial institutions (such as one of the large UK banks) and other corporates. For this latter category, UK corporation tax (currently at 28 per cent) is payable upon any gains realised, subject to specific reliefs such as the substantial shareholding exemption.[8]

7 Section 100 of the Taxation of Chargeable Gains Act 1992.

8 Schedule 7AC of the Taxation of Chargeable Gains Act 1992.

2.5 Incentives for the executives of the investor

It is often the case that the executives of the investor will have an indirect or direct interest in Newco (often held through a nominee) by reason of his or her participation in the investor's carried interest or co-investment schemes. The executives' tax concerns in relation to their interests in Newco will largely mirror those of the managers (see section 4 below), namely:

(a) they will wish to ensure that there is no income tax or NIC charge on acquisition of the interest in Newco; and
(b) they will wish to ensure that, upon a sale of their interest in Newco, they are subject to capital gains tax rather than income tax and NIC.

Accordingly, it would usually be the case that any participation in the carried interest will be structured, so far as possible, to fall within the terms of the HMRC/BVCA Memorandum of Understanding in relation to carried interest arrangements.[9] This remains an area of significant political scrutiny in the UK following the Treasury Select Committee's probing of the industry in June 2007.[10]

3 Tax issues for Newco

There are usually deal-specific tax issues which affect Newco in relation to its acquisition of Target. However, in addition to these specific issues, the following issues commonly arise:

(a) whether Newco will obtain a tax deduction for interest payable upon the investor debt;
(b) assuming a deduction is available, when it will be available;
(c) understanding the tax deductions available to Newco in respect of fees incurred during the acquisition of Target; and
(d) the VAT recoverability position in respect of fees incurred during the acquisition of Target.

3.1 Tax deductions for interest

When carrying out its financial modelling in respect of an investment,[11] the investor will make certain assumptions regarding whether interest payable upon the investor debt will be tax deductible for Newco. For advisers it is important to understand the assumptions that have been made regarding the tax deductibility of such interest, as the failure to obtain anticipated deductions may affect the economic viability of the investment. There are a number of

9 Issued on 25 July 2003.
10 See also chapter 1, section 2.2.
11 See further chapter 1, section 3.3.

bases upon which HMRC could seek to deny a tax deduction in respect of the interest upon investor debt.

3.2 Distribution treatment

To the extent that the interest upon the debt represents more than a *reasonable commercial return*, the excess will be treated as a distribution for tax purposes and therefore not tax deductible.[12] The question of reasonableness falls to be applied at the time the debt instrument is issued and takes account of all circumstances including the creditworthiness of the borrower and the quality of any security. To the extent that this provision is found to apply it is only the excess which is treated as non-deductible. Given the other provisions available to it (and in particular the transfer pricing provisions referred to in section 3.3 below), this provision is not generally the first line of attack by HMRC.

Where there is a connection between the shares held by the investor and the debt instrument (and in particular where there are features which suggest that they are stapled together) then the whole of the interest upon the debt may be treated as a distribution and hence not tax deductible.[13] It is commonly considered that this provision is company-specific (i.e. in order for it to bite, the shares and debt must be in the same company). This is one reason for a double (or more) Newco structure being used (i.e. to ensure that the investor's shares are held in a different company to that in which it holds the debt).[14] In this way, it is considered that this provision is of no application.

3.3 Transfer pricing

UK transfer pricing rules[15] apply where a provision between two persons who satisfy a statutory connection test differs from what would be the arm's length provision between two independent enterprises. Where the rules apply, the profits and losses for the purposes of corporation tax are adjusted to reflect the profits and losses that would have resulted had the provision been at arm's length. For the transfer pricing rules to apply, it is necessary for the provision to have been made or imposed as between any two connected persons. Persons are connected for these purposes where:

(a) one of the persons is directly or indirectly participating in the management, control or capital of the other; or
(b) the same person or persons is or are directly or indirectly participating in the management, control or capital of each of the affected persons.

12 Section 209(2)(d) of the Income and Corporation Taxes Act 1988.
13 Section 209(2)(e)(vi) of the Income and Corporation Taxes Act 1988.
14 See also chapter 3, section 2.3, in relation to multiple Newcos.
15 Schedule 28AA of the Income and Corporation Taxes Act 1988.

As a result of the statutory connection test, generally the rules apply in the context of transactions within a group, certain joint ventures, or other transactions between parties under common control or where one controls the other.

Until 2005, it was commonly considered that in most cases the transfer pricing rules had no application in relation to the debt financing of Newco by a private equity investor where the investor was structured as one or more limited partnerships, due to there not being the requisite degree of connection between the investor and Newco, although HMRC now disputes this view. However, the debt financing of Newco by the investor in most private equity transactions will now fall within the transfer pricing rules because, with effect from 2005, the rules were extended to apply to financing arrangements where;

(a) the lender and other persons acted together in relation to such arrangements; and
(b) the requisite degree of connection would be satisfied if all the rights and powers of the other persons are attributed to the lender.[16]

In the context of a typical private equity transaction, it is likely that all the shareholders of Newco and all its finance providers will be regarded as so acting together, with the result that the transfer pricing rules are applicable to the debt financing provided by the investor.

Where transfer pricing legislation applies in respect of the investor debt, Newco will be unable to obtain a tax deduction for any interest which is considered to be in excess of an arm's length amount. In the context of private equity transactions, this has two potential applications as follows:

(a) to the extent that the rate of interest charged is in excess of an arm's length rate that amount of interest is not tax deductible – the arm's length rate is the rate at which a third party lender (with no equity interest in Newco) would lend to Newco; and
(b) more importantly, to the extent that the debt itself would not have been lent by an independent third party, then the interest upon such debt is not tax deductible at all. This is the so-called 'thin capitalisation' rule; i.e. where there is a highly leveraged Newco, HMRC may argue that an independent third party (such as a bank) would not have lent some or all of the debt to Newco, and to the extent it would not have lent such amount, the interest in respect of that debt is not tax deductible.

3.4 Timing of any interest deduction

Where Newco is entitled to a tax deduction, the timing of such deduction is very important. Whenever Newco obtains a tax deduction in respect of the interest on the investor debt, this will generally result in Newco incurring a taxable loss

16 Paragraph 4A of Schedule 28AA to the Income and Corporation Taxes Act 1988.

in the relevant accounting period (as the amount of such interest often exceeds the taxable profits of Newco for that period). In such circumstances, Newco will be able to surrender such loss against the profits of Target by way of group relief on a current year basis.[17] Thus, in effect, the interest costs incurred by Newco are off-set against the trading profits of Target. Newco is only able to do this on a current year basis. Thus, if in any accounting period the losses within Newco exceed Target's profits for that period, the excess cannot be offset against the profits of Target for any other period. Whilst the losses can be carried forward (and to a limited extent back) against the taxable profits of Newco, in reality Newco will usually have very little by way of taxable profits. Hence, the losses become trapped in Newco and are largely worthless.

There are two possible times at which interest may be deductible, namely:

(a) as the interest accrues; or
(b) when it is paid.

Where interest is paid regularly (i.e. it is not rolled up), then there should be no practical difference regarding when the tax deduction may be taken. Any deduction within Newco for such interest is likely to be of real benefit to the Newco group.

Where interest is rolled up then, even if Newco is entitled to a deduction in respect of such interest, in certain circumstances that interest is only deductible in the accounting period in which it is paid, i.e. not when it accrues.[18] This is likely to be highly disadvantageous because:

(a) in the meantime, taxable profits within the Newco group will be higher than would otherwise be the case if the interest was deductible as it accrued; thus, there will be a real cash flow cost during the life of the investment;
(b) if the interest is only deductible as and when it is paid, it is likely that at the time of payment there will be a very large tax deductible amount which may result in losses in Newco which exceed the taxable profits of Target for the corresponding period. For the reasons outlined above, such excess losses are likely to be trapped in Newco and to become worthless.

The rules which defer a tax deduction until such time as the interest is paid do not apply to interest which is paid within twelve months of the accounting period in which it accrues. Thus, where the interest is not rolled up, it will be deductible as it accrues. Further, where the lender is within the charge to corporation tax in respect of the interest, interest will be deductible as it accrues even where the interest is rolled up. Subject to these exceptions, the rules which defer a tax deduction generally apply where:

(a) the lender is a company and controls the borrower (or *vice versa*) or they are under common control;

17 Section 402 of the Income and Corporation Taxes Act 1988.
18 Paragraph 2(2) of Schedule 9 to the Finance Act 1996.

(b) the borrower is a close company and the lender has the requisite degree of connection with the borrower; or
(c) the lender is a company and has a major interest in the borrower (or *vice versa*).

Until 2002, there was an exception which resulted in most investments made by a private equity investor structured as a limited partnership being regarded as not having the requisite degree of connection, with the result that there was no deferral of the tax deduction for Newco in respect of rolled up interest on the investor debt. However, the current exceptions are significantly more tightly drawn, with the result that in many cases they will not apply to prevent the deferral of the tax deduction for rolled-up interest.

Subject to transitional provisions, in respect of accounting periods beginning on or after 1 April 2009, the rules which apply to companies and which defer a tax deduction for late paid interest have been narrowed. Broadly, where the lender is a company, the rules will only apply if it is resident or effectively managed in a non-qualifying territory. For these purposes, a qualifying territory comprises the UK and jurisdictions with which the UK has a double taxation treaty which contains a non-discrimination article. Thus, non-qualifying territories will mainly comprise tax havens.

As highlighted in chapter 3,[19] interest is often rolled up because Newco does not have the cash flow to service the debt, particularly in the earlier years of an investment. However, as noted above, rolling up interest may adversely affect the timing of any tax deduction. One way commonly used to overcome this issue is to satisfy the accruing interest by the issue of 'payment in kind notes' ('PIK notes'). Rather than interest being rolled up, Newco will issue further notes to the investor with a face value equal to the accrued interest. The issue of PIK notes will be treated as payment for tax purposes[20] and thus, assuming a tax deduction is available in respect of the interest, it enables Newco to obtain such deduction in the accounting period in which the PIK notes are issued, rather than when any cash is paid. However, issuing such notes has two other consequences:

(a) It triggers the withholding tax issues referred to in section 2.2 above. Where tax is required to be withheld, Newco is required to withhold PIK notes with a value equal to income tax on the deemed interest at the basic rate and pay them over to HMRC.[21]
(b) It may trigger a tax liability for the private equity investor (or its investors) in respect of that interest notwithstanding that all that has been received is a further note rather than cash.

19 See chapter 3, section 2.2(b).
20 Section 413 of the Corporation Tax Act 2009.
21 Section 929 of the Income Tax Act 2007.

Where the debt financing is provided in the form of a deep discounted bond, there are similar rules (to those which apply to interest) which may apply to defer a tax deduction for the discount to when it is paid (rather than the deduction being available on an accruals basis).[22]

3.5 Deductibility of fees

Newco will incur a substantial amount of fees in relation to the acquisition of Target. It will wish to maximise the corporation tax deduction for such fees. The basic position is as follows:

(a) To the extent that the fees relate to the debt issue, then such costs will generally be accounted for in accordance with FRS4 and the tax treatment will follow the accounting treatment. This generally means that costs directly connected with the issue of the debt instrument will be amortised for tax purposes over the anticipated duration of the debt, and thus will give Newco a tax deduction for such costs over the life of the loan. Such costs will include the bank arrangement fees, due diligence fees incurred in relation to the raising of the debt and legal fees incurred in relation to the debt instrument.

(b) Whether or not other expenses incurred by Newco will be tax deductible will depend upon whether they are capital or income. Generally speaking, expenditure relating to general consideration or appraisal of opportunities will be tax deductible, but expenditure incurred once a target is identified and the acquisition process begins will not be tax deductible.

Disputes with HMRC regarding the extent to which transaction fees incurred by Newco are tax deductible are common. HMRC often disputes the availability of any deduction for the fees which relate to the transaction (other than fees which relate to the debt instrument) on the basis that such fees have been incurred once a target is identified and the acquisition process begins. The precise boundaries of this test have not yet been tested by the courts, but are likely to be tested within the next few years.

3.6 VAT recovery

In order for the VAT upon deal costs to be recoverable by Newco, it must be VAT registered, and therefore must be:

(a) carrying on a taxable business such as providing management services; if this route is adopted, then the VAT recovery position of Newco will depend upon being able to demonstrate that it is carrying on a taxable business, and that the deal costs relate to such business; or

22 Section 407 of the Corporation Tax Act 2009.

(b) included within a VAT group with the investee company; if this route is adopted, then the VAT recovery position of Newco will depend upon the underlying VAT recovery position of the investee company.

It is generally the case that the latter approach is adopted, so that an application is made for Newco to join a VAT group with the investee company with effect from completion of the investment.

Where fees are incurred by other parties (e.g. the bank) and are being met by Newco, then Newco will not be in a position to recover the VAT upon such fees (this has been the settled position for some time, although it is considered likely that this view may shortly be the subject of a test case). Accordingly, the legal adviser who acts both for the investors on their investment and for Newco on its acquisition of Target must raise distinct invoices for the two separate pieces of work, the former being an invoice addressed to the investor but payable by Newco as a third party (and on which VAT is not recoverable by Newco).

4 Tax issues for managers

There are a number of tax issues that arise on private equity transactions which are relevant to the managers. The two most fundamental tax issues for the managers subscribing for shares in Newco are:

(a) whether they are liable to income tax upon acquiring their Newco shares; any such charge will be highly disadvantageous, not least as the managers may not have the cash to meet the charge; and
(b) when selling their Newco shares will they be liable to income tax or capital gains tax (CGT) upon any gains. If the shares are within the CGT regime, the rate of tax is 18 per cent and, where entrepreneurs relief is available, the effective rate of CGT is only 10 per cent on up to £1 million of gains.[23] If the shares are within the income tax regime, the rate of tax will be higher (currently the higher rate is 40 per cent). In addition, if income tax is payable, then generally employees NIC will be payable by the managers (generally at the rate of 1 per cent) and Newco will be liable to employers NIC (currently at the rate of 12.8 per cent).

The potential tax charges described below apply where a manager acquires shares by reason of his employment or directorship or any prospective or former employment or directorship. There are various deeming provisions which have the effect that a manager will be deemed to acquire his Newco shares by reason of his employment/directorship.[24] Thus the rules below apply to all managers whether MBO or MBI candidates, if directors (whether they are executive or non-executive), and even where the Newco shares are received

23 Chapter 3, Part V, of the Taxation of Chargeable Gains Act 2002.
24 Section 421B of the Income Tax (Earnings and Pensions) Act 2003.

as consideration for selling shares in Target (for example, on a secondary buy-out). The effect of the deeming rules is that it is no longer possible to rely upon the 'founders' argument, which historically allowed managers to argue that their shares had been acquired in their capacity as the founders of Newco, rather than by reason of employment/directorship.

The potential charges described below refer to the Newco shares acquired by the managers. However, the provisions are equally applicable to other types of securities, such as loan notes.

4.1 Tax on acquisition of Newco shares

There is a basic tax charge (known as the 'general earnings charge') which arises whenever an employee or director acquires shares at an undervalue.[25] For example, an employee acquires 100 shares for £1,000 but the market value of those shares is £11,000. The employee is treated as having received employment income of £10,000 and will be charged to income tax on that amount in the same way as if the employee had received any other benefit in kind.

This creates a difficulty for the managers as the question of whether or not a charge arises will depend upon the value of the Newco shares and valuation is not a precise science; thus there is some uncertainty for the managers. It was partly to address this uncertainty that the HMRC/BVCA memorandum of understanding (see section 4.4 below) was introduced.

4.2 Restricted securities

The provisions referred to below will apply where the managers' shares are 'restricted securities' for the purposes of the Income Tax (Earnings and Pensions) Act 2003.[26] Due to the rights which typically will attach to the managers' shares (such as leaver provisions, restrictions on transfer, pre-emption, drag along clauses and restricted voting rights),[27] it is almost inevitable that such shares will be regarded as restricted securities for these purposes.

The effect of the shares being restricted securities is that some part of the ultimate sale proceeds may be subject to income tax. To determine the amount which may be subject to income tax, one first ascertains the value of the shares at the date the manager acquires them, taking account of all the restrictions (this is known as the 'restricted market value' or 'actual market value' (AMV)). One then ascertains the value of the shares at that date ignoring all the restrictions (this is known as the 'unrestricted market value' (UMV)). If the manager pays less than the UMV for the shares, then the amount by which he pays less than UMV is expressed as a proportion of UMV, and upon a sale of those shares a corresponding proportion of the sale proceeds is subject to income tax.

25 Section 62 of the Income Tax (Earnings and Pensions) Act 2003.
26 Chapter 2, Part 7, of the Income Tax (Earnings and Pensions) Act 2003.
27 As explained in more detail in chapter 5.

For example, if the AMV and UMV of 1,000 Newco shares is £9,000 and £10,000 respectively. and the manager acquires 1,000 shares for £9,000, there is no general earnings charge on acquisition (as described in section 4.1 above) as the manager will have paid the AMV for the shares. However, the price paid by the manager for his shares represents a 10 per cent discount to the UMV of those shares. If the manager subsequently sells the shares for £100,000, 10 per cent of that amount (i.e. £10,000) will be subject to income tax.

Given that the managers' overall objective will be to acquire the shares at a low value and to dispose of them at a higher value, it is highly desirable to avoid an income tax charge on disposal. Broadly, there are two ways in which to avoid such a charge arising in the circumstances referred to above, as follows:

(a) enter into a section 431 election (see section 4.3 below); or
(b) pay full UMV on acquisition; thus, in the example above, no income tax or NIC charge would have arisen on the sale of the shares if the manager had paid £10,000 for the shares at the outset.

4.3 Elections

The managers have the option of electing wholly or partly out of the restricted securities regime by entering into a section 431 election. The effect of making the election in whole is that no part of the ultimate sale proceeds is subject to income tax under the restricted securities rules described in section 4.2 above. Such election must be made within fourteen days of the acquisition of the securities, and must be made jointly between the manager and the manager's employing company. The election is irrevocable and must be made in a standard format. An election is not submitted to HMRC, but is merely kept for future reference.

The other main effect of making an election is that, for the purposes of computing any general tax charge (see section 4.1 above), it is the UMV, and not the AMV, of the shares which is taken into account. As the UMV will almost inevitably be higher than the AMV of the shares, this may result in an income tax charge (or a greater income tax charge) for the manager on acquiring his Newco shares.

Using the example set out in section 4.2 above, if the manager enters into an election, then he will have a general earnings charge on £1,000. This is because as a result of making the election it is the UMV (not the AMV) of the shares which is now relevant for the purposes of determining whether any such charge arises (and, if so, the extent of such charge). The manager has acquired shares for £9,000 whereas the UMV is £10,000. As previously, the differential is 10 per cent. Entering into the election means that the manager has to pay income tax on that 10 per cent differential at the time of acquisition when the differential is worth just £1,000 (rather than at the time of disposal when, in the example above, the differential is worth £10,000). When the manager subsequently sells the shares for £100,000, the whole of that amount is sheltered from income tax under the restricted securities regime because of the election. The whole of the gain will be subject to CGT rather than income tax unless HMRC can apply certain other provisions (see section 4.5 below).

As will be noted, there are potential downsides to making an election. First, the initial general earnings charge is calculated by reference to UMV rather than AMV. Secondly, there is no guarantee that the shares will increase in value. Should the value of the shares decrease, there is no mechanism for the manager to reclaim any general earnings charge which arises as a result of its being computed by reference to UMV. Despite these potential downsides, it is usual for a well-advised manager to enter into an election. Even if the parties are confident that UMV is being paid on acquisition, it is still advisable to make an election to prevent any future disputes. Usually, the investor will require the managers to enter into such elections[28] – the reason being that it will want to avoid any employers NIC charge accruing to Newco in the event of a subsequent exit (which would be the case if elections are not entered into, and the managers pay less than UMV for their shares), as any such charge may impact the value realised by the investor on an exit.

4.4 HMRC/BVCA Memorandum of Understanding

Following the introduction of the employment-related securities legislation, there was significant disquiet as to the uncertainty created by the fact that immediate and future tax charges depended upon the valuation issues referred to above. As a result, a Memorandum of Understanding (MOU) was agreed between HMRC and the BVCA.[29] The MOU introduced certain 'safe harbours'. The effect of falling within a safe harbour is that there is no general earnings charge for a manager and no income tax charge on an exit under the restricted securities legislation – this is on the basis that HMRC accepts that a manager has paid UMV for his shares. Given this acceptance, there is no reason for a manager also to have to enter into a section 431(1) election in relation to his shares. However, it is invariably the case that a manager will still enter into such an election as a precautionary measure.

The conditions which must be satisfied to fall within the MOU are as follows:

(a) The managers' shares must be ordinary share capital.
(b) Finance provided by the investor in the form of preference shares or loan stock must be on commercial terms. This will be the case if the rate of return is at least as expensive as the most expensive debt provided by a

28 This is often achieved by an express obligation on the managers to enter into such elections in the investment agreement.
29 Issued on 25 July 2003, also referred to in chapter 3, section 3.1.

non-shareholder (e.g. the senior and mezzanine debt providers). Note that reference is made to the single most expensive rate, and not a blended or average rate. Where the finance is in the form of preference shares, the rate of return is adjusted (for the purposes of determining whether this condition is satisfied) to take account of the fact that dividends on preference shares are not tax deductible for Newco. Generally, any warrants granted to senior or mezzanine debt providers are disregarded for the purposes of making the comparison.

(c) Subject to there being no ratchet[30] in place, the price paid by the managers for their ordinary shares must not be less than the price the investor pays for its ordinary shares. Where there is a ratchet in place, the original MOU condition stated that the price which the managers paid for their shares as a proportion of the total amount subscribed for all the equity shares must not be less than the maximum proportionate share of the sale proceeds which the managers could obtain on an exit. Since the MOU was first introduced, HMRC has changed its guidance on this point, so that arguably all that the managers have to pay is the same price per share as the investor pays per share for its shares. However, it is generally still the case that transactions where there is a ratchet will be structured so as to comply with the original guidance.[31]

(d) The managers must acquire their shares at the same time as the investor acquires its ordinary capital.

(e) The managers' shares must have no features that give them or allow them to acquire rights not available to the other holders of ordinary share capital. The exception to this is that it is permissible for a ratchet to apply in favour of the managers' shares (without causing this condition to be breached) provided that:

   (i) the ratchet arrangements work by altering the entitlements of the managers according to the performance of Newco or the Newco group or according to the investment returns of the investor; the ratchet must not alter the entitlements of the managers by reference to their personal performance; and

   (ii) the ratchet arrangement must be in place when the investor acquires its shares.

(f) The managers must be fully remunerated as to salary (and bonuses) through a separate employment contract.

Commonly, the most difficult MOU condition to satisfy is that referred to in (b), particularly if any mezzanine or other second-tier debt finance is being provided to Newco as in that case the return on such finance is often relatively high (and hence the coupon on the investor debt must be correspondingly high).

30 For ratchets, see chapter 3, section 3.2, and chapter 5, section 4.6.

31 Resulting in the structuring implications referred to in chapter 3, section 3.2.

However, given the certainty offered by the MOU, most investors and managers will always seek to structure a deal in order to satisfy its conditions.

4.5 Potential income tax charges on exit

Sections 4.1 to 4.4 above describe the tax charge that can arise when the managers acquire and dispose of restricted securities. However, Part 7 of the Income Tax (Earnings and Pensions) Act 2003 imposes income tax (and possibly NIC) charges in a far broader range of circumstances such as:

(a) *Convertible securities.*[32] If the manager shares are convertible into another class of shares, then on a disposal of such shares (or, if earlier, upon their conversion or upon the shares ceasing to be convertible), an income tax charge may apply. Broadly speaking, the income tax charge is levied on the value attributable to the conversion right (or, as appropriate, on any consideration given for the release of a right to convert or the receipt of money or money's worth received in connection with the conversion right).

(b) *Securities with artificially depressed or enhanced market value.*[33] This applies where the market value of the securities have been artificially depressed or enhanced by more than 10 per cent. It is comparatively rare for securities with artificially depressed value to be an issue in typical private equity transactions. Where managers hold shares and the rights to such shares (or to shares held by others) are varied, with the result that the manager shares increase in value, then a charge may arise under the provisions relating to artificially enhancing the value of the manager shares.

(c) *Securities acquired on deferred terms.*[34] A manager may agree to pay market value for shares but defer the payment until some later event. No general earnings charge arises for the manager in relation to such arrangement as the manager is obliged to pay market value for his shares. However, the amount outstanding is taxed as if it were an interest-free loan from his employer, with the result that the manager is treated as having an annual taxable benefit in kind equal to a notional interest charge on the amount outstanding. Further, if the shares are disposed of without the manager paying the amount outstanding, or if that amount is waived, the manager will be treated as having taxable income of a corresponding amount. This provision arises most commonly where the manager shares are issued nil or partly paid, or their shares are bought on deferred payment terms.

(d) *Securities disposed of for more than market value.*[35] This is designed to catch arrangements which give a manager a disproportionate amount of consideration for the securities being disposed of. Upon a sale of the entire

32 Chapter 3, Part 7, of the Income Tax (Earnings and Pensions) Act 2003.

33 Chapters 3A and 3B, Part 7, of the Income Tax (Earnings and Pensions) Act 2003.

34 Chapter 3C, Part 7, of the Income Tax (Earnings and Pensions) Act 2003.

35 Chapter 3D, Part 7, of the Income Tax (Earnings and Pensions) Act 2003.

issued share capital of Newco to a third party where the manager receives his strict *pro rata* share of the proceeds of sale (in accordance with the rights attaching to his shares), this provision will generally not be relevant. Examples where it may be relevant include:

(i) on an exit, if the manager, taking into account the rights attaching to his shares, receives more than that to which he is entitled; or
(ii) the manager sells his shares in advance of the exit (say, under the leaver provisions common in the articles of association of Newco); in this case, even if the shares are sold at what is described as a fair price, HMRC is likely to regard this as exceeding their market value if the price is not discounted to reflect that a small minority holding is being sold; or
(iii) if the shares are sold to Newco, the investor or any related party, and the price paid to the manager is not discounted to reflect that a small minority holding is being sold.

(e) *Post-acquisition benefits from securities.*[36] There is a wide-ranging provision pursuant to which HMRC may seek to tax 'special benefits' derived from the manager shares as employment income. The scope of this provision is unclear: on one reading, it could catch any benefit received from employment-related securities or from their sale. HMRC has tried to develop arguments that this provision allows it to tax some or all exit proceeds as employment income rather than capital gain in cases where it perceives there to be some abuse. Two situations in particular in which HMRC has suggested that these provisions may apply are where there is a ratchet or where a company is perceived by HMRC to be thinly capitalised (i.e. the level of debt compared to equity is high).

HMRC now accepts that, where the MOU applies, there will be no income tax liability arising under this provision as a result of the operation of the ratchet. HMRC has not formally accepted that this provision is not applicable in situations where the MOU conditions are not satisfied. However, HMRC has retreated somewhat from its original stance, although it will scrutinise a ratchet very carefully to determine whether or not any amount paid under the ratchet will attract income tax. To minimise the chances of the HMRC successfully applying this provision in the context of a ratchet, it is advantageous to structure the ratchet in the manner referred to in section 4.4(e), and also to satisfy the condition referred to in section 4.4(c).

4.6 PAYE/NIC

If the managers have an income tax charge upon acquiring their Newco shares, the question to be determined is whether their employer is obliged to account

36 Chapter 4, Part 7, of the Income Tax (Earnings and Pensions) Act 2003.

for that income tax through the PAYE system or whether the managers are liable to pay the income tax through their personal tax returns. If PAYE is applicable, then NIC (both employers and employees) will also be payable.

Generally, there will be an obligation upon Newco to apply PAYE and NIC if the shares are 'readily convertible assets'.[37] For these purposes, shares will be readily convertible assets if:

(a) they can be realised upon a recognised investment exchange (i.e. broadly where they are listed shares) or there are trading arrangements in place (or which are likely to come into place) in relation to the shares (e.g. an internal market or other mechanism through which the shares can be bought and sold); or
(b) the conditions which must be satisfied for the employer to secure a corporation tax deduction under Schedule 23 to the Finance Act 2003 in respect of the managers' acquisition of shares are not so satisfied.

If an income tax charge does arise, and the employer is obliged to account for any income tax through PAYE, the obligation on the employer is to pay the 'best estimate' of any PAYE due.[38] It is possible, once the shares have been acquired by the managers but before the PAYE is due, to agree the value of the shares for PAYE purposes so that the employer can discharge its PAYE obligations. This valuation does not bind HMRC, in that if it later comes to a different view of the valuation it can seek to obtain further income tax from the managers.

If any PAYE is due from the employer and the manager does not reimburse the PAYE to the employer within ninety days, an amount equal to such PAYE will itself be taxable as a benefit in kind and attract further income tax and NIC.[39] If the managers reimburse the employer after the expiry of the ninety-day period, such benefit in kind charge stands notwithstanding such reimbursement.

If the managers are liable to any of the other income tax charges referred to in section 4.5, it is likely that most will arise in circumstances requiring the employer to account for such income tax through PAYE (and thus for NIC to also be payable).

5 Conclusion

Since 2003, there has been a significant amount of change in the tax regime applicable to private equity investors and their investments. As a result of the buyout boom, and the subsequent credit crunch and economic downturn, there has been a particular focus upon the taxation of the returns paid

37 Section 702 of the Income Tax (Earnings and Pensions) Act 2003.
38 Section 696(2) of the Income Tax (Earnings and Pensions) Act 2003.
39 Section 222 of the Income Tax (Earnings and Pensions) Act 2003.

to private equity executives under carried interest and co-investment schemes. The replacement of the historic taper relief regime with a flat CGT rate was, in part, a response to the widespread media coverage of the 2007 Treasury Select Committee – and in particular the headline-grabbing comments that private equity executives were paying a lower rate of tax than their cleaners. The amount of debt within private-equity-backed investee companies has also resulted in many such companies paying little or no corporation tax on profits, and the extension of the transfer pricing rules referred to above is an attempt to address a number of concerns raised in that context.

With the private equity industry continuing to be the focus of much political comment on a UK, European and worldwide basis, it seems inevitable that the taxation of the industry and its investments will continue to be scrutinised, and that there will be further changes in what is already a complex area.

10

Public-to-private transactions

1 Introduction

In this chapter, we will look at the specific issues relevant to a public-to-private (also often referred to as a 'take private') transaction. A public-to-private transaction involves the acquisition by a private-equity-backed vehicle of a public target company (which we will refer to in this chapter as 'P2P Target'), and as a result combines the features of a traditional private company management buyout with the structural and regulatory requirements of a public company takeover.

In this chapter, we explore some of the particular features which are inherent in such a structure, and the ways in which the private equity and bank funding documents need to adapt to suit the particular requirements of this type of transaction. Other features common in a public bid (for example, the absence of warranties beyond title and capacity) can create challenges for the typical private equity investor. There can be reduced access for the purposes of due diligence, and the regulatory framework and timetable in which a public offer must be made in the United Kingdom has caused such deals to be an increasingly differentiated part of a private equity offering (in the sense that some houses are better equipped, and experienced, to complete them than others). However, with appropriate consideration, they can afford excellent opportunities to private equity investors looking to acquire good businesses with strong management teams.

This chapter highlights the key issues which are likely to arise, and which should be appreciated by the private equity investors and the P2P Target management team from the outset. The chapter is split into three sections:

(a) the issues which are specific to public-to-private transactions;
(b) a brief overview of some of the key takeover rules relating to public takeovers; and
(c) specific issues in relation to the funding to be provided to the Bidco making the offer.

Much of the content in this chapter relates to the issues on the assumption that the transaction is structured as a public offer. However, in recent times, public-to-private transactions have also been effected by way of a scheme of arrangement which is considered in section 3.8 below. This chapter does not set out a full discussion of all the issues involved in a public offer in the United Kingdom, but it does highlight the particular considerations which affect private equity as the funders to Bidco.

2 Issues specific to public-to-private transactions

2.1 The City Code on Takeovers and Mergers

As with all public company takeovers, the City Code on Takeovers and Mergers ('the Takeover Code'), as applied by the Panel on Takeovers and Mergers ('the Takeover Panel'), will regulate the conduct of the transaction.

The Takeover Panel will provide guidance on the application of the Takeover Code to the advisers to the private equity investors, Bidco and P2P Target itself, each of whom will liaise closely with the Panel to ensure that the structure and conduct of the transaction is consistent with the Takeover Code. The Takeover Panel has statutory powers and can apply to the court for enforcement of the Code.

2.2 Conflicts of interest

Those directors of P2P Target who will form the management team of the new group going forward must first deal with their existing responsibilities to P2P Target. Specifically:

(a) as a director, each has fiduciary duties, including a duty to promote the success of the company for the benefit of its members as a whole;[1] and
(b) as an executive, each has obligations to P2P Target under an employment contract.

There is an inherent conflict of interest for the P2P Target directors who will be participating in the proposed offer. For example, the directors of P2P Target will be obliged to secure the best price for their shareholders before deciding to recommend any offer to their shareholders, which will be in direct conflict with the interests of the private equity investors and Bidco in obtaining control of the company on the most attractive terms practicable. Many of the issues discussed in this chapter stem from the need to recognise, and manage, that conflict and to prevent any suggestion that a conflict of interest has inhibited the directors of P2P Target from acting in the best interests of its shareholders.

In dealing with the conflict of interest in this situation, public appearances are particularly important. Not only must everybody act properly in relation to any conflict, they must be publicly seen to do so. Any perception in the market

1 See further chapter 11, section 6.4.

that shareholders' interests may have been affected by a conflict of interest could prejudice the success of a public-to-private offer and have adverse reputational consequences for all concerned.

This issue gives rise to several specific considerations which are explained in more detail in the following sections. Advisers must also remain aware when advising any director of the provisions in the P2P Target's articles, and the Companies Act 2006,[2] on directors' interests, as well as the requirements of the Takeover Code.

2.3 Board approval to pursue offer

Any directors of P2P Target who are contemplating becoming involved in an offer for the company should take independent legal advice at the outset, before notifying the chairman of the board of such proposed involvement. In particular, there are strict obligations on a director not to be in a situation where he has any interests which may possibly lead to a conflict with his duty to P2P Target unless he first obtains authorisation at a meeting of the board of P2P Target. Generally, the board acting by its unconflicted directors can give this authorisation (rather than needing to refer the matter to shareholders for a decision), although the articles of association of P2P Target should be checked on this point. The board may, of course, impose conditions on any such authorisation, and in any event is likely to keep the position under review.

A director will not be able to pursue the possibility of an offer for P2P Target without the full approval of the board of P2P Target given by the other, unconflicted directors. Without this approval, he would inevitably breach his duties to P2P Target at some stage. For example, his involvement is likely to involve a significant time commitment during business hours, which is inconsistent with his obligations under his service contract. Participation would also inevitably involve the disclosure by him to potential funders of confidential, unpublished information about P2P Target, which would also need P2P Target's authority.

If the independent directors do decide that it is in the best interests of P2P Target and its shareholders to allow the relevant directors to explore the possibility of a buyout, that consent should be formally minuted and recorded, ideally in a letter between P2P Target and the relevant directors. The letter should set out the terms of the consent and the ground rules to be followed by the directors and their advisers to ensure that the conflict of interest and Takeover Code issues described below are properly handled.

A director of P2P Target who is involved in the offer need not, with these safeguards, resign his directorship. However, he will continue to be bound by his fiduciary duty to act in the best interests of P2P Target; an approval to pursue the opportunity does not override that fundamental duty.

2 See further chapter 11, section 6.

2.4 Appointment of independent committee of directors

As soon as it becomes apparent that any of the P2P Target directors may be involved in a proposed offer, P2P Target should form an independent committee of directors. This will be important to those directors forming part of the offer, as it helps demonstrate that P2P Target shareholders' interests have not been affected by the conflict of interest. The function of the committee will be to consider the proposals to be made by the private equity investors and Bidco, and to advise P2P Target's shareholders on whether or not to accept any offer from Bidco. The non-independent directors should not participate in the decision of their board colleagues to set up an independent committee (and will typically be precluded from doing so under P2P Target's articles of association).

The independent committee should be comprised of P2P Target directors who are independent of, and unconnected with, the private equity investors and Bidco. This means that any director who could have an ongoing role after the buyout may be regarded as not independent. Note 4 to rule 25.1 of the Takeover Code provides that, for this purpose:

> a director will normally be regarded as having a conflict of interest where it is intended that he should have any continuing role (whether in an executive or non-executive capacity) in either Bidco or the offeree company in the event of the offer being successful.

Typically, the independent committee would consist of non-executive directors satisfying the independence criteria, as they are likely to be least affected by an offer being successful or otherwise. The identification of those directors who are independent, and those who are not, will need care. The choice of the independent committee will also need to recognise that the position of individual directors, and particularly the nature of their proposed involvement in a buyout, may change as the transaction progresses.

It is possible that there might be no independent directors. In such cases, P2P Target's financial advisers would often take the role of the independent committee and advise P2P Target's shareholders on the merits of the offer.

The directors who are involved in the proposed offer should not be entitled to attend meetings of the independent committee or any part of board meetings at which the proposed offer is discussed. They should not have access to documents generated by or for the benefit of the independent committee or otherwise relating to the company's consideration of the proposed offer. Consideration should be given to the scope of the matters to which access should be restricted, balancing the need for a director to continue to receive certain information to allow him to perform his functions as a director against the interests of P2P Target in restricting his access to information which it would not be appropriate for such a director to receive.

Initially, the independent committee will need to consider whether or not it is in the interests of P2P Target's shareholders for it to co-operate with the formulation of an offer by a bidder vehicle in which some or all of P2P

Target's directors are involved. It will also ultimately fall to the independent committee formally to recommend the offer to its shareholders, or to decide not to do so. In practice, the public-to-private transaction is unlikely to proceed unless it is recommended to the P2P Target's shareholders by the independent committee.

2.5 Appointing independent advisers

Rule 3.1 of the Takeover Code provides:

> The board of the offeree company must obtain competent independent advice on any offer and the substance of such advice must be made known to its shareholders.

Note 1 to that rule goes on to provide:

> The requirement for competent independent advice is of particular importance in cases where the offer is a management buyout or similar transaction … In such cases, it is particularly important that the independence of the adviser is beyond question. Furthermore the responsibility borne by the adviser is considerable and, for this reason, the board of the offeree company should appoint an independent adviser as soon as possible after it becomes aware of the possibility that an offer may be made.

The board of P2P Target will often appoint the company's existing broker (or nominated adviser, if admitted to trading on AIM) as its rule 3 adviser. It is usual for Bidco to appoint its own independent financial adviser for the purposes of the transaction. Bidco's adviser will negotiate the commercial terms of the bid, ensure compliance by Bidco and its shareholders with the Takeover Code, make the necessary cash confirmation required by the Code, effect any purchases of P2P Target shares in the market before or during the course of the bid, and advise generally on bid tactics.

2.6 Due diligence

As the acquisition of P2P Target will be made by public offer, rather than by private sale, Bidco will not obtain the benefit of any warranties from the shareholders of P2P Target about the company and its business. In the absence of such warranty protection, any equity or debt provider to Bidco is likely to require extensive due diligence on P2P Target.

There is no general restriction on the dissemination of publicly available information about P2P Target. However, as outlined above, disclosure by any director of information, except in accordance with the terms of the consent from the independent committee, could constitute a breach both of his contractual obligations to P2P Target and of his fiduciary duties as a director. The receipt of such information by funders could also expose them to liability to P2P Target, particularly if they are aware that the disclosure is unauthorised.

The independent directors will be particularly concerned to control the release of information concerning P2P Target to potential bidders, as those directors have specific obligations under the Takeover Code in this area. Rule 20.2 of the Takeover Code provides:

> Any information ... given to one offeror or potential offeror, whether named or unnamed, must, on request, be given equally and promptly to another offeror or bona fide potential offeror even if that other offeror is less welcome. This requirement will usually only apply when there has been a public announcement of the existence of the offeror or potential offeror to which information has been given or, if there has been no public announcement, when the offeror or bona fide potential offeror requesting information ... has been informed authoritatively of the existence of another potential offeror.

P2P Target directors who are involved in an offer will already have a great deal of detailed information about P2P Target, which may have been amassed over many years. It would not be practicable to make all such information available to other offerors. This situation is dealt with in note 3 to rule 20.2 which provides:

> If the offer or potential offer is a management buyout or similar transaction, the information which this rule requires to be given to competing offerors or potential offerors is that information generated by the offeree company (including the management of the offeree company acting in their capacity as such) which is passed to external providers or potential providers of finance (whether equity or debt) to the offeror or potential offeror. The Panel expects the directors who are involved in making the offer to co-operate with the independent directors of the offeree company and its advisers in the assembly of this information.

In order to ensure compliance with this requirement an independent committee would usually seek undertakings, both from Bidco's independent advisers and from potential equity and debt providers to Bidco, that information will only be disclosed to them with the consent of the independent committee, or at least only if it is provided to them at the same time. This requirement obviously gives rise to practical difficulties when it comes to monitoring compliance, and when dealing with meetings and other situations where oral information is passed to funders.

Note 3 to rule 20.2 covers information generated by P2P Target directors only where it is generated by them in their capacity as directors of P2P Target. Such directors would not be required to make available to another offeror any information generated specifically for the purpose of the bid. For example, another bidder would not be entitled to see the Business Plan. There may be circumstances where the distinction between information generated for the purpose of the company and that generated for the purpose of the offer may be less clear. This is sometimes an area of debate.

These rules are designed to ensure that all potential bidders are treated equally. They might require that information which has been disclosed to an outside financier is also provided to a less welcome bidder, such as a trade competitor. As a result, the rules need to be considered with care by both the bidding directors and the independent directors.

2.7 Copy of information to the independent committee

Rule 20.3 of the Takeover Code deals with a related issue – the rights of the independent directors to be supplied with all information provided by the buyout team to their funders. This requirement reflects the concern that a management buyout team might be in possession of information about P2P Target which gives them an unfair advantage over the independent directors. The rule provides:

> If the offer or potential offer is a management buyout or similar transaction, the offeror or potential offeror must, on request, promptly furnish the independent directors of the offeree company or its advisers with all information which has been furnished by the offeror or potential offeror to external providers or potential providers of finance (either equity or debt) for the buyout.

It should be noted that, unlike rule 20.2, the provision of information under rule 20.3 is not restricted to information generated by P2P Target or by the management of P2P Target acting in that capacity. The independent committee can request all information provided to funders of Bidco, including any information generated by management solely for the purpose of the proposed offer. Unlike information generated by P2P Target, information supplied back to the independent directors under rule 20.3 which has been generated by the buyout team in that capacity does not need to be supplied to competing bidders under rule 20.2.

2.8 Management equity participation and terms

The directors of P2P Target who are involved in the offer would normally expect to subscribe for shares in Bidco (or the ultimate holding company of Bidco), as in any other buyout. If they hold shares in P2P Target, the subscription price for their shares in Bidco will usually be satisfied, in whole or in part, by the transfer to the Bidco of their shares in P2P Target. Bidco will not generally be in a position to offer the other shareholders of P2P Target the opportunity to subscribe for shares in Bidco as consideration for the transfer of their shares on acceptance of the offer.

Rule 16 of the Takeover Code provides that:

> Except with the consent of the Panel, an offeror or persons acting in concert with it may not make any arrangements with shareholders and may not deal or enter into arrangements to deal in shares of the offeree

> company, or enter into arrangements which involve acceptance of an offer, either during an offer or when one is reasonably in contemplation, if there are favourable conditions attached which are not being extended to all shareholders.

Therefore, an arrangement to acquire shares held by the management buyout team in consideration for the allotment of shares in Bidco is one falling within rule 16, and requiring the consent of the Takeover Panel.

This situation is anticipated by note 4 to rule 16 which provides, by reference to note 2 to that rule:

> Sometimes, an offeror may wish to arrange for the management of the offeree company to remain financially involved in the business. The methods by which this may be achieved vary but the principle which the Panel is concerned to safeguard is that the risks as well as the rewards associated with an equity shareholding should apply to the management's retained interest. For example, the Panel would not normally find acceptable an option arrangement which guaranteed the original offer price as a minimum.

There are two further requirements imposed by the Takeover Code in relation to such arrangements:

(a) first, the Panel will require a public statement from P2P Target's independent financial adviser that, in their opinion, the arrangements with the management of P2P Target are fair and reasonable; and
(b) secondly, the Panel will also require that the management arrangements are approved at a general meeting by the P2P Target shareholders (where the bidder and relevant management would be disenfranchised and the vote would be taken on a poll).

The parties will need to consider carefully the structure of Bidco to ensure that management comply with the Takeover Panel requirement that they participate in the risks as well as the rewards associated with an equity shareholding. Provisions requiring management's shares in Bidco to be offered round for sale at specified prices in given circumstances (most obviously, Good/Bad Leaver provisions[3]) need particular care. Compulsory transfer provisions providing for the transfer of management's shares if they cease to be employed by Bidco cannot provide that such a transfer will be at a guaranteed minimum price, for example.

In giving its consent to any favourable conditions, the independent committee will be concerned to ensure that the directors receiving shares in Bidco are not receiving a greater value of consideration than that being offered to other shareholders under the terms of the offer. In recent transactions, a statement has appeared in the offer document to the effect that the price paid by

3 See chapter 5, section 4.16.

management for its shares in Bidco was the same as that paid by the private equity providers, on the basis that the value of management's shares in P2P Target is the bid price under the offer.[4]

Under rule 24.5 of the Takeover Code, full details must be set out in the offer document of any special arrangements between Bidco, or any person acting in concert with it, and any of the directors, recent directors, shareholders or recent shareholders of P2P Target connected with the offer. This disclosure requirement would cover any favourable conditions falling within rule 16. It would also cover any proposed service agreements to be entered into, and any termination arrangements agreed with any of the directors of P2P Target, whether or not the relevant directors are involved in the offer.

Any payment for termination of the appointment of any P2P Target directors would also need to be approved by P2P Target's shareholders under the terms of section 219 of the Companies Act 2006 if it exceeds the amount properly payable for breach of contract.

3 Overview of other key issues and provisions relating to public takeovers

3.1 Financial support and exclusivity (inducement and break fees)

It is unlikely that a management team would be able, and/or that the debt and equity providers to Bidco would be willing, to underwrite the costs of professional advisers in preparing a public-to-private offer should the offer not be successful. For that reason, it is not uncommon to agree with the independent directors a basis upon which some fee compensation (characterised as an inducement or break fee) would be payable by P2P Target in certain circumstances where management's offer is not successful. This is a complex area, given the duties of the independent directors and legal restrictions on public companies providing financial assistance for the purchase of their own shares.[5] The Takeover Code permits this kind of fee arrangement in limited circumstances (set out in rule 21.2), principally that:

(a) the inducement fee must be *de minimis* (no more than 1 per cent of the offer value);
(b) both the board of P2P Target and its financial adviser must confirm the following in writing to the Takeover Panel:
    (i) that the inducement fee was agreed as a result of arm's length commercial negotiations;

4 For tax reasons, this would usually be the case on any buyout. See further chapter 9, section 4.4.

5 Note that, under section 678 of the Companies Act 2006, the giving of financial assistance remains unlawful for public companies. However, in this context, market practice is to rely on the argument that an inducement fee of no more than 1 per cent of the offer value does

(ii) the circumstances in which the inducement fee will become payable and the basis on which such circumstances were considered to be appropriate;
(iii) any relevant information concerning possible competing offers;
(iv) that there are no side agreements or understandings that have not been fully disclosed; and
(v) that they believe the fee to be in the best interests of P2P Target's shareholders;

(c) the arrangements must be fully disclosed to shareholders in the announcement of a firm intention to make a bid and in the offer documents; and
(d) the Takeover Panel should be consulted at the earliest opportunity where an inducement fee or similar arrangement is being proposed.

The independent committee will be under a duty to negotiate the lowest fee possible.

The size of fee, and the circumstances in which it becomes payable, will often be a contentious area. A break fee arrangement will often include an agreement by P2P Target not to solicit competing offers from other bidders for a certain period of time. This kind of exclusivity agreement will not prevent other bidders tabling offers or gaining access to P2P Target's information under rule 20.2, but will give the bidder some comfort as it incurs costs in preparing its offer.

3.2 Insider dealing

The existence of the prospective transaction will almost certainly constitute price-sensitive information. Great care therefore needs to be taken in making others 'insiders'. This could arise either by making other parties or persons aware of the transaction itself, or by disclosing to them confidential information about P2P Target which is sufficiently material to be price-sensitive. The insider dealing provisions of the Criminal Justice Act 1993 could apply criminal sanctions in the event of dealings (or encouraging others to deal) in P2P Target's shares or the disclosure of information about the proposed offer in breach of the provisions of that Act.

The acquisition of shares in P2P Target by Bidco in order to facilitate the bid in circumstances where the only inside information known to Bidco and its advisers is the fact that a bid is in contemplation ought to be permissible, although detailed analysis and advice should always be sought. Similarly, such behaviour ought not to amount to market abuse under section 118 of the Financial Services and Markets Act 2000, although again detailed advice will be necessary.

not constitute a material reduction of net assets and therefore is not 'financial assistance' as defined by section 677 of the Companies Act 2006.

Rule 4.1 of the Takeover Code provides that:

(a) No dealings of any kind in securities of the offeree company (including options and derivatives in respect of or referenced to such securities) by any person, not being [Bidco], who is privy to confidential, price-sensitive information concerning an offer or contemplated offer may take place between the time when there is reason to suppose that an approach or an offer is contemplated and the announcement of the approach or offer or of the termination of the discussions.
(b) No person who is privy to such information may make any recommendation to any other person as to dealing in the relevant securities …

3.3 Dealings of Bidco and concert parties

A number of provisions of the Takeover Code affect concert parties, both of Bidco and of P2P Target. In particular, restrictions on dealings in shares in P2P Target are imposed on concert parties, and some previous dealings by a bidder vehicle's concert parties can require a change in the terms proposed for the offer itself.

Under the Takeover Code, persons acting in concert broadly are those who, pursuant to an agreement or understanding (whether formal or informal), co-operate to obtain or consolidate control of a company or to frustrate a successful bid by a third party. The Takeover Panel will make certain presumptions as to persons acting in concert for the purposes of the Takeover Code unless the contrary is established. In a public-to-private transaction, Bidco's concert parties will be deemed to include the private equity investors and the management team. More complex is the question as to whether, and, if so, which, companies in the investors' investee group are deemed to be acting in concert with Bidco. Debt providers, where no warrants or other equity element in the Bidco are involved, would not normally be treated as acting in concert; however, the Takeover Panel should always be consulted if there is any doubt.

Examples of issues which can arise for Bidco and concert parties of Bidco include the following matters.

(a) Prohibition on sale

Rule 4.2 of the Takeover Code prohibits Bidco or its concert parties from selling any shares in P2P Target without the Takeover Panel's consent during an offer period.

(b) Rules concerning offer terms

Under rule 6 of the Takeover Code, where Bidco or its concert parties have purchased shares in P2P Target in the three-month period before the offer, the offer to shareholders of the same class must not be on less favourable terms.

Similarly, under rule 11 of the Takeover Code, where 10 per cent or more of the shares of P2P Target have been acquired by Bidco or its concert parties within the twelve months preceding the offer, the offer must include a cash offer at not less than the highest price paid to acquire those shares.

In addition, an acquisition of shares by Bidco or its concert parties during an offer period for cash at a higher price than the offer price will require the terms of the offer to be revised to include a cash offer at that price.

(c) Mandatory offer

Under rule 9 of the Takeover Code, if persons acting in concert acquire shares carrying 30 per cent or more of the voting rights in a company to which the Takeover Code applies, or increase a holding of between 30 per cent and 50 per cent, they will be required to make a mandatory offer for the remaining shares in that company.

There are onerous restrictions on the terms of a mandatory offer. In particular:

(a) a mandatory offer will be conditional only on 50 per cent acceptances;
(b) the offer must include a cash offer at the highest price paid by Bidco and its concert parties for shares in P2P Target in the preceding twelve months.

A bank lending to a bidder vehicle is likely to seek assurance that Bidco and its concert parties have not acquired and will not acquire interests which could trigger a mandatory offer.

3.4 Announcements

Rule 2.2 of the Takeover Code sets out the circumstances in which an announcement of a proposed offer is required. Rule 2.2(e) provides that such an announcement is required when negotiations or discussions are about to be extended to include more than a very restricted number of people.

The Takeover Panel places very great emphasis on this provision, and wishes to be made aware of any prospective public-to-private transaction before any Bidco begins approaching prospective funders. In general, the Takeover Panel will seek to restrict discussions with prospective funders and shareholders before an announcement, but this will depend on the specific circumstances.

Rule 2.2 of the Takeover Code also sets out other circumstances when an announcement is required, including the following:

(a) when a firm intention to make an offer is notified to the board of P2P Target; and
(b) when P2P Target is subject to rumour or speculation or there is an untoward movement in its share price.

P2P Target will need to be mindful of its obligations to avoid the selective disclosure of price-sensitive information. While P2P Target and Bidco may have similar interests so far as the desirability of announcing the transaction is concerned, this will not necessarily be the case. Bidco's directors should be aware that a decision by P2P Target on whether it should make an announcement will be made by the independent directors, in conjunction with P2P Target's advisers. During the period before P2P Target has been approached, the responsibility for making an announcement lies with the bidder. Once an approach has been made, the primary responsibility for making an announcement will shift to P2P Target.

It is not uncommon for a company to make a 'holding announcement'. This would state that it has received an approach from certain directors which may, or may not, lead to an offer being made for P2P Target. Such announcements are of important tactical significance, alerting potential third party bidders to P2P Target's position, but facilitating the due diligence process by making the existence of a possible offer public knowledge. It is quite common for companies to have prepared a draft holding announcement, so that it is ready for an announcement to be made in an urgent situation.

To a far greater extent than in other management buyouts, in a public-to-private transaction there is always the risk of a competing bid emerging and the management bid failing. If a competing bid is made, P2P Target will have to consider it, even if it has already recommended the management bid. It is partly to avoid prompting competing bids that bidders try to delay any announcement as long as possible; once a public company is known to be 'in play', anything can happen.

3.5 Obtaining control

Under rule 10 of the Takeover Code, it must be a condition of the offer that the offer will not have effect unless Bidco has acquired or agreed to acquire shares carrying over 50 per cent of the voting rights in P2P Target. In practice, Bidco will wish to obtain far more than a 50 per cent acceptance level; typically, an offer will be conditional on either 75 per cent or 90 per cent acceptances depending on how the deal is structured.

The effect which each of the different levels of acceptance will have on Bidco's ability to influence and control P2P Target is as follows.

(a) 50 per cent shareholding

Once Bidco has over 50 per cent of the voting rights of P2P Target, it has the power to dismiss the directors of P2P Target and gain effective control of the P2P Target's board. However, while a greater than 50 per cent shareholding will enable Bidco to have effective control of the business of P2P Target, it will not be able to make structural changes to P2P Target that need a higher threshold of shareholder approval or require change to be made to the constitution. In particular, it will not be able to procure that P2P Target grants security to a bank which has funded the offer, because it will not be able to approve the necessary re-registration of the company from plc to private which requires the approval of the holders of 75 per cent of votes cast.[6]

(b) 75 per cent shareholding

Once Bidco has acquired 75 per cent of the voting rights of P2P Target, it has the power to pass a special resolution. Certain fundamental matters, typically relating to the underlying structure and constitution of a company, must be determined by such a resolution. These include resolutions to:

- re-register the company as a private company;[7]
- commence a members' voluntary liquidation;[8]
- change the name of the company;[9]
- change the articles of association of the company.[10]

The re-registration of Bidco as a private company will be necessary to enable P2P Target to give security for the debt finance used in the transaction. Even though Bidco will have the power to pass such resolutions with a 75 per cent holding in P2P Target, it must take account of the following issues:

(a) In order to pass any resolution, Bidco will need to call meetings of P2P Target, and the statutory notice periods and procedures for meetings will apply.
(b) Section 994 of the Companies Act 2006 contains provisions for the protection of minority shareholders.
(c) While a resolution to re-register P2P Target as a private company can be passed by a 75 per cent shareholder, the resolution is subject to a statutory twenty-eight-day period for challenge by minority shareholders where it has not been passed unanimously (see further section 4.2 below).

(c) 90 per cent shareholding and the compulsory acquisition procedure

The desired level of acceptances will most usually be 90 per cent, since this will trigger the compulsory acquisition procedures (also known as 'squeeze out' rights) set out in sections 979–982 of the Companies Act 2006. These provisions provide that, where an offer has been made to acquire all of the shares of a particular class, if Bidco has acquired or unconditionally contracted to acquire 90 per cent in value of the shares to which the takeover relates and 90 per cent of the voting rights carried by those shares, it may compulsorily acquire the remaining shares. In this way, Bidco would be able to buy out any

6 Section 283 of the Companies Act 2006; on the bank funder's requirements, see further section 4.2 below.
7 Section 96 of the Companies Act 2006.
8 Section 84(1)(b) of the Insolvency Act 1986.
9 Section 78 of the Companies Act 2006; note that the articles of association of the company may also now permit a change of name by other means.
10 Section 21 of the Companies Act 2006.

minority shareholders who had not accepted the offer and thereby acquire all of the shares in P2P Target.

If, during the course of the offer, Bidco acquires any shares in P2P Target for more than the offer price, that higher price must also be paid to shareholders whose shares are compulsorily acquired. The procedure provides for a six-week period for minority shareholders to make application to the court for an order that Bidco is not entitled to acquire the shares or that the terms of the acquisition should be different from those specified by Bidco.[11]

The compulsory acquisition procedure under sections 979–982 of the Companies Act 2006 applies only where an offer is made to acquire all of the shares of the relevant class in P2P Target which are not already held by Bidco. If the management buyout team owns shares in P2P Target and the offer is not made to acquire their shares, Bidco would *prima facie* not be entitled to rely on the compulsory acquisition procedure.

To avoid this problem, section 975 of the Companies Act 2006 provides that the reference to shares held by Bidco includes shares which Bidco has contracted to acquire. Accordingly, the offer is not made in respect of those shares. Any of the management buyout team who holds shares in P2P Target will instead contract to sell those shares to Bidco, usually in consideration for the issue of shares in Bidco (or its ultimate parent company). Bidco will only wish to purchase shares, and the management buyout team will only wish to sell shares, if the offer is successful, and therefore the contract is likely to be conditional on the offer being declared wholly unconditional. Changes introduced by the Companies Act 2006 make clear that such a conditional contract is sufficient to fall within the provisions of section 975.

By falling outside the offer, however, the management buyout team's shares will not be included for the purpose of ascertaining whether or not the 90 per cent acceptance level has been achieved, triggering the compulsory acquisition procedure. This may be significant if the management buyout team has a substantial shareholding in P2P Target.

3.6 Irrevocable undertakings

Before making the offer, the management buyout team and Bidco's funders will want to obtain as much assurance as possible that the offer will be successful. In order to get this comfort, Bidco will seek irrevocable undertakings from P2P Target's more significant shareholders that they will accept the offer. The shareholders giving these undertakings will then be bound to accept the offer, and may appoint Bidco as their attorney to do so. Irrevocables are usually obtained shortly before the offer is made, as they will create a disclosable interest in P2P Target's shares. In addition, pursuant to rule 8 of the Takeover Code, any irrevocable commitment which is procured during an offer period (which

11 Section 986 of the Companies Act 2006.

commences upon the announcement of any proposed or possible offer (with or without terms)) must be announced on the day following that transaction.

Irrevocable undertakings may also be sought from the management team and their family members. Where shares are held by trustees on behalf of family trusts, care will need to be taken to confirm that the trustees have authority to enter into an irrevocable undertaking to accept an offer.

An irrevocable undertaking may be either 'hard' (binding in all circumstances), 'soft' (ceases to be binding if a higher offer emerges) or 'semi-hard' (ceases to be binding if a higher offer emerges which exceeds the existing offer by an agreed amount). Some shareholders that are unwilling to give an irrevocable undertaking may be prepared to sign a letter of intent to accept the bid. Although clearly of less value, letters of intent may still give the bidder some comfort as to sentiment towards the offer.

3.7 The formal public documents

Under rule 19.2 of the Takeover Code, the offer document and any other document issued in connection with the offer must contain a statement that the directors of Bidco or the directors of P2P Target, as appropriate, accept responsibility for the information contained in that document.

On a conventional offer, all P2P Target directors would assume responsibility for any recommendation to shareholders to accept the offer and for all information in the offer document relating to themselves and their families or relating to P2P Target. In a public-to-private transaction, under note 3 to rule 25.1 of the Takeover Code, the P2P Target directors who are involved in the offer will have a conflict of interest and accordingly will not be required to accept responsibility for any recommendation to shareholders to accept the offer. However, they will remain responsible (along with the independent directors) for any information relating to P2P Target, even though the prime responsibility for preparation of that information may have fallen on the independent committee of the board of P2P Target. If they are also directors of Bidco, the P2P Target directors who are involved in the offer will also be required to give a statement accepting responsibility for the other parts of the offer document, namely, those relating to themselves, Bidco and its financing.

Note 5 to rule 19.2 of the Takeover Code extends responsibility for the offer document to any company which has control of Bidco. In the case of a public-to-private transaction, the Takeover Panel will require a responsibility statement from the directors of the private equity provider, or alternatively from the private equity investors' credit committee which has approved the offer. The exact application of this requirement to the private equity investors will depend on the structure of the fund, and the nature of the fund's internal approval processes.

Under note 1 to rule 19.2 of the Takeover Code, where P2P Target's response to the proposed offer is delegated to an independent committee, each director of P2P Target (including those involved in that offer) must disclose to the committee all relevant facts directly relating to himself, and other relevant facts known to him or opinions held by him. For example, a director involved in the proposed offer would need to disclose any negotiations he was having with third parties concerning proposals for the continuing operations of the company after the offer had completed.

3.8 Schemes of arrangement

In recent years many takeovers of public companies have been structured as schemes of arrangement rather than as offers. A scheme of arrangement is a court-approved process governed by Part 26 of the Companies Act 2006 and the Takeover Code (note in particular the contents of Appendix 7 to the Takeover Code, which sets out some of the specific rules which apply to such arrangements).

Bidco and its advisers will need to determine on the facts how best to structure a proposed 'take private' transaction. If a scheme of arrangement is preferred, this will only be possible with the co-operation of P2P Target. Such arrangements are typically structured as a 'cancellation scheme' whereby P2P Target cancels its shares and issues new shares to Bidco in return for Bidco's payment of the bid consideration to P2P Target shareholders.

Some of the more significant features of a scheme of arrangement include the following matters.

(a) A scheme requires the approval of P2P Target shareholders representing a majority in number, and not less than 75 per cent in value, of those voting and present. Any shares held by the private equity investor, the management team and Bidco will not form part of the class of shareholders for the purposes of the vote approving the scheme.

(b) A scheme must be sanctioned by the court. Once sanctioned, a scheme is binding on all P2P Target shareholders and therefore nothing further is required compulsorily to acquire the shares of those who failed to vote or voted against the scheme.

(c) A scheme is an arrangement between the P2P Target and its shareholders. By contrast to an offer, P2P Target therefore has control of the transaction process and key documentation relating to the transaction (i.e. a circular to P2P Target shareholders describing the scheme and containing notices convening the relevant shareholder meetings), albeit that the takeover will be on a recommended basis and the parties will have set out the terms of their co-operation in implementing the scheme in an implementation agreement.

(d) Given the timescales of obtaining court sanction, a takeover offer may establish majority control of P2P Target more quickly than a 'take private' by way of a scheme. However, the time period for achieving 100 per cent control of P2P Target can be shorter via a scheme.

(e) A scheme is less flexible than an offer: the terms of a scheme cannot be changed without the proposal of a new scheme. This may put Bidco at a disadvantage if a competing bid materialises, although it is possible to switch to an offer with the consent of the Takeover Panel.

(f) Stamp duty (at 0.5 per cent) is not payable by Bidco on a scheme. This can be a material advantage over an offer in large transactions.

4 Funding issues on a public-to-private transaction

4.1 Equity funding: the investment documents

The investment documentation on a public-to-private transaction is very similar to the documents found on a private company buyout. The majority of the provisions in the main investment documents will be unchanged, although there are some key differences as highlighted below.

(a) Conditionality: cash confirmation

The first key difference is that the investment agreement will be signed immediately before the announcement is made of a firm intention of Bidco to make the offer, but completion will not take place until a few weeks later (as the first drawdown of monies from the investors will not be required straight away: see further subsection (b) below). The issue therefore arises of the conditionality which the investors may attach to such funding being advanced after signing.

Rule 24.7 of the Code requires that the financial advisers to Bidco provide a cash confirmation (in the offer document) confirming that Newco has the funds available to finance the cash element of the bid. Such confirmation is required to demonstrate that Bidco has taken all reasonable care to ensure that the finance will be available. The financial advisers need to be comfortable that, once the investment agreement has been entered into, the investors' monies will be available when the offer becomes or is declared unconditional in all respects. The cash confirmation exercise usually involves the engagement of separate lawyers to look specifically at the conditions in the investment agreement and the banking documents to ensure that the cash confirmation can be given.

The investment agreement on a public-to-private transaction will therefore typically have only one condition: i.e. that of the offer becoming or being declared unconditional in all respects. This can be contrasted with the situation found in most buyout investment agreements, where a raft of conditions is included to serve as a checklist of the investors' requirements before monies will be advanced, even though, in practice, it is usual in that situation for the signing of the agreement and the investment funding to take place simultaneously.[12]

It is usual to see a provision in the investment agreement that the parties will use their reasonable endeavours to seek to satisfy that condition. Sometimes, an

12 See further chapter 5, section 3.2.

additional 'get out' clause is included, stating that the investors will not be under an obligation to advance its monies if the bank funders withdraw their funding commitment. In reviewing any conditionality wording, including 'get out' provisions, it is essential to ensure that any conditions in the banking documents will either be satisfied pre-exchange, or be within Bidco's control/gift to satisfy once the offer is declared unconditional. It is also important to review any other documents that are to be signed on or prior to exchange (for example, any agreement under which the management team conditionally agrees to exchange their shares in P2P Target for shares in Bidco or its ultimate parent company), to check that the only condition that applies is that of the offer being declared unconditional.

(b) Timing of funding

Once the offer has become or been declared unconditional in all respects, Bidco will be under an obligation to pay the following consideration for the shares (in practice, these amounts are paid to receiving agents, who receive the same on behalf of the relevant shareholders):

(a) for those P2P Target shareholders who have accepted the offer before it becomes or is declared unconditional in all respects, the consideration should be paid on the fourteenth day after the offer has become or been declared unconditional in all respects;
(b) for those P2P Target shareholders who accept the offer subsequently but before the final closing date, they should be paid within fourteen days after receipt of such acceptance.

The mechanics for payments on a public-to-private transaction are therefore more complex than for a private company buyout. Care is needed from a practical perspective to ensure there is sufficient time to deal with shareholders holding shares in dematerialised form under the CREST system. The investment agreement will typically state that, once the condition has been satisfied, completion will take place at a time that Bidco, the investors and the managers agree, but in any event no later than close of business on the thirteenth day after satisfaction of the relevant condition, to ensure there is sufficient time for such logistics to be handled.

Private equity investors may require drawdown notices to be served and other internal processes to be completed before funds can be made available. In the case of managed funds, notice periods of ten business days (or even longer) may be required for the drawdown of funds. Time periods should be checked with care – it may even be necessary to serve drawdown notices before the offer has become unconditional.

(c) Obligations on the management team and Bidco

It is important from the investors' point of view that it has appropriate controls over Bidco's conduct of the offer, given that the management team will often be the owners and directors of Bidco during this period. As has been highlighted throughout this chapter, there are various obligations on Bidco under the Takeover Code in particular, and the investors will wish to ensure that all of such matters are controlled.

Therefore, in addition to the typical business conduct obligations that are found in any investment agreement, it is usual to see a number of additional obligations placed on Bidco that run from the date of exchange. Examples of such obligations include:

(a) an obligation on Bidco to take all steps in connection with or relating to the offer or the proposed acquisition of P2P Target as may be reasonably required by the investors;
(b) an obligation on Bidco to comply with the relevant 'squeeze out' provisions once acceptance in respect of 90 per cent of the shares to which the offer relates has been attained;
(c) an obligation on Bidco to apply for cancellation of P2P Target's listing on the London Stock Exchange or on AIM, as the case may be;
(d) an obligation on Bidco to procure that P2P Target convenes a shareholder meeting to pass a resolution to re-register P2P Target as a private company.

There are also a number of further undertakings that investors will usually seek from the management team that are specific to a public-to-private transaction, such as undertakings:

(a) to disclose to the investors, before the offer is declared unconditional, anything of which they become aware that could or may be likely to affect the conditions in the offer, or that could or may be likely to constitute a breach of the warranties in the investment agreement (see further below);
(b) not to declare the offer unconditional as to acceptances, or fully unconditional, unless the Takeover Panel requires otherwise;
(c) not to issue any advertisement or announcement in connection with the offer;
(d) not to agree or announce any extension of the offer, revise the terms or conditions of the offer, increase the price offered, or propose any alternative consideration under the offer;
(e) not to exercise any of Bidco's rights pursuant to the irrevocable undertakings given by any of P2P Target's shareholders;
(f) not to purchase any shares in P2P Target or otherwise deal in securities in P2P Target (which obligation should also be given in respect of any relevant persons who might be construed as acting in concert with Bidco, such as close relatives and family trusts);
(g) to comply with the Takeover Code, and to procure that Bidco complies with the Takeover Code and behaves in a manner consistent with the statements of intention attributed to Bidco in the offer document.

(d) Warranties

On a public-to-private transaction, it is not possible to obtain a full set of acquisition-type warranties, as there is no sale and purchase agreement. As we saw in chapter 5, the warranties that are given to the investors under the investment agreement usually have as their main purpose the flushing out of information, and so are often viewed more as an extension of the due diligence process, rather than offering any meaningful economic redress if the warranties prove to be false.[13]

On a public-to-private transaction, the issue of warranties can become an area of much debate. On the one hand, the absence of any acquisition warranties from the sellers, and potentially more limited due diligence, may lead the investors to insist that management give more extensive warranties concerning P2P Target. On the other hand, concerns as to the economic worth of the managers as warrantors, and the obvious difficulties with being seen to take legal action against members of a management team that the investors have backed, remain equally valid on a public-to-private transaction.

Another related issue is the question of when any warranties are given. As we have seen, where there is a delay between exchange and completion, the warranties given by the relevant sellers are usually repeated at completion.[14] In a public-to-private transaction, however, it is more common that any warranties to be given by the managers are given only when the investment agreement is entered into, immediately before the offer is announced. As noted above, an obligation is then imposed on the management team in the investment agreement to disclose to the investors full details of any material fact or circumstance of which they become aware prior to the offer being declared unconditional which is likely to be relevant to the conditions of the offer. This is mainly a reflection of the fact that the repetition of warranties before completion is unlikely to offer any remedy to the investors in any event; the degree of cash confirmation required means that it is extremely unlikely that the investors will be able to back out of the deal should something significant occur between exchange and completion.

It is also prudent for investors to include some additional warranties from management specific to the offer, for example:

(a) that the information in the offer document relating to Bidco and the management team, and so far as the managers are aware in relation to P2P Target and its directors, is correct; and
(b) that the management team and Bidco have complied with the requirements under the City Code.

13 See chapter 5, section 3.4.
14 See chapter 4, section 2.6(b).

Warranties such as these will help to focus the minds of members of the management team on the content of the offer document, and their obligations under the Takeover Code.

4.2 Bank funding

Debt providers must be prepared to commit to lend on the date Bidco announces its offer, and fulfil that obligation at a future date, even though there may be an intervening breach by Bidco, Topco or any subsidiary of Topco (including the members of the Target group upon acquisition) of the terms of the relevant facility agreements (except for certain fundamental breaches discussed in more detail below). This, of course, contrasts sharply with an acquisition of a private company, where the debt providers will be entitled to withdraw their finance if there are breaches of representations and warranties, or of the financial covenants or other events of default set out in the debt documentation.

The only events of default which may exempt the debt providers from their obligation to lend in a public-to-private transaction (other than the relevant offer not being declared unconditional in all respects) are typically restricted to:

(a) non-payment by Bidco of sums due under the debt documents;
(b) insolvency events in respect of Bidco, any Midco or Topco;
(c) invalidity of the financing documents;
(d) breaches of covenants relating to the conduct of the offer;
(e) breaches by Bidco, any Midco or Topco of the restrictions in the debt documents relating to mergers, acquisitions (other than the acquisition of Target), granting of security (other than the security in favour of the debt providers) and incurrence of financial indebtedness (other than under the debt documents);
(f) breaches by Bidco, any Midco or Topco of the representations as to their legal status and existence, the legal and binding nature of the debt documents, their power and authority to enter into the debt arrangements and the validity of the debt documents.

Given that Bidco, any Midco and Topco are new companies incorporated for the purposes of making the offer, the only liabilities they will have incurred and will anticipate incurring before an offer is declared unconditional will be in connection with the offer and the funding of the offer. As a result, it is difficult to envisage how any such breach may occur from a practical point of view.

Lending into default is one the idiosyncratic features of the debt funding of public-to-private takeovers. It runs contrary to the normal principles of bank lending, but the credit committees of lenders have become comfortable with the concept. A more concerning feature of public-to-private takeovers for debt providers is the inevitable delay there will be in obtaining security over the assets of the P2P Target group, or, in the worst case scenario, the possibility that they may end up with no security at all. This delay arises because the guarantees and security from P2P Target and its subsidiaries cannot be provided until P2P Target has been re-registered as a private company. Public companies cannot grant financial assistance for the acquisition of their own shares and, in addition, the subsidiaries of P2P Target cannot give financial assistance while their parent is still a public company. As noted in section 3.5 above, the re-registration of P2P Target as a private company requires a special resolution of the shareholders of P2P Target. Consequently, the debt providers will be keen to ensure that the offer cannot be capable of being closed unless and until they are sure that this special resolution can be passed.

In light of this, it will be common to see a covenant in the debt documentation that will restrict Bidco from declaring the offer unconditional as to acceptances unless the level of acceptances of the offer (when combined with the number of shares in P2P Target already held by Bidco) represents either:

(a) not less than 90 per cent of each class of share capital of the P2P Target; or,
(b) in some circumstances, not less than 75 per cent of the issued share capital of the P2P Target.

In the former case, the debt providers can take comfort from the fact that, once the 90 per cent threshold is reached, Bidco can invoke the compulsory acquisition provisions referred to in section 3.5 and acquire the remaining shares leading to 100 per cent ownership. In these circumstances, they will be certain that the necessary resolution will be obtained. In the latter case, the position is slightly more problematic. Control of 75 per cent of the issued share capital of P2P Target would be sufficient to pass the necessary special resolutions. However, during a period of twenty-eight days following the date of the resolution, members representing not less than 5 per cent of the issued share capital of the P2P Target, or being not less than fifty in number, can apply to the court for the cancellation of the resolution re-registering the P2P Target as a private limited company (provided that those shareholders did not vote in favour of the special resolution).[15]

Debt providers will look to build certain protections into the debt documentation addressing each of these potential issues, which may take one of a number of forms:

(a) A covenant that Bidco will not declare the offer wholly unconditional at the 75 per cent acceptances level unless the debt providers are satisfied that there is no reasonable likelihood of a shareholder or group of shareholders looking to have the required resolution cancelled.
(b) An event of default in circumstances where the security to be given by P2P Target is not supplied by a certain date. This would trigger a potential acceleration of the debt and the obligation of Bidco to repay the whole of the funding. It should be noted however, that this is clearly of limited value as the repayment obligation, whilst crystallised, is still an unsecured obligation of the group.

15 See section 98 of the Companies Act 2006.

(c) Increasing the interest rate applicable to the debt in the event that the security to be given by P2P Target is not supplied by a certain date. Such an increase in interest would be sized to reflect the increased risk perceived by the debt providers.

5 Conclusion

In the market conditions being experienced at the time of writing this book, many public companies are viewed by commentators as undervalued. Their share prices having fallen dramatically – either in line with the market due to the general macro-economic environment, or perhaps due to specific shortcomings in their business model to tackle more challenging times. In principle, it might be assumed that such conditions would result in an increased volume of public-to-private transactions, with private equity bidders more likely to be able to fund a comparatively attractive offer.

However, the reality is that there have been relatively few recent public-to-private transactions completed. In an illiquid market, share prices are volatile; small volumes of trading in a company's shares may have a disproportionate effect on share price (particularly in the case of small and medium-sized companies). Valuing a company in these conditions becomes difficult, and there is often a marked difference in expectations between the board and shareholders of a public company on the one hand and a private equity buyer on the other. Market volatility therefore inevitably serves to heighten the risk that a potential public-to-private transaction will fail due to a disagreement on valuation, sometimes at a point when a large amount of time and cost has been invested in conducting due diligence. This heightened execution risk, coupled with the uncertainty that a takeover offer will be successful, and the complexities of the process that we have explored in this chapter, is enough to deter some private equity investors from embarking on 'take private' transactions as a matter of principle. The significant costs of a public-to-private can also be a deterrent, particularly for those public companies with a low market capitalisation.

It is unsurprisingly those public companies with features that may mitigate some of these execution risks that tend to make more attractive targets. For example, a public company with a concentration of shares in the hands of a small number of shareholders, possibly including members of the board, who can be persuaded to give irrevocable commitments to accept an offer will make a far more attractive proposition to a potential private equity bidder than a company with a diverse shareholder register, or with no significant institutional or management shareholdings. As market volatility is replaced with some sense of order in the markets, public-to-private transactions still offer good opportunities for those private equity houses with the capabilities to identify the best deals and deliver them.

11

Living with the investment

1 Introduction

In this chapter, we will look at some of the issues faced by the private equity investors and the managers during the lifetime of the investee company. In particular, we will look at issues related to the ongoing funding of the business, underperformance of the investment, parting company with a manager, and restructurings including debt capitalisation. These are challenges in all markets, but have become ever more pressing in the market conditions prevailing from 2008 onwards.

Such matters put to the test the mechanisms included in the documentation at the time of the buyout, and afford the opportunity to see how theory and practice combine to protect the interests of both the company and the investors. The implications of employment law, the relationships between the investors, the management team and the senior lenders, the taxation aspects of any changes to the deal structure and the overriding objective to protect and, where possible, enhance the value of the investment must all be considered. Such factors operate to set the environment in which often challenging business decisions must be made and implemented under tight commercial time pressure.

We will also examine directors' duties and, in particular, the new statutory code relating to directors' duties in the Companies Act 2006. Conflicts of interest can be particularly acute given the various agendas of the parties to the investment, and their different roles and responsibilities. This is especially the case in an underperformance situation, but the duties of directors exist at all times, and are of increasing importance as a result of ever closer governmental, regulatory and media scrutiny of the industry.

2 Monitoring the investment

2.1 Approach to monitoring

An important part of the activities of the private equity firm, on behalf of its underlying investors, is the monitoring of its portfolio of investments.

Monitoring enables the private equity firm to report regularly to its own investors, and periodically to review its own internal valuation of the investment. Monitoring also ensures a continued review of the strategies adopted for the purpose of achieving the ultimate aim of a successful exit.

In general terms, two different approaches are seen as to who carries out such monitoring. In some cases, the executives within the private equity house who negotiated the original transaction are also involved in its monitoring, whilst other private equity firms prefer to separate out their 'deal-doing' executives from their portfolio executives, and transfer much of the day-to-day monitoring of investments to a separate portfolio team. There are advantages and disadvantages to each approach. Those who favour the deal executives continuing with the monitoring of the investment argue that this helps preserve the personal relationships created on the original buyout with the management team, and ensures that executives responsible for the transaction remain responsible for the performance of the investment they have backed. Others argue that the management of the portfolio requires a different skill set to the origination of transactions, and that a separated approach ensures that the investee company will always have access to a contact at the private equity firm irrespective of whether the 'deal-doers' are in the midst of a time-consuming new transaction. In some firms, a combined approach is seen, where specialist portfolio executives work alongside the original investment executive to monitor the investment and manage the ongoing relationship.

Investors also differ in their level of engagement with the investee company. Some are very active and 'hands on' in their approach, such that the private equity investor directors or portfolio managers are almost a day-to-day part of the business, with a detailed knowledge of what is happening within the business and changes to its prospects. Others have a more passive monitoring role, watching the management accounts as they come in, but only becoming active if a possible exit opportunity arises, if something alarming is detected, or if a consent matter is brought to them. The approach is largely influenced by factors such as the number and size of the investments in the investor's portfolio, and the relative size of the private equity investor's stake. If investors have a minority stake with relatively weak controls, their ability to manage and influence the investment in a 'hands on' way will be much diminished. On balance, however, the push towards investor-led equity positions, and the increasing complexity of the financial gearing involved in larger buyouts, have tended to push all funds towards a more 'hands on' approach.

2.2 Tools for monitoring

The private equity investors will be able to keep a close watch on what is happening to its investment through the appointment of investor directors or observers to attend board meetings. In addition, the investment documents will contain various provisions enabling the investors to monitor performance.

(a) Financial and other information

Whichever approach to monitoring is adopted, monitoring begins with the financial and other information to which the private equity investors are entitled under the investment agreement. The investment agreement will require that Newco send the investors monthly management accounts, usually showing in detail how performance compares against the Business Plan or the latest annual budget, and the key banking covenants. Investors will also usually be entitled to receive details of other significant matters such as material litigation, or correspondence with the bank outside the ordinary course.[1]

(b) Annual budget

Another important part of the monitoring process is achieved by the requirement for agreement of an annual budget. The investment agreement will require that the annual budget for each financial year of Newco and its group must be approved in advance with the investors, usually around thirty to forty-five days before the start of the financial year to which it relates. The Business Plan at the time of the buyout is normally used as the budget for the financial year in which the buyout occurs. Going forward, however, there will invariably be changes to the business and its evolution compared to what was assumed and forecast in the Plan. The annual budgeting process enables the parties to reassess matters in light of their ongoing experience with the business, and the prevailing environment and trading conditions in which the business has to operate. This process necessarily involves investors understanding the business, and being briefed by executive management on the state of the business and its prospects for the next financial year. This is a useful check back on the decisions underlying the investment's strategy, and allows a continued review of the positioning of the business towards a suitable exit.

(c) Investor consents

The investor consent requirements (whether under the investment agreement or the articles of association) also fulfil a monitoring role. The need for the managers to seek approval to material matters, or indeed any matters outside the ordinary course of business, acts as a warning mechanism to alert the investors on significant matters arising within the business.[2] The annual budget will set out that year's provision for key expenditures such as material property or business acquisitions, or other capital expenditure. To ease the investor consent process for some matters, investor consents may be tied in to the budgeting process, such that the need for investor consent is limited to any expenditure that represents a departure from that agreed budget provision.

1 For information requirements, see chapter 5, section 3.11.
2 For more detail on investor consents, see chapter 5, section 3.12.

(d) Post-completion action plan (90 or 100 Day Plan)

As we have seen,[3] the investors will usually require an action plan to be prepared and actioned immediately following completion of the buyout, to identify those activities that must be undertaken to ensure a smooth transfer of ownership of the business, and to address any pressing issues highlighted by due diligence that were not addressed before completion of the acquisition. The progress of such action plan will usually be monitored by way of reporting back and discussion at board meetings in the first few months after completion of the transaction. The investment agreement may include specific obligations on the managers to procure that such plan is finalised and actioned within the relevant timescale, and for regular written reports of progress to be provided to the investors until all steps set out in the plan have been concluded.

(e) Interaction with bank monitoring and consent mechanisms

In most deals, there is significant third party debt in the structure. As illustrated in chapter 6, the banks providing senior debt will also have an active interest in monitoring the business, and will impose a consent regime for material matters in the business that may alter their lending risk or security.[4] The private equity investors will also wish to see copies (preferably in advance) of any financial or other information that is to be supplied to the banks or any other funders, in case that information may suggest a breach of covenant or other difficulty in the business now or in the near future. The same point arises on any application for a consent or waiver from such funders. Prior notification of any such information to be supplied, or consent or waiver to be sought, gives the private equity investors an opportunity to mitigate any problem, or possibly to influence the decisions to be taken by the bank lenders when difficulties do occur.

2.3 Remedies to facilitate monitoring

Monitoring is important. Private equity investors can become particularly concerned if there is any delay in the preparation of management accounts or other financial information, or any serious doubts about the adequacy and reliability of that information. They will also become extremely frustrated if managers take their responsibilities under the investment documents for granted; whilst the occasional brief delay in delivering information due to the need to address issues within the business may be tolerated, regular failures to provide what the investors require, on the basis that was agreed and documented at the time of the original deal, will be frowned upon.

As an ultimate measure, the investment agreement will normally reserve the right for the private equity investors to appoint investigating accountants to check and/or obtain the necessary information if there is any delay or default

3 See chapter 1, section 3.2.
4 See chapter 6, section 4.1(f).

in the preparation of financial information. If the investors were to exercise that right, it is usual that the cost of the review is borne by the investee company. It is relatively rare for such clause to be relied upon in practice, but the threat of this as an ultimate sanction may often help ensure that corporate governance procedures are improved, and that the appropriate level of information is provided in a timely fashion. The confrontational nature of such remedy means that this provision is sometimes known as the 'blockbuster clause'.

In extreme cases, a material or persistent breach, or a material misreporting, will undermine the confidence between the private equity investors and the managers (or some of them), particularly if real problems are being hidden or their discovery delayed. This may in turn lead to disciplinary matters under the service agreement, or even to a termination of the employment of the manager(s) concerned, which is considered in section 5 below.

3 Further funding

3.1 Reasons for seeking funding

Sometimes, private-equity-backed companies will require further funding beyond the levels provided for at the time of the buyout. For some venture or development capital deals,[5] this is part of the original model – the initial funding commitment is staged as a series of fixed instalments, and linked to the achievement of particular milestones (for example, in relation to the testing and licensing of a drug being produced by a pharmaceutical or biotech company, the opening of new retail outlets, and so on). Generally, in the case of the buyout of a mature company, all the funding that is expected to be required is made available as part of the initial funding round (albeit that some of the senior debt may be on revolving credit terms), and accordingly the intention of the parties is that upon completion it should have adequate funding in place or committed from the banks and investors for its foreseeable needs. The investors and other funders would not choose to go into an investment knowing that the core funding levels are not adequate, given the risk of any further funding not being available in future, or only being available on unattractive terms.

Although there is usually only one formal funding round envisaged in the documentation, circumstances could arise where a further funding round is desirable or even necessary in the business. This most frequently arises in an underperformance situation, which is also considered in section 4 of this chapter. However, other opportunities may also arise which require further funding, for example the company may be able to make a strategic acquisition or expansion of its business which was not part of the original Business Plan but nevertheless has a very significant potential advantage to the company. In this situation, a revised Business Plan would inevitably be required from the

5 See further chapter 1, section 2.1.

management team to enable the private equity investors to see the advantages of the further funding and to obtain the necessary internal approvals. A similar process is likely to be required by the bank if additional bank debt is to be sought as part of the funding.

3.2 Dilution and the structuring of further funding

As we have seen, a key feature of a buyout is that the private equity investors put in proportionately more money for their equity than the managers. The use of debt funding by private equity investors to 'sweeten' the equity deal for managers is inherent in most buyouts, as is discussed in more detail in chapter 3.[6]

Where further funding is required from private equity investors during the life of the investment (typically, only when the bank funder(s) cannot provide the full amount required), the question arises as to whether that too should be in such a blended form, or whether all of such funding should be provided in the form of equity or possibly debt. Also, the issue arises of the price at which any new equity should be introduced, or the interest rate that should be attached to any debt instruments.

Managers would normally share in the right to participate in any new equity fundraising; that is to say that they would be entitled to subscribe for a proportionate amount of any new shares at the same price per share as the investors. In theory, therefore, managers have a protection to avoid being diluted provided they put in their fair share. However, in practice, private equity investors are usually in a much stronger financial position to provide any extra funding required. As a result, there is a very real possibility that management's equity percentage will be diluted because they cannot afford to put in the necessary monies to take up their new equity in full. Even if the new money goes in on arm's length terms, so that the dilution is one of percentage rather than of value (the argument being that management's smaller stake has the same, or substantially the same, value as before due to the new monies being introduced – a smaller share in a bigger pie), there can be both emotional and practical consequences in having a reduced equity percentage.

Where the funding is related to a good news situation (for example, a strategic opportunity), it is possible that the private equity investors and the banks will be persuaded to fund it on a non-dilutive basis. In that case, the new money will come purely in the form of debt (or, perhaps, preference shares) which will require an appropriate, or even generous, return, but the private equity investors would not seek to have a higher proportion of the equity. Of course, if the return is too generous, the dilutive effect of the more expensive debt instrument may in itself have an adverse effect on the motivations of management.

Irrespective of the split between debt and equity, there can be tax implications for the management team in a new equity fundraising. This is particularly

6 See in particular chapter 3, section 2.

the case if, as a consequence of the terms of the fundraising, it is necessary to alter any ratchet[7] or similar mechanism that formed part of the original transaction. However, if the opportunity is good enough and the parties can agree the broad commercial criteria of the deal, it is usually possible to plan this in a tax-efficient manner.

Where the news is not so good, and the further funding is required to rectify some problem in the balance sheet or to persuade the senior lender or other funders not to take more drastic steps to protect its existing position, the private equity investors are far less likely to offer any sweet deal to managers for the further funding. In those cases, the managers often do not put in any new money, and are simply diluted by the further funding. As has already been explained in chapter 3, management equity ranks at the bottom of the pile on a failure of the investment and, as such, management's investment is fully at risk in the event of an underperformance. Having said that, if management are to remain motivated to ensure that the business is turned around following an underperformance, some form of incentive will usually be necessary, whether within the funding structure or otherwise.[8]

3.3 Further funding checklist

When drafting documentation for a new funding round, the existing investment documents must be reviewed carefully to ensure that any relevant procedures for the new investment are followed. The existing documents must also be checked to ensure that any new commercial requirements are properly incorporated within the existing structure, and that any obsolete or redundant provisions are varied or removed accordingly.

The circumstances that give rise to a need for further funding, and the commercial terms agreed between the parties to reflect those circumstances, will vary. As a result, the requirements in terms of legal documentation will also be specific to the situation in which the investee company has found itself. Generally speaking, the documentation for a further funding round will include a supplemental investment agreement, revisions to the articles of association, and (where debt investment is involved) modifications to the intercreditor agreement with the bank and possibly the banking facilities. Points to be checked by the legal adviser on a further funding round include the following:

- obtaining full details of all funding to be provided, and the parties providing it, including the interest rate (or dividends accruing, as the case may

7 For ratchets generally, see chapter 3, section 3.2, and chapter 5, section 4.6.

8 See further chapter 7, section 5, concerning management incentives. Incentives of the type made available to second-tier managers on a successful buyout may also be used for senior managers in an underperformance situation, either on a stand-alone basis or in combination with the existing equity stake.

be) and repayment dates for any loans or preference share instruments, and confirmation of whether any loans will be secured;

- where shares are to be issued, the class in which shares will be issued to each subscriber (or, where the rights attached to the shares differ from the existing classes, or rights attached to any of the existing classes are to be varied, details of the rights to be attached to each relevant class);
- the procedure for issuing new shares as prescribed by the existing investment agreement and articles;
- details of whether any further debt funding is to be secured and, if so, the ranking of that debt against the existing secured loans, both in terms of repayment in the ordinary course and in the event of a default;
- clarification of whether the Business Plan is to be updated and, if so, whether it should be warranted by the management team (whilst this is invariably a prerequisite to the initial deal, it may not be commercially viable on a further funding round, depending on whether the further funding offers any benefit for management);
- details of any other warranties that may be required from management, if these can be negotiated, for example to confirm that no material issues have arisen since the time of the original buyout other than those of which the investors are aware;
- confirmation of whether any individuals who were not party to the original investment agreement will become a party at this stage of the refinancing, so that they give warranties (where relevant) and are bound by the restrictive covenants and other obligations set out in that document (which is often relevant, as a further investment is often accompanied by a change or addition to the management team);
- checking the investor consents required, and consents required under the banking documents, and ensuring that all such consents are in place;
- clarifying who is currently a director and will be a director of each relevant company in the group going forward, and the quorum requirements under each relevant set of articles of association for approval of the funding documents and completion of the investment;
- checking adherence requirements for new debt funders to become a party to the intercreditor arrangements, where relevant; and
- carrying out new money-laundering checks where necessary for the investors, and carrying out company searches and bankruptcy searches to ensure there are no new issues revealed before the further investment takes place.

4 Underperformance and debt restructuring

4.1 Background and reasons for underperformance

Underperformance is a major issue for private equity investors. Most private equity investors will have, at any one time, some underperforming assets in their portfolio. The private equity investment model depends upon a number of very successful investments producing sufficient profit and gain not only to cover the ailing or failing investments, but also to produce (on an aggregated basis) the overall returns that are attractive to the private equity fund's own investors.

What is meant by underperformance, and its implications, will vary from deal to deal. More often than not, the most simple evaluation is to measure profits achieved against those forecast in the Business Plan, as this usually has a direct and proportionate impact on the likely exit valuation, and therefore the investors' ultimate return. The consequences of underperformance will also depend on what was negotiated at the time of the deal. In some cases, it may simply cause bonuses to be missed, whilst in others it will also give rise to enhanced rights for the investors (for example, to appoint further directors, to exercise a drag along right unfettered, or to have enhanced voting rights). Occasionally, it may even give rise to an express contractual right to terminate the manager's employment.

Of course, where the underperformance is so material as to jeopardise the relationship of the business with key customers, suppliers or regulators, or to risk or cause a breach of bank covenants, far greater issues may arise for the investors, the company and the managers.

Where it becomes apparent to the private equity investors from their monitoring that an investment is underperforming, they will begin by looking to understand the reasons for this. It may be that the underlying business is performing well but the structure is excessively leveraged, or that assumptions underlying key parts of the funding structure have changed in a way which is adverse to the business (for example, adverse interest or currency movements beyond any hedging arrangements, or changes in the taxation treatment of particular aspects of the deal structure). In some cases, underperformance may arise due to timing differences in certain of the assumptions underlying the Business Plan, or changes to the market in which the company is operating (new entrants, changes in regulatory environment, new products and services taking market share). In other situations, it may result, for example, from problems in the company itself, or in its supply chain or customer base.

Private equity investors will want to understand the reasons for the underperformance and what steps the managers propose in order to address the situation. Where the underperformance is material (in particular, if it could risk jeopardising bank covenants), then the private equity investors may well seek external professional advice on the proposed steps suggested by the managers, or require that a further Business Plan be prepared. If not satisfied with the outcome, the 'blockbuster clause' (see section 2.3 above) may even be invoked to enable a review of the business by professional advisers against management's wishes.

4.2 Steps the investors may consider

Where there is an underperformance that cannot readily be explained and addressed, the parties may consider several alternative solutions to the problem, for example:

- changing the strategy of the business and the Business Plan;
- seeking further funding from the bank, or variations to the banking terms (for example, an extension of the facilities by altering the repayment dates);
- further funding from the private equity investors or other shareholders;
- adding to the management team, and/or parting company with one or more members of the management team;
- restructuring of the balance sheet, for example through capitalisation of existing shareholder debt (see further below);
- selling the investment; and
- in extreme cases, administration or other insolvency processes.

Where an underperformance arises that could lead to a breach of the covenants in the banking documents, it is important to speak to the bank at an early stage. Generally, a sensible dialogue with the bank is likely to lead to a more satisfactory overall resolution of the issues of underperformance than would result from a last minute conversation on the imminent occurrence of a material breach of covenant. That said, where time allows, investors will usually want to have had an opportunity to decide on the best strategy for tackling the underperformance (at least in outline) so that the bank is presented with possible solutions and not just a problem.

As noted above, in many underperformance situations it may well be necessary to strengthen the business with further funding from the private equity investors or the bank. Another possible solution, however, is to write off, or capitalise (i.e. issue shares in the capital of Newco, or possibly other companies in the group, in satisfaction of), some or all of the debt and interest that exists in the structure. Either approach is designed to preserve value so far as practicable for the existing funders, and to leave the business in the most viable state either to trade out of the difficulties or to maximise the realisation if there has to be a forced exit at this stage. A capitalisation or waiver of existing debt may also be crucial to motivate a management team whose equity is otherwise significantly underwater.

Some of the issues that a lawyer must consider when further funding is required are outlined in section 3 above. We will now consider further the issues that arise in the event that debt is to be waived or capitalised, and the influence that the bank will bring to bear as senior lender.

4.3 Debt waivers and capitalisations: tax consequences

The waiver or capitalisation of senior and investor debt gives rise to a number of specific tax issues, relating both to Newco and its group and to the investors.

Such issues are usually a key driver in determining the steps to be taken for any proposed restructuring following underperformance.

Assuming that the relevant investee company is within the charge to UK corporation tax, the most common tax issues that need to be addressed are:

- whether any tax liability will arise in Newco or its group as a result of the debt waiver or capitalisation;
- correspondingly, whether the creditor (i.e. the investors or bank funders capitalising the debt) will obtain any tax relief;
- whether any withholding tax issues will arise in the context of a debt capitalisation; and
- whether a capitalisation can give rise to unexpected degrouping charges and/or the stranding of valuable tax assets.

(a) Tax arising in Newco

When a company is released from a liability to repay senior or investor debt (often referred to as a waiver, or writing off, of the debt), the general position is that the company is treated as realising an amount of taxable income equal to the debt released.[9] No such income will be treated as arising for the investee company in question if the creditor is a company that is connected with the investee company in the accounting period in which the release occurs.[10] This connection test is satisfied in the event that one of the companies controls the other, or both companies are under common control.[11] Whilst this may offer a way to avoid a taxable income arising, in most private equity investments there will not be the relevant degree of connection (as no single investor will usually control the underlying investment), and as a result one often cannot rely upon this exception.

Another exception to the general position is where the release forms part of a formal insolvency arrangement.[12] However, this is unlikely to be of much assistance in the context of a restructuring of an investee company, the aim of which is most usually (amongst other things) to avoid a formal insolvency arrangement and the adverse consequences that flow from that.

For this reason, many private equity restructurings are effected by capitalising the relevant debt rather than a simple debt waiver. This is because a company will not be treated as realising taxable income upon the release of debt where that release is in consideration of an issue of ordinary shares.[13] For these purposes, the term 'ordinary shares' has a special tax meaning and, broadly speaking, will comprise any shares other than fixed rate preference shares. This approach is also particularly helpful in that there is no requirement that the ordinary shares have an equivalent value to the face value of

9 Section 307 of the Corporation Tax Act 2009.
10 Paragraph 358 of the Corporation Tax Act 2009.
11 Section 466 of the Corporation Tax Act 2009.
12 Sections 322(3) and 358 of the Corporation Tax Act 2009.
13 Sections 322(4) and 358 of the Corporation Tax Act 2009.

the debt released. Therefore, it is possible to issue relatively worthless ordinary shares in consideration of the release of the debt without triggering a tax charge within the investee company – meaning that investor debt or even bank debt can be capitalised for a shareholding which represents whatever commercial value the parties agree.

(b) Tax relief for the creditors

The question then arises of the impact of such debt for equity capitalisation in the hands of the relevant creditor. A financial trader, such as a bank, generally will account for its debt instruments on a mark to market basis. As a result, senior lenders will usually obtain tax relief in respect of distressed investee company debt as and when it is written down in the relevant bank's accounts. Other companies within the charge to UK corporation tax will similarly expect to obtain tax relief for any losses arising upon releasing an investee company from its obligation to repay investor loans. Therefore, upon a debt capitalisation, the creditor will usually be treated as releasing the debt in return for the shares issued and, if the creditor is not connected to the investee company, this should give rise to tax relief for the creditor in respect of the loss on the debt. This is therefore one of those rare occasions where there is tax asymmetry in favour of the taxpayer, as the investee company is not taxed on the release, but the creditor company obtains tax relief.

However, subject to one exception noted below, no relief will be available if in the relevant accounting period the creditor and investee company are connected with each other.[14] This is the counterbalance to the fact that, as noted above, an investee company is not treated as having any taxable income upon the release of debt where the creditor is a connected company.

It is possible that, as a result of the capitalisation, the creditor company becomes connected to the investee company. If this were the case, in the absence of any special relief, this would result in the creditor company being denied relief for the debt released in return for the shares issued. However, in order to facilitate these types of balance sheet restructurings, a creditor company is still able to secure relief if it becomes connected as a result of the capitalisation provided that it was not previously connected with the investee company in the relevant accounting period.[15] This should enable most investors who are not connected to the investee company concerned prior to the capitalisation to obtain the necessary relief.

Particular care is needed where a creditor becomes connected with the investee company as a result of a debt capitalisation and continues to hold other debt in the investee company, as this can trigger certain liabilities in the investee company if the remaining debt is impaired.[16] In such circumstance, a

14 Section 354 of the Corporation Tax Act 2009.
15 Section 356 of the Corporation Tax Act 2009.
16 Sections 321 and 322 of the Corporation Tax Act 2009.

full review of all the debt held by the creditor should be carried out before the debt capitalisation proceeds.

(c) Withholding tax

Subject to a number of exceptions, an investee company is obliged to withhold tax (currently at 20 per cent) from payments of interest. The main exceptions are where the interest is paid on certain bank debt or to a UK company.[17]

In many private equity investments, interest will have been rolled up on the investor debt and added to the principal. Where shares are issued in satisfaction of the debt (including the rolled-up interest), that will constitute payment of the interest for tax purposes,[18] thus triggering a withholding tax obligation unless one of the exceptions referred to above applies.

Such obligation is generally satisfied by withholding some of the shares and paying them over to HMRC. However, this requirement may be waived if HMRC accepts that it is impracticable to do this.

(d) Degrouping issues

As noted in chapter 3,[19] the debt investments of the senior lenders and the private equity investors (and any other debt funders) will generally be held not in the top company in the structure, but rather in a company further down the group structure. As a consequence, the issue of shares in the debtor company to the investor may result in the debtor company (and its subsidiaries) being degrouped for tax purposes from those companies above it in the group.

If there have been intra-group transfers of assets between the debtor company (or its subsidiaries) and companies higher up the group structure, this could result in tax degrouping charges in the debtor company (or one of its subsidiaries).[20] In addition, it could also result in tax reliefs arising higher up the group structure being unavailable to offset against profits arising in the debtor company (and its subsidiaries).[21] Although these issues do not usually arise in a private equity context (as such intra-group transfers up the structure would be unusual), they must be borne in mind whenever shares are to be issued in a subsidiary company.

4.4 Debt capitalisations and restructurings: the bank's influence

Inevitably, the senior lenders have a significant influence in determining the measures to be taken on underperformance. Not only are they usually the largest creditor, but they have an inherent superiority in the funding structure,

17 Sections 879 and 993 of the Income Act 2007.

18 Section 413 Corporation Tax Act 2009 and section 939 Income Tax Act 2007.

19 See chapter 3, section 2.3.

20 See section 179 of the Taxation of Chargeable Gains Act 1992, and Schedule 29 to the Finance Act 2002.

21 See Chapter IV, Part X, of the Income and Corporation Taxes Act 1988.

and an ability to call in working capital from the business if there has been a default.

The interests of the company's management team and the private equity investors are often aligned on an underperformance, with both trying to persuade the bank either to continue with the current funding or at least to agree to a restructuring that leaves something in play for the owners. The historic performance of the borrower and its future prospects will be key factors. In terms of prospects, the bank will invariably focus on whether any proposed restructuring can produce a better realisation to enable the bank to get paid (or at least to minimise the bank's loss). In many situations, this will mean allowing Target to trade as a going concern, rather than suffering the adverse consequences (in terms of relationships with customers, suppliers and employees) that can so often arise if the business enters into administration or other insolvency processes, reducing the amount that the bank ultimately recovers.

The restructuring of a private equity company may involve the capitalisation of a significant amount, or even all, of the private equity investors' subordinated debt. However, the bank will not necessarily escape completely unscathed, even though it holds the prior-ranking debt. In return for agreeing to capitalise a substantial part of its investment, the investors may insist either that the banking facilities are revisited (for example, to reschedule repayment dates, revisit covenant thresholds that have proven to be too tight, or waive breaches of covenant that have occurred) or at the most extreme that the senior bank funders also waive or capitalise part of its debt into some form of equity instrument.

A number of 'debt for equity swaps' (where the senior bank funders capitalise part of their existing loans into equity) have already taken place in the aftermath of the economic turmoil triggered by the credit crunch and related banking crisis during 2008. The extent of the stake to be sacrificed to the bank will vary from transaction to transaction and from bank to bank, and depends to a large extent on whether the senior debt is simply being rescheduled or must actually be sacrificed.

Where a rescheduling is all that is required, the bank(s) may be satisfied simply to take additional fees, or warrants to subscribe for equity shares akin to those held by mezzanine funders. This brings with it the advantage that the bank will not usually become a shareholder until immediately before exit, with less influence on the business until that point. Where a bank takes warrants, the commercial issues to be considered in agreeing the terms of the warrants are generally consistent with those which are negotiated with mezzanine funders. As such, many private equity investors are more comfortable in this area.[22]

However, where a sacrifice of monies owed to the bank is required, banks are increasingly capitalising part of their debt into an equity shareholding.

22 See also chapter 3, section 2.4, and chapter 6, section 4.2(b).

In that case, the negotiations can become much more protracted. Banks will often look for status akin to a material and independent minority investor in a private equity syndicate. As such, they may well expect to be a party to the investment agreement, and request vetoes and consents similar to those granted to the private equity funders. A balance must be struck here. The provision of financial information should not be controversial for example, and often only reflects what the lender may receive under the banking documentation as senior funder anyway (although a bank will usually insist on separate rights in its capacities as a lender and as a shareholder, should the two interests become separated in the future). At the other extreme, both private equity and management shareholders will not be attracted to the possibility of the bank's consent being required before any trading contracts can be entered into or management remuneration changes effected (provided that these have been blessed by the existing private equity funders and will not result in a default under the senior debt documents).

The outcome is often to define two differing levels of investor consent: a 'lead investor consent' (which requires only the blessing of the original private equity fund(s)); and an 'all investor consent' (requiring the consent of both the private equity investors and the bank). The same result can also be achieved by leaving the existing investor consents as they are, and including a shorter, watered-down consent list for the bank. Where the bank takes a direct equity stake, it is more likely (and the banks would argue more reasonable) that the bank will also have the right to appoint a director, or at least an observer.

Control of exit will invariably be a key concern for the private equity investors. Whilst some degree of protection is acceptable to ensure that exit proceeds cannot be manipulated away from the bank's equity stake, it would be unusual for a private equity firm to accept that the bank must actually consent to a proposed exit. Similarly, drag along rights will usually stay within the control of the current private equity investors, with the bank being subject to such rights alongside the management shareholders. Of course, banks will look for the same position as the private equity investors on the question of warranties on exit, i.e. warranties as to title and capacity to sell their own shares only.[23]

Different considerations apply if the underperformance is so serious that the debt to be sacrificed by the bank would be sufficient to give the bank a majority interest. In those cases the bank will rule the roost, and may argue that it should 'take the keys' and run the business as it chooses without the involvement of the private equity investors at all. In those cases, the relevant private equity firm may be willing to continue as a passive, minority investor, or may accept that the game is up and agree to a restructuring which removes them from the business altogether. That said, it is not usually the case that a bank can simply step into the shoes of the existing owners and continue to support the running of a business as a going concern. Save where security is

23 For the position of investors on exit, see chapter 13, section 3.3.

enforced and a formal administration process takes place (perhaps as a precursor to a 'pre-pack' deal, where a buyer has already been identified to acquire the business from the administration process), a bank will usually need the presence of either the existing private equity investor(s), or replacement investors (such as a specialist turnaround fund), for the ongoing support and monitoring of the business.

5 Parting company with a manager

5.1 Background

It is not uncommon in an underperformance situation that one or more of the managers may leave the investment at that time, usually coupled with recruiting or promoting others to fill the role of the departing manager. Sometimes, this is because the trust and confidence of the private equity investors and the bank in the individual manager has been called into question by the factors leading to the underperformance. In other situations, it may be that one or more of the managers lack the necessary skill set to handle the business in a revised funding structure and operational climate. Occasionally, particularly where the management equity has been diluted, managers may wish to leave the investment if no sensible incentive mechanism can be found to keep them in the business.

Of course, managers can leave in other circumstances even if there is no underperformance, for example due to death, ill-health or normal retirement. Similarly, a manager may wish to leave because he has spotted a better opportunity, or may be asked to leave as a result of gross misconduct or other issues touching on his suitability as a senior employee in the company. If the investors or other managers feel that an individual is not making as significant a contribution as was hoped, then steps may be taken to deal with that even if the performance of the other managers, or the business as a whole, is such that there is no underperformance occurring at all.

5.2 Claims and rights to be considered

Whatever the circumstances of a manager's departure, the rights and possible claims of the manager must be considered carefully. In this context, there are three different capacities in which such rights or claims may arise:

(a) as a director;
(b) as an employee; or
(c) as a shareholder.

These different roles interact, and can even conflict, with the result that the negotiation of the terms of an individual's departure can often be complex and protracted, particularly if the circumstances of departure are acrimonious.

5.3 Directorship

Directorship is a fiduciary office. It brings certain duties and responsibilities,[24] and indeed a breach or underperformance of these duties may well lie behind the decision to part with a manager. However, it also confers certain rights on the office holder (subject to any express terms of the articles of association). For example, a director has a right to be informed of and to attend all board meetings. He also has the right to access a company's premises generally, and to inspect the books and records of the company.

This is not usually a position that the other parties would desire should continue following a cessation of employment, particularly in circumstances where a possible claim or dispute may arise (whether on the part of the manager or the company). At its simplest, it can be difficult for the board to take the decision to terminate a service agreement in the first place, or to consider related employment rights, claims and compromises, if the director has a right to be aware of, and to be present at, all board meetings. Similarly, during any notice period or period of garden leave,[25] or during the period of negotiation of any claims, the exercise of these rights could be a frustration or otherwise contrary to the interests of the other shareholders. Whilst a garden leave clause in a service agreement usually allows the company to limit or exclude all duties that the manager has in his capacity as an employee, and to bar him from or limit his access to company premises, personnel and records accordingly, it is not clear how effective this is in the context of the manager's duties and rights as a director.

As a result, as highlighted in chapter 7, service agreements generally contain an obligation on the manager to resign his directorship if his employment ends for any reason (often coupled with a power of attorney if he refuses or is unable for any reason to resign, so that this resignation can be effected for him). However, this is not always a watertight remedy either, as if care is not taken in the drafting it only operates when the employment actually ends (rather than on giving or receiving notice). If there is any material delay before the employment ends, or any dispute as to whether or when it is ended, the directorship may still be active. Even if the obligation to resign is expressed to be triggered at the start of the notice period, there remains the possibility (depending on the circumstances of departure) that the manager may be able to allege that the company is in repudiatory breach of the service agreement, and cannot therefore seek to rely upon the provision to procure such resignation or invoke any related power of attorney. Regardless of whether such claims are ultimately successful, the fact that it can give rise to some doubt as to whether he is still a director gives the director a nuisance value at least, especially in an underperformance situation where the board may need to make tough

24 See further section 6 below.
25 See chapter 7, section 2.3.

decisions in a short timescale, and third parties (such as the bank) will be very sensitive to any procedural irregularity or challenge to the validity of the board proceedings.

Sometimes, the obligation to resign is in the investment agreement – this is thought to be safer from the risk of an allegation of another party's repudiatory breach releasing the manager from the obligation. That risk is not completely negated, however. The safest approach, therefore, is to have a suitable provision in the articles, so that the directorship can be ended by notice from the investors. It is more protective if this is an absolute right for the investors such that it does not depends on the status of the employment relationship. The use of the power may increase the risks of other claims, but should at least resolve the legal issue of whether the manager is still a director. In a group structure, it is also important to cascade the decision to other relevant subsidiaries.

Of course, the shareholders do have the separate statutory right under section 168 of the Companies Act 2006[26] to remove a director by ordinary resolution, but the procedural protections and timescales afforded by these provisions[27] makes it a remedy of last resort, and inferior to a properly crafted express right in the constitution of the company. This is an important area to address upfront at the time that the articles are first adopted, long before any dispute arises.

The investors should equally be careful before agreeing to any class right that would give the manager a hard right to reappoint himself to the board. This defeats the purpose of ensuring that the directorship can be cleanly ended where appropriate to do so, and should only be agreed to if there is a strong commercial justification. Such an enshrined right to be a director would be unusual in most buyouts, although there are occasions when a manager may have more valid grounds to justify such a request (for example, on a secondary transaction where a founder manager is rolling over a significant amount, and therefore requests the directorship right in that capacity to protect the rolled investment).

The challenge of how to make the initial decision to terminate a manager's employment without having to invite the manager in question to the relevant board meeting (which is not usually the easiest or most productive scenario for obvious reasons) can also in part be addressed by the remuneration committee.[28] If the power to suspend or terminate the employment of a manager is vested in the remuneration committee, typically comprising just the non-executive directors (or perhaps the non-executives and the chief executive, other than when considering the chief executive himself), then it may be possible for that committee to take the initial decision without needing to convene a full board meeting including the manager.

26 Previously, section 303 of the Companies Act 1985.

27 Section 168(2) states that special notice is required and section 169 includes rights for the director concerned to have his or her views heard.

28 See further chapter 5, section 3.10.

5.4 Employment rights and claims

Chapter 7 sets out more details of the rights and claims that a manager may have in the context of his employment and its purported termination.[29] Certain claims arise by statute, and as a result cannot be excluded by contrary terms in the service agreement. Possible claims for breach of contract must also be considered.

As summarised in section 5.1 above, the circumstances in which the decision is made to terminate the employment of an executive will not always amount to gross misconduct or otherwise entitle dismissal of the individual without notice. This can occur (even in businesses that are not underperforming, of course) and, when it does, the risk of employment claims is much reduced. More often, however, it arises in less clear-cut circumstances, for example a breakdown of the trust and confidence of the investors or other managers in that individual that gives rise to the decision to terminate (or, perhaps, that manager being offered up by his colleagues as a scapegoat – because someone has to take commercial responsibility for the problems for the rest to move on). For less senior employees, coaching, mentoring or redefining an individual's role may address personal underperformance issues. Such steps (and the period of time that the employer ought to wait to look for improvement) are less likely to be considered acceptable in the context of a senior manager.

This need for expedition (which can also arise to short-circuit the due process of disciplinary procedures, even in a suspected gross misconduct case) means that there is a higher than average risk of an unfair dismissal claim arising when the employment of a senior manager is terminated. In effect, this forms part of the cost to the business of parting with the manager (or, looking at it another way, of backing the wrong person in the first place).

5.5 Rights as a shareholder

The termination of employment and the directorship can also give rise to a potential claim by the manager in his capacity as a shareholder. There is a respectable line of authorities, going back to the decision in *Ebrahimi* v. *Westbourne Galleries*,[30] that suggests that a shareholder may be able to petition for a winding up of the company (based on the 'just and equitable' ground under what is now section 122 of the Insolvency Act 1986) where the company was in effect a form of quasi-partnership, such that the individual's employment was an expected incidence of his membership of the company. That said, such agreements are harder to apply to private equity cases for two reasons:

(a) the elaborate provisions designed to allow termination of employment, with related restrictive covenants and a mechanism for the clawback of equity

29 See in particular chapter 7, section 4.
30 [1973] AC 360.

shares (which is normally discretionary),[31] makes it harder to suggest that there was an implicit agreement that any form of quasi-partnership existed justifying a winding up on departure; and

(b) more recent case law has suggested that the jurisdiction of the court in relation to unfair prejudice (a shareholder remedy conferred by what is now section 994 of the Companies Act 2006, and which did not exist at the time of *Ebrahimi*) offers a more suitable approach for the court in many situations.[32] The court has a wide discretion as to what is a suitable remedy if an unfair prejudice claim is successful, such that winding up is not the only (or even the most likely) outcome. A more typical remedy is that a successful claimant is bought out at fair value (although in many cases such valuation may be determined without discount for any minority interest).

If an unfair prejudice action were successful, the valuation of the leaver's equity may be more attractive than under the mechanism contained in the articles of association on any clawback of shares, especially if the circumstances would result in a 'Bad Leaver' valuation, or treat only part of that manager's equity as vested.[33] For this reason, in many situations, a claim for unfair prejudice is asserted or threatened following a departure. However, in practice, it is rarely pursued. Usually, it is alleged as part of a 'kitchen sink' negotiation tactic, to attempt to maximise the value of the departing manager's compromise package. Where the company itself is underperforming or in financial difficulty, the claim may not have much merit in any event, as the difference between the court's valuation and the valuation under the relevant articles would be little, if any.

In practice, and excluding those cases where the matter becomes seriously contentious (which is the minority of cases), the question of valuation of the sale shares is usually a straightforward discussion at the time of departure. Where the company is insolvent or seriously underperforming (so that the equity is unquestionably underwater), a nominal consideration, or perhaps a token larger figure, will be agreed. In these cases, the manager will usually have little bargaining power beyond any delay that going through the formal clawback mechanism would cause, and any independent valuation costs that would be incurred. Where the business is solvent but not strongly performing, buying out at initial subscription cost, or such cost and a little extra, may well be a compromise. Cost price is often a key driver for a manager, who may have taken out personal loans to raise funding for his initial share subscription.

The hardest cases are those where the equity is in value. In theory, the formal valuation mechanism in the articles may be needed in these cases,

31 See chapter 5, section 4.11.

32 See, for example, *Re Woven Rugs Ltd* [2008] BCC 903.

33 See further chapter 5, section 4.11.

although in practice a price is usually agreed in the context of the overall compromise package.[34] Sometimes, the manager is allowed to keep his shares (or at least some of them), though this is unusual unless there has been a secondary buyout, or there are other circumstances resulting in part or all of the manager's equity being outside the leaver mechanism.

The leaver mechanism is an important protection in the circumstances of a manager's departure. Properly drafted and exercised, it will enable his shares to be acquired. As explained in chapter 5, much time and attention is put into settling these terms at the time of the buyout, and subtle nuances are often reflected in the precise wording. The negotiation of a deal or the exercise of the formal clawback mechanism can take time. Where there is real value in the equity it is important for the company and its investors to be mindful of any time period applicable to the leaver mechanism, to ensure the clawback right is not lost simply because negotiations drag on beyond such period.

During any period of negotiation, the manager will remain a member. Depending on the articles, this may entitle him to vote on shareholder resolutions or to participate in a rights issue. This is not always what is desired by the other shareholders in the circumstances of a departure, however, so the articles will often contain a provision either expressly removing some or all of these rights (sometimes by reclassifying the shares to a non-voting class), or at least entitling the board or the investors to remove the rights in question by written notice. Typically, such provisions are triggered as soon as notice of cessation of employment is given (whether by Newco or by the manager), rather than the date on which the employment actually ends or any leaver provisions are triggered. The interests of the other shareholders (and in particular the investors) are often best protected by keeping the leaver and disenfranchisement mechanisms as independent of each other as possible. In certain cases, it may not be intended to exercise the clawback rights (or at least not at once), but the disenfranchisement right may still be useful, especially in an underperformance situation when shareholder resolutions may be needed in a hurry and the interests of the departing manager (if entitled to vote on the resolutions) may not be aligned with the other shareholders.

5.6 Non-compete, confidentiality and related matters

One issue of sensitivity in any negotiations around a departing manager is the non- compete, non-poaching and confidentiality restrictions that were put in place at the time of the buyout. These will typically be found in both the service agreement[35] (made with and in favour of Newco) and in the investment agreement[36] (made with and in favour of the investors, and sometimes also in

34 See also chapter 9, section 4.5(d), for discussion on how a sale in these circumstances can trigger PAYE and National Insurance liabilities.

35 See chapter 7, section 2.6.

36 See chapter 5, section 3.7.

favour of Newco). These can be important protections for the group – especially where the departure is as a result of a manager choosing to leave.

As noted in chapter 7, the restrictive covenant in the service agreement may be in jeopardy if there is any real suggestion that the dismissal itself (or the way in which it was done) constituted a repudiatory breach by the employer company. This is one of the reasons for the separate covenants in the investment agreement, so that there is no doubt that these covenants will be binding even if repudiatory breach of the service agreement is alleged. A compromise agreement will often include a restatement of such provisions, or confirmation that the original provisions continue in force and effect, to avoid any uncertainty following the manager's departure.

5.7 Anticipating issues in the original documents

The interaction of employment, directorship, shareholder and possibly contractual claims can make the decision and process of parting with a manager difficult. The key to a successful outcome (from the point of view of the continuing shareholders) is to have anticipated the most likely scenarios in advance at the time of the buyout and to ensure that the documentation (in particular, the articles and the service agreement) provide the maximum flexibility and strongest bargaining position to reduce the risk that the departing manager can assert claims that would be highly disruptive to the business (especially in an underperformance or rescue situation).

At the time of negotiating these documents, individual managers can sometimes be resistant to a number of these mechanisms. It is often persuasive to explain at that time that a performing manager is far more likely to stay than to leave, and that the best interests of all remaining shareholders (not just the private equity investors) are protected by a strong hand being dealt in advance to Newco in those situations where departures are necessary. While this 'divide and conquer' principle may seem to contradict the strong team spirit that is usually a feature of a good management team, it does reflect commercial reality and, properly explained and appreciated, can lead to a robust position being accepted upfront by all concerned. Having set out the position in this way, it is important that Newco (and the investors) are careful at the time of departure to ensure that the mechanisms are followed strictly, and in particular that any relevant time periods are met.

6 Directors' duties and conflicts of interest

6.1 Background to directors' duties

In this section, we consider the duties that are owed by directors, and the particular implications that such duties may create in a private equity environment. The new codified duties set out in the Companies Act 2006 have provided a substantial framework from which to begin such analysis, although there is other legislation that is relevant (particularly in an insolvency situation) as well as a substantial body of case law. Throughout this section, we refer to duties being owed to a *company*. In the context of a private equity transaction, it is important to remember that an individual will owe separate duties to every company in the Newco group structure of which he is a director, as well as any companies outside that group.

Consideration of the responsibilities of directors in a private-equity-backed deal emphasises the different relationships that particular individuals may face. Key managers will be directors of one or more companies in the group, as well as employees and shareholders. The chairman will usually be both a non-executive director and a shareholder, often in various different companies outside the Newco group. The investor directors appointed by the private equity investors will often be senior executives (and sometimes even directors) within the relevant private equity manager firm, and sometimes in one or more of the underlying investors themselves, and will have a direct financial interest (in the form of carried interest, and possibly a co-investment) both in Newco and in other investments in the private equity investors' portfolio. The investor director may also be an investor director or observer in other portfolio companies in which that same investor has a stake.

Before the 2006 Act came into force, the regime of directors' duties was a mixture of statute and case law, with some of the cases dating back 100 years or more. One of the aims of the 2006 Act was to make the area of directors' duties more accessible, to address the question of 'In whose interest should companies be run?' to reflect modern business needs, and to bring corporate social responsibility further into the boardroom. The aim of the new statutory duties was: (a) to embed in statute the concept of 'enlightened shareholder value', by making clear that directors must promote the success of the company for the benefit of its shareholders, taking into account factors such as employees, suppliers, customers and the effect of decisions on the environment; and (b) to introduce a statutory statement of directors' duties to clarify their responsibilities and improve the law on regulating directors' conflicts of interests.

The codification of duties under the 2006 Act does not cover all of the general duties that a director owes to a company. Some will remain unmodified, such as considering the interests of creditors in circumstances of potential insolvency.[37] Directors' duties are therefore now governed: (a) by the common law; (b) by the new codified duties under the 2006 Act; and (c) by other specific statutory duties. There are a large number of specific statutory duties, such as those under the Health and Safety at Work Act 1974 and employment legislation; directors must remain abreast of their responsibility under all relevant legislation.

Under the 2006 Act, there are seven codified duties of directors, which are considered in turn in sections 6.3 to 6.9 below. Although strictly outside the

37 See further section 6.12 below.

codified duties, there is also a statutory requirement under section 182 of the 2006 Act for directors to declare their interests in any existing transactions or arrangements that have been entered into by the relevant company, as outlined in section 6.10 below. There are also certain requirements for particular arrangements between a company and a director to be approved by the shareholders, which are considered in section 6.11.

For completeness, there are certain specific duties imposed on directors under the 2006 Act, for example those duties requiring directors:

- to maintain proper tax and accounting records giving an accurate statement of the company's financial position;
- to maintain the statutory registers of the company;
- to prepare the company's annual accounts and return for submission to the Registrar of Companies;
- in the case of public companies only, to hold an annual general meeting.

The sections that follow provide an overview of the main duties referred to above, and, where relevant, offer additional guidance on the ways in which such duties may have particular implications for a private-equity-backed company. Finally, an overview is provided of the key duties that must be considered in an insolvency context.

6.2 To whom are the duties owed?

Generally, directors owe their duties to the company alone, which means to the present and future shareholders of the company and not to any one shareholder individually. Before October 2007, if the directors had breached their duties, then, generally speaking, the members had to look to the board to enforce such breach on behalf of the company, although if the board failed to take action the members could resolve that the company do so. In general, minority shareholders cannot sue for the wrongs done to their company, although there were certain statutory and common law exceptions to this general rule, for example where the wrongdoers are themselves in control.[38] This has meant that derivative claims brought by shareholders in the name of the company have been very scarce.

However, this may change as a result of the new derivative claims procedures under the 2006 Act. Under sections 260–264 of the 2006 Act, a derivative claim may be brought by any shareholder in respect of a cause of action arising from an actual or proposed act or omission involving the negligence, default, breach of duty or breach of trust by a director of a company.

Any shareholder can bring a claim under this provision – all they need is one share and, critically, they do not have to have been a shareholder at the time of the alleged wrongdoing. There has therefore been speculation that this

38 The principle established in the case of *Foss* v. *Harbottle* (1843) 2 Hare 461.

new action will allow activists or other pressure groups to bring troublesome claims, or could lead to spoiling tactics in the context of transactions. A good example might be in relation to a recommended takeover, which might result in redundancies, where a trade union acquires a shareholding to bring a claim against the directors (on the basis that the interests of the employees have not been properly considered in light of the concept of enlightened shareholder value)[39] to frustrate a transaction.

There are, however, some safeguards against speculative claims. First, the new derivative action is a two-stage process. A claimant must establish a *prima facie* case before being given permission by the court to proceed with any claim.[40] Secondly, the 2006 Act contains a list of matters that the court must take into account when considering whether or not to grant such permission. These include:

(a) whether the shareholder is acting in good faith;
(b) the importance that a hypothetical person acting in accordance with the duty to promote the success of the company would attach to continuing the claim; and
(c) whether the act or omission complained of is capable of being, and would be likely to be, authorised or ratified by shareholders.[41]

At the time of writing, it is unclear how rigorously the courts will interpret the new legislation. The first cases will be crucial. Notwithstanding the statutory safeguards, and the historic reluctance of the courts to become involved in second-guessing the commercial judgments of directors, the fear remains that, unless the courts throw claims out at the initial permission stage, shareholders will achieve their objectives even if they lose their case, because they will have delayed (and possibly therefore frustrated) implementation of the board's decision and damaged the company as a result.

Since directors' principal duties are owed to the company, the company may ratify the actions of a director who is in breach of his duties, or who has exceeded his authority, by way of a shareholder resolution. There are exceptions to this, the main one being that the company cannot ratify an act which the company itself has no power to do. Also, where the director concerned (or any connected person) is a shareholder, they will not be counted in any vote to ratify such a breach of duty.

Although directors' duties are owed mainly to the company, directors must also have regard to the interests of creditors and employees, and must not treat minority shareholders unfairly or oppressively. The duties that directors owe to creditors are relevant mainly in the context of an insolvency or potential insolvency of the company concerned, discussed further in section 6.12 below.

39 Under section 172 of the Companies Act 2006: see section 6.4 below.
40 Section 262 of the Companies Act 2006.
41 Section 263 of the Companies Act 2006.

6.3 Duty to act within company's powers (section 171)

This provision is a simple codification of the law that was in force before the 2006 Act[42] and states that a director of a company must:

(a) act in accordance with the company's constitution; and
(b) only exercise powers for the purposes for which they are conferred.

A good example of how this duty might be breached in a private equity context would be if the directors used their power to issue shares (a power designed to raise capital) to dilute a minority shareholder when no real need to raise the capital existed. In a takeover scenario, such power might also be abused by Target to ward off an unwanted bid by the strategic selection of shareholders to whom shares are issued.

6.4 Duty to promote the success of the company (section 172)

This new duty replaces the pre-2006 Act duty of loyalty, i.e. to act in what the director in good faith considers to be the best interests of the company.[43] Arguably, this is the most demanding provision of the entire 2006 Act, as it is this new duty that introduces the concept of 'enlightened shareholder value' into UK legislation.

There are effectively two limbs to this duty:

(a) first, a director must act in a way which he considers, in good faith, would be most likely to promote the success of the company for the benefit of its members as a whole; and
(b) secondly, in doing so, the director must have regard to (amongst other matters) the six factors listed in Figure 11.1. The words 'amongst other matters' make the list non-exhaustive; the list simply illustrates the broad areas of particular importance, reflecting a wider expectation as to what constitutes responsible business behaviour.

The decision as to what will promote success, and what constitutes success, is one for a director's good faith judgment. This ties in with the historical approach of the English courts, which has been to defer to the honest commercial judgment of the directors (who were chosen by the shareholders, at least in theory, to run the company's business) as to what is in the best interests (or, under the new regime, most likely to 'promote the success') of the company.

Given the extensive and non-exhaustive nature of the list of factors to be considered, it is quite difficult to imagine what else might be included. Possible additions include the interests of subsidiaries, and consideration of health and safety issues. The important point to bear in mind is that the overriding duty of

42 See, for example, *Howard Smith Ltd* v. *Ampol Petroleum* [1974] AC 82.
43 See, for example, *Charterbridge Corporation Ltd* v. *Lloyds Bank Ltd* [1970] Ch 62.

The duty to promote the success of the company requires that a director must act in the way he considers, in good faith, would be most likely to promote the success of the company for the benefit of its members as a whole, and in doing so have regard (amongst other matters) to:

- the likely consequences of any decision in the long term
- the interests of the company's employees
- the need to foster the company's business relationships with suppliers, customers and others
- the impact of the company's operations on the community and the environment
- the desirability of the company maintaining a reputation for high standards of business conduct
- the need to act fairly as between members of the company.

Figure 11.1 Promoting the success of the company – the six factors to consider

a director is to promote the success of the company. This avoids the numerous contradictions that would otherwise arise. For example, if an energy company is considering building a new power station, this is likely to have an adverse environmental impact, but that does not mean *per se* that the power station should not be built. Building the power station may be fundamental to the success of the company, but the environmental impact must be borne in mind. Another example of where a conflict may arise is in the case of redundancies, where the interests of the company and those of a number of its employees are likely to be at odds. Helpfully, the UK government has stressed that the over-reaching principle needs to take precedence, i.e. to promote the success of the company.

6.5 Duty to exercise independent judgment (section 173)

This is a codification of the principle that directors must exercise independent judgment, i.e. they must not fetter their discretion.[44] The provision states that the duty is not infringed by a director acting:

(a) in accordance with an agreement duly entered into by the company that restricts the future exercise of discretion by its directors; or

44 See *Kregor* v. *Hollins* (1913) 109 LT 225.

(b) in a way authorised by the company's constitution.

From a practical perspective, this means that there is no problem, for example, in a company entering into a contract for the sale of one of its subsidiaries and agreeing not to compete with the business of that subsidiary for a period of time. That amounts to a commercial agreement permitted by this provision. Where this provision may prevent a fetter on the directors' discretion by agreement is if, for example, they decided to undertake never to recommend a takeover bid. Whilst they might contractually agree to do this, it is hard to imagine that a court would uphold such a decision as it is depriving them of their independent judgment in the future. Also, whilst it must be independent in the sense of its being a director's own judgment, it is not intended to prevent a director from relying on advice (e.g. legal advice), and indeed in some cases not taking advice may amount to a breach of a director's duty in itself.

In a private equity context, this can give rise to a particular concern for an investor director who has a role to represent the interests of the private equity investors on the board of the company. In exercising his discretion, what weight can he attach to the views and interests of the private equity investors above those of other shareholders? The wording in the section, that the duty is not infringed by the director acting 'in a way authorised by the company's constitution', offers a potential solution here; wording in the articles of association of the company may protect the investor director by stressing that he may have due regard to the interests of the investors (or similar wording), and market practice is heading in this direction. A balance must be struck when incorporating such a provision, however. Whether the section is broad enough to enable wording to go into the articles which renders the investor director a mere automaton, doing solely what the investors say, is debatable (not least because not all the duties of a director offer the same exclusion based on authorisation by the company's constitution).

6.6 Duty to exercise reasonable care, skill and diligence (section 174)

This duty amounts to a codification of existing case law,[45] but also closely follows the provisions in the Insolvency Act 1986 for wrongful trading.[46] The test here is both objective and subjective. Exercising care, skill and diligence means:

> the care, skill and diligence that would be exercised by a reasonably diligent person with:
>
> (a) the general knowledge, skill and experience that may reasonably be expected of a person carrying out the functions carried out by the director in relation to the company; and
> (b) the general knowledge, skill and experience that the director has.

45 The authority most often cited was *Re City Equitable Fire Insurance Co. Ltd* [1925] 1 Ch 407.
46 Section 214 of the Insolvency Act 1986; see further section 6.12(b) below.

This effectively means that there is a minimum standard required by law of all directors, which is increased should the director have a higher standard of actual knowledge, skill and experience. A director cannot rely on the fact that he is generally incompetent to impose an incredibly low standard of skill and care. However, a director is not expected to have a highly specialised level of expertise in all areas, only those where he has particular skill and experience. For example, a director on the audit committee who happens to be a qualified accountant would have a greater duty of care than a director who is not so qualified. It should also be noted that executive directors might often have a degree of skill and care imposed by their service contracts which is greater than the statutory one.

6.7 Duty to avoid conflicts of interest (section 175)

The common law on conflicts prior to the 2006 Act required that a director did not put himself in a position where his personal interests conflicted with those of the company, unless the shareholders had consented to such conflict. In line with the general trend towards increased board scrutiny and accountability, the 2006 Act introduces a new statutory duty for directors to avoid any situation in which he has or can have an interest, direct or indirect, which conflicts (or could conflict) with the interests of any company of which he is a director.

The main difference is that, under common law, when a conflict of interest arose, directors would be expected to take steps to mitigate the situation, whilst, under the 2006 Act, the new duty obliges directors not to let the conflict situation arise in the first place. However, there are three statutory exceptions where the duty would not be breached:

(a) where the relevant matter cannot reasonably be regarded as likely to give rise to a conflict of interest;
(b) where the relevant matter involves a transaction or arrangement with the company; this distinguishes the situational conflicts that arise generally (covered by section 175) with transaction-specific conflicts (where the matter would need to be declared to the board under sections 177 or 182 of the 2006 Act);[47] and
(c) where the relevant matter has been authorised by either the shareholders or the unconflicted directors.

There is no statutory definition of a conflict of interest. However, section 175 is very widely drafted in that it catches situations that *possibly may* result in a conflict. The 2006 Act makes it clear that this includes the exploitation of property, information or opportunity, and the fact that the company itself could not take advantage of that property, information or opportunity is irrelevant. The sort of conflict situations which could be caught include cross-directorships

47 See sections 6.9 and 6.10 below.

(whether within or external to the group); being or representing a significant shareholder in the company (such as an investor director); being on the board of the company's pension trustee company; or owning a piece of land next to the company's premises, the value of which could be affected by the company's activities. A useful general rule is to regard an 'interest' as a very broad term that includes any thing (or any connection) which could potentially divert a director's mind from giving sole consideration to promoting the success of the relevant group company.

The concept of boards authorising conflict situations was introduced by the 2006 Act. Whilst only conflict situations that arise after 1 October 2008 need to be authorised, it is considered best practice also to authorise any conflict situations in existence before 1 October 2008. Directors should go through a process of identifying their conflict situations, and then make arrangements for such situations to be authorised. This new duty to avoid conflict situations is a statutory one that each director has a personal responsibility to perform. Ideally, directors should complete a questionnaire to flush out any direct or indirect conflict situations, and such conflict situations that do not fall within the exceptions should be authorised by the shareholders or the unconflicted directors.

As for the duty to exercise independent judgment,[48] it is becoming common for the articles of association in a private-equity-backed company to pre-authorise the situational conflicts inherent in a buyout. For all directors, this will include the situational conflict that arises as a consequence of a director being a director of other group companies. In the case of an investor director, a situational conflict also arises as a consequence of the individual being an employee or representative of the relevant private equity firm, and having a direct financial interest in the return achieved by the investor shareholders by way of carried interest or any relevant co-investment. Investor directors and other non-executive directors may well sit on the boards of other companies, that could include customers, suppliers or even direct competitors. The wording that is now generally being included in the articles of association of investee companies is therefore quite extensive, to ensure that any such conflicts are pre-authorised in so far as that is possible.

The advantage to including such provisions in the articles from the outset is that all directors (and, in particular, the investor director) can be certain from the beginning of an investment that these inherent conflicts are approved, and that he will not be in breach of his duties to Newco under the Act, or dependent on managers to pass resolutions at board level to approve the situation. The same mechanism in the articles can also confirm the ability of the investor director to pass confidential information to the investors, or protect the investor director from any claim that could otherwise arise for not passing to Newco any confidential information of which he becomes aware through his involvement in the private equity investors or one of its other investee companies. It

48 See section 6.5 above.

would not be practicable to manage a private equity portfolio if the duties that an investor director owed to one company required him to disclose to that company confidential information relating to other companies in the portfolio.

6.8 Duty not to accept benefits from third parties (section 176)

A director must not accept a benefit from a third party conferred by reason of (a) his being a director, or (b) his doing (or not doing) anything as director. There is an exception that states the duty is not infringed if the acceptance of the benefit cannot reasonably be regarded as likely to give rise to a conflict of interest. Directors will therefore need to consider carefully whether they are able to accept corporate hospitality, and each benefit would need to be considered in context.

There is no definition of benefit in the 2006 Act, and there is no *de minimis* threshold. As a result, a common sense approach, with a hint of caution, needs to be taken. Companies may wish to amend their internal codes of conduct or policies to enshrine this approach.

In private equity situations, it is not uncommon for investors to agree that particular directors (for example, its appointed chairman, or a trouble-shooter appointed on an underperformance) should be remunerated directly by the investors – typically to motivate an exit by agreeing to pay the director concerned a share of the investors' exit proceeds. Historically, such arrangements might even be entered into behind the scenes, without the knowledge of the other directors or shareholders. Such an agreement could fall foul of this section if there is any argument that the conduct which is necessary to trigger the payment might in any way conflict with the interests of the company. To avoid any doubt, such exit incentives may be better paid by the company itself rather than the investors, and with the full knowledge and authorisation of the other directors or shareholders.

6.9 Duty to declare interests in proposed transactions or arrangements (section 177)

If a director has an interest, whether direct or indirect, in a proposed transaction or arrangement with the company, then he must declare the nature and extent of that interest before the transaction or arrangement is entered into. This provision deals with so-called 'transactional' conflicts, i.e. a conflict that arises as a consequence of a particular transaction that is to be entered into, in contrast to the 'situational' conflicts covered by section 175.

There are a number of ways a director may declare the interest. It may be made at the first board meeting after which his interest arose or he became aware of it, or it may be made by way of written notice which must be read out at the next board meeting. Finally, a director can give a general notice to the board that he is deemed to be interested in all transactions with a particular organisation. Many articles of association stipulate that a director cannot vote at, or be counted in the quorum of, a board meeting at which the proposed contract is to be considered; this must be checked where any such transaction or arrangement is to be approved.

Such transactional conflicts arise all the time on private equity transactions. All such interests must be considered and declared by management and investor directors alike. As shareholders in the company (or investor directors with an interest in the underlying performance of the investor shareholders), directors will inevitably have a personal interest in matters to be considered by the board relating to the initial transaction, further refinancings or restructurings, and the ultimate exit. It is important to ensure that all of such interests are declared, and carefully minuted.

6.10 Declaration of interests in existing transactions (section 182)

Whilst not strictly one of the codified directors' duties, there is also a requirement for directors to declare an interest (direct or indirect) in an existing transaction or arrangement entered into by the company.

This declaration must be made as soon as reasonably practicable, and may be made by way of written notice or general notice. The notice must state the nature and extent of the director's interest in the body corporate or firm, or the nature of the connection with the person. The general notice must be given either at a meeting of the directors, or the director has to take reasonable steps to ensure it is brought up and read at the next directors' meeting after it is given. If a director has declared an interest in accordance with section 177 (i.e. at the time the transaction or arrangement was proposed and before it was entered into by the company), then there is no need for the director to repeat the declaration under section 182 when the proposed transaction or arrangement becomes an actual one.

6.11 Transactions between companies and directors

In addition to the new statutory duties of directors, the 2006 Act provides that certain contracts between a company and its directors are prohibited unless shareholder approval has first been obtained. For these purposes, shareholder approval means an ordinary resolution, unless the articles of association prescribe a higher threshold. Most of these rules also apply if the director in question is a director at the holding company level (i.e. a director of a holding company must seek approval from the shareholders of that holding company where such matters are transacted by the relevant subsidiary of that holding company).

(a) Directors' long-term service contracts (sections 188 and 189)

Directors' service contracts in excess of two years' duration (previously five years), and incapable of termination by the company before the end of such term or capable of termination during that term only in specified circumstances require shareholder approval.

(b) Substantial property transactions (sections 190–196)

Substantial property transactions with directors (or shadow directors) or connected persons, where the assets transferred exceed £100,000 or, if lower, 10 per cent of the company's net assets require shareholder approval. Assets worth less than £5,000 (previously £2,000) are not included.

(c) Compensation for loss of office (section 215–222)

Shareholder approval is necessary for a range of payments connected with a director losing the office of director or retiring from that position. Additional payments requiring approval include:

(a) payments for the loss of any other office or employment connected with managing the company or any subsidiary undertaking;
(b) payments on retirement from any other office or employment connected with managing the company or any subsidiary undertaking;
(c) payments to any persons connected with the director who loses office/retires; and
(d) payments by a company to a director of its holding company who loses office/retires.

However, there are a number of exceptions to the need for shareholder approval, for example in relation to payments to discharge an existing legal obligation[49] (which captures most circumstances where a *bona fide* payment is made under a compromise package for the termination of a manager's employment), and certain small payments.[50]

(d) Loans to directors (sections 197–214)

The general prohibition on loans to directors that subsisted under the Companies Act 1985 has been abolished by the 2006 Act. A company can make a loan to a director of a company, or of its holding company, and provide guarantees or security to a person who has made a loan to such a director, but only once shareholder approval has been obtained.

Quasi-loans (e.g. for season tickets) and credit transactions (e.g. arranging credit card facilities for a director's use) are still permissible, but in the case of public companies (and private companies associated with public companies) these also require shareholder approval.[51]

There are a number of exceptions to the requirement for shareholder approval, notably a small loan exception which applies to loans of £10,000 or less (up from £5,000).[52]

49 Section 220 of the Companies Act 2006.
50 Section 221 of the Companies Act 2006.
51 Section 198 of the Companies Act 2006.
52 Section 207 of the Companies Act 2006.

6.12 Corporate directors and insolvency

The insolvency of companies and the responsibilities of directors of insolvent companies are governed by the Insolvency Act 1986 and the Company Directors Disqualification Act 1986. These statutes place some of the strictest standards on directors in carrying out their duties.

A company is insolvent where:

(a) it is unable to pay its debts as they fall due; or
(b) the value of its assets is less than the amount of its liabilities, taking into account its contingent and prospective liabilities.

The consequences of a company insolvency can be extremely serious for a director, not least because he can leave himself open to personal liability and disqualification. In order to minimise his potential liability, a director should inform the board as soon as he suspects that the company is heading for insolvency. He must also ensure that accurate and up to date financial information is available to the board.

If there are cash flow problems, steps should be taken to alleviate the difficulties, such as realising assets and chasing debtors, raising additional equity capital or arranging for a sale to a larger organisation able to assist the company with its difficulties. If the cash situation is so critical that future trading becomes impossible, the directors must either reach an informal arrangement with the company's creditors or follow the formal insolvency procedures. Professional advice is essential in such circumstances.

(a) Fraudulent trading

If any business of a company has been carried on with intent to defraud creditors of the company, or creditors of any other person, or for any fraudulent purpose then:

(a) every person (including a director) who was knowingly a party to the carrying on of the business in that manner is liable to imprisonment (up to ten years) or a fine (unlimited) or both (and this applies whether or not the company has been, or is in the course of being, wound up); and
(b) if it appears in the course of winding up a company that this has been the case, the court may, on the application of the liquidator, declare that any persons (including directors) who were knowingly parties to the carrying on of the business in that manner are to be personally liable to make such contributions to the company's assets as the court thinks proper.[53]

The classic example of fraudulent trading is where a company continues to carry on business and to incur debts at a time when there is, to the knowledge of the directors, no reasonable prospect of the creditors ever receiving payment of those debts.

53 Section 213 of the Insolvency Act 1986.

The fraudulent trading rules have not been particularly successful because persons have escaped liability due to the absence of actual knowledge, fraudulent intent or bad faith, or because no new liabilities have actually been incurred. The remedy of wrongful trading, however, imposes liability in cases where directors have failed to exercise sufficient diligence in monitoring the company's affairs, and to take corrective action in the face of insolvency.

(b) Wrongful trading

Wrongful trading is a civil remedy and only applies where a company has gone into insolvent liquidation.

The courts are empowered, on the application of the liquidator, to order a past or present director (or shadow director) to contribute to the assets of the company where, prior to the commencement of the liquidation of the company (whether voluntary or compulsory), the director knew or ought to have concluded that there was no reasonable prospect of the company avoiding an insolvent liquidation.[54]

The function of the courts in dealing with wrongful trading is to compensate the creditors rather than to penalise the directors. Consequently, the amount that a director will be ordered to contribute will be the amount by which the company's assets have been depleted as a result of that director's conduct. A lack of fraudulent intent on the part of the director will not necessarily restrict his contribution to a token amount. The director will also be ordered to pay interest on the amount of his contribution from the date of commencement of the liquidation, and will have to pay the legal costs of the person taking the action.

The director will be able to avoid liability if he can show that, once he knew or ought to have concluded that there was no reasonable prospect of the company avoiding an insolvent liquidation, he took every step that ought to have been taken to minimise the loss to the company's creditors.[55]

The standard to be applied in determining what steps a director ought to have taken is that of a reasonably diligent person having:

(a) the general knowledge, skill and experience to be expected of a person carrying out the director's functions; and
(b) the knowledge, skill and experience that the director actually possesses.[56]

In other words, the standard includes both objective and subjective elements, similar to those imposed on directors generally under the new duty to exercise reasonable care, skill and diligence.[57] The court will have regard to the functions carried out by the director in question, as well as to the particular company and its business.

54 Section 214(2) of the Insolvency Act 1986.
55 Section 214(3) of the Insolvency Act 1986.
56 Section 214(4) of the Insolvency Act 1986.
57 Section 174 of the Companies Act 2006; see also section 6.6 above.

What will constitute 'every step' will depend on the particular circumstances, but could include the sale of assets to meet liabilities, the cessation of trading, the prompt obtaining of professional advice, or the appointment of an administrator. It is unlikely that simply resigning will absolve the director from responsibility, although it may do so if he resigns because his fellow directors will not take the appropriate action.

If the court makes an order for contribution against a director, it is also empowered to make a disqualification order against that director.

Wrongful trading issues must be considered in any situation where an underperformance arises that is of such significance that it may call the future solvency of the investment into question. A wrongful trading action may be brought against shadow directors as well as actual directors. As a result, the issue is relevant not only to managers and investor directors, but also potentially to observers or other executives at the private equity firm in the event that the board is accustomed to acting at the direction of those individuals. Professional advice is essential in such circumstances – not only when the issue is first brought to the attention of the individuals concerned, but also as any negotiations for a proposed restructuring of the investee company are continuing.

6.13 Practical guidance on directors' duties

It should be apparent that the law governing the duties of directors is extensive and far-reaching. It includes substantial historic case law, the new codified duties, insolvency legislation and specific obligations. The question a practitioner is often asked, therefore, is whether any practical, easily digestible, guidance can be offered to enable directors to understand the general nature of their duties, the pitfalls to look out for, and the steps that can be taken to avoid potential claims.

At the time that the new general duties were introduced, the Department of Trade and Industry published a high-level summary of what directors should and should not do,[58] which included the following general principles:

- Act in the company's best interests, taking everything you think relevant into account.
- Obey the company's constitution and decisions taken under it.
- Be honest, and remember that the company's property belongs to it and not to you or its shareholders.
- Be diligent, careful and well informed about the company's affairs. If you have any special skills or experience, use them.
- Make sure the company keeps records of your decisions.
- Remember that you remain responsible for the work you give to others.

58 Companies Act 2006; DTI, *Duties of Company Directors: Ministerial Statements* (June 2007).

- Avoid situations where your interests conflict with those of the company. When in doubt disclose potential conflicts quickly.
- Seek external advice where necessary, particularly if the company is in financial difficulty.

In addition to this guidance, there are also some practical steps that can be taken to mitigate against potential claims such as:

- Ensure that all new and existing board members are fully briefed on their new statutory duties.
- When preparing board papers, ensure that any declarations of interest are correctly minuted, and that all relevant factors are properly considered.
- Review director and officer liability insurance policies, to ensure that adequate protection is in place for any actions that may arise for breach of the new codified duties.

7 Conclusion

In this chapter, we have considered some of the issues that can arise during the lifetime of an investment, and how the documentation and procedures put in place at the time of the original deal seek to anticipate and regulate these issues. The importance of good planning (and learning from past mistakes) when drafting the initial deal documents cannot be understated. When the time comes to rely on these provisions, the interests of the various participants can diverge markedly, particularly in an underperformance situation. The documentation can strengthen the hand of a party, even though the underlying economics will normally drive the overall outcome.

We have also highlighted the vulnerability of the management equity in an underperformance situation. It is the instrument that gets the best overall return per pound invested when all goes well but, by the same token, it is the first to lose value and to become worthless. This can create challenges for the investors and the bank funders, however, given the need to motivate the remaining and/or replacement managers to turn around the company's fortunes.

There are numerous inherent conflicts of interest in private equity transactions, particularly when considering the interests of the various directors, and the investor director(s) in particular. Investors and management teams alike must take all appropriate steps to regulate their behaviour against the background of the codification of directors' duties, as well as being mindful of their duties to creditors should underperformance suggest a risk of insolvency.

Enhancing value during the life of the investment is key to maximising the interests of all parties to a private-equity-backed deal. For this reason, many private equity investors will be sensitive to the need to maintain a good working relationship with their management teams, and do not always press home the full legal or economic strength of their position either at the time the deal is negotiated or afterwards. When that trust and confidence has evaporated, the need to move quickly and decisively to protect the investment becomes paramount. If a private equity investor ever has to use (or threaten the use of) the big stick that the key protections in the investment documents provide, the chances are that the investment is already significantly weakened if not fatally undermined. There may be no choice – but the outcome is rarely satisfactory, and can also have reputational consequences for both the private equity firm and the investee business.

12

Secondary buyouts

1 Introduction

In a secondary buyout (often referred to simply as a 'secondary'), a company which has already been subject to an existing management buyout is sold by its existing private equity backers and management to a new company backed by a separate private equity investor and some or all of the same managers. The typical feature, therefore, is that there is a change of private equity investor (and, sometimes, some of the managers), with many or all of the existing shareholding managers who obtained equity in the first buyout carrying over some of their investment into the new buyer vehicle. Whilst the investors and any managers who are not to continue with the business will sell their shares for cash, the other managers (often referred to as the 'rolling managers') will choose, or may perhaps be required, to sell their existing shares in exchange, in part at least, for shares in the new Newco. Of course, there can be many variants on this typical model, but the key feature is a change of private equity investor and a broad continuity of managers.

There is no reason why this second buyout company cannot itself later be sold to another company backed by a third set of investors with some or all of the same managers (a 'tertiary') and so forth. In this chapter, however, we will refer to all such transactions as a secondary, as the differences between a secondary and a tertiary is more one of history in terms of the investment than of form and substance in terms of the principal transactional issues. There are also some transactions which, on first impression, look similar to a secondary – for example where the incoming new investor is a separate fund within the same private equity stable (which can create some acute conflicts and other sensitivities), or a transaction where an existing private-equity-backed business is sold to a new company backed by different private equity investors and a separate management team (i.e. not based principally on rolling managers) – but neither of these is a true secondary for the purpose of this chapter.

2 Features of a secondary buyout

2.1 Reasons for a secondary buyout

A secondary is an exit opportunity for the selling private equity investor and an investment opportunity for the new private equity investor. On first impression, a secondary therefore seems a strange transaction. Why is one private equity investor a willing seller at a particular exit value when another private equity investor is a willing buyer at that same price? During the 1990s, many investors were cynical about secondaries on exactly that basis (i.e. that there must always be a winner and a loser). However, it is now widely acknowledged that there can be all manner of reasons to justify a secondary from both sides, for example:

- The existing investor is reaching the end of its fund life and wishes to realise assets in its portfolio.
- The investment requires a further injection of capital to take it to the next stage and existing funders are either unwilling or unable to back this.
- There needs to be succession within the management of the business, and the existing investor has less confidence in the new team.
- There is a change of strategy or of investment profile on the part of the existing investor.
- There has been an auction to facilitate a sale, and a secondary has emerged at a good price and with good prospects of execution.
- The new investor believes that it can obtain more value out of the investment, for example through their increased sector expertise or other 'value adds'.
- The new investor is attracted to working with a proven management team and wishes to invest in a proven business, leading to a very attractive price being offered.

From the point of view of the rolling managers, a secondary can also present some useful opportunities, including:

- An opportunity to cash in some of the value added to the business (and invest those monies in a different way), but with the chance to continue to have an active stake in the future growth opportunities of a business they know and understand.
- A chance to work with a new investor, and to negotiate investment terms, as a more sophisticated and proven management team (which can lead to a considerably improved offer for management, especially if there is bidding tension between two or more new backers).
- Access to a deeper investment cash resource (particularly relevant if the existing investor lacks the funds or has rejected requests for further funding).
- The opportunity to raise money and seek growth on the back of a revised Business Plan, which may present a very different capital requirement and risk and reward profile to that which underlay the original transaction.

- The chance to address any succession issues within management. Although not always the case, a secondary often involves some of the more senior members of the management team either exiting completely or reducing their role and commitment to, and stake in, the business. This has the consequence of enabling junior colleagues (or sometimes newly appointed buyin candidates) to take over the principal managerial responsibilities for the business.
- In certain market conditions, a secondary may present an exit opportunity or, at least, a partial exit opportunity where a full trade sale would either not be possible, or would not reflect the future growth value which management believes can be achieved in the business.
- In some situations, a secondary may facilitate an exit where the investment has been underperforming, and the existing private equity investor is no longer willing or able to back the existing venture. This is an opportunity only likely to be attractive to those investors specialising in rescue and turnaround situations.[1]

2.2 Seller conflicts of interest

All the conflicts of interest that arise in any buyout, or on any sale of a private-equity-backed business, arise on a secondary. However, the particular features of a secondary can often seem to magnify some of these conflicts and, in particular, can cause both sets of conflict to arise at the same time.

This issue is made more acute where the rolling managers will have a higher proportion of the shares in the equity structure of the second Newco than in the present company (although, in reality, higher gearing in the second Newco may well mean that this higher equity stake sits behind a more significant amount of debt). On the one hand, the rolling managers are, in part, sellers and have an economic interest in maximising the sale price (at least to the extent to which they are actually releasing value for themselves as part of the disposal transaction). However, as a prospective shareholder in the buyer, they have an interest in keeping the sale price as low as can be negotiated, and ensuring that any identified risks are left behind or are adequately covered by all of the sellers (or by warranty insurance paid for by all of the sellers). It is this dual role of being both seller and buyer which distinguishes their position from the original buyout (where they were usually only buyers, albeit with responsibilities as employees, and often directors, of the seller or Target), and from a trade sale (where their interests will principally be as sellers – particularly if they are not required to have any executive role in the business after the sale and have no economic interest in it).

In practice, the circumstances surrounding the approach that leads to the secondary, and the overall sale process, may either alleviate or heighten this potential conflict. Where the selling private equity investor has proposed a secondary as a feasible exit route, or has persuaded the managers to accept a

1 On different types of investor, see chapter 1, section 2.3.

significant rollover so as to maximise the cash proceeds of the selling investor, then the selling investor will regard the prospect of a secondary buyout more positively, and will be less concerned that any offer may not be at arm's length. In other situations, for example where the approach has come from management (or the new investor is associated with management), and the existing private equity investor had been less focused on a possible sale at the time, there may be more of a concern that the managers are aware of some opportunity likely to lead to increased value in the business. Similarly, if the principal members of the existing management team are also exiting at the time of the sale, with the secondary leading to a succession of management either to a second tier or to buyin candidates (or a combination), the selling private equity investor may be more comfortable that at least some of the managers have a more perfect alignment with its own economic interests. At the end of the day, of course, the attractiveness of the price paid is the key factor.

Where these conflicts exist, it is usually familiar territory for the selling investor and the managers. Similar conflicts may well have arisen at the time of the original buyout, where there was a risk that the interests of the managers were not fully aligned with the interests of the then sellers. These concerns can be alleviated somewhat if there is a formal sale process (whether or not an auction). Corporate finance advisers retained in the sale process are often keen to ensure that the managers are actively co-operating in the best interests of the sellers as a whole, and not allowing any particular interest they may have (or hope to have) in the secondary to interfere with the sale process. In particular, they will usually require that any potential buyers (whether trade buyers or private equity) only channel approaches to the sellers through the corporate finance adviser or some other approved route. This is designed to reduce, or at least postpone, the chance that some or all of the management team may be tempted to think of themselves more as a buyer than a seller, and accordingly become aligned more with the second Newco and its funders than with the sellers. Clearly, this must be matched with the desire on the part of the other sellers and their corporate finance advisers to obtain a satisfactory sale. If the secondary offers the best prospect, then it is both important and sensible (from the selling investor's and any exiting manager's perspective) to allow the necessary degree of collaboration between the rolling managers and the funders to the secondary Newco.

2.3 The selling private equity investors

In essence, any selling private equity investors would prefer to treat a secondary in exactly the same way as any other share sale exit, as discussed in chapter 13. In particular, they would normally seek to take a typical institutional position on warranties and indemnities, with each investor agreeing only to warrant title to the shares which it is selling, and its capacity to sell them together with a release of any claims which it may have against the Target group and its employees (including, of course, the managers). They would not expect to take any further commercial risk on the history of the investment or its underlying business.[2]

To date, new investors engaging in secondaries have recognised this approach and have accommodated it, not least because they are familiar with the same approach themselves on exit. Any gap in the warranty cover may, in suitable cases, be plugged by warranty insurance to the extent to which insurance is available and covers the risk in question. Given that such a warranty gap exists, a good-quality disclosure exercise by the management team and accompanying due diligence exercise will be critical for the secondary Newco and its funders.

Assuming the customary investor seller position is adopted such that no commercial warranties are given by the investors, any significant issues that arise during due diligence will either be reflected in a price adjustment or, in the most extreme situation, by a complete refusal from the secondary Newco to buy. Alternatively, to the extent that managers are realising cash on sale, the issue may be covered by such managers (whether rolling or exiting managers) agreeing to part of their cash consideration being held in a retention account to stand behind warranties, indemnities or other provisions addressing those identified due diligence risks. This inevitably leads to a significant conflict of interest between the selling private equity investor and the managers (in particular, rolling managers), particularly if the rolling managers are being required by the secondary Newco and its funders to roll over a larger proportion of their proceeds than they would wish.

It follows that, in some situations, private equity investors may have to be more flexible to facilitate the deal, for example by agreeing to contribute to such a retention, or by paying its *pro rata* share of any costs to insure against the specific risks. After all, if the alternative is no exit at all, or a reduced price reflecting the worst case scenario for the issue concerned, the exiting investor may have no alternative to accepting a contingent element to its price. In those cases, however, the investor will expect any such mechanism to be drafted as precisely as possible – in particular to ensure that its share of the proceeds is only available to satisfy a proven claim on the specific issue concerned, and there is an appropriate cap to the amount of its contribution and a time limit during which such a claim can be made. Such protections are essential to enable the private equity fund to provide the clarity and certainty required to its own ultimate investors.

2.4 Exiting managers

As has already been mentioned, it is not uncommon in a secondary for one or more of the existing senior members of the management team to leave the

2 For more on the typical investor position on warranties, see chapter 13, section 3.3.

business (or at least to step down to a non-executive role) and to realise the whole of his value on exit. This often makes sense, and indeed may well be one of the factors that drove the secondary in the first place. For example, a manager may feel that, for reasons of age or health or ambition, he has added all he is likely to be able to contribute to the growth of the business, and now would be a good time to cash in that value and perhaps retire to pursue other business or personal interests. Similarly, his keenness to see the business adopt a more expansionary growth strategy (offering perhaps both increased risk and increased return for the investment) may be less than that of his colleagues, particularly if this new strategy will take time to implement. Sometimes, a whole tier of management can exit in this way, and the secondary is one way of achieving a succession in the management of the business to the next tier.

On other occasions, a particular manager is out of step with other members of the management team for other reasons. Sometimes, particularly if the exiting manager is still a key member of the management team at the time of the secondary, he may be expected to stay on for a while in a non-executive or consultant capacity. This may be particularly useful in dealing with customers, suppliers, regulators (where relevant) and other key relationships, and assisting the transition of management to the new team. The precise terms on which any such continued role in the business will take place (and in particular whether the exiting manager retains any equity incentive or is required, despite his departure, to roll over some of his value into the new structure – for example, by way of loan notes) will be a matter of bespoke negotiation at the time. In other cases, all concerned are happy for the exiting manager to depart as soon as possible.

It should be borne in mind, however, that an exiting manager is likely to be in a different position to the selling private equity investor in one particular way, in that he is likely to have to give commercial warranties as part of the sale process, and to enter into restrictive covenants. To this extent, he is like any manager in a typical trade sale of a private-equity-backed business. However, because he has no interest in the new structure, he is likely to wish to minimise his exposure in this context as much as possible, and therefore will most likely have a very different perspective to his rolling colleagues.

3 Implications of a secondary on the legal documentation

3.1 Structure and classes of instrument(s) held

As explained in chapter 3,[3] rolling managers will have two distinct interests in the new business: a proportion of the institutional strip alongside the new investors; and a share in the sweet equity (alongside any new managers taking equity for the first time). The proportion of the sweet equity to be held by each individual manager will be a matter for negotiation, and does not necessarily reflect

3 See chapter 3, section 3.5.

the proportions in which any rolling managers hold their respective shares in the institutional strip. The allocation of the sweet equity (as between all managers, whether rolling or new shareholders) is instead determined applying the same principles which would apply to the allocation of equity value in a regular management buyout – in other words, based on their anticipated contributions towards achieving the strategy set out in the new Business Plan, and largely disregarding the fact that some of those managers may have a separate rolled interest in the secondary Newco based on value created to date.

Although there is no reason why the rolled investment could not be into the same class of shares and loan notes as will be taken by the private equity investor in the secondary Newco (and this is sometimes seen), the rolled investment will often be represented by a separate class of shares and related loan notes having the same overall economic rights as the private equity shares and loan notes, but without the same class rights and other vetoes and protections. In this way, the private equity investors do not run the risk that rolling managers will have a say as part of the investor classes (so that, for example, their shares are not taken into account when determining whether a requirement for an 'investor majority consent' has been obtained under the articles of association). In terms of ranking for payment of interest, dividends or capital, the managers' rolled investments will usually rank *pari passu* with the private equity investor strip (even though it may be in a different class of share and loan note), although sometimes the commercial circumstances surrounding the deal may be such that the rolled management investments are subordinated behind the investments held by the investors.

As highlighted in chapter 3, it is common for a series of loan note and/or share exchange agreements to be entered into by the rolling managers, to ensure that they ultimately hold their own shares and loan notes in the correct corporate entities in the secondary Newco group. Tax considerations will drive both the structure and the timing of the rolled investment, as is discussed in more detail in section 3.5 below.

3.2 Implications of departure of manager

The sweet equity and the rolled investment held by the rolling managers are usually treated differently on the departure of a manager. It should be expected that the sweet equity will be subject to all the usual clawback arrangements that would apply to manager shares in a typical buyout, irrespective of whether the holder of the shares is a new manager or a rolling manager. However, the rolled equity strip is generally not subject to compulsory transfer provisions (although it is usual for investors to insist that the voting rights attached to any rolled equity are removed if the relevant rolling manager ceases to be employed, as for any leaver who retains equity for whatever reason[4]). Even

4 On voting, see further chapter 5, section 4.3.

though the manager's rolled investment may be into different classes of securities to those held by the investors, such rolled value is nevertheless seen as a permanent part of the structure of the secondary Newco.

The fact that a manager's rolled value remains secured within the business following his or her departure is not always seen as an advantage by a rolling manager. This is especially the case if some of his non-rolling colleagues were able to take their value in the business in full at the time of the secondary (in the form of cash sale proceeds), whereas he has been expected to lock a substantial proportion of his value into the second Newco until such time as the next exit is achieved. In effect, should a rolling manager leave after the time of the secondary, material value which he has rolled into the secondary Newco will be fixed in that venture even though he is no longer part of the team, and has no particular ability to influence the outcome of the investment. For this reason, rolling managers sometimes wish to negotiate that their rolled loan notes should be able to be realised if they cease to be employed (either as a general principle, or at least if they leave in circumstances justifying a 'Good Leaver' treatment).[5]

As a general rule, any proposals obliging the second Newco to repay the rolled investment if a rolling manager's employment ends will be strongly resisted by the private equity investors. The value rolled over may well be significant, and therefore it will not always be practicable for the business to repay that value. As a result, if the loan notes were repayable on cessation of employment, this could have the commercial effect of providing disproportionate security of employment to the rolling manager (i.e. he would never be dismissed on the basis that the company could not afford to repay the investment as a consequence of his departure). In practice, the bank funders to the secondary Newco are unlikely to accept substantial value being repaid to a manager before exit in this way either. Whilst finding a relatively small sum to buy out sweet equity may be manageable for both the bank and the investor (particularly if that equity is to be acquired at cost), seeing subordinated debt repaid ahead of the bank and the investor is a very different proposition. An investor will most usually argue that this is part of the bargain when taking a share of the institutional strip.

Whether there is any scope for loan notes being repaid on departure is a matter of bargaining power and negotiation between the parties. The best that management might expect is some form of non-binding side letter, stating that if the employment ends (either generally, or perhaps limited to a 'Good Leaver' situation) there is an understanding that the loan notes will be repaid if possible, but without giving rise to a formal contractual debt capable of demand. Any such repayment would also be stated to be subject to bank consent, and perhaps to a requirement that the directors (or the private equity investor) are of the view that it would not adversely prejudice the business or prospects of the group going forward.

5 For more on Good/Bad Leaver treatment, see chapter 5, section 4.11.

3.3 Negotiation of terms: use of equity termsheet or questionnaire

One of the perceived advantages for management of a secondary is their ability to negotiate an improved deal with the new private equity investor, in relation both to their economic interest in the structure, and also the restrictions or other provisions in the equity documentation and service agreements. The rolling managers will already have some experience of working with private equity, and there may well be particular issues which have proven to be a problem in their relationship with the existing investor. The managers may also feel that a proven business which has already delivered against a previous Business Plan (assuming that is the case) should be subject to less stringent restrictions or underperformance provisions second time around. Further, as the rolling managers will be rolling real value into the new structure, this may well change not only the bargaining power between the parties, but also some of the alignment and thinking which underlies the more typical stance taken in a buyout, where the only stake which the managers will hold in Newco is sweet equity.

Often, the new private equity investor will offer to adhere to the same position as was agreed on the original transaction on key issues such as 'Good Leaver' and 'Bad Leaver', restrictive covenants and so on. This is usually put forward as an advantage, on the basis that it will enable the documents to be agreed more quickly, particularly if the dialogue between the new private equity investor and the managers takes place only after exclusivity has been granted, and at a time when there is considerable pressure from the sellers to close the transaction. Whilst there are undoubtedly advantages in following the original deal, management and their advisers should consider whether any specific provisions ought to change in the new environment or, perhaps, to reflect changes in market practice since the first buyout.

In many ways, an equity questionnaire or termsheet is even more important in a secondary than in a normal buyout. A secondary may well arise in a competitive situation – either because both trade and private equity buyers are looking at a business, or as a result of two or more private equity buyers competing for the same opportunity. In this situation, provided that the sale process allows it, the rolling managers will often look to elicit at an early stage the position of the potential investors on some of the key issues that typically arise when negotiating the investment agreement, articles of association and service agreements. Clearly, there can be a strategic advantage for the rolling managers in creating some competitive tension between private equity bidders in this scenario. As a consequence, when compared with a primary buyout, any equity termsheet or questionnaire is more likely to be driven by management's advisers rather than by advisers to the private equity investor on a secondary. The termsheet may effectively serve as a 'wish list' for management, or may alternatively take the form of a questionnaire requesting investors to confirm their position on key points, thus enabling the rolling managers to compare rival bids (and perhaps to choose those aspects which appeal from the different proposals for negotiation with the final selected bidder). If a termsheet can be finalised before exclusivity is granted to any particular bidder then it can be a very effective negotiation tool in a competitive process.

However, this approach does not always align with the best interests of the other sellers. Where there are sensitivities around the conflict of interests that might arise for the rolling managers, or indeed a concern as to whether a sale process will be successful at all, the other sellers may seek to limit or prevent this more detailed dialogue between the new investors and management until exclusivity has been granted to a preferred bidder. The process will vary according to the competitiveness of the sale process, the relationship between the rolling managers and the other sellers, and their respective bargaining power.

3.4 Warranty cover

One key area where there will often be a departure from the previous deal is in respect of warranty limitations. As for any buyout, it is necessary on a secondary to distinguish the warranties given in the acquisition agreement from the warranties given in the investment agreement. The warranties in the acquisition agreement are given to the buying Newco by the sellers, and in general terms cover matters relating to the historic affairs and liabilities of the Target group.[6] The warranties in the investment agreement are given by the managers to the investors, and are predominantly designed to enable the investors to elicit details of the manager's personal history, and any information the managers may have which qualifies the due diligence reports or the Business Plan.[7] On a secondary, of course, each of the rolling managers will be a warrantor under both documents.

As discussed in chapter 5,[8] the monetary limit on the liability of a manager under the investment agreement warranties is typically based on a multiple of that manager's annual salary (two times salary being a regular compromise position). In the context of a secondary, for any new manager who is only taking sweet equity and is not rolling any investment the same stance may be expected. However, where there are rolling managers, this particular monetary limit may not be considered to be appropriate by the investors for those individuals. Private equity investors are keen to ensure there is some potential pain in the investment warranties, so that the managers take the due diligence and disclosure exercises seriously. Where they have cash from the sale, a limit based simply on a multiple of salary may not be sufficiently large to create that pressure.

Where the rolling managers have a strong negotiating position, any suggestion that their liability for investment agreement warranties should be higher than that of the new managers investing for sweet equity may well be resisted. It might be argued that their exposure under the acquisition agreement

6 See chapter 4, section 2.7.
7 See chapter 5, section 3.4.
8 See chapter 5, section 3.6.

warranties and the investment agreement warranties should properly be distinguished, such that it is unreasonable for the rolling managers to be expected to bear a higher exposure on those warranties which are more forward looking in nature, and are predominantly designed to elicit disclosure.

If this position is not accepted by the investors, then a compromise might be to see the monetary limit under both sets of warranties limited to the cash proceeds which each manager has received for his shares (but not the full consideration, i.e. ignoring the value of the rolled investment). Clearly, this is potentially a much higher exposure for the managers than the usual salary-based cap in the investment agreement, but it at least ensures that the warranty claims under both agreements cannot exceed the cash that the managers have actually received. A position might be agreed between these two extremes depending on the circumstances – for example, limiting the rolling managers' exposure under both documents to a proportion of the cash consideration, rather than the full amount. Whatever the compromise reached, it is important that any possible liability under both documents is considered in tandem. Investors also need to bear in mind that, as funders to the buying Newco, the rolling managers will suffer financial detriment if the value of their rolled investment diminishes as a consequence of a failing within the business – and that, as for any sale, it is a far more attractive proposition for the investor to pursue exiting sellers for a warranty claim, rather than their own management team.

One other legal provision which may require a different treatment in a secondary is the back-to-back warranty, that is to say the warranty usually sought by private equity investors in the investment agreement that the management team is not aware of any claims under the acquisition agreement.[9] Whilst this is not uncommon in a typical buyout, there may be less obvious justification for it in any secondary buyout, in particular if all the managers under the investment agreement are also sellers in the acquisition agreement.

3.5 Tax considerations for the rolling managers

The rolling managers will wish to ensure that the exchange of their shares in Target for an issue of loan notes and/or shares in the new Newco is treated as a rollover for tax purposes (a 'tax rollover'),[10] as the result is that no capital gains tax is triggered in respect of the Newco loan notes and/or shares received. Instead, tax only arises on disposal of such loan notes and/or shares.

To achieve a tax rollover, a number of mechanical conditions must be satisfied. In the context of a secondary, the main point to note is that to secure a tax rollover it is the buyer (i.e. Bidco) which must issue the loan notes and/or shares to the rolling managers. Where there is more than one Newco in the acquiring structure, it would be usual for Bidco to issue loan notes to the

9 For further discussion, see chapter 5, section 3.5.
10 Meaning it falls within the provisions of section 135 of the Taxation of Chargeable Gains Act 2002.

rolling managers with those loan notes then being exchanged for loan notes and/or shares up through the chain until such point as the rolling managers hold shares and/or loan notes in the right vehicle in the chain. Each such exchange is also structured to be a tax rollover. These so-called 'flip up' arrangements are illustrated in chapter 3.[11]

In order to achieve a tax rollover, one of the conditions which must be satisfied is that the issue of loan notes and/or shares is effected for *bona fide* commercial reasons, and does not form part of a scheme or arrangement of which the main purpose or one of the main purposes is avoidance of liability to tax (this is known as the 'motive test').[12] Where a rolling manager holds no more than 5 per cent of any class of shares in the Target (taking into account any shares held by connected persons such as relatives), there is no need to satisfy the motive test in order to obtain a tax rollover.[13] In other cases, it is possible to apply in advance for confirmation from HMRC that it accepts that the motive test is satisfied.[14] It is not a pre-condition in order to obtain a tax rollover that an advance clearance is obtained, but it would be usual for clcarance to be sought, and the timetable for any secondary buyout will therefore generally accommodate the time required to seek such confirmation.

In certain circumstances, HMRC can tax some or all of the proceeds of a disposal of shares in the same way as a dividend rather than as capital proceeds.[15] In order to do so, HMRC must give notice to counter the tax advantage which it identifies as having arisen on the disposal. It may do so if any one of five sets of circumstances is satisfied. One of them would be satisfied if a person receives consideration which represents the value of assets which are or would be available for distribution by way of dividend in such a way as to avoid a charge to income tax. Arguably, this could be the case where a Target has distributable reserves available to it (taking account of any reserves of its subsidiaries). This is disadvantageous because the effective rate at which tax is paid on dividends is currently 25 per cent compared to the capital gains tax rate which is currently 18 per cent.

The treatment referred to above does not apply in relation to a rolling manager if the manager can demonstrate that:

(a) the transaction is carried out for *bona fide* commercial reasons or in the ordinary course of making/managing investments; and
(b) the transaction is not carried out with the object (or a main object) of avoiding tax (this is often referred to as the 'escape clause').[16]

11 See further chapter 3, section 3.5.
12 Section 137(1) of the Taxation of Chargeable Gains Act 2002.
13 Section 137(2) of the Taxation of Chargeable Gains Act 2002.
14 Under section 138 of the Taxation of Chargeable Gains Act 2002.
15 Under section 684 of the Income Tax Act 2007.
16 Section 685 of the Income Tax Act 2007.

It is possible to apply in advance for confirmation from HMRC that it accepts that the escape clause applies,[17] although there is no requirement to seek such confirmation. In recent years, it has been relatively common for HMRC to refuse to give such confirmation for rolling managers receiving cash and/or loan notes as part of their consideration for selling their shares in Target where such managers as a whole are increasing their equity stake, and/or the aggregate equity stake of the managers in the new Newco is 20 per cent or more.

The effect of HMRC refusing clearance is not that it will seek to tax the cash and/or loan notes received in the same way as a dividend, but rather that it is reserving its right to seek to do so at a later stage.

4 Conclusion

Secondary buyouts represented a significant proportion of private equity transactions in the UK market in the buyout boom period from 2005 to 2007. In an economic climate where it is proving more difficult to raise debt finance for acquisitions, there have inevitably been fewer secondary transactions. Generally, secondaries tend to involve a higher consideration than first generation buyouts – resulting in the need for more significant debt funding. A trade buyer, perhaps sitting on firmer funding, able to offer more security or, in particular, having significant cash already in its balance sheet, will be in a better position in many circumstances to close a transaction, and should therefore be able to offer greater transaction deliverability. However, in time, we are likely to see the return to prominence of the secondary as a transaction which helps to oil the wheels of private equity, by encouraging the churn of investments which has traditionally driven growth in the sector. Secondaries by rescue or turnaround funds should also prove prominent during more challenging economic times.

It remains to be seen if, in the more challenging environment being experienced at the time of writing, selling private equity investors will be able to preserve their 'take the cash and don't look back' approach by refusing to offer general commercial warranties on sale. In the UK at least, the no-warranties policy adopted by most private equity firms has weathered significant pressure in the past. It is perhaps most likely that the practice on secondaries will follow any trend that emerges on share sale exits to trade buyers, given that secondary interest and trade buyers will be competing to acquire more attractive businesses. However, it may be that an investor buyer on a secondary deal is more sympathetic to the absence of warranty cover than a trade buyer (the secondary investor's investment documents will no doubt include provisions stating that they will not give warranties on exit, making it more difficult for those investors to argue that the selling investors should accept a different position).

17 Section 701 of the Income Tax Act 2007.

Secondaries represent a hybrid between a typical management buyout and a trade sale. Issues of conflict can often arise, most notably for the rolling managers who must balance their interests as both seller and buyer. The more significant investment which a rolling manager makes in a secondary also brings legal complications – in particular, concerning the ranking of the various loan notes and shareholdings that emerge in the structure, and the consequences for a rolling manager if his employment is terminated. That said, with sufficient focus on the specific issues that arise on a secondary, the standard model for a private equity transaction in the UK can readily be adapted to suit these transactions.

13

Exits

1 Introduction

In this final chapter, we turn to look at some of the issues that arise on a successful exit by the investors from a private-equity-backed company. We will concentrate on two types of transaction in particular: a share sale; and an Initial Public Offering (IPO).

In relation to share sales, this chapter will touch on some areas that are relevant to any disposal of a private company. However, the main focus will be on those specific issues that can arise on the sale of a company that is private-equity-backed, and the consequences for each of the parties to the transaction. This approach is consistent with the approach taken in chapter 4, where the specific issues that arise on a share purchase by a private-equity-backed buyer were highlighted; inevitably, many of the areas considered overlap, although the position taken by the buyer and the seller(s) on such issues can be markedly different.

On the face of it, an IPO is a very different transaction to a share sale, not least because of the highly regulated environment in which the transaction is taking place, and the high profile and publicity it attracts. However, many of the same features and commercial concerns for the private equity investors and managers can arise, and it is informative to see how these consistent issues are addressed in the two different exit transactions. Either exit will tend to require the unpicking of the funding structure from the buyout, and the repayment or refinancing of the debt put into the structure at that time. There may also be a need to involve regulators and other third parties, for example in respect of pension schemes, competition matters, or key customer or supplier relationships. The transaction may therefore involve many more parties than simply the selling shareholders and the buyer.

Before considering the specific issues on these two types of exit, however, it is worthwhile reflecting on how the focus on an ultimate exit lies at the heart of any private equity investment from the very beginning.

2 Exit focus

2.1 The importance of the exit and exit planning

It is sometimes said that a private equity investor plans for the exit even before it acquires Target. This does not mean to say that it has already lined up a profitable buyer – if that were the case, then the sellers' marketing exercise has missed a good opportunity. However, being as certain as they can be that there will be a sale opportunity for an investment is a critical part of the assessment of a potential investment before the private equity investor completes the acquisition. It would be usual, however, for the investor to have asked its financial and commercial due diligence advisers to consider the various routes to exit, including identified buyers (whether trade or financial buyers) and any IPO prospects, as part of their remit.

This does not mean to say that the business can simply be carried on 'as is' for a period, and sold in the state in which it is bought. As we have seen, the Business Plan will envisage changes to the structure of the business to increase its value. This may include further expansion of the business, the launch of new products or services, rationalising parts of the cost base and/or splitting up and dividing the business. Other possible models could include the introduction of an 'opco/propco' structure (whereby a company which owns the property in which it operates restructures itself to a trading company occupying that property pursuant to a lease, enabling a separate sale of the freehold), or some other change to the business model such as the manner in which it deals with its customers, suppliers or employees.

Some businesses by their nature are more attractive to trade buyers as a future exit opportunity, and some may be more suited to other private equity houses via a secondary deal, particularly where Target is in a sector which is favoured by that market. Other businesses may be more suitable to an IPO or other transaction involving the public markets. It is not essential that the private equity investor has determined precisely how it will sell the business at the time of purchase. What matters is that there is a good prospect of being able to exit the investment at a successful valuation in a sensible timeframe.

Everything that the private equity investor does in relation to the investment both during the acquisition and in the life of the investment is therefore focused upon ensuring these exit opportunities are available, and maximising the overall exit value. Value in this context means the combination of the proceeds received on the exit and the length of time before the exit occurs – both elements are key in the private equity evaluation of the business opportunity, as they will determine the key measure of return to their ultimate investors, being the internal rate of return (IRR) (as explained in section 3.4 of chapter 1).

2.2 The role of due diligence

This exit focus should be on the minds of the investor, and all relevant advisers to the investor, throughout the acquisition due diligence process. In order to maximise the ultimate gain on exit, it is essential to buy at the right price, and otherwise on the right terms, at the start of the process. Accordingly, the Newco buyer backed by private equity funding will utilise the acquisition due diligence as fully as possible, in order to ensure that any risks or liabilities identified in the business are either left with the seller, or otherwise underwritten by the seller, to the fullest extent possible. Ideally, the investor will look to factor any material issues into the price on acquisition (which can lead to strained negotiations as transactions enter exclusivity, as sellers to private equity may sense the investors taking any opportunity to 'price chip', as discussed in chapter 2).[1]

Following the acquisition, however, the acquisition due diligence can be equally important as a way of ensuring that the problems and opportunities are, where necessary, addressed at a sensible cost and in a realistic timescale. As we have seen,[2] good legal due diligence will distinguish between those fundamental issues which must be addressed by way of price adjustment, indemnities, warranties or other protections at the time of the deal, and those which may be addressed by suitable remedial action post-completion. As noted in earlier chapters, it is common for the private equity investors to require the managers, with the assistance of the relevant due diligence providers, to produce a document (often referred to as the 90 Day or 100 Day Plan, reflecting the period following completion in which it is prepared) setting out a sensible plan for rectifying any such issues, together with a timescale, costings and suitable milestones for monitoring progress. If these remaining issues are not addressed after the acquisition, they will usually still exist at the time that the owners are seeking to exit the investment. The focus on exit requires that the private equity investors and the managers put the business into the best state possible to maximise exit value, by utilising the issues identified in due diligence and, where it is sensible and cost-effective to do so, rectifying them.

2.3 Exit focus during the life of the investment

Of course, during the life of the investment, other issues and opportunities will arise that were not known or identified at acquisition. From a legal perspective, changes in law and practice, or in the regulatory environment, can create a potential problem within Target, or may create a possible solution for an already known difficulty. In the wider sense, commercial opportunities and threats will emerge on a continuing basis. The investor and managers will be keen to understand all of such issues as fully as possible and, where necessary, to address them in a way that best preserves or enhances the exit value. The exit focus means that there is an ongoing exercise to maximise value and to quantify, reduce or eliminate risk and liability. For these reasons, private equity is often championed by its supporters as an environment that stimulates

1 See chapter 2, section 3.3.
2 See chapter 2, section 4.3.

value creation; the interests of the shareholders and the management team are aligned to create meaningful and sustainable value in the business over the medium term, rather than having a focus on short-term profit distributions or remuneration.

Even in underperforming investments, the major decisions that may have to be made and that were explored in chapter 11 (for example, in relation to refinancing, restructuring or changes to the management team or Business Plan) will be made with a sharp focus on exit value – even though, on these facts, that may well be with a view to minimising the loss rather than maximising the gain. The private equity investor only stops thinking about an exit when there is no prospect of preserving any of the value already invested and no sensible case for investing further funds – only at that stage is any realistic hope in the investment lost.

3 Share sale

3.1 Parties

As explained in chapter 4, a share sale of a UK company typically proceeds by way of a formal written contract between the existing shareholders (sellers) and the buyer.[3] When a private-equity-backed company is sold, therefore, the sellers are the private equity investors and the managers. In some cases, other people may become shareholders in the company just before the sale, and join in to receive some of the consideration – this could arise, for example, if the holders of employee share options choose to exercise their options, or a bank or mezzanine lender elects to exercise its warrant to become members and to share in the gain on the sale. In many cases, however, such option or warrant holders receive a cash cancellation payment instead from the buyer, and do not actually exercise their rights to become a member of the company (and accordingly do not become sellers in the share sale). Another seller sometimes seen is an employee benefit trust (EBT), if any of the shares are held in such a trust. Again, practice varies as to whether the shares held by the EBT are sold by the EBT with proceeds passed to the employee beneficiaries, or the shares are transferred out to such beneficiaries before the time of the sale, so that the proceeds end up directly in their hands.[4]

The special factors that arise when the transaction is a secondary buyout are considered in more detail in chapter 12. When an auction arises, there may well be tension between any possible trade buyer and the prospect of a secondary buyout. This chapter will focus on a full exit, that is to say where

3 See chapter 4, section 2.1. Target itself will not usually be a party.

4 See further chapter 6, section 4.2(b), on mezzanine warrants; and chapter 7, section 5, on share options and similar incentives.

the managers either leave the business altogether at completion of the sale, or stay on as employees but have realised their full capital gain by selling all of their shares on sale. In some cases, the managers may go on to hold shares in the buyer (for example, if a listed company is the acquirer, it may issue its own shares to the sellers as part of the price); however, in those circumstances, the sellers have typically agreed to sell on those terms because they considered it to be the best deal on offer overall, rather than because those individuals are expected to be material equity participants in the buyer's business going forward. Many of the issues outlined in this chapter will also be relevant on a secondary deal.

3.2 Typical features of a share sale exit process

Chapter 2 summarises, from a buyer's perspective, the steps involved in a typical share sale transaction.[5] Whilst the precise process will vary depending on the factors explored in detail in that chapter, it will typically involve the following steps:

- selection of advisers;
- initial marketing process;
- non-binding offers;
- heads of offer letter agreed with preferred buyer;
- due diligence;
- share sale agreement drafted and negotiated;
- share sale agreement signed;
- conditions satisfied post-signing (where relevant); and
- sale completes and price paid.

We shall now examine some of these steps in more detail, and in doing so highlight the differences that can arise from a seller's perspective when the Target is private-equity-backed.

(a) Selection of advisers

In most transactions, the sellers will retain a number of advisers, including at least a corporate finance adviser and a legal adviser to act for them on the sale. In the sale of a private-equity-backed company, the investors will generally have the final say on the choice of advisers, unless they are in a minority equity position. The firms selected often have a delicate balance to strike, especially if any real issue arises between the investors and the managers. Most managers tend to regard such advisers as inclined more to the views and interests of the private equity investors, especially when they are the majority equity owners. Whilst the investor preference generally prevails on the choice of corporate finance adviser in particular, the management team may be able to exert more

5 See chapter 2, section 2.

influence on the choice of legal adviser – as the remainder of this chapter highlights, the managers will invariably have a greater need for legal advice, and engagement in the legal process generally, than the investors.

(b) Marketing process

The managers have a key role to play in this process, not only in providing detailed information about the existing business, but also in the preparation of future forecasts, and the other aspects of the marketing dealing with prospects and outlook. Potential bidders will usually want to meet the managers, especially private equity bidders. A formal process and firm regime are usually in place to ensure that this is done in a way which best protects the interests of all sellers, normally in the form of formal management presentations.

(c) Due diligence

The preferred buyer will inevitably wish to undertake due diligence. In some auction processes, the sellers will already have undertaken substantial vendor due diligence to be made available to the bidders (or, at least, to the preferred bidder). This is intended to shorten the due diligence process and timetable, with the intention that any further buyer due diligence will be very limited (if it is permitted at all), and principally confirmatory. It also has the advantage of allowing the advisers who carried out the due diligence exercise for the investors on the original buyout simply to update their reports, rather than a prospective buyer's advisers having to start the whole exercise from scratch. As discussed in chapter 2, in the height of the seller market in the UK during 2006 and 2007, there was a considerable emphasis on auction and similar processes, and an extensive use of vendor due diligence and other techniques to maintain a tight timetable pressure. The change in market conditions since then has led to a more orthodox buyer-driven process, where the buyer will prefer to take its time and undertake relevant due diligence itself, through its own nominated advisers. The precise scope and nature of the due diligence will vary according to the size of the deal, the sector in which Target operates, and the nature of the assets and liabilities (or potential liabilities) relevant to Target. Whatever the form of due diligence undertaken, the managers are a key part of the process on behalf of the sellers, as they will be best placed to provide the access and information that the preferred bidder will need.

(d) The share sale agreement[6]

In all share sales, the share sale agreement is the key transactional document. The key commercial issues that arise on that document which are specific to a private equity sale are discussed in sections 3.3 to 3.8 below.

6 For a more comprehensive analysis of some of the content and features of acquisition agreements, see chapter 4, section 2.

(e) Share sale agreement signed

The process of signing ought to be relatively straightforward, although in practice the substantial number of documents that typically accompany any deal mean that the act often occurs during a demanding completion meeting. In private-equity-backed deals, there can often be a relatively large number of sellers; there may be several investors investing on parallel terms, several managers, and possibly additional employees, option holders or other external shareholders (where there is a historic reason for an outsider to hold shares, for example where a manager has left the business but retained an equity stake). It would be rare for all the investors to be separately represented at signing – powers of attorney are very commonly used – but it is important for the legal advisers to the sellers to ensure that these are arranged in good time. Some investors, especially those based outside the UK, may have considerable formality, both internal and, sometimes, external to comply with (for example, involving a notary) before a power of attorney can be granted and delivered. Managers are more likely to attend in person, but powers of attorney are also advisable here, especially if manager shares are more widely held by family members or trusts, or by a larger pool of employees. Powers of attorney are always advisable in reserve even if there is only a small number of managers, as availability (and deal timetables) can often change at the last minute.

(f) Completion

This will typically be a straightforward mechanical process where the parties comply with their respective responsibilities, the shares are transferred, and the price paid. A private-equity-backed deal will also involve the settlement of the buyout finance and the unpicking of the related debt and equity documentation. Although this is a more elaborate process than would be found, for example, on the sale of a subsidiary by its parent, it is mainly a question of good preparation, and does not raise any significant issues not encountered on other corporate disposals. Completion will often occur immediately following exchange of the sale agreement, which is most straightforward (and preferred wherever possible by both buyers and sellers for that reason). Where conditionality is unavoidable (to deal with a competition or other regulatory clearance, or shareholder approval for the buyer, for example), the process can require more diligent preparation.[7]

3.3 Warranties and covenants: the institutional position

One of the biggest differences in UK practice between most other share sales and the sale of a private-equity-backed company is the attitude of private equity investors to warranties, covenants and other restrictions or risks that

7 See chapter 4, section 2.5, on conditionality generally; and chapter 4, section 4, in relation to competition clearance.

may survive and cause some problem for, or claim against, them after completion of the share sale. In other private share sales in the UK, the sellers will generally give warranties where their liability is capped at the full value of the consideration received, or a proportion of that full value which is accepted to be sufficient cover to the buyer. Sometimes, special deals are agreed allowing certain sellers to avoid giving warranties (for example, where some shares are held by junior employees, or family members or trusts) but, in general terms, the starting-point at least is warranty cover of an amount equal to the full consideration. The precise content of the warranties, and the extent to which recovery is legally possible, will still depend on bargaining power and skill in negotiations, but the general assumption remains that all sellers will provide adequate warranty cover to the buyer.

By their nature, private equity investors take a different approach. They will strongly insist that they sell on what they will describe as standard institutional terms. By this, they mean that they will warrant their title to the shares that they sell, and their capacity to enter into the sale, but no further. They will not give commercial warranties about the company itself, its business, assets or liabilities. Nor will they give any deed of covenant about its tax affairs, or any indemnities concerning the business or (for example) its environmental or pension funding status.

In many ways, this stance is consistent with the approach of any seller (private or institutional) in a takeover bid or other sale of listed shares. However, it often surprises trade buyers in the context of a private sale who are not generally accustomed to the approach, particularly if based outside the UK. The investors are often the majority shareholders in the company, and therefore will be receiving the greater share of the consideration. As we have seen, they will also normally have had board representation (or at least the right to appoint a director), and will have received management accounts and other ongoing information about Target during the life of their investment. Key decisions will have been influenced, or actually effected, by the private equity investors under their veto and consent mechanisms in the equity documentation. They are likely to be far more informed about the affairs of the company than any market seller of listed shares, or many sellers of shares in other private companies who will give full value warranties.

In response, however, the private equity investors will cite the unquestionably well-established practice of their market. The practice has arisen, and been accepted, as the majority of investors have invested third party funds, which need to be repaid to their clients (or reinvested) as soon as a disposal has completed. Their own model of operating, and its attractiveness to their own investors, would be substantially diminished if sale proceeds have to be retained in anticipation of the possibility of warranty claims or, worse still, investors have to be approached to meet a claim after proceeds have been paid out to them. It should be noted that, generally speaking, this approach is upheld by all private equity investors in the UK, including those who are captives of established UK banks or other financial institutions, or who are themselves listed or publicly traded.

Generally, if reluctantly, buyers will accept this approach. From the sellers' perspective, however, if the private equity investors do not give commercial warranties or indemnities, these risks inevitably fall upon the shoulders of management. A lively debate as to exactly what risks might arise, and on what basis management will give warranties and indemnities on the exit, often therefore ensues between the management sellers and the buyer. In an attempt to ensure that such debate is generally concluded in favour of the traditional stance of investors, the investment agreement on the initial buyout will usually include an express acknowledgment by the managers that they will be required to provide customary warranties and indemnities on any exit, and that the investors will not be required to do so beyond their own title and capacity.

If the managers have a significant stake in the business, warranties from those managers may well offer a material degree of comfort to the buyer. However, the smaller the management stake in the business, the greater the risk the buyer will face by limiting its redress solely to managers (as it would be usual for the managers to limit their risk to their share of the proceeds, or a proportion of those proceeds if they can get away with it). In many cases, the managers will have a relatively small stake, such that, even if the managers were (unusually) willing to accept a greater risk than their proceeds, it is doubtful whether this would actually confer much additional value or protection for the buyer. This is because the managers may well have very little real wealth beyond their proceeds, and a right to sue them is of little comfort if they are not good for the claim. Accordingly, there is a risk of a substantial gap in the warranty cover available to the buyer.

One way of addressing this is the use of *warranty insurance* which, in some circumstances, has been used to give comfort to a buyer for that part of the value of the sale proceeds (or sometimes a lower figure) not covered as a result of the private equity investors not providing warranties. There are limits to the matters which warranty insurance would cover but, for a premium based on the amount of cover required, it can afford a degree of comfort in particular circumstances. Although private equity investors will not give commercial warranties, they have been known to contribute towards the cost of this insurance (at least in proportion to their equity stake), although the exit expectation clause in the investment agreement referred to above may look to discount that possibility too. Where the investors do agree to contribute, a buyer may elect to put such insurance in place at its own expense, and make a corresponding adjustment to the overall price paid for the company (thereby affecting all sellers proportionally).

3.4 Completion accounts and locked box mechanisms

One arrangement often seen on share sales which, at first impression, may appear to be a departure from the standard institutional stance on commercial risk is the willingness of institutional sellers to agree to the use by the buyer of completion accounts to test the net assets, working capital or another key financial measure of the business as at completion. As explained in chapter 4, this is a mechanism often used by buyers to check the actual state of the business at the time of purchase, and will be linked to a price adjustment mechanism (usually on a pound-for-pound basis) if the level of net assets (or other measure) delivered at completion is found to be below a specified target level, or to be more than an agreed tolerance below that level. Sometimes, the mechanism will be an either-way mechanism, with the price also increasing if the net assets are higher than expected.[8]

Generally, private equity investors may be willing to contribute towards any shortfall that results from the application of completion accounts, if this is necessary to close the deal. Investors rationalise this on the basis that delivery of the appropriate level of net assets (or other measure) is a fundamental assumption in setting the price, and so, where such value has diminished at the time of sale, it is only fair that the sellers bear that price reduction *pro rata*. It can be distinguished from commercial warranties, where the warrantors are largely taking a risk on unknown commercial matters latent in the business (any known matters would not tend to be dealt with by way of warranty cover, as any identified problems should be included in the disclosure letter, leaving the buyer unable to make a claim against the warrantors in any event).

That said, investors are alert to the possibility that completion accounts could, in certain circumstances, be used as a device to ask them to accept commercial risks in the business, and they will introduce policies or safeguards to protect themselves against that risk. For example, investors would normally insist that the completion accounts are drawn up on the same basis, and using the same policies and practices, as were applied in preparing the last statutory accounts of the company as much as possible, and may well resist the otherwise common practice of including specific provisions in completion accounts to deal with particular identified risks (such as a bad or doubtful debt provision) on a basis that is stricter than that applied in the accounts. Taking that specific example, an accounting policy used in the preparation of completion accounts which includes a more onerous policy for providing for bad or doubtful debts and which has a knock-on effect on the price paid arguably, indirectly, amounts to a warranty on the collectability of the company's book debts (which is a matter that private equity sellers would not normally warrant). Similarly, if the investors were to allow the completion accounts to be prepared on a basis which is consistent with UK generally accepted accounting practice, rather than in a manner consistent with the last audited accounts, by agreeing to be subject to the completion accounts price adjustment the investors are, indirectly, warranting the compliance of the last accounts with UK practice.

8 For more information on completion accounts generally, see chapter 4, section 2.2.

Where private equity investors do accept their share of the risk on completion accounts, they would invariably expect this to be on a several basis, with each investor being liable for that proportion of any shortfall in the same ratio as its share of the equity. The private equity investors would not accept a situation where the whole of the shortfall could be claimed from them, leaving them to seek contributions from other sellers (i.e. from the managers).

Similarly, a private equity investor would normally seek to cap its exposure under a completion accounts or other price adjustment mechanism. Sometimes, a retention account is used, and each investor's exposure is capped at the amount placed on behalf of that investor into the retention account. Even if there is no formal retention account, the private equity investor would usually withhold an amount equal to the capped figure (for example, by asking the solicitor acting for the sellers to retain such amount in a deposit account), and will only distribute the net surplus to its ultimate investors once the outcome of the completion accounts exercise has been completed (to avoid the unattractive position described above, where the private equity firm has to go back to the clients to ask them to return to the buyer part of the consideration which had been received and paid out to them). Sometimes, the managers may enjoy a proportionate cap on their own exposure, whilst in other situations they may have to agree to take up any excess over the capped amount on their own account without contribution from the investors. This very much depends upon the negotiation strength and bargaining power of the managers, the investors and the buyer at the time – although a buyer is unlikely to be sympathetic to not having an ability to recover if there is a significant shortfall, and investors will argue that management are sufficiently informed to agree a cap to the investor exposure which provides management with more than enough headroom.

As mentioned in chapter 4,[9] a locked box mechanism is sometimes used as an alternative to completion accounts. A locked box mechanism is more attractive than completion accounts to the sellers (and, in particular, to private equity sellers) because the seller knows that, provided it has not had any payment except for a permitted payment (as defined in the agreement), there will be no adjustment to the price. This gives certainty, saves cost and delay, and maximises the ability of investors to return proceeds promptly and fully to clients. From the managers' perspective, it also avoids the additional exposure and possible conflicts that can arise from a completion accounts mechanism. For the same reasons that investors will wish to control their possible exposure under a completion accounts mechanism, investors will wish to ensure that their liability for any leakages from the locked box is limited to such amounts as they have actually received, and that they are not required to confirm the accuracy of the underlying locked box accounts by virtue of any warranty or indemnities included in the acquisition agreement to underpin the locked box mechanism.

9 See chapter 4, section 2.2(b).

3.5 Other arrangements to deal with seller risk

There are some other ways in which private equity investors may be viewed as entering into 'behind the scenes' arrangements with managers to deal with warranty and similar risks, or at least to soften the exposure of the managers under them. For example, a substantial part of the time spent by legal and accounting advisers will be to deal with due diligence, negotiation of warranties and similar provisions and the related limitations, and preparing and settling the disclosure letter. Even though the private equity sellers are not exposed to warranty risks, and so in that sense get no direct benefit from this work, they will almost invariably agree to meet their *pro rata* share of that cost as part of the overall costs of sale. This is standard and not particularly controversial; after all, if this work is not carried out, then there will be no exit for the institutions, so in that sense it is a 'cost of the deal'. In other (more exceptional) situations, investors may agree to meet more than their own share of costs, or to meet other more personal costs of the selling managers (e.g. in relation to tax planning).

There have also been rare examples of private equity investors agreeing to stand behind the managers (to an extent, and always within a capped amount) in the event of a warranty claim. This is usually structured without the private equity investors directly being liable to the buyer or giving warranties on the face of the sale agreement, in order that investors may maintain their 'hard line' policy. It remains to be seen whether the market conditions prevailing in the credit crunch will lead to a weakening of the standard institutional stance – or, perhaps, to an increase in the use of these 'behind the scenes' mechanisms.

3.6 Restrictive covenants

Another area in which a private equity investor will adopt a stance that differs to a management seller is the area of restrictive covenants. Usually, the ability to restrict the sellers from competing with the company, or seeking to solicit its customers, suppliers or employees, is a valuable protection for the buyer. As indicated in chapter 4, English common law would treat all these agreements as *prima facie* void unless the parties can show that the covenants are designed to protect a legitimate business interest, and go no further than is reasonable (both as between the parties and in the public interest) to protect that interest.[10] There is a legitimate public interest in seeking to protect the goodwill sold in companies (without this, a buyer would pay less if anything for that goodwill, and sellers would be less motivated to set up and grow businesses) and, accordingly, reasonable restrictive covenants will normally be enforceable against sellers.

10 On restrictive covenants generally, see chapter 4, section 2.10, and chapter 5, section 3.7.

Managers would normally give reasonable restrictive covenants without difficulty but, generally, private equity investors will not. The reasons usually given for this are as follows:

- market practice (just as for commercial warranties, the UK institutional position is simply not to do so);
- the duties owed by the private equity investor to its own funds are inconsistent with its fettering its investment discretion in this way; for the same reason, a private equity investor would not agree in an investment agreement not to invest in another company in the same sector as the investee under that agreement, for example; and
- the private equity investor is simply a financial backer, and is not itself an active competitor in the company's business sector; such a covenant would be inconsistent with that role (in the same way, for example, that a bank would not expect to be precluded from lending to two businesses in the same industry).

This refusal has been long-standing in the industry, and it seems unlikely, even in the market conditions that exist following the credit crunch, that any private equity fund is likely to agree to provide restrictive covenants. To do so could preclude investors from pursuing another opportunity which it considers to be particularly attractive.

3.7 Confidentiality

A seller of private company shares (or, at least, a seller who has been an insider in relation to its affairs and is likely to have received confidential information) will usually also be expected to agree to respect the confidentiality of any information of the company or group being sold which is in that seller's possession. Private equity investors are generally reluctant to give this comfort if it can be avoided (even though they have had such information during the life of the investment), largely because of their desire to be able to 'close the book' once the sale has happened without worrying about the possibility of a residual claim. An argument might be cited that investors do not as a matter of practice share confidential information, but they would not wish to be subjected to a speculative claim in the event that a competitor of the business were to come into possession of that information by some other means in the future. This reluctance is, however, sometimes overcome. In those cases, the legal adviser to the sellers will look to ensure that any provisions are tightly drawn, so as to limit the obligation of the investors to a prohibition of any disclosure by that investor only of information that is actually in its possession, possibly with the additional benefit of a time limit to the obligation.

3.8 Other matters

Certain other matters arising on a share sale exit are worthy of mention for a private-equity-backed company.

(a) Cancellation of earlier agreements

It will be a normal part of the completion exercise on a share sale exit that the investment agreement and other documents put in place as part of the original buyout will be cancelled. Generally, this is uncontroversial, and an appropriate agreed form document will be entered into by all relevant parties, including the private equity investors. Cancellation would normally include a release of claims by all parties, and will be conditional upon completion occurring.

(b) Repayment of debt

The completion mechanics will also include the obligation to procure the repayment of the senior debt, mezzanine debt and any investor loan notes, and the cancellation of any relevant security. In practice, the buyer will usually provide the funding needed by the company to repay the borrowings, with the headline price paid being reduced accordingly from the 'debt free' enterprise value to the actual value of the shares sold. It is unlikely that the company will be able to repay such debt without the buyer's funding.

(c) Allocation of seller completion obligations

Certain matters will need to be effected by the sellers at completion. Some of these are typical to any share sale (such as the delivery of stock transfers and share certificates, the resignation of officers and the passing of board and shareholder resolutions); others are peculiar to private equity (such as the cancellation of the original buyout documentation and repayment of debt referred to above). Although all these matters will need to be addressed (and all sellers have a commercial incentive to see them done), there will normally be an allocation of specific responsibility as between the managers and the private equity investors. The private equity investors will generally only accept responsibility for matters under their own control (such as the delivery of share certificates and stock transfers for their own shares, and the execution by them of documents to cancel the buyout arrangements). However, they do not want to face a claim for failing to do something that is outside their own unilateral ability or which cannot readily and fully be performed at completion. Similarly, the obligation will generally be several, with each private equity investor only committing to what it can do rather than the investors collectively entering into a joint obligation. Other seller matters, such as the delivery of company assets or convening of group company board meetings, are usually only obligations of the management sellers. In practice, the buyer is rarely concerned with this, as it can ensure that any key actions are transacted as part of the completion process, and usually reserves the right not to complete until all relevant steps have been taken.

(d) Powers of attorney

It is not uncommon for a buyer of shares to ask that the sellers provide the buyer with an irrevocable power of attorney so that the buyer may exercise any voting rights attached to the sale shares pending stamping and registration of the relevant stock transfer forms. Until stamping has been completed and the name of the buyer is entered into the register of members, the sellers will remain the members of the company and, accordingly, will be the legal persons entitled to pass shareholder resolutions notwithstanding the fact that they have sold the shares to the buyer. Private equity investors are generally reluctant to grant powers of attorney to third parties, however, and may even be prohibited by their constitutional documents from doing so. In part, this is because they often execute documents themselves on behalf of their managed funds by way of power of attorney, and such powers of attorney often do not permit such sub-delegation. In other cases, there may be an institutional reluctance to grant powers of attorney to anybody outside their own organisation. Usually, therefore, private equity investors will try to persuade the buyer that they should stamp the stock transfers as soon as possible and manage without a power of attorney. As a compromise, the investors may instead agree to an obligation to sign written resolutions or appoint proxies in respect of the sale shares for a limited period after completion as the buyer directs, to offer some comfort if a period between completion and registration of the transfers is unavoidable.

(e) Further assurance

It is a normal feature of most share sales that the sellers give a contractual further assurance to the buyer, committing to do whatever is necessary to enable the buyer to have the benefit of the agreement and the rights attached to the sale shares. This is the case even where there is no immediately obvious issue that may need to be addressed in the future. There will be exceptions to this in most deals (for example, it is not usual for the sellers to pay stamp duty on the sale), and there may well be a debate about who meets any out-of-pocket expenses (such as professional fees) that the sellers might incur in complying with the further assurance obligation. There may also be a longstop date (say, six or twelve months) after which the obligation will lapse. Consistent with their general desire to close the book at completion, private equity investors will be very reluctant to give such further assurance at all. If they are persuaded to do so, it will be for a fixed (usually very short) period, will be several (each private equity investor speaking only for itself), and will normally be at the cost of the buyer in respect of any out-of-pocket expenses incurred. More often than not, no such further assurance is agreed to, and the buyer will simply be asked to focus on the specific actions which are actually required to ensure title in the relevant shares is transferred, and clarify before contract any specific actions or documents required from the sellers in that context.

4 Initial Public Offerings (IPOs)

4.1 Introduction to IPOs

In the turbulent market conditions experienced at the time of writing this book, an exit via an IPO is highly unlikely. However, whilst a return to the benign conditions of the last few years may be some way off, institutional investors in the London public markets traditionally have had an appetite for high-quality, UK domestic businesses. An IPO is therefore likely to remain a viable exit route for private equity investors in the medium term.

Indeed, a recent Cass Business School survey of IPOs during the period January 1995 to December 2006[11] indicates that 22 per cent by number and 27 per cent by value of all IPOs during that period were of companies with private equity backing. IPOs have compared surprisingly well against trade sales and secondary buyouts as an exit route over that same period: more than 16 per cent of exits were via IPO and sales of listed equities post-IPO (compared with approximately 21 per cent via trade sale and 4 per cent via secondary buyouts). If the availability of debt remains constrained (and/or the cost of debt remains high) for a prolonged period, we may well see an increase in the use of the public equity markets as an exit route compared to the number of trade sales and secondary buyouts which have been such a feature of the last few years.

4.2 Identifying a viable IPO candidate

Not all companies in a private equity investor's portfolio will be suitable businesses for IPO, particularly given the current market conditions and the investment environment in which we are likely to be operating for the next two or three years. As a starting-point for assessing a company's suitability for IPO, any investor will need to consider:

- the company's track record of delivering growth in revenue and profit;
- the strategy of the company, and prospects, for delivering future growth;
- the company's market position and barriers to entry in its markets; and
- the experience of management, especially the CEO and CFO, in delivering results.

A high-quality IPO candidate will rank highly in all of these areas, making an attractive investment case for new investors. However, there may be additional factors which make an IPO a more compelling exit route, such as the ability to use publicly traded securities as an acquisition currency, or the opportunity to attract public (or retail) investors in the company as part of the IPO process, thus enhancing awareness of the company's brand among its customers and raising the company's profile in domestic or global markets.

11 Cass Business School, *The London Markets and Private Equity-Backed IPOs – A Report by Cass Business School* (April 2008).

4.3 Typical transaction structure

A typical IPO of a private-equity-backed company will involve a placing of shares in the company with institutional investors on a global basis, in combination with admission of the company's share capital to trading on a public market. Unlike America, in the UK a public offer to retail investors is relatively unusual. The placing will often involve both the issue of new shares by the company (to raise new capital for the repayment of debt, the funding of its future strategy and for working capital, as well as to pay the fees connected with the IPO and fundraising), and the sale of existing shares by the private equity investors.

It is unusual for the investors to achieve a full exit in an IPO; most often, investors will retain a stake post-IPO. The level of the retained stake will often be a function of the level of demand from investors in the IPO: the company will often require a fixed amount of new capital to satisfy working capital requirements and therefore a private equity investor will only be able to sell to the extent there is excess demand for shares from investors. In addition, investors may well wish to see the private equity investor retain a stake to demonstrate an alignment of its interests to those of the new investors.

Given the likelihood of a retained stake in the business, not surprisingly a private equity investor will be cautious about preparing a company for IPO if it does not have faith in that company's ability to produce long-term growth and value for shareholders such that the investor will be able to achieve a full exit over a one to two year timeframe at least at the valuation set at the point of IPO, or better. The prospect of a retained stake in the company beyond IPO also gives rise to a number of corporate governance issues which the private equity investor should consider at an early stage in the process – in particular, the retention of board representation by the private equity investor, and the nature of any restrictions on the future sale of that stake (see further sections 4.6 and 4.7 below).

The liquidity of the company's shares in the after-market will be important in achieving good share price performance (and thus ultimately realising value for the private equity investor with a retained stake), and in giving the private equity investor the best possible chance of trading out its position over the long term. The initial valuation and free float at IPO are key factors in determining initial liquidity in the market. The market on which the company's shares are admitted will also have an influence. The London Stock Exchange's AIM market for growth companies has attracted criticism from investors and other market participants for poor liquidity and underperformance, particularly among many of the smaller companies admitted to that market. As a result, if the company in question satisfies the criteria for admission to the London Stock Exchange's Main Market and for admission to the Official List, then this is likely to be the preferable route to market as it will give access to a wider potential investor base. In the current climate, a company should have a minimum valuation of £100 million and a free float of at least 25–30 per cent at IPO to make the transaction viable.

4.4 Grooming a company for IPO

A company contemplating an IPO should start preparing itself well in advance for the rigours of life as a public company. At least twelve months prior to starting the IPO process itself, thought should be given to a number of key areas of the business, and steps taken to remedy any issues, including:

(a) *The executive management team.* Are the CEO and CFO of the company of the right calibre to lead the company through an IPO process and in its initial stages as a public company? The team will be responsible for leading the business through an intense period of preparation during the IPO process and, crucially, will be key in selling the company to potential investors. In just the same way as the private equity investor has relied heavily on the skills of the management team in delivering value during its period of investment, potential institutional investors in the IPO will be looking for the same qualities of leadership and confidence in their ability to deliver shareholder value following the IPO. If additions or changes to the management team are necessary to achieve an IPO, then the changes will need to be implemented and given time to demonstrate value well before an IPO is launched.

(b) *Non-executive directors.* The board may well comprise a number of non-executive directors, but again their experience of the public markets should be considered. In most circumstances, UK corporate governance standards are likely to demand that the majority of the board (excluding the chairman) comprises independent non-executive directors. It may be necessary therefore to consider augmenting the existing board with additional directors, or to consider certain changes to the board in order to achieve an appropriate balance of independence and expertise. The role of chairman will be particularly important for a public company and should be someone with appropriate 'City' credentials. As a public company, the company will also need to establish audit, remuneration and nominations board committees; the board should include an independent non-executive director with appropriate financial experience to chair the audit committee.

(c) *Potential due diligence issues.* The IPO process will include a rigorous commercial, financial and legal due diligence exercise. Thought should be given well in advance to any areas of the business which may need to be addressed, for example consistency of application and presentation of accounting policies, the level of distributable reserves and any dividend traps in the group, any key commercial contracts with unusual or onerous terms (especially change of control clauses which may be triggered by the IPO), the terms of existing debt facilities (especially any covenants which may need renegotiating as part of the IPO process), the share capital structure of the company (including the terms of any warrants and options) and the changes necessary to achieve a single class of shares at the IPO.[12]

12 Including any changes necessary to give effect to a proceeds ratchet: see chapter 5, section 4.6.

4.5 Starting the IPO process

The first step in the formal IPO process is for the company to appoint an investment bank to act as financial adviser, sponsor and underwriter to the IPO. These roles may be fulfilled by more than one investment bank, although a syndicated approach is only usual where a large fundraising is involved.

The selection of the right investment bank is key to the success of the transaction. Although it is ultimately the decision of the board of the company, it is typical to find the private equity investor taking an active role in the selection process. Aside from the obvious issue of valuation, the selection process should focus on the bank's sector expertise, the rating of its research analyst in the sector, and the commitment of its sales team to the transaction. Wherever possible, the company's management and the private equity investor should meet with the relevant research analyst[13] and the head of sales at the bank concerned to get an understanding of their initial opinions on the company and their commitment to the process. Although the track record and personal chemistry with the advisory team at the bank are important, the research and sales sides of the bank will be instrumental in selling the IPO, and fundamental to the company's life as a public company post-IPO.

In many instances, not enough attention is paid to the key commercial terms of the fundraising at this early stage. The company and private equity investor should seek to agree a number of important terms with the investment bank before awarding the mandate and signing an engagement letter with the bank. Although the underwriting fees and commissions are a key component of this, it is sensible to agree a termsheet with the bank concerned at this stage which covers all of the key terms of the underwriting agreement whilst the company is in a strong negotiating position.

4.6 Key terms of the underwriting agreement

The key terms of the underwriting agreement should be agreed with the investment bank in the form of a termsheet at the outset of the transaction, prior to agreeing to the bank's engagement terms, as set out below.

(a) Fees and commissions

These vary widely depending on the size of the fundraising and market conditions. It is often the case that the bank will ask for a fixed advisory fee (often payable in whole or in part even if the transaction ultimately fails) plus commissions for a successful fundraising. Private equity investors often complain that the most unattractive aspect of an IPO is the uncertainty as to valuation and

13 Pursuant to the UK Financial Services Authority's Conduct of Business Sourcebook, an analyst producing independent investment research is prohibited from participating in a pitch by an investment bank for new business. However, those restrictions do not apply to an analyst producing non-independent research (a more common business model among traditional UK mid-market-focused investment banks).

therefore realisation on exit. Consideration should be given to incentivising the bank appropriately to maximise value by building in a ratchet to the commissions earned by reference to a range of valuations (although the highest valuation at IPO will not necessarily attract long-term investors and produce the best share price performance in the after-market). An alternative commission structure which has been in vogue in the last few years is to include a discretionary element to the commission (0.25–0.5 per cent), payable at the discretion of the board of the company if the bank has performed well. However, in practice it is rare for this payment not to be made if the IPO occurs.

It is usual for the company to also reimburse the bank for its expenses, such as legal fees. These can be considerable and costly to bear if the transaction aborts, so thought should be given to negotiating caps or discounts in respect of the bank's expenses in the event of an aborted deal or a mechanism agreed for pre-approval by the company of significant expenses.

(b) Warranties and indemnities

The company will be expected to give the underwriter a wide range of warranties relating to the disclosure document (most commonly a prospectus) to be published in connection with the IPO and generally in relation to the company and its business, as well as an indemnity for claims or losses incurred by the bank in certain circumstances. Banks will often seek to assert that others connected with the transaction should provide the same comfort, especially the directors and proposed directors of the company and any shareholders selling shares in the IPO. This gives rise to two issues for a private equity investor:

(a) *The scope of any warranties and indemnities to be given by the investor.* Private equity investors will be reticent to provide any warranties or an indemnity to the underwriter in respect of the transaction. However, in most transactions, a compromise position is reached where the private equity investor provides a restricted scope of warranties only, relating to a limited range of matters relevant to the investor itself such as ownership and title of shares, capacity to enter into the agreement and the accuracy of information relating to the investor contained in the disclosure document. Given the fundamental nature of these warranties, it is not unusual to see such warranties given without any contractual limitations, such as a monetary cap on liability or any restriction on the time within which a claim must be made, although these are clearly areas for negotiation on a case-by-case basis.

(b) *The scope of any warranties and indemnity to be given by any representative of the private equity investor who is to remain on the board of the company as a non-executive director at IPO.* There is often a distinction drawn in an underwriting agreement between executive and non-executive directors of the company both in terms of the scope of contractual comfort they provide to an underwriter and in terms of the limitations on their liability. This is not a reflection of the position at law – all directors, regardless of title and function, have potential liability for a prospectus and statements made by the company during the IPO process. In the context of an IPO, non-executive directors can often be relatively new to the business and, in any event, due to the nature of their duties, do not have the intimate knowledge of the business that the executive directors possess. On that basis, the underwriter is often prepared to accept a lesser level of contractual comfort from the non-executive directors compared to the executive directors. One common compromise position is that the non-executive directors will only give warranties on an awareness basis as to the accuracy of the disclosures in the disclosure document and warranties as to personal information relating to themselves, with liability often limited in both time and amount. The private equity investor will be keen to understand the precise nature of the liability its representative is being asked to assume, and to ensure appropriate insurance is in place to cover the risks.

(c) Lock-up

An underwriter will expect to obtain the agreement of all existing shareholders that they will only transfer or dispose of interests in shares following the IPO with its prior consent. This is to ensure an orderly market in the company's shares following the IPO. Many private equity investors initially look to resist such a lock-up although, in practice, most will eventually agree to such a restriction for a limited period of time, ranging from three months to twelve months, provided it is subject to certain exemptions (such as acceptance of a recommended takeover offer and intra-group or intra-fund transfers).

4.7 Relationship agreement

If a private equity investor holds a substantial shareholding in the company following an IPO, it is likely to continue to exert significant influence on the company and its board. Depending on the size of its stake, it may be able to achieve a certain amount of control of the company through its voting power at shareholder meetings. It may be the case that the company agrees with such an investor that it should retain the right to nominate a representative to the board of the company.

In any of these circumstances, it is likely that potential investors in the IPO will expect to see, as a matter of good corporate governance, a relationship agreement in place at IPO between the company and the private equity investor which seeks to regulate the dealings between the private equity investor (as a substantial, or controlling, shareholder) and the company. The key elements of a typical relationship agreement include:

(a) the agreement of the relevant shareholder to interact with the company in all dealings with it on an arm's length basis and on normal commercial terms;

(b) if the shareholder has the right to appoint a director to the board of the company, details as to when this right will terminate; typically, such right will exist for so long as the shareholder retains a shareholding in excess of an agreed level (often a 10 per cent stake);
(c) restrictions on the exercise of voting rights by the shareholder in relation to the approval of any dealings between the shareholder and the company;
(d) limited shareholder protections, which may be negotiable in specific circumstances; and
(e) restrictions on the ability of the board representative to pass confidential information to the shareholder and restrictions on share dealings by the shareholder in certain circumstances.

4.8 IPO process

The overall timetable for a London IPO from the time of appointment of advisers to admission of the company's shares to trading on the market will vary depending on a range of issues, such as the scale of the company's business (and therefore the extent of the due diligence exercise which will need to be undertaken), the complexity of any restructuring that may need to be undertaken prior to IPO, the number of issues which may need to be addressed as a result of due diligence prior to IPO, the structure of the fundraising and the nature of the disclosure document (for example, a prospectus will require the prior approval of the UK Listing Authority, whereas an AIM admission document will not). As a general rule, the IPO process is likely to take at least twelve weeks, and perhaps longer.

The key work streams, many of which will run in parallel, are as follows:

(a) *Due diligence.* This will usually comprise a full commercial, legal and financial review of the business. This will result in a detailed written report by both a firm of reporting accountants and the company's legal advisers. In some cases, more specific commercial due diligence may be commissioned by the investment bank concerned, for example a valuation report in respect of a real estate portfolio or a geological report in respect of a mining company.
(b) *Pre-IPO research.* The investment bank's research analyst will prepare a research note on the company which will be issued at least two weeks prior to any formal marketing of the IPO by the company or its advisers. This will be key to beginning to educate potential institutional investors on the investment case for the company, and establishing an independent view on valuation of the business based, in part, on the analyst's financial projections for the company. This research will be informed by data provided by the company, but will represent the analyst's own views. In reality, it is a key part of the marketing process, and will set the market's expectations as to the company's future performance.

(c) *Investor presentation.* This will be the key marketing document used by management of the company to present the company's story to potential investors in a series of short meetings, known as a 'roadshow'. These meetings will take place in the last two to three weeks of the process prior to listing, and are the key tool in testing market appetite for the IPO. The investment bank's sales team will follow up each roadshow meeting with a telephone call to the potential investor to seek to elicit an order. This process results in a book of orders at a range of prices which will inform the investment bank's final recommendation as to the price at which the IPO should be launched and the shares sold. The final decision as to price should take into account not only the range of prices in the order book, but also the nature of the investors. Those institutions which are known to be longer-term investors may be preferred to a shareholder register comprised of hedge funds with a shorter-term investment horizon, which could have a negative impact on share price performance.
(d) *Disclosure document.* The preparation of a prospectus (or AIM admission document, if appropriate) will be a key focus of the company's advisers. This will also be a key part of the marketing process, as well as satisfying the relevant disclosure requirements of the Prospectus Rules and/or the AIM Rules for Companies.
(e) *Underwriting agreement.* This agreement will be negotiated between the investment bank and its legal advisers on the one hand, and the company and selling shareholders and their respective legal advisers on the other. It will set out in detail the mechanics of the fundraising and admission process as well as dealing with the matters referred to in section 4.6 above.

A private equity investor should be heavily involved throughout this process; a thorough process and well-presented investment case will maximise value for shareholders. The investor should ensure representation on the steering group for the project and be closely involved in the key stages of the process. For example, the appointment of independent non-executive directors to the board will be a key decision, not only because of the positive effect this may have on the marketing of the IPO, but also (and more importantly for the private equity investor) because this group of directors, plus the investor's own nominee, are likely between them to have the majority vote at board meetings. The composition of the board thus becomes key to the investor's confidence in the leadership of the business, and its ability to deliver shareholder value following the IPO.

The private equity investor will naturally be involved in the final decision as to pricing of the IPO, but equally important is the publication of research earlier in the process. This will set the market's expectations of the company's future performance, and in turn will inevitably influence the company's future share price performance and hence directly impact the private equity investor's realisation of value.

4.9 Post-IPO

Following admission of the company's securities to a public market, the private equity investor and its board representative will need to operate within the regulatory regime for UK publicly traded companies. Particular care will be needed to ensure compliance with insider dealing laws, the Financial Services and Markets Act 2000, the Disclosure and Transparency Rules and the City Code on Takeovers and Mergers.

The private equity investor will need to ensure it has sufficient internal systems and procedures in place to ensure compliance with its obligations, for example monitoring its dealings and interests and making disclosures to the company and the market where appropriate.

The presence of a board representative may increase the risks of insider dealing and/or market abuse to the extent unpublished price-sensitive information is known to the board member, who will in any event be bound by the company's sharedealing code. This is an area where the private equity investor and the individual board member should take specialist advice about the appropriate procedures to implement.

5 Conclusion

In this chapter, we have examined the two most hoped for forms of exit for a successful private equity investment: the private company sale; and the IPO. We have also looked at the importance of exit focus in the overall analysis of a transaction from the outset, and the particular factors that can arise on each type of exit. A recurring theme is the desire for investors to achieve maximum liquidity with minimum redress, and to be in a position to return the proceeds to the underlying investors in the funds as soon as possible. For many businesses, a trade sale will be the most efficient method of achieving the objectives desired, and it would be fair to say that this is usually the investor's preferred exit route given the relative certainty and liquidity inherent in the transaction when compared with an IPO. However, there will be circumstances where an IPO creates the best opportunity for maximising value on the investment and, where relevant, enabling the private equity investors to maintain an ongoing (albeit diluted) stake in the business going forward. An IPO may also be attractive to the managers, who may wish to guide the business to the next stage of its evolution in the very different business environment of the public markets.

As has been highlighted throughout this book, the period leading up to the summer of 2007 was something of a boom period for private equity. The apparently ever-increasing private equity marketplace, and the willingness of banks and others to provide liquidity, generated very significant returns for the majority of investors in the period prior to the credit crunch. The market conditions since the credit crunch, with restricted liquidity and general hesitancy over asset valuations (not to mention the increased focus that investors have had to place on their existing portfolio companies) has led to a reduction in market activity both in terms of investment and exits. However, the considerable contribution that private equity has made to UK industry in recent years, and the opportunities which it affords both to investors and to managers by aligning their interests in the ownership and management of businesses, means that there is likely to remain an ongoing role for private equity for many years to come. The flexibility shown by the private equity industry to date suggests that it has the will and the resourcefulness to adapt in the ever-changing conditions which we now face.

Index